A HISTORY OF THOUGHT ON ECONOMIC INTEGRATION

Also edited by Fritz Machlup

ECONOMIC INTEGRATION: WORLDWIDE, REGIONAL, SECTORAL
Proceedings of the Fourth Congress of the International Economic Association held in Budapest, Hungary.

A History of Thought on Economic Integration

FRITZ MACHLUP

Columbia University Press
New York   1977

© Fritz Machlup 1977

Published in 1977 in Great Britain by
THE MACMILLAN PRESS LTD
and in the United States of America by
COLUMBIA UNIVERSITY PRESS

Printed in Great Britain

Library of Congress Cataloging in Publication Data

Machlup, Fritz, 1902 —
A history of thought on economic integration

Bibliography: p.
Includes index.
1. International economic integration. I. Title
HF1007.M175   1977   382.1   76-54770
ISBN 0-231-04298-1

Contents

Preface

The Fourth World Congress of the International Economic Association, held in Budapest in August 1974, had as its theme 'Economic Integration: Worldwide, Regional, Sectoral'. My presidential address was on 'The History of Thought on Economic integration'. In my research for this intellectual history, I had collected far more material than I could possibly pack into the limited space of a paper for oral delivery. I therefore selected only a few pages for full presentation and several sections for condensed presentation at the Congress and I briefly reported on the existence of additional material to be published soon at an appropriate place.

My address to the Congress is being published in the volume of proceedings, *Economic Integration: Worldwide, Regional, Sectoral* (London: Macmillan, 1976, and New York: Halsted Press, 1977) in a version expanded beyond what I had time to present orally, but still abbreviated compared with what I had accumulated in preparing for my task. No matter whether that address will be considered an abridged version of this book, or whether this book will be regarded as an expanded version of the address published in the conference proceedings, the historical survey offered here is still incomplete in several respects. The chief limitation is that it covers publications in only a few languages: English, French, German, and a few items in Italian. This limitation is surely understandable, but since the Congress was attended by economists from 77 countries, I apologised for my disregard of the literature in other languages. I am painfully aware of another deficiency: even in the languages covered in this survey I have probably been rather arbitrary in the selections made of particular authors or specific contributions and also regarding the space or emphasis given to writers and issues selected for inclusion.

My book is divided into three main parts. The first deals with

the *term* and its history, the second with the *idea* and its different strands. The reason for this partition is immediately obvious.
Words are supposed to convey ideas, but neither words nor concepts remain for ever unchanged. New terms are introduced to
convey old concepts, and old concepts are modified, enlarged or
restricted, often without change in the terms employed. The history of an idea must therefore be distinguished from the history
of the word attached to it at present or at any one time.

The third part is a review of the *contributors* to the idea of
economic integration. The separation of intellectual history into
a part dealing with thought without naming the thinkers and
another part presenting the authors but offering only brief statements of their chief contributions to the subject is, I admit, an
unusual procedure. I chose this design for several reasons. Among
them was the realisation that my sources were in no small part
outside the domain of economics in the professional sense.
Political historians, statesmen, and men of letters have had much
to say on our subject and their contributions ought to be considered.

If I am criticised for giving the third part of this study the
shape of an annotated bibliography rather than a traditional
history of thought, I accept this criticism as largely justified. I
believe, however, it will prove useful to many. As a bibliography
it provides information usually withheld in bibliographical references. It gives the fully spelled out first names of all authors —
which ought to be helpful to users of library catalogues, where
searches are made unnecessarily time-consuming when only the
initials of the authors' first names are known — and it states the
years of birth of all living authors and the years of birth and
death of those deceased. Such information, though trivial for
most readers, may make this book a useful reference work to
some.

The definition of economic integration used in this book
makes the theory of international integration almost co-exten-
sive with the theory of international trade. Though my conception may be regarded by some of my colleagues as excessively
broad, it has led me to produce a book that can qualify as a text
in International Economics. While this was not my intention
when I embarked on writing it, I do not regret the result.
Students may be pleased to see an advanced text that succeeds
in explaining complex economic arguments without the use of a
single mathematical equation or of any graphical demonstration.
In these days, exclusively verbal expositions of economic theory
are not easy to come by.

I have alluded to the reasons for separating the survey of ideas from the survey of contributors: Chapter 4 presents ideas and arguments without naming their authors, and Chapter 9 gives the sources with only brief allusions to the ideas and arguments. This arrangement may have a special appeal to some teachers in that it makes the book a good instrument for 'open-book examinations'.

Acknowledgements are due to many who need not be listed here: scores of economists who responded to my request for information unavailable in our libraries on their years of birth and their first names (kept secret by inconsiderate editors and publishers). I must also thank several research assistants for their help in library research; but only one of them should be named here: Miss Jessica Kennedy, who diligently and resourcefully obtained or verified for me much of the bibliographical information needed for Chapters 5 and 8.

One of my friends may be credited or blamed for the existence of this book. When I was thinking about the choice of topic for my presidential address to the Congress of the International Economic Association, my notorious penchant for conceptual analysis and semantic exercises was driving me to write a paper confined to the meanings and definitions of economic integration. It was Professor Harry G. Johnson who encouraged me to undertake the more ambitious task of 'A History of Thought on Economic Integration'. I can only hope that my readers will not regret that I followed Harry's advice.

FRITZ MACHLUP

New York University

Part One
The Term, its History, and its Meaning

The word 'integration', taken from the Latin, is of course very old. In Latin, *integratio* was mostly used in the sense of 'renovation'. The *Oxford English Dictionary* gives 1620 as the date for the first use in print of integration in the sense of 'combining parts into a whole'.

I have not undertaken to find out in what fields of systematic knowledge the word had its earlier uses. I did however inquire into the history of the term in economics and, especially, in international economics. The first chapter is to report my findings of this research. In the course of this inquiry I became impressed with the wide spectrum of meanings which had been attached to the term even in the presumed narrow sense of spatial or geographic economic integration. I felt compelled to let the chapter on 'The Use of the Term in Economics' be followed by one on 'The Meaning of the Term'.

1 The Use of the Term in Economics

In economics the word was first employed in industrial organisation to refer to *combinations of business firms* through agreements, cartels, concerns, trusts, and mergers — horizontal integration referring to combinations of competitors, vertical integration to combinations of suppliers with customers.[1] In the sense of *combining separate economies* into larger economic regions the word integration has a very short history.

NOT USED UNTIL RECENTLY

I have tried to find the earliest uses of the word in this meaning. It had not been so used anywhere in the old, chiefly historical, literature on the economic amalgamation of the nation-state, nor in the literature on customs unions, including the *Zollverein*, nor in the literature on international trade before the 1940s. No subject index of any book that I know on international economics prior to 1953 contains the entry 'integration'.

The Encyclopaedia of the Social Sciences, published in 1937, did have the word in its index, but as 'Integration, industrial — see Combinations, industrial' (Vol. XV, p. 629) and the cited article began by distinguishing between horizontal and vertical combinations through mergers, concerns, and cartels (Vol. III, p. 664). The new *International Encyclopedia of the Social Sciences*, published in 1968, does include 'International Integration', indeed four articles. Three of them — one on 'Regional Integration', another on 'Global Integration', the third on 'Func-

---

[1] I have dealt in detail with the differences between the integration of enterprises or industries and the integration of economies in my essay 'Integrationshemmende Integrationspolitik', in *Bernhard-Harms Vorlesungen* 5/6, ed. by Herbert Giersch (Kiel: Institut für Weltwirtschaft, 1974). There I explained why sectoral integration may be a serious hindrance to general economic integration.

tional Integration' — were written by political scientists.[2] Only
the fourth article, on 'Economic Unions', was by an economist
(Vol. 7, pp. 541—6).

Let me offer one other piece of circumstantial evidence for
my supposition that we have here an instance of a rather sudden
change in terminology. When Jan Tinbergen published in 1954
his book on *International Economic Integration*, he told us in
the Preface that its predecessor edition, published in 1945, had
borne the title *International Economic Co-operation*. We see
that a larger family of words — ranging from economic rapprochement via co-operation and solidarity to amalgamation,
fusion, and unification — had been given a new name; economic
integration. But who did it? Who was or who were the terminological innovators?

THE FIRST USERS: A DETECTIVE STORY

My search for the first user or users has had all the characteristics
of a detective story. There were several suspects, wrong clues,
vain efforts, surprising discoveries, and much suspense (for
example, when a new clue was perceived and a new track followed). A few times the search seemed successfully completed,
but then a still earlier source was found and possible links had
to be investigated. Indeed, I cannot be sure that I have tracked
down all writers responsible for the novel use of the old term. I
can well imagine that a rival detective will come up with a new
find, making my own findings nugatory.

There is the possibility of multiple invention, several persons
independently hitting upon the same terminological innovation.
I have tracked down several writers — between 1930 and 1942 —
who could have been independent users of the term in its new
meaning. At least they did not cite or refer to any other author.
Yet I have found numerous links among most of these writers,
which make it more likely that their use of the term was not
original but derivative. There is nothing wrong with adapting to
the technical language of other writers without paying any atten-

[2] In political science, the term 'political integration' within and among
countries had been used earlier, at least since the late 1920s. The following
statement may be quoted in support of this opinion: '. . . the "appearance
of political integration" which the League has already produced in some
measure, is to find its economic complement. . .' The complement, however,
was still called 'European economic solidarity'. Harry D. Gideonse, 'Economic Foundations of Pan-Europeanism', *The Annals of the American
Academy of Political and Social Science*, Vol. CXLIX (May 1930) p. 155.

tion to the question whether a certain special term was novel or
original with the scholar from whom it has been taken over. My
hypothesis is that the term in its new meaning was original with
two books, completely independent of each other, but derivative
in the other publications. The first of these books was by two
German writers on trade statistics, published in 1933. The other
was the English translation by Mendel Shapiro of the first Swedish edition of Eli F. Heckscher's work on *Mercantilism*. The
Swedish edition was published in 1931, the English in 1935. For
reasons which will soon be apparent I choose to talk first about
the Heckscher volumes.[3]

The Swedish edition does not contain the word 'integration'
except as an adjective — an 'integrating state policy' — not its
opposite, 'disintegration'. It does, however, employ such words
as *splittring* and *upplösning*, which could be rendered in English
as splintering, fragmentation, decomposition, or dissolution, but
were in fact translated as disintegration. Thus we read how 'mercantilism as a unifying system' attempted to overcome the
'economic disintegration' that had been caused by feudal powers,
by the system of river tolls and road tolls (p. 36), and by 'local
disintegration in other spheres' (p. 110), until at last 'victory of
the [nation] state over particularism' (p. 137) was achieved. The
'unification' was, of course, limited to the national economy
and inter-provincial trade.

Heckscher's work was widely read and one may assume that
among its readers was a group of five writers who used the term
economic disintegration not only for intranational but also, or
chiefly, for international trade. It happens that close links and
associations existed among these five economists. They published
their relevant studies between 1938 and 1942; three of them
were residents of Geneva, two were teaching at the London
School of Economics: I refer to Wilhelm Röpke, Ludwig Mises,
Moritz Bonn, Friedrich Hayek, and Folke Hilgerdt. Perhaps it is
also significant that, like Heckscher, Hilgerdt was Swedish, and
that Röpke published one of his relevant pieces as an article in
Swedish; that Mises and Röpke were colleagues at Geneva; and
that Bonn and Hayek, both in London, belonged with Röpke
and Mises to the same circle of liberal (libertarian) economists.

Röpke's article on 'Decisive Problems of the Disintegration of

---

[3] Eli F. Heckscher, *Merkantilismen* (Stockholm: Norstedt & Söners, 1931).
English editions: Eli F. Heckscher, *Mercantilism*, authorised translation by
Mendel Shapiro (London: Allen & Unwin, 1935); revised edition, edited by
E. F. Söderlund (London: Allen & Unwin, 1955). The second edition is
enlarged by additional notes and chapters, but the text itself is unchanged.

World Economy',[4] appeared in *Ekonomisk Tidskrift* in January 1939. Röpke's book, on which he had worked for several years, appeared under the title *International Economic Disintegration* (Edinburgh: Hodge, 1942). He showed that a process of international economic integration, from about 1700 to 1914, was followed by economic disintegration, which was still going on when he was writing. Röpke found that socio-political and economic integration were interrelated, as were also the disintegration movements in both spheres.

In 1938 both Röpke and Mises had contributed to a volume on *The World Crisis*, a collection of essays by professors at the Graduate Institute of International Studies in Geneva. The essay by Mises in this volume carried the title 'Disintegration of the International Division of Labour'. It was largely a critique of the political and economic arguments against free trade and of the nationalist tendencies of the time which had halted the earlier progress towards freer movements of goods, capital, money, and people. The words integration and disintegration, however, were not in the text of the essay: the fact that 'disintegration' appeared in its title suggests that Mises liked Ropke's usage of the term, but had learned it only after he had completed his manuscript.[5]

In the same year, 1938, Moritz J. Bonn, who since his emigration from Germany had been teaching at the London School of Economics, published a book with the title *The Crumbling of Empire: The Disintegration of World Economy* (London: Allen & Unwin). As in the cases of Heckscher and Mises, only the negative noun, not the positive 'integration' was used. 'Disintegration

[4] Wilhelm Röpke, 'Världshushållningens förfall och därmed sammanhängande grundfrågor', *Ekonomisk Tidskrift*, Vol. XLI (January 1939) pp. 11—29. The English rendition of the Swedish title is by Röpke himself (in the Preface of his 1942 book, p. v); it may be noted that disintegration is not a literal translation of the Swedish word *förfall*.

[5] I may record here another instance of a writer using the negative of our term in the title only, and not in the text. Dag Hammarskjöld, the Swedish economist (later Secretary-General of the United Nations), contributed a 'Note on a Desintegrated, Provisional Standard as a Basis of Stabilization' to *The Problems of Monetary Stabilization*, Part II of a volume published by a Joint Committee of the Carnegie Endowment and the International Chamber of Commerce (Paris: International Chamber of Commerce, 1936), pp. 384—96. Hammarskjöld thus has priority in the economic use of 'desintegrated', but he applied the verb not to potential trade and factor movements but to an exchange-rate system in which several countries or groups of countries pursue separate (and therefore 'disintegrated') policies of monetary stabilisation and exchange-rate adjustment. Note that Hammarskjöld was Swedish and wrote his paper one year after the English edition of Heckscher's work was published.

appears in the title of Bonn's book, in its Introduction, and as
the title of its Part II (p. 99). Yet Chapter 2 in Part II is called
'Economic Separatism' (p. 120). There Bonn recounts how 'continental nationalism joined hands with colonial nationalism in
revolting against the empire of Free Trade which England was
trying to establish' (p. 122). Elsewhere in the book, Bonn speaks
of 'economic isolation' (p. 196) and of 'regional economic
nationalism' (p. 214) as two of the movements that have contributed to the 'complete disintegration of the Western world'
(p. 17) and have halted the earlier trend toward 'economic .
universalism'. However, Bonn believed that 'the choice lies between conquest and federation, or rather between compulsory
and voluntary federation' (p. 402). In any case, 'the day of a
federated Central Europe is bound to come' (p. 421).

In September 1939, Hayek published an article on 'Economic
Conditions of Inter-State Federalism' (*The New Commonwealth
Quarterly*, Vol. V), discussing 'Union Now', the movement for
an Atlantic Union which had been promoted by Clarence Streit.
Hayek, like Heckscher, Bonn, and Mises, spoke only of 'disintegration', not integration, for example, when he credited the Constitution of the United States with having helped 'to prevent an
even more rapid disintegration into many separate economic
areas' (p. 144).

Folke Hilgerdt, the fifth writer in this group, was an economist
and statistician with the League of Nations in Geneva. Regarding
the links that may connect him with earlier writers on international economic integration, we should consider several possibilities. As I have said, he was a Swede, like Heckscher, and he
resided in Geneva, like Röpke and Mises. But he was chiefly
working on trade statistics, and thus was probably acquainted
with the work of the two German statisticians whom I have
mentioned as probably independent originators of the term in
its new meaning. This is then the place to introduce Gaedicke
and von Eynern.

In a series under the editorship of Alfred Weber (who is best
known for his theory of economic location) there had appeared
in 1933 a two-volume work by Herbert Gaedicke and Gert von
Eynern on *Die produktionswirtschaftliche Integration Europas:
Eine Untersuchung über die Aussenhandelsverflechtung der
europäischen Länder* (Berlin: Junker und Dünnhaupt, 1933).
Part I contained the text, Part II statistical tables. In a literal
English translation the title would read 'The production-econo-
mic integration of Europe: An investigation of the interweaving
by foreign trade of the countries of Europe'. The authors set them-

selves the task of showing statistically the 'integration of
Europe's economy', that is, the degree to which the economies
of the individual countries were interrelated ('interwoven')
through supplying one another with raw materials and intermediate products (p. 2). Statistics of foreign trade were used fo
the measurement of this integration, and the conclusion was th:
there existed a 'high degree of export integration', chiefly of
continental Europe, but also of all Europe and 'all Europe inclu
ive of Russia'. The trade data indicated that this integration wa
substantially disturbed through the First World War (p. 28). Th
authors broke down their figures by countries and commodity
groups; they also distinguished between *Kerneuropa* (core-
Europe) and *Randeuropa* (peripheral Europe). Their statistical
techniques were primitive, but their effort to measure or apprai
the 'degree of integration' merits respect.

Hilgerdt's task was more ambitious inasmuch as his study
comprised the whole world. He produced the volume *The Network of World Trade* (Geneva: Economic Intelligence Service,
League of Nations, 1942). He computed the matrices of international trade to show the changing patterns of world trade.
These patterns had become increasingly complicated with the
'steady integration of economic activities in different continents'
which despite the deterioration of the system during the 1920s
and 1930s 'remained a central factor in the mechanism tending
to render the world an economic unit' (p. 67). Hilgerdt was the
first to present statistical evidence pointing to the 'world-wide
integration of the economy of different countries' (p. 88).[6]

The term in its new connotation crossed the Atlantic, I sup-
pose, in 1941. Perhaps it did so in the luggage of Mr Hilgerdt,
when the Economic Intelligence Service of the League moved t
Princeton. (Indeed, *The Network of World Trade* was printed a
the Princeton University Press.) But the first American user of
our term was John S. de Beers, an economist in the US Treasur
Department, in an article on "Tariff Aspects of a Federal Union
(*Quarterly Journal of Economics*, Vol. LVI, November 1941).
There was a table with the caption 'Economic Integration of
Certain Areas and Groups of Countries as Indicated by Foreign
Trade Statistics' (p. 67). The term does not appear anywhere el
in the 52 pages of this piece.[7]

---

[6] One year earlier, the volume on *Europe's Trade*, also published by the
League of Nations [1941] had not yet contained the term integration;
'interdependence', 'trading groups', and 'intra-trade' were the closest rela-
tives present.

[7] Dr de Beers cannot remember how he came to use 'economic integra-

In December 1942 two papers using our term were presented at the Washington meeting of the American Economic Association, one by Folke Hilgerdt on 'The Case for Multilateral Trade', the other by Antonin Basch on 'European Economic Regionalism' (*American Economic Review*, Papers and Proceedings, Vol. XXXIII, March 1943). Hilgerdt spoke of 'the multilateral exchange of goods and services that provides for the international economic integration of countries in a manner profitable to all' (p. 406) and he suggested that 'the international integration we have in mind will have to be achieved by co-ordination of national economic policies, particularly in the field of foreign trade' (p. 407). Basch discussed the case 'for a reversal of the prewar movement towards self-sufficiency of all kinds' and for 'inter-European trade . . . to achieve a greater integration of the European economy' (p. 409).

ADOPTION OF THE TERM FOR OFFICIAL USE

I still had to find out when and how the term invaded the official language of Washington, London, Paris, and other centres of government.[8] The term was not yet in Winston Churchill's speech in which he, in September 1946, called for the 're-creation of the European family', nor in the resolution of ECOSOC (the Economic and Social Council of the United Nations), recognising, in the same autumn, the necessity of 'regional economic co-operation'. Nor was the term used in March 1947 in the Fulbright Resolution of the United States Congress, favouring 'the creation of a United States of Europe within the framework of the United Nations'. And, more surprising, the term was not yet in George Marshall's address at Harvard on 5 June 1947, in which the Secretary of State observed that 'visible destruction [in Europe] was probably less serious than the dislocation of the entire fabric of European economy . . .' and that 'the modern system of the division of labor upon which the exchange of products is based is in danger of breaking down.' This address was the launching of the Marshall Plan, the European Recovery Programme.

---

tion' in the caption of his table. His article was based on a term paper which he had written for a seminar of Professor Jacob Viner at the University of Chicago.

[8] In this search I was greatly helped by Professor Sidney Ratner, who referred me to some of the pertinent publications. Without his knowledge of the period and its literature my detective work would have been much more difficult.

Marshall's address might have included the term under review because among the documents underlying the drafting was the outline of a paper by three young economists working in the State Department, sent to George F. Kennan, Director of the Policy Planning Staff, early in May 1947, in which the writers called for 'a coordinated European Recovery Program' directed 'toward a strong and economically integrated Europe'.[9] The three economists were Harold Van B. Cleveland, Ben T. Moore, and Charles P. Kindleberger.

During the weeks in which this memorandum was being prepared and discussed the term integration appeared in various documents, most of them 'Top Secret' and circulated only among the top members of the government departments. There was a 'Report of the Special "Ad Hoc" Committee of the State War-Navy Coordinating Committee' (Washington, 21 April 1947),[10] which in Annex A of Appendix A employed the term in question in two consecutive paragraphs in two different meanings. In paragraph 30 we read of the need for 'successful integration and coordination of the economic programs in the critical countries' — which, of course, is not what we are now searching for — but only three lines later, in paragraph 31, we read of the hope for 'reintegration of these countries into healthy regional and world trading and production systems' — which is precisely what we *are* talking about.

On 23 May 1947, a memorandum from George F. Kennan to Dean Acheson, Under Secretary of State, spoke of what 'action should be taken in the immediate future to halt the economic disintegration of Western Europe.[11] On 27 May 1947 a memorandum from William L. Clayton, Under Secretary of State for Economic Affairs, sent to Acheson (and probably read by and discussed with Secretary Marshall) stated the opinion that 'without further prompt and substantial aid from the United States, economic, social and political disintegration will overwhelm Europe.[12]

---

[9] Quoted from Joseph M. Jones, *The Fifteen Weeks*, New York: Viking Press, 1955, pp. 243—4. Jones quotes also from a speech which Dean Acheson, Under Secretary of State, had delivered earlier that year in Mississippi and which contained the idea of integration but not the word. It spoke of the necessity of the 'various parts of Europe's economy . . . working together in a harmonious whole' and of 'a coordinated European economy' (p. 280).

[10] US Department of State, *Foreign Relations of the United States, 1947*, Vol. III (Washington: 1974) pp. 214—15.

[11] Ibid., p. 225.

[12] Ibid., p. 231. Clayton was recommending a generous grant: 'This three

One other memorandum from the collection of official papers may be quoted here, particularly because it put our term into the mouth of a foreign diplomat. In this memorandum, written two weeks after the Marshall Address (and following an article in *Pravda* of 16 June 1947, which had made American officials wonder about the position of the countries of Eastern Europe), Benjamin V. Cohen, Counselor in the Department of State, reported his conversation with the Polish Ambassador. According to Cohen, the Ambassador 'pointed to the role that Poland had played in the creation of the ECE and the fact that Poland had decreased the proportion of her exports going to the Soviet Union as evidence of Poland's desire to *integrate her economy with that of Western Europe*'.[13]

During 1948 we find the term used in an increasing number of speeches and documents. The most conspicuous use of 'economic integration' in an official pronouncement came on 31 October 1949, when Paul Hoffmann, the Administrator of the ECA (Economic Cooperation Administration) addressed the Council of the OEEC (Organisation of European Economic Co-operation). Hoffmann urged faster progress toward 'an integration of the Western European economy" and explained its meaning in these words:

> The substance of such integration would be the formation of a single large market within which quantitative restrictions on the movements of goods, monetary barriers to the flow of payments and, eventually, all tariffs are permanently swept away.

The Paris correspondent of the *New York Times* of 1 November 1949 observed that

> Mr Hoffmann used the word 'integration' fifteen times or almost once to every hundred words of his speech. It is a word that rarely if ever has been used by European statesmen having to do with the Marshall Plan to describe what should happen to Europe's economies.

---

year grant to Europe should be based on a European plan which the principal European nations . . . should work out. Such a plan should be based on a European *economic federation* on the order of the Belgium-Netherlands-Luxembourg Customs Union. Europe cannot recover from this war and again become independent if her economy continues to be *divided into many small watertight compartments* as it is today' (p. 232, italics not in the original).

[13] Ibid., p. 261. Italics not in the original.

It is strange that Mr Hoffmann's agency, the US Economic Co-operation Administration, in its quarterly reports to Congress had always spoken of economic co-operation, liberalisation, unification, and customs unions. The first use of the word integration that I could detect in this source was in the *Fifth Report to Congress*, transmitted on 15 November 1949, in relation to a Scandinavian customs union. It mentioned, in the section on 'Customs Unions', that 'further progress has been made toward the achievement of economic integration among the Scandinavia countries' [p. 6]. But, in any case, the term was 'in'; it had taken the place of all previously used synonyms in practically all languages in which such matters are talked about.

2 The Meaning of the Term and its Scope

Now that we know, or believe we know, the history of the term and its new meaning, we must admit that this meaning is by no means clear. Let me quote a footnote from a historian's work published in 1955.

> The term 'integration' came into general ECA usage . . . reflecting an adaptation to diverse currents of thought on both sides of the Atlantic. The word, though never precisely defined, connoted more than casual co-operation but less than full unification. Marjolin of the OEEC later [in a book published in 1953] spoke of integration as embracing all the steps taken toward unification, even though they might fall far short of that ideal . . .[1]

If one could reasonably say, twenty years ago, that the term had never been precisely defined, one must say now that we suffer less from a lack of definitions than from an abundance of mutually contradictory definitions.

UNANIMITY, CONSENSUS, DIVERGENCE

Users are virtually unanimous on one question: that integration can be understood either as a process or as a state of affairs reached by that process. Whether that state has to be the terminal point or any intermediate point in the process is not always clear, but this ambiguity can be taken care of by distinguishing between complete and incomplete integration. More difficult is

---

[1] Harry Bayard Price, *The Marshall Plan and Its Meaning* (Ithaca, NY: Cornell University Press, 1955) p. 122, footnote 7. The reference in the quotation is to Robert Marjolin, *Europe and the United States in the World Economy* (Durham, NC: Duke University Press, 1953).

the question of what it is that is to be integrated: people, areas,
markets, production, goods, resources, or what? If areas are
meant, do they have to be national territories? The most important questions, however, ask (1) what is the substance, what are
the essential criteria of such integration and (2) by what indications, or symptoms, can one decide whether there is or is not a
process at work, or a state of affairs attained? These are very
different questions. Users of the term may agree on what the
substance is and yet disagree on how one can find out or what
one should observe; conversely, some might agree on possible
indicators without agreeing on the essentials, on what it is all
about. Just to give one example, there is fundamental disagreement on the relation between economic integration and equalisation of incomes (or of the prices of productive services) in differ
ent areas, some writers regarding equalisation as the essence of
integration, others as a possible consequence, others as the main
target, others as an indicator, and others as merely incidental or
even unrelated to economic integration.

A wide consensus exists on three issues: one, that economic
integration refers basically to division of labour; two, that it involves mobility of goods or factors or both; and three, that it is
related to discrimination or non-discrimination in the treatment
of goods and factors (for example, with regard to origin or destination). This consensus does not imply agreement on a definition. We shall have to discuss all three issues before we can
decide on their comparative significance.

Many disagreements about the most appropriate definition
can be disposed of by the use of adjectives modifying the noun.
When Bela Balassa presented us with a very helpful review of
definitions,[2] he proposed the rejection of some definitions as
being too wide. Yet one does not have to reject a definition on
these grounds as long as the concept can be narrowed through
the use of a qualifying adjective with the term. For example,
Balassa wanted the definition of economic integration to restrict
the process or state of affairs to different *nations* joining in a
regional group or bloc. This is an unnecessary restriction, and an
uneconomical one, because the economics of the matter is the
same whether it is different provinces of a state that become
'more integrated', or different nations within a bloc, or different
blocs in the world as a whole. One can easily differentiate by

[2] Bela Balassa, 'Towards a Theory of Economic Integration', *Kyklos*, Vol.
XIV (1961) pp. 1—17; also *The Theory of Economic Integration* (Homewood, Ill.: Irwin, 1961) pp. 1—3.

speaking of *national* (interprovincial, intranational), *regional* (multinational), and *worldwide* (global, universal) integration.

Similarly, instead of arguing whether certain arrangements for co-ordination or unified management of particular sectors of two or more economies (say electricity, mining, transportation, communication, etc.) deserve to be called economic integration — I would be inclined to deny it — one may agree to speak of such arrangements as *sectoral* integration, as distinguished from *general* economic integration. The use of 'general' in contradistinction to sectoral or partial integration is intended to produce in the reader's or listener's mind an association with general-equilibrium theory, a system of interactions and interdependences in the sense that any activity is directly or indirectly related to any other activity in the economy (seen as a system or region).

Again, instead of arguing whether a very small increase in the division of labour deserves or does not deserve to be regarded as economic integration (seen as a process), one may agree to speak of attaining higher and lower *degrees* of integration. On closer inspection, however, we shall find that the idea of degrees involves the possibility of quantification, measurement or estimation, and that we still have much to learn on these matters.

Several different techniques, forms, or aspects of general economic integration are hard to distinguish by mere adjectives or by a few explanatory words. For example, international economic integration can be attained — this has been stated as one of the issues on which a wide consensus exists — through movements of people, funds, and products, all three or any two, or only one. This has been well-known long before the term economic integration was introduced, and some writers on integration have stressed this distinction, as, for example, Tinbergen in 1952. Balassa proposes that we distinguish *trade* integration, *factor* integration, *policy* integration, and *total* integration. One wonders, however, to what extent factor integration presupposes trade integration, and to what extent *policy* integration presupposes trade and factor integration. Moreover, one may ask whether factor integration refers to all types of factors of production and to what extent it would co-exist with unrestricted movement of goods. (There will later be an occasion to reflect on the theory that free mobility of products across national frontiers can, under ideal conditions, achieve the same results as could be attained by perfect mobility of labour and capital.) Perhaps we had better speak of common or integrated product markets, labour markets, and capital markets. The term *market* integration was proposed by Vajda.[3] It is a useful term, but one should understand that the economic implications of market integration are very different if only *some* markets — say, for certain agricultural and industrial products, or for certain kinds of labour — are integrated or if *all* markets are integrated. In the former case, there may be only little progress toward general economic integration, and perhaps even net retardation. The distortion in the economy through partial, selective, sectoral integration may be so serious that the effects may be damaging, rather than beneficial, on balance.

DIVISION OF LABOUR, MOBILITY, AND NON-DISCRIMINATION

Complete integration of markets implies adequate mobility of whatever it is that is supplied in the markets in question and non-discrimination in the sense that neither sellers nor buyers are influenced by the origin or destination of the thing bought or sold. Mobility need only be adequate (rather than perfect) because it is not necessary that every single unit of the product or factor of production be movable; it suffices for all practical purposes if a certain part of the total supply can be moved without undue cost or trouble.

Let us try to illustrate the condition of perfect mobility and non-discrimination separately for product markets, labour markets, and capital markets. One may regard the wheat market in the United States as fully integrated if the buyer does not care whether the wheat was grown in Iowa or in Kansas, and the seller does not care whether it is shipped to California or to New York. The wheat market in the European Community would be regarded as fully integrated if the buyer did not care whether the wheat was grown in France or in Germany, and the seller did not care where it was being shipped — each of which is made difficult because of a variety of formalities, restrictions, and border taxes or adjustments according to CAP regulations (Common Agricultural Policy).

One may regard a labour market, say for unskilled factory workers in the United States, as fully integrated if the employer does not care whether the worker comes from Ohio or from

[3] Imre Vajda, 'Integration, Economic Union and the National State', in Imre Vajda and Mihály Simai, eds, *Foreign Trade in a Planned Economy*, (Cambridge: Cambridge University Press, 1971) p. 33. Vajda wanted 'market integration' to be supplemented by 'production and development integration' (pp. 35ff.).

Tennessee, and if the worker does not care (apart from the cost of moving) whether the job is in Pennsylvania or in Illinois. The market for the same type of labour in the European Community would be regarded as fully integrated if the employer did not care whether the worker came from Belgium or from Italy, and the worker did not care (apart from the cost of moving) in which of the Common Market countries his job might be. These conditions seem to be approachable, since there are no governmental restrictions, but language barriers make things more difficult.

The capital market in the United States is fully integrated if the buyer of shares of stock does not care whether the issuing corporation has its headquarters or most of its assets in Delaware or in Minnesota, and if the corporation does not care who its stockholders are or where they reside. The analogous indifference does not prevail in the European Community, where most stockholders hold shares of stock in corporations domiciled in the same country and where the acquisition of foreign securities and the sale of securities to foreign buyers may be subject to governmental restrictions and controls.

These illustrations may have given some idea of how both mobility and non-discrimination are related to economic integration. It seems that it would be more to the point to look at both as necessary conditions rather than as the essentials in the definition of integration. If, for example, mobility of a part of the supply suffices to attain the allocation or distribution that corresponds to the economic optimisation model, why should the definition of economic integration require mobility of the *entire* supply? However, if we are satisfied with 'adequate' mobility, we obviously think of adequacy for a purpose, namely, for the attainment of complete general economic integration — and this clearly marks integration as something other than mobility of products and/or factors. The same holds for non-discrimination; it is a necessary (though not sufficient) condition for economic integration.[4]

[4] Whenever it is less than worldwide, integration implies both discrimination and non-discrimination. Regional integration, for example, requires non-discrimination among products and factors coming from (or going to) countries *within* the region, but discrimination against products or factors coming from (or going to) countries *outside* the region. Assume three separate countries, A, B and C, had separate import tariffs, so that each discriminated against the products of the other two in favour of its domestic products; if A and B now form a customs union, B-products will no longer be discriminated against compared with the domestic products of A, but there will be discrimination against C-products in favour of those of A and B.

Can we take division of labour to be an essential part of the definition of economic integration? If we do, we carry out, I believe, the intentions of most users of the term; I believe also that we thereby conform to the ideas of socialist as well as of free-enterprise economists. A very neat formulation in terms of an analogy helpful in explaining the essence of general economic integration has recently been offered by a Polish economist, Stanislaw Chelstowski. As he puts it, in an article on 'CMEA and Integration' (*Polish Perspectives*, Vol. XV, December 1972), it means 'tailoring the economic fabric of each country to the requirements of an international division of labour' (p. 10). But how much international division of labour has to be arranged for? Is there a minimum and/or a maximum of exchange of products that makes it economic integration?

ACTUAL VERSUS POTENTIAL: OPPORTUNITIES REALISED AND UNREALISED

I submit that the idea of complete integration implies the *actual* utilisation of all *potential* opportunities of efficient division of labour. The notion of taking advantage of an existing but hitherto unused opportunity relegates the entire conception from the domain of recorded observations to the domain of delicate calculations based on data not publicly available and not recorded anywhere. For, alas, whether an unused opportunity for a beneficial exchange of potentially produced goods exists cannot be shown except by a benefit-and-cost analysis in which benefits as well as costs are hypothesised with the help of an imaginative marginal calculus.

If progress in the degree of international economic integration is made by increasing trade, but only such trade as benefits the economies affected, and if complete integration is attained when all opportunities for beneficial expansion of trade are exhausted, two important inferences follow. First, it is conceivable that some increase in the exchange of goods does not constitute a higher degree of integration, because the calculations of the opportunity costs of production and exchange may have been faulty or neglected. (Exports may have been subsidised at the expense of forgone alternatives.) Secondly, it is possible that in the cases of certain countries a relatively small volume of foreign trade represents complete integration between the countries concerned — because there may not be any more opportunities for gainful trade left unused — and that, in other cases, a large volume of foreign trade represents a still very incomplete integration of the economies in question, because so many opportunities for efficient division of labour remain unused.

The calculations relevant for the evaluation of actual and potential exchange are so delicate and complex because they involve an indefinite number of inputs and outputs indirectly related to one another by alternative employment and alternative production. General economic integration of the economies under consideration does not refer to particular industries or sectors, nor to particular factors or products, intermediate or final, but rather to the *entirety of economic activities* of the region (country, bloc, or world). It is an integration of all productive resources available anywhere in the region for the production of all the many goods and services demanded under actually or potentially realised conditions. It is constituted by a complete interweaving and interdependence of *all* economic sectors, industries, branches, and any activities whatsoever, in the closest possible approximation to the theoretical model of general equilibrium in a system with unrestricted mobility of all movable factors and products, intermediate and finished.[5]

The essential criterion of complete general economic integration is commonly seen in equality of prices of equal goods and equal services. That is to say, that all means of production (original or intermediate) in the integrated economic region which are both perfectly mobile and perfectly substitutable for one another (hence, genuinely equal) will receive the same prices and will have the same marginal net value productivity in all their uses. Of course this also implies that unequal means of production (i.e., those not perfectly substitutable for one another) will not command equal prices (except by sheer coincidence). Equality of prices despite inequality of the marginal net value productivities — for example, due to lower efficiency or unfavourable location — is a typical form of discrimination, which may meet some standards of social justice but definitely violates the principle of general economic integration.

The economically optimal relationships among all costs and prices in the completely integrated area can be determined only in a system of perfect interdependence. This presupposes that all enterprises and all agencies in charge of planning and allocation have to make their calculations on the basis of opportunity cost. Every means of production, wherever actually used, has to be valued according to the social utility that could potentially be

[5] Fritz Machlup, 'Integrationshemmende Integrationspolitik', *Bernhard-Harms-Vorlesungen* 5/6 (Kiel: Institut für Weltwirtschaft, 1974) p. 43.

derived from alternative uses. Such alternative uses may be anywhere in the (supposedly) integrated region and in any sector,
industry, or branch, however remote. All means of production
have to 'compete' for all possible uses, and all branches of production have to 'compete' for all possibly usable means of production. In market economies this competition includes effectiv
competition among enterprises; in comprehensively planned
economies it involves competition among all conceivable altern;
tives in the considerations of the decision-making agencies or
boards. Expressed in a slightly modified way: all inputs are con
sidered eligible to compete for uses in the production of all
conceivable outputs, and all outputs are considered eligible to
compete for allocations of all conceivable inputs. In this inter-
relatedness and interdependence among all economic activities I
see the essence of general economic integration. This is the prin
ciple, and it applies equally to a single country, a group of
countries, or the whole world.[6]

FREEDOM FROM RESTRICTIONS VERSUS SELECTIVE ACTIVISM

While unrestricted movements of all kinds of labour, capital, an
products may be necessary conditions of general integration of
any economy or combination of economies, the *freedom* of
travel and migration, capital transfer, and trade may not be
sufficient for the attainment of full integration. Ordinarily,
various institutions and policies are needed to secure the full
utilisation of all efficient possibilities of division of labour. This
is most readily seen if one reminds oneself of the facts that trad
calls for payments, that capital movements call for the exchange
ability of different currencies, and that migrations on a large
scale call for chances to take possessions along and to remit earr
ings. Hence an international payments system that allows payments and foreign-exchange transactions without restrictions or
controls — in short, monetary integration — is an integral part o
complete economic integration. One can understand, therefore,
why several writers add *policy* integration and *institutional* integration to integration of the markets for labour, capital, and
products.

If governments of countries with free enterprise are intent
upon promoting international economic integration, regional or
worldwide, they will have to act in these three ways: to remove

[6] Ibid., pp. 44—5.

restrictions on the movements of people, funds, and goods; to pursue policies designed to correct wrong signals of the free market and to strengthen the effects of correct signals; and to create permanent institutions without which the integrating forces of free markets may be too weak to be effective. Jan Tinbergen proposed to speak of the first of these techniques as *negative* integration, and of the two others as *positive* integration. He may only have wanted to contrast the removal of old governmental policies and institutions (namely, of those that prevent integration) with the establishment of new policies and institutions (designed to aid integration). But the evaluative connotations of negative and positive make these into loaded words. The removal of discriminatory and restrictive institutions and thus the grant of freedom of economic transaction is called negative, while the establishment of policies and institutions endowed with the coercive powers of the state is called positive; *ergo*, freedom is negative, coercion is positive.

Those who see in liberalisation (of trade, payments, travel, migration, and financial transactions) the strongest force in general economic integration do not deny that certain governmental institutions are necessary if the profit motive is to call forth the right kind of spontaneous actions of free, private decision-makers. There is certainly need for a legal system that safeguards property rights and enforces contracts. There is need for a monetary system that facilitates foreign payments by securing the interchangeability of different currencies or, better still, by replacing the separate national currencies with an international one. Tax harmonisation would avoid some distortions in resource allocation and consumption if indirect taxes, such as sales taxes or value-added taxes were made uniform for all goods and services all over the area to be economically integrated. Yet I have a strong suspicion that the actions recommended to or adopted by several governments in the name of monetary integration and fiscal harmonisation are counterproductive. Let me state my reasons for saying so.

MONETARY AND FISCAL INTEGRATION

The most urgent prescription which the money-doctors (or money-quacks) gave to governments desiring *monetary* integration was fixed exchange rates with the smallest possible bands for permissible oscillations around parities. This prescription would be fine if the countries were prepared to give up their autonomy over credit policy. Fixed exchange rates were possible

as long as governments did not pursue monetary policies designed to aim at other targets, such as maintaining full employment
accelerating economic growth, counteracting fluctuations in
business activity, or keeping price levels more stable than they
are abroad. With other targets proclaimed as national goals to
be attained or aided by monetary policy, a system of fixed exchange rates became inoperable.

Determined advocates of fixed rates, nevertheless, stuck stub-
bornly to their prescription and, in order to avoid or postpone
adjusting rates that had become unrealistic, resorted to foreign-
exchange restrictions, controls of capital movements, and even
outright impediments to trade. Thus, a policy advertised as instrumental to the achievement of monetary integration and as
conducive to greater economic integration became in effect a
'positive' obstacle in the way to integration, setting back genera
economic integration by many years. Even after most men in
charge of national monetary affairs had realised that some kind
of floating-rate system was inevitable, they maintained much of
the arsenal of control devices, continued to restrict internationa
movements of capital, and prolonged the disintegration of
capital markets to the best of their ability.

What should we, then, make of the term monetary integration? Should we allow it to be used for policies and institutions
flagrantly impeding integration? We cannot prevent people from
using words any way they like, but we may warn against misleading and deceptive usage.[7] I propose that the term monetary

---

[7] 'The hallmark of monetary integration as defined here is a permanent,
unalterable fixity of parities. It may or may not entail the use of a commo
currency.' Bela Balassa, 'Monetary Integration in the European Common
Market', in Alexander K. Swoboda, ed., *Europe and the Evolution of the
International Monetary System* (Leiden: A. W. Sijthoff, 1973) p. 101, n.
17. Balassa is fully aware of the fact that fixed rates can be maintained onl
if certain prerequisites are accepted. But the omission of these prerequisite
from the definition may lead to serious errors of policy. The chief trouble
with 'monetary integration' is that most users of this term confuse official
commitments to fixed or 'unalterable' exchange rates with (a) automatic
mechanisms guaranteeing that flows of monetary reserves will be translate
into adjustments of national money stocks, (b) effective co-ordination of
monetary policies requisite to the permanence of exchange-rate stability,
or (c) free foreign-exchange markets and unrestricted payments in current
as well as capital transactions. As long as there are national authorities witl
power to influence national money stocks and aggregate spending (in pursuit of any goals other than exchange stability) or to restrict the free interconvertibility of currencies (in pursuit of maintenance of fictitious stability
of official exchange rates), commitments to unalterable exchange rates are
practically worthless.

integration be used only for measures, policies, or processes that facilitate monetary transactions by anybody or for any purpose. Absence of restrictions is the minimum meaning of the term; the maximum is monetary unification, the use of a single, uniform currency. Somewhere in the spectrum is co-ordination of national monetary policies, which however is a practical-political impossibility under present-day ideologies concerning the functions of national central banks. It does not now qualify as a practical instrument of monetary integration.

If a group of countries is determined to give the strongest possible support to economic integration for the region, the member countries will have to abolish their independent national central banks and adopt a uniform currency, issued by a Community Central Bank. If they are not prepared to do so without a lengthy transition period, they can speed up the process toward a uniform currency by adopting a parallel standard, with both national and regional (international) currencies circulating side by side, not linked by fixed exchange rates, and with no restrictions on the use of the regional (or international) currency in payments, contracts, and settlements, foreign or domestic. If the members of the group of countries are not prepared to follow such a plan of gradual substitution of an international currency for their own, the only contribution to the attainment of general economic integration which they can make through monetary arrangements is to continue to let their currencies float, but to remove all restrictions on payments and financial transactions.

Harmonisation of *fiscal* institutions, particularly the tax system, has been an important subject of analysis, discussion, and positive government action in recent years. It is firmly believed that equalisation of indirect taxes in all member countries of a common market is an important step on the way to higher degrees of general economic integration. This is an especially strong preconception with regard to sales taxes, turnover taxes, and value-added taxes; bureaucrats in the finance ministries as well as businessmen are convinced that these taxes ought to be refunded to exporters and collected from importers if they are not to impair the competitive position of the industries concerned. That this is wrong, at least if the tax rates are not different for different goods, has been known since Ricardo and has been repeatedly restated, most recently by Gottfried Haberler.[8] Yet,

[8] Gottfried Haberler, 'Probleme der wirtschaftlichen Integration Europas', in *Bernhard-Harms-Vorlesungen 5/6* (Kiel: Institut für Weltwirtschaft, 1974) pp. 23—6.

in deference to the practitioners' beliefs and pressures, the member countries of the European Community, although they abolished customs duties on intra-Community trade, make border tax adjustments, collecting from importers and refunding to exporters. These import taxes and export premiums have been established and maintained as compensatory adjustments in line with the principles of harmonisation and integration. What these 'positive' measures imply is the maintenance of checkpoints at the frontiers between the countries of the presumably integrated group. These measures preserve some of the previous economic separation of the countries concerned. Any German product shipped to France will at the border be processed, with all due formalities, to arrange for tax refunds to the exporter and tax collection from the importer.

Would it be unreasonable to suggest that a highly significant trait or probe of economic integration may be the non-existence of any checkpoints at the frontiers between member countries? What the authors of the Constitution of the United States of America recognised almost 200 years ago is far from being realised by the architects of the Common Market: that a shipment from Germany to France must not be treated differently from a shipment from Bavaria to Baden-Württemberg, or from Burgundy to Normandy. Perhaps one may go even farther and say that full economic integration between two or more countries with market economies is not reached as long as they still know the volume of trade between them. No statistic tells us what the trade volume is between Pennsylvania and Ohio. (I fully realise that these remarks do not apply to economic integration among centrally planned economies, where the plans always imply quantitative decisions and controls.)

DEGREES OF ECONOMIC INTEGRATION

With so many different conditions helpful or harmful to the progress of economic integration it is difficult, or perhaps impossible, to find any comprehensive description, let alone any short formula, to express the combined effects to be expected. How much do the formalities and bureaucratic delays at the border interfere with the movement of goods? If, on balance, the border tax adjustments favour export to other member countries, are they possibly discriminatory, favouring the wrong products? If controls on payments hinder monetary transactions with other member countries, how can the effects on trade and on capital movements be appraised separately? How can changes in people'

propensities and in institutional arrangements, promoting or dis-
couraging movements of people, funds, and goods, be analysed
for their separate and combined effects on mobility?

I wish I were able to propose a neat and concise verbal formulation describing the different degrees of mobility of different
types of factors and products — but I do not know how this
could be done. And perhaps we ought to shy away from any
attempt at devising numerical indices of the degree of economic
integration achieved as a result of so-called 'positive' policies
and institutions and of the different degrees of mobility of
factors and products effected by 'negative' measures to remove
restrictions. Yet, one should not give up. I look forward to studying the papers of Working Group A of the Budapest Congress,
which may give us new insights into the problem of 'Measuring
the Progress or Degree of Economic Integration' or, more likely,
of devising separate indices of different conditions and different
effects that seem to be sufficiently relevant to give meaning to
the confident assertions as to how far the existing regional blocs
have progressed toward their professed objectives.

The difficulty or impossibility of measuring economic integration, or even of suggesting methods of doing it, is embarrassing.
There are philosophers' dicta to the effect that a concept ought
to be subject to *operational definition* and that propositions
employing the concept ought to be subject to *operational test-
ing.* I am inclined to disregard these dicta as neopositivistic pre-
judice, and to reject the still more extreme position which denies
that anything but empirical operations can give meaning to concepts and to propositions involving them. Thus I insist that the
concept of a degree of economic integration has meaning even if
we do not know how to measure it. However, if one asserts that
a concrete historical situation represents a higher degree of integration than another such situation, one cannot reasonably
refuse to tell on what evidence this assertion rests. For example,
if somebody compares the progress made or degree attained in
the economic integration among the CMEA countries and the
EEC countries (or among the states of the USA, or between the
USA and Canada) he has to present statistical evidence — and
present also the theoretical basis on which one can agree that it
really is evidence for what is being asserted. This holds also for
comparisons of the progress of integration in a given area over
stated periods of time.

The indices offering themselves for comparisons of this sort
refer either to *conditions* or to *effects.* Among the conditions
are those that are likely to affect *mobility*, and among the effects

are actual *movements*. Both mobility (the elasticity of responses to stimuli) and actual movements refer to goods, people, capital funds, and enterprise and management. Mobility of goods can be affected by tariffs and customs formalities (with their delays and chicaneries), quotas, licence requirements, payments restrictions, currency allocations, deposit requirements, and all sorts of controls, regulations, and their operations. One can furnish similar lists for conditions affecting travel, migration, trade credits, capital transfers, securities purchases, direct investments, and whatever else may contribute to economic integration.

The effects of mobility may be seen not only in actual move-ments of goods, people, and capital funds but also in relative prices; hence, comparisons of relative prices of goods, labour services, loanable funds, and securities in the supposedly integra-ted countries are valuable tests of the adequacy of mobility, on the one hand, and on the degree of integration achieved, on the other. For standardised products such tests are easier than for differentiated ones. The simplest tests are based on the rule that, in the absence of restrictions, prices for the same commodity will not differ from one place to another by more than the trans-port cost between these places and, if one of the places in ques-tion is the site where the good is produced, the prices should not differ by less than the transport cost. Tests for prices of the same securities on different stock exchanges are even simpler, whereas tests of interest rates for loanable funds are complicated by the fact that various risks — risks of default or future restrictions on payments, exchange risks, etc. — are involved and may be differ-ently evaluated by different lenders for different borrowers. Tests for prices of the 'same' kind and quality of labour in differ-ent countries are very difficult: first because one can never be sure that the efficiency of the workers is really the same; second, because differences in working conditions, fringe benefits, and non-pecuniary advantages and disadvantages of residing in differ-ent places and countries are hard to take into account; third, because variations in exchange rates may play havoc with the comparisons; and fourth, because adjustments of existing differ-ences in earnings through migration are very slow, what with the risky investment in moving expenses and the psychological ob-stacles to moving to a foreign country.

One of the most widely used tests consists in comparisons of various trade ratios: what portion of total purchases in any part of a supposedly integrated (or intentionally to be integrated) region is of goods and services produced in that same part (pro-vince, state, country), what portion is of goods and services produced in other parts of the region, and what portion is of things produced in the rest of the world? Analogous tests are made for total sales of output: what portion is sold to residents of the same part of the region (province, state, country), what portion sold to other parts of the region, what portion to the rest of the world? Studies of this sort have been made, with most surprising results. They show a remarkable provincialism in Europe, where in the larger countries the bulk of all purchases are of goods and services produced in the same country, and the bulk of all sales are to residents of the same country. Analogous estimates for the United States yield very much larger shares of purchases and sales, respectively, from suppliers and to buyers residing in other states of the union.

Translated into the thinking of the man in the street, this type of provincialism is reflected in the fact that in Europe everybody is aware of the origin of his motor car: he is fully conscious of his driving a French, a German, an Italian car; in the United States nobody ever thinks of the fact that he drives a car made in Michigan or assembled, say, in Maryland.

The tests discussed, and probably several other tests not discussed here, with all their weaknesses, probably shed some helpful light on the meanings and connotations of economic integration. Yet none of the tests can be admitted as conclusive in an attempt to measure the degree of economic integration attained. The main reason for this scepticism lies in the fact that integration is essentially, as I have said before, a *relative* achievement, a ratio of actually realised to potentially realisable opportunities for effective division of labour. We may have learned how to measure actual trade, actual migration, actual capital movements, but we have not yet learned how to measure the unused potential.

DEGREE OF INTEGRATION VERSUS EXTENSION OF INTEGRATED AREA

Additional difficulties of a conceptual nature arise from the fact that economic integration is relative not only to unknown potentials but also to the area under consideration. We must distinguish the *degree* of integration achieved within a *given territory* from the *extension of the territory* to be integrated.

If new territory is added to a region with the intent of having the resources and activities in the new territory integrated with those of the 'old' area, one must expect a reorganisation of some of the activities and a reallocation of its resources in both parts

and, of course, more trade between the old and the new parts of
the extended region. (This calls for caution in appraisals of the
degree of integration, especially if actual movements of goods
and factors are measured and the results are considered as aids in
such appraisals.) Any increased division of labour between the
old and the new parts of the extended region should express itself in new trade flows which increase the share of intraregional
trade in total world trade. Of course, the combined shares of
domestic trade and of what was previously counted as intraregional trade within the old region may then be lower. This reduction should not lead to wrong conclusions concerning the
degree of integration either in the old or in the extended region.
As the network of trade widens and the relative share of trade
among the closest neighbours is reduced in the process, it would
surely be erroneous to infer from this that the extension of external trade and the smaller relative share of internal trade mean
a lower degree of general economic integration within the origin
al 'home area'.

Let us then affirm that the notion 'degree of integration' calls
for a specification of the area or combination of areas to which
it is supposed to apply. We should note that different degrees of
integration may have been reached (*a*) within the old region;
(*b*) between the old region and one newly joined with it; (*c*) between the old region and the rest of the world; and (*d*) between
the extended region (the combined area) and the rest of the
world. If other regional blocs exist, even more combinations
would be interesting, especially the degree of integration (*e*) between the extended region and the other regional blocs.

If we then accept the idea that the degree of integration may
be estimated (or at least a rough impression formed) separately
for each area and for each combination of areas, we shall find it
possible to speak of a relatively high degree of integration within
area A, a lower degree with area A + B, a still lower one within
A + B + C, and so on until we have the entire world. This is not
inconsistent with expressed policy statements of several governments. They are, as a rule, determined to take advantage of all
efficient opportunities for division of labour within their own
country; they very much want to utilise many such opportunities within the regional group of which they are a member; they
hold that considerable gains could be derived from trade with
other regional blocs (for example, East-West trade) or in general
with the rest of the world. It would be unnecessarily confining
to estimate the degree of integration just for the economic activi
ties within the regional bloc. The concept makes sense for any

and all combinations of territories, even if we are still far from knowing how to measure it.

ECONOMIC INDEPENDENCE AND THE FEAR OF FOREIGN BLACKMAIL

A particular motive for extension of an integrated area merits brief attention: the desire to have an outside source of supply of a 'strategic' produce or material incorporated into the area and thus to achieve 'independence'. The meaning of strategic is perhaps obvious: a shortage or lack of the good in question would starve or strangle the economy. The meaning of independence is less obvious; most reasonably it refers to the possibility of hostile control over the source of supply being used to subject the country or bloc (which for its survival depends on adequate imports of the strategic goods) to blackmail or gross extortion. This argument for incorporation of, or integration with, a country hitherto outside the expansionist country or bloc is sometimes based on pure geopolitics, sometimes on poor economics. There was much propaganda, in the nineteenth century and the first third of the twentieth, especially in Germany and to some extent in France, in favour of expansion toward the eastern 'bread basket' of Europe in order to achieve 'independence' from overseas imports of grains. This was largely poor economics — unless the expansionist argument could be based on a genuine probability of extortion or war by any overseas enemies. Some arguments for independence from 'foreign' supplies may be sound, or at least reasonable, provided they include a political analysis of the dangers of military or economic warfare and an economic analysis of the alternatives, including the cost of domestic or intra-regional production of substitutes for the strategic imports. (We recall that the distinction between integration by conquest and integration by agreement may be pertinent in arguments for extension of the area with the goal of independence from foreign domination.)

POSITIVE ECONOMICS VERSUS WELFARE ECONOMICS

Several times in this discussion I have used such words as beneficial and gainful in connection with extensions of trade and opportunities for division of labour. As long as nothing but a 'more efficient' use of resources is involved and efficiency is understood to refer to additional output (measured at given prices) without regard to its distribution, the relevant propositions may still be regarded as being within the limits of positive economics. As soon as we realise that gains from trade are divided among the partners, and that changes in the terms of trade may increase the gains of one country at the expense of another country, we enter the domain of welfare economics. How much of the analysis of economic integration will be welfare economics?

It is often considered best professional practice to avoid value judgements — judgements as to whether a change is for the better or for the worse — and stay within positive economics. In the theory of economic integration one cannot get very far with such purity. Any reallocation of resources, any reorganisation of economic activity will be beneficial to some, harmful to others. Thus the attempt to judge whether a particular change will be 'on balance' helpful or harmful to the residents of an area, a combination of areas, or the whole world, cannot help being 'evaluative', that is, welfare economics.

Judgements of the beneficial or harmful effects of economic integration depend therefore on the interests which the economic advocate has most at heart. He may be concerned with local, provincial, national, regional interests or he may be cosmopolitan and think chiefly of the world at large. Some 'classical' economists were staunch cosmopolitans and would regard a change as beneficial even if their own country were a loser in the deal, provided some net benefit accrued to the inhabitants of the world. Several of these authors made strong pronouncements about the 'desirability' of some measure or development without even realising (or at least without warning) that they were thinking of the world community, not of the narrow interests of the nation. Since all plans for more extended economic integration assume that gains will be derived from it, it will be necessary to make clear, more than has been done in much of the literature, which parts of the world will be major beneficiaries, which minor beneficiaries, and which possibly losers.

The possibilities are so manifold, depending on a host of conditions and circumstances, that the task of distributing the gain in even the simplest of theoretical models is most demanding; it calls for analytical skills of the hairsplitting variety. Assume, to indicate the type of reasoning to be employed, a world of four countries, A, B, C and D, each of them having some trade with the other three, and each using tariffs to protect some of its domestic producers. Now, recognising the advantages of more extended trade, A and B join in a customs union and abolish the duties on imports from each other. A will now buy from B some goods which it used to make at home and some which it used to import from C. The substitution of imports from B for domestic production represents an increase in foreign trade and, therefore, 'trade creation', whereas the substitution for imports from C represents 'trade diversion', to use the important dichotomy introduced by Jacob Viner.[9] Thus far things are not too difficult, especially if we confine ourselves to the effects on the efficiency of production: the trade creation has involved the displacement of a less efficient source of supply (namely, the previously protected domestic producers in A) by a more efficient one in B; and the trade diversion has meant that a more efficient source of supply (namely, producers in C who were the most competitive suppliers of A, as long as A's tariffs were the same regardless of the origin of the goods) has been displaced by less efficient producers in B (who became A's suppliers only because the duty on their products was abolished while that on C's product was kept). If the volume of trade creation exceeded that of trade diversion, welfare will have increased in A and probably also in the three countries combined; it cannot be said yet how B and C have fared, for thus far we do not know how B will deal with its export surplus and (perhaps) overemployment and what C will do with its trade deficit and unemployment. The story, therefore, must go on and, alas, there are too many plots to choose from.

Let us see what some of our choices have to offer. Assume that B has previously had unemployed labour and excess plant capacity, which it now uses to produce its new exports to A; that C suffers an increase in unemployment because of its losses of exports to A; and that A too suffers an increase in unemployment because its domestic production was reduced. What will B do with its new income and what will C do with its unemployed resources? The simplest plot would be to let B use its additional income to buy something from A and something else from C. This would restore balance in their trade and put the unemployed in A and C to work. But this outcome is too simple and too dull; let us assume instead that B uses its extra income to buy from D, and C uses its extra workers to make something to sell to D; since D's exports to B exceed its imports from B, it has still some income left to buy enough from A to absorb A's unemployment. Still too simple? More interesting plots would bring us sophisticated complications arising from various ordinary or extraordinary elasticities of supply and from especially entertaining income-

---

[9] Jacob Viner, *The Customs Union Issue* (New York: Carnegie Endowment for International Peace, 1950), pp. 43—55.

and price-elasticities of demand for domestic products and various imports.

In the preceding paragraph only positive economics was involved. But now let us call in our best experts in value judgements and have them first reach an agreement on what is most likely to happen and then what the net benefits and net losses will be for A, for B, for C, for D, for A and B together, for C ar D together, for A, B and C together, and for all four.

The task sounds formidable. The question is whether one ma be satisfied with one of the simpler plots and with some simple rules of thumb for judging the effects on welfare. Most of the economic advocates seem to think so and I can only hope that they are right.

A TAXONOMIC AND SEMANTIC SUMMARY

I have proposed that much of the ambiguity of the term economic integration may be avoided by the use of qualifying adjectives, and I have also discussed some of the adjectives that have attained wide currency. A warning may be in order, however, not to expect that the proposed adjectives remove all vagueness Unfortunately, some of the adjectives have been used as ambigu ously as the noun. Here is a sample:

Regional has been used to mean

   (i) provincial, any part of a state;
  (ii) multinational, two or more states but less than the wor!
 (iii) any territory, such as a province, a nation, a group of nations but also the whole world.

Viner can be cited as one who used region in the first sense, that is, to mean a part of a country;[10] Ohlin used region mos often in the third sense, that is, to refer to the area that happened to be relevant in the context;[11] in the last two or three decades most writers have been thinking of groups or blocs c countries, hence, of regions in the second sense.

Global has been used to mean

  (i) worldwide, comprising the entire globe;
 (ii) comprising all activities and all sectors of any region.

[10] Jacob Viner, *Studies in the Theory of International Trade* (New Yor! Harper, 1937) p. 595.

[11] Bertil Ohlin, *Interregional and International Trade* (Cambridge, Mass. Harvard University Press, 1933) p. 67.

In the first sense global is meant to be the opposite of regional in sense (ii), in the second sense global is meant to be the opposite of sectoral.

Universal has been used to mean

(i)   worldwide;
(ii)   comprising all parts (or sectors) of the relevant region.
In the first sense universal is a synonym for global in sense (i), in the second sense it is the opposite of partial.

Sectoral has been used to mean

(i)   limited to particular industries or sectors of the economy or economies concerned;
(ii)   gradual, proceeding successively from sector to sector.
In the second sense sectoral was used in a report prepared for an international conference.[12]

Functional has been used to mean

(i)   gradual, proceeding successively from sector to sector;
(ii)   by means of price incentives operating in the free market.
In the first sense, functional is equivalent to sectoral in sense (ii); it is so used by many political scientists.[13] However, political scientists have also used functional in the second sense, roughly equivalent to 'liberalist'.[14]

Institutional has been used to mean

(i)   by means of *dirigiste* administrative commands and prohibitions;
(ii)   by means of adaptations of national or international institutions (in the widest sense of the word, for example monetary practices and arrangements).
In the first sense, institutional is the opposite of functional in sense (ii) and has been so used by the writers who wanted to

---

[12] Fritz W. Meyer, *Die Europäische Agrargemeinschaft und ihre Auswirkungen auf die gegenwärtige und zukünftige Handelspolitik und das Transferproblem*. Gutachten für die deutsche Delegation bei dem Vorbereitenden Arbeitsausschuss der Konferenz für die Organisation der Europäischen Agrarmärkte, 15 September 1952.

[13] Peter G. Bock, 'Functionalism and Functional Integration', *International Encyclopedia of the Social Sciences* (New York: Macmillan, 1968) Vol. 7, pp. 534—41.

[14] Rolf Sannwald and Jacques Stohler, *Economic Integration: Theoretical Assumptions and Consequences of European Unification* (Princeton: Princeton University Press, 1959, 2nd ed., 1961) p. 84.

stress this pair of antonyms. The second sense has been more customary.

THE INCLUSION OF PUBLIC GOODS

Definitions of integration that stress the opportunities for division of labour in the production of goods and services are likely to focus on economic criteria and to leave political and other aspects aside. A disregard of political concerns disturbs those who like to integrate all social sciences into a unified science of society. A good way to satisfy some of these unitarians was shown by Richard Cooper, when he, in a most stimulating paper prepared for the Budapest Congress, widened the focus of our economic analysis to include *public goods* (usually intangibles) besides the private goods which have long monopolised the economic theorists' attention.[15]

Many of these public goods are what social scientists (economists included) have regarded as the satisfaction of non-economic, social or political objectives (of groups, communities, nations, or groups of nations). If the attainment of widely held collective objectives — such as nationalism (anticosmopolitanism national or international egalitarianism, or the cultivation of par ticular artistic and literary tastes — is regarded as a public good, the most effective division of labour in producing this public good may well call for very different territorial delimitations than would be compatible with efficiency in the production of privat goods and services. Some years ago, Harry Johnson, and Charles A. Cooper and Benton F. Massell (in independent articles to be cited later in Chapter 9) called attention to these matters; now Richard Copper did us a service by incorporating them into a conceptual framework for our thinking about the geographic extension of international economic integration.

The trouble with most of these public goods is, in my view, that they are wanted by a public that does not know their costs. Even if we presented the most sophisticated benefit-and-cost analyses for each of the public goods, we could not make most people comprehend that they must pay for them and how much Many things that flatter the nationalistic sentiments of a people

---

[15] Bananas are private goods, most cheaply acquired in exchange for a domestic product; but the pride of having bananas grown at home, rather than acquired by trade, is a public good. Some non-conformists may not share this pride. To their tastes, this public good would be a nonsense and a nuisance.

are fervently and zealously wanted as long as people think that the cost is reasonable or is being paid by others. If each of the public goods had to be paid for out of taxes and each citizen knew how much his own share of the cost would be, we might see that the effective demand for many public goods is not so strong as the proponents had thought it was. I cannot furnish empirical support for this statement, but I am highly sceptical about the strength which the demand for public goods would have if the citizens were fully cognizant of the unavoidable assessments of the individual contributions to the cost of providing many of these public goods. My doubts refer to a large variety of collective undertakings, ranging from defence and armament via national airlines and protected steel mills to subsidised arts and sciences.

As we learn that many public goods can be more efficiently provided by a smaller club of provinces or countries than by a larger (more cosmopolitan) group of countries, we ought to take notice of the fact that the opportunity cost of providing these collective goods will be increased by the decision to forgo the greater efficiency with which private goods could be produced if division of labour were extended over a much larger territory, probably the entire world. In other words, the provision of public goods in the smaller geographic area that appears optimal for their production may be subject to heavy external costs which burden the production of private goods for an unduly limited market. These external costs would surely escape the attention of the tax accountants, but would probably be missed also by the benefit-and-cost accountants looking at their items and numbers through rose-tinted glasses.

In the history of the idea of economic integration not much has been written on public or collective goods in an explicit fashion, except when some arguments against free trade, and in favour of protection of domestic production, were made with reference to collective objectives such as military preparedness for the next war (to secure an ample supply of soldiers from a robust rural population and of arms from a strong defence industry). The overwhelming part of the literature, when the cases for national, regional, or global integration were argued, focused on short- and long-run economic efficiency in the production of ordinary (that is, private) goods and services as the major objective — and I cannot help thinking that the conventional writers' judgement in choosing this focus was sound.

Part Two
The Idea and its Different Strands

Part One contained a historical inquiry in Chapter 1, where the history of the use of the term 'integration' in national and international economics was explored. Part Three will be predominantly historical, as it will review the expressed opinions of hundreds of men who wrote and talked about economic integration. The two chapters of *Part Two*, however, cannot be called historical in character — unless one is prepared to have history without names and without dates. Time, place, and people are part and parcel of historical research, and none of these will be found in Part Two. Nevertheless, a strong claim can be made for its relevance in a history of thought, for it is devoted to an analysis of the idea the history of which will be presented in Part Three.

In Chapter 3 a few brief and rather general reflections will be offered on the differences between economic thought and economic analysis, and then on the relations between economic and political thought. Chapter 4 will be a somewhat novel undertaking: to break up the complex idea of general economic integration into its many elements; or, to use another metaphor, to disentangle the many different strands from which its conceptual yarn has been spun.

3   Economic Thought, Economic Analysis, and Political Aims

This will be a brief chapter in defence of distinctions which according to some schools of thought are not justified by genuine differences. To differentiate between economic analysis and economic thought may be to judge the former as rigorous and the latter as superficial, or to suggest that the former develops generalisations while the latter offers generalities. Such judgements would be offensive to many. On the other hand, there is much to be said in favour of the distinction, especially if it serves to contrast pure with applied theory.

The distinction between economic and political thought is rejected by those who find that attempts to separate economic and political forces are methodologically unsound, tainted by a biased *Weltanschauung*, and counterproductive if the aim is a real understanding of social reality. Yet, no matter how closely politics and economics are interlocked in reality, it is surely possible intellectually to keep them apart; of course not by assuming away the existence of one or the other, but rather by taking one of them as given and unchanged for the run of a train of reasoning. Such analytical procedures have been not only possible but also intellectually rewarding and of great heuristic value in the search for generalisations of considerable explanatory and predictive power.

ECONOMIC THOUGHT AND ECONOMIC ANALYSIS

In distinguishing economic thought and analysis I follow the example of Joseph Schumpeter.[1] There had been many comprehensive works on the history of economic thought or economic doctrines, but Schumpeter found their scope too wide for the

---

[1] Joseph A. Schumpeter, *History of Economic Analysis* (New York: Oxford University Press, 1954) p. vii.

careful theoretical dissecting that he set out to do on the economic literature. There was more than enough to say on economic analysis alone, unencumbered by discussions of applied economics and broader economic thought that was not sufficiently sharp, clean-cut and generalised to be regarded as analysis.

In a history of the idea of general economic integration it would surely be too restrictive and too pretentious to limit oneself to pure economic analysis. However, one may still recognise Schumpeter's distinction by sorting the contributions into different categories, one of which is labelled 'Economic Theory'. This will contain economic analyses of the abstract issues raised in the theory of economic integration, ranging roughly from the theory of division of labour and comparative costs, via the theory of factor movements and factor prices and the theory of the effects of trade expansion and trade restriction on national income and its distribution, to the theory of the economic effects of customs unions and full-fledged economic union.

The segregation of economic theory from broader economic thought on economic integration will not involve us in issues of great subtlety. By and large, the decisions on just where particular contributions to economic thinking should be treated will be guided by their immediate reference to concrete situations. Plans and policy recommendations for particular times and places will not be reviewed under the heading of economic theory but among the contributions by political economists, statesmen and other proponents, promoters, or opponents of integration schemes. Details on the classification of economic thought by the sources of the contributions will be set forth in the introduction to Part Three.

ECONOMIC AND POLITICAL THOUGHT

Apart from Marxian economics, the literature of economics has for almost two centuries attempted to make as clean-cut a separation of economic from social and political thought as its writers were capable of achieving. This general statement holds, notwithstanding the now fashionable bow to interdisciplinary research, for the majority of fields and areas of specialisation. The topic of economic integration, however, does not belong to this majority, except as far as its theoretical foundations — the pure theory of international trade — is concerned.

In a history of the idea of national and international economic integration the separation in question is difficult to carry through, because the social and political issues of any area and period are inseparably linked with economic ones. Indeed, the fundamental question of means and ends may militate against monodisciplinary thinking and require interdisciplinary inquiry. The literature is full of statements contradicting one another in the identification of target and instrument. There are many for whom peace and political unity is the target, and economic integration the instrument; but there are others who see in economic integration the target and in political integration (federation, confederation, supranational authorities, etc.) the needed instrument.

One might think that on this question economists and political scientists are neatly divided, but this is not so. We find mixed company on both sides of the issue. A good many economists have declared that a customs union was politically impossible without simultaneous or preceding political integration. Other economists, however, were convinced that closer political relations and, eventually, peace among the nations, could be achieved only by means of economic co-operation and co-ordination ahead of political unification. For example, Vilfredo Pareto, speaking at a Peace Congress in Rome, in 1889, saw customs unions and other international economic arrangements as means to better political relations and eventual pacification.[2] Similar statements were made in 1900 at a Political Science Congress on 'Les Etats-Unis d'Europe'.

Several apodictic assertions about the impossibility of customs unions in the absence of political unification have been disconfirmed by historical events: first by the formation of the German *Zollverein* and again by the formation of the European Common Market. Other, more vaguely formulated propostions claiming much weaker preconditions were not falsifiable. For example, the frequent claims that some unspecified measure of 'national sentiment' or 'cultural affinity' is a necessary condition for achieving closer economic ties can neither be proved nor disproved. What was the role of national sentiment in the economic unifications of the kingdoms on the British Isles, of quadrilingual Switzerland, or of the multilingual, pluricultural Austria of the Hapsburgs?

For some targets of integration it is difficult to decide whether they are economic or political. I admit to serious confusion when I read a few eminent economists who include equality (or 'less inequality') of income among the criteria of integration. If

[2] *Atti del Congresso di Roma per la pace e per l'arbitrato internazionale,* Maggio 1889 (Città di Castello, 1889).

this is to refer to the earnings of labour, it would be a serious blunder to forget that the homogeneous factor L (of uniform quality) is a purely mental construct designed to explain the equalisation of factor prices in an abstract model of imaginary countries under perfectly free trade and under several other counterfactual assumptions. This factor L is neither the same as nor related to real-world labour of various types working with different efficiency under different conditions in different real-world countries. Yet we find that a substantial reduction, if not removal, of existing national and international differences in the earnings of labour is stipulated by some economists among the targets of economic integration or among the indices of their being approached or attained.

Perhaps I have misunderstood Jan Tinbergen[3] and Gunnar Myrdal[4] and their heavy emphasis on redistribution within and among countries. I cannot help thinking of Jacob Viner's[5] reference to the income differentials of farmers within the United States, where the average income per man was more than 39 times higher in the richest agricultural county than in the poorest. With perfectly free interstate trade and a common market for products, with perfect mobility of capital, and substantial mobility of labour within the United States, this nation had surely attained a higher degree of internal economic integration than any larger region or the whole world is likely to achieve in decades to come. Should we as responsible theoretical and political economists encourage or even entice our students to jump from idealised explanatory models to practical (or rather impractical) political problems of the real world?

[3] Jan Tinbergen, *International Economic Integration* (second, revised ed., Amsterdam: Elsevier, 1965) p. 78.

[4] Gunnar Myrdal, *An International Economy: Problems and Prospects* (New York: Harper, 1956) pp. 1—4.

[5] Jacob Viner, *International Economics and Economic Development* (Glencoe, Ill.: Free Press, 1952) p. 65.

4   The Main Strands of the Idea

Every serious discussion of economic integration, national, multinational, or worldwide, is based on concepts and issues of international-trade theory. Movements of goods, services, people, capital funds, and moneys across natural or political frontiers are what interregional and international economic relations are all about — and all of these movements are part and parcel of economic integration. Trade is usually regarded as the quintessence of economic integration, and division of labour in several of its aspects as its underlying principle. This holds for intranational as well as international trade.

DIVISION OF LABOUR

'Division of labour' has become such a common catchword that several variants of the phenomenon are confounded or overlooked. Sometimes inadequate attention is given to the fact that the division may be a way of organising the production of a *particular* good (or a particular line of joint or otherwise related products) but also the production of *different*, largely unrelated goods for sale or exchange against other goods.

In the division of labour in making a particular good (or line of goods) it may be important — especially for questions of income distribution — to distinguish between (1) the combined activities of teams of workers who in close physical collaboration handle and finish each single unit of the product; (2) the work of persons who perform different tasks in completing the product, perhaps in a definite succession as in an assembly line; (3) the progress of work where an intermediate product is passed on from one team (department) to another, again in a definite succession, but still in the same establishment ('intraplant' division of labour); (4) the division of labour among different establishments (plants), with intermediate products transported from

43

one place to another, sometimes over considerable distances, but still under the same management ('intrafirm' division of labour, 'vertical integration'); and (5) the division of labour in the production of particular products or product lines where some intermediate products or materials, fuel, energy, etc., are acquired from different plants managed by different firms ('interfirm' division of labour). Frequently it is difficult (or extremely arbitrary) to describe the progress of work in a definite sequence, for example, when several parts of a machine are made at different places, either by the same firm or by different firms, and then put together in an assembly plant. It hardly needs saying that the first three types of division, all 'intraplant', are also 'intranational', whereas division of the fourth and fifth type may be international. The other category of division of labour — the division of labour in making different goods — can be either within a country or between different countries.

The fact that intraplant division of labour is always intranational does not make it irrelevant for the theory of international trade and economic integration. For example, some ways of organising the production of goods call for division of labour among large numbers of workers turning out very large quantities of output; however, a country may not be large enough to absorb these quantities at home, so that the use of such efficient large-scale production will become possible or efficient only when an export market is added to the home market. This fact was recognised by the very first expositors of the concept of division of labour.

THE EXTENT OF THE MARKET

It was understood that the possibilities of division of labour were limited by the extent of the market and that the extent of the market, in turn, was limited by natural and artificial barriers to transportation. Tolls, taxes, and customs duties were the major artificial barriers, and economic integration therefore was promoted by the reduction and abolition of such imposts. The question of the optimum size of the integrated territory — beyond the nation — arose early in the game. (A pertinent statement made in 1691 will be quoted in Chapter 9).

For several centuries, however, the main concern of the promoters of economic integration was to unite the counties, provinces, and splinter-states into an integrated nation state. Although there were a few forward-looking proposals for multinational and even worldwide economic integration, the discussion of such plans was largely a matter of the nineteenth and twentieth centuries. Nevertheless, most classical writers were agreed on the proposition that every extension of the market conferred economic advantages on those involved: 'In proportion as the market is extended, the people of every country are enabled to make the best division of their labour, and the most advantageous use of their exertions' [Ricardo, 1817; in similar vein, Smith, 1776.]

SPECIALISATION

The increase in productivity through appropriate division of labour has much to do with the greater efficiency of specialisation. Again, different aspects have tended to get confused. There is, first, specialisation dictated by *natural differences* ('soil, climate, and situation', but also the energy, diligence, and talents of people), which received top billing in most models that were designed to show the greater output attainable through international division of labour (say, wine being grown in climatically favoured Portugal and exchanged for cloth made in England). There are, secondly, the *artificial differences* in skill acquired by *workers* in years of specialisation in the performance of particular tasks; and thirdly, the likewise artificial differences in speed and accuracy through the use of special *equipment* (machines, apparatuses, and instruments) which can be efficiently employed only in specialised mass production.

Fourthly, there are the *changes in the proportions* in which different goods are produced in the regions or countries in or between which economic integration is intensified or extended; the essence of these changes is that people elsewhere, that is, in another province or country, produce the goods, or more of the goods, that require relatively larger amounts of such productive factors as are relatively scarce 'at home'. It does not have to be 'complete' specialisation; indeed, interregional and international division of labour with incomplete specialisation may afford the participants benefits that are more substantial and more evenly distributed than complete specialisation is likely to provide. Provinces or countries involved, instead of entirely *abandoning* the production of the goods for which larger input-ratios of (originally) dearer productive factors are needed, merely *reduce* the production of these goods (and import the resulting shortfall) and *increase* the production (and export the resulting surplus) of the goods that require more of the (originally) more abundant factors.[1]

Only the first of the four types of specialisation — and, in some limited sense, the second — need involve differences (heterogeneities) in the resources or factors of production available to the trading partners. For the understanding of important principles of trade theory one has to bear in mind that international division of labour can be efficient even without any differences in the gifts of nature, in the characters and talents of people, in the state of the technical arts, in the stock of capital, and even in the proportion of quantities in which any productive resources are available in the different countries; all it takes to make division of labour efficient under such circumstances is that consumers' tastes are different enough to make some factors of production relatively more demanded in one country than in the other. This strand of the idea — demand-related differences in factor endowment — is perhaps less pertinent to the issue of specialisation than to the issue of factor incomes, which we reserve for discussion a little later.

ABSOLUTE AND COMPARATIVE ADVANTAGE

Early writers on international trade had explained the advantages of international division of labour by pointing to 'absolute' cost differences (in terms of labour used) in the production of different goods. The notion of 'absolute' cost differences, or 'absolute' advantages in production, has bothered many students who correctly saw that differences and advantages must always be relative to something. These costs and cost differences are expressed in terms of a standard unit of a productive factor, say, standard labour. That wine is cheaper in sunny Portugal than in England if its cost is compared in hours of labour required per unit of output seems trivially obvious. If cloth could be produced in England with less hours of labour per unit than in Portugal, the advantages of trade would seem self-evident in terms of 'absolute' input-output ratios. Things would be different, however, if both

[1] Students may be easily confused by writers speaking of 'specialisation in the production of good *A*' without making it clear whether they mean the process of producing *more* of product *A* and less of *B*, or the state of producing *only* product *A* (complete specialisation). In the former case, the country merely changes the proportions in which it produces goods *A* and *B*; in the latter case, it has abandoned the production of *B* — which has significant implications for the relevance of certain theorems to be discussed later.

wine and cloth, and perhaps all other products, required less labour per unit of output in Portugal than in England. Would it still be beneficial for the two countries to trade? This was the question which was affirmatively answered by reflections on 'comparative cost differences', or comparative advantage.

The invention of the law of comparative advantage may be regarded as one of the greatest achievements of economic theory. The law is derived from two propositions and their corollaries. The first proposition is that all it takes for a country or a region to have comparative advantages in the production of some things is to have worse (absolute) disadvantages in the production of other things. Since it is practically impossible for any economic region (province, country, group of countries) to be equally inefficient in all conceivable activities, it is virtually certain that every region will have comparative advantages in some of them. The second proposition is more hypothetical; it states that the money prices of goods and services offered by producers under pure and perfect competition in perfect markets, in the absence of external economies and with perfectly adjusted exchange rates, will reflect the comparative advantages in producing these goods and services. Hence, any distortion of these competitive prices through tariffs or other restrictions will adversely affect the people who could potentially benefit from trading the goods they could produce with a comparative advantage against goods they could produce with a comparative disadvantage.

Comparative advantages and disadvantages are 'measured' by marginal cost — where costs are, of course, the values of all inputs required for the production of the particular output and fully reflect all opportunities forgone by employing the inputs for this rather than any alternative output (hence, the 'opportunity costs'). It should be noted that under perfectly free trade in equilibrium, that is, when no further increase or decrease in the trade of any commodity seems advantageous, the marginal costs of production (including transport) would have become equal in the trading countries. Thus, the initial differences in marginal costs would have disappeared and, consequently, measurements of marginal costs would no longer reveal any comparative advantages and disadvantages. These advantages and disadvantages could be shown only if there were no trade or, at least, less trade than in free-trade equilibrium. This consideration is sometimes overlooked by econometricians who undertake to test whether there really exist calculable cost differences in the production of the exports and of the domestic import-substitutes in the countries in question.

Full understanding of the logic of the law of comparative advantage, sound judgement of the strength and significance of its underlying assumptions, and ability to appraise the practical implications of the argument — these are prerequisites of any intelligent discussion of economic integration. That any seemingly cogent implications for commercial policy may still be overpowered by extraneous considerations must be conceded for this as for any other essentially political question.

FREE-TRADE DOCTRINE: ADHERENCE AND DISSENT

A few writers on trade and integration accepted the general implications of the law of comparative advantage at their face value and favoured worldwide free trade without any reservations: they recommended unilateral free trade, that is, abolition of tariffs against imports into their own country even if all other countries were resolved to maintain their tariff walls. Other advocates of free trade accepted the implications of the law of comparative advantage only after they had come to the judgement that the assumptions on which it rested were, though not 'realistic', approached closely enough by conditions prevailing in reality. A third group conceded the existence of wide deviation of real conditions from the heuristic assumptions of the law, but concluded that in most situations the imposition of tariffs or other trade restrictions could not compensate for the various types of 'market failure' but would more likely worsen the resulting distortions of the structure of prices and production.

The rank of dissenters was recruited from several quarters. There were those who simply failed to understand the logic of the argument. A second group felt itself justified in rejecting an argument out of hand when it was based, even provisionally, on unrealistic assumptions; they did not consider it worth their while to examine the degree to which weaker (less restrictive, less unrealistic) assumptions would impair the conclusions reached on the basis of stronger assumptions. A third and more thoughtful group of dissenters singled out some particularly unrealistic assumptions as liable to vitiate the law or its applicability to real-world conditions. Some stressed the existence of externalities (deviations of social from private costs or benefits) others the prevalence of monopoly or oligopoly positions in industry, or obstacles to adequate mobility of labour within the country or region, or rigidity of wage rates, or chronic disalignments of exchange rates.

A fourth group entertained special views about the international division of the possible gains from trade and suggested that a clever or 'scientific' tariff policy might secure to a country substantially more favourable terms of trade and thereby an income gain that could outweigh the associated loss in productive efficiency. A fifth group of writers championed the welfare of particular industries, sectors, or classes, and advocated protection designed to increase the income share of their favourites. Somewhat different was the nature of the dissent of a sixth group of specialists in international trade and integration: they proposed to minimise the significance of considerations based on existing conditions and to place almost exclusive emphasis on potentialities which they devined to become attainable at some future time: 'development of the nation's productive powers' was the goal of their programme, and protection of currently inefficient production its major instrument.

All of these views merit inclusion in this survey. If any attention is to be paid to historical sequence in the literature of the field, we should first turn to the question of the division of the gains from trade among the trading countries.

DIVIDING THE GAINS FROM TRADE

Efficient division of labour through international trade yields an increase in the combined output of the countries involved. How is this increase, this 'gain from trade', divided among the countries? Early economic analysts made several errors of reasoning on this subject. A primitive idea to the effect that the 'two countries' involved in the extension of trade would share the gain fifty-fifty was quickly discarded. Was it possible that one of the countries would take all and the other would get nothing? If the terms of trade, that is, the exchange ratio between the 'two goods' traded — or rather the change in the exchange ratio before and after the extension of trade — determined how the gain from the trade was divided, then the question was merely pushed a little further back: what determines the terms of trade and their changes due to incremental trade?

This question led to the very ingenious theory of reciprocal demand (or reciprocal offers), which compares the countries' willingness or eagerness to acquire imports in exchange for their exports (or to offer exports in exchange for their imports). There were some writers who held that the larger and more powerful country would impose on its smaller and weaker trading partner such terms as would allow the former to grab the entire gain and

leave the poorer with no gain at all. The opposite outcome, ho-
ever, was seen to be far more likely, if not absolutely certain: a
small country could never export enough to satisfy fully the
demand of a much bigger country; hence, the latter would still
have to produce some of the good which it could produce only
at a comparative disadvantage; the price ratio between the 'two
goods would therefore have to be such that both goods could b
made in the large country while the small country could completely specialise in the one good in which it had the comparati
advantage. At constant costs, the terms of trade would be equa
to the unchanged cost ratio that prevailed in the larger country
at increasing cost of production, the imports into that country
would permit a reduction in output and hence a cost reduction
The smaller country, specialising in the production of its expor
good, would pocket the entire gain from the trade if constant
cost prevailed in the large country; and it would pocket the
larger, perhaps overwhelming, part of the gain if increasing cost
prevailed in the large country.

This solution was later qualified in two respects. As it applie
to two goods only, it was suggested that a situation in which or
of the countries engaged in trade without any gain to itself wou
be unlikely to last: there would soon be a third and a fourth
good becoming tradable with at least some gain accruing to the
larger country. Another qualification related to the lack of
generality of the solution, as the underlying argument jumped
from the size difference of the two countries to rather specific
conditions of reciprocal demand. A more general solution woul
simply state that the country which, in consequence of the extended trade, experienced the largest change in the price ratios
of the goods consumed would be the biggest gainer.

The formulation of a correct and more complete theory of
the determination of the terms of trade was a difficult task,
especially as the earlier attempts with models of only two countries, two goods, and one factor of production (labour) were
clearly unsatisfactory. The first extension was in the number of
goods. It was possible to arrange an unlimited number of goods
producible in two countries in the order of their comparative
cost advantages and to show that varying money wage rates and
foreign-exchange rates would, for balanced trade (or, in later
formulations, for any given trade balance designed to match a
capital balance), simultaneously determine which goods would
be exported and which imported and at what terms of trade and
hence, with what division of the gains from trade. Further extensions regarding the number of countries and the number of

factors came much later and are rarely presented even in advanced courses on international economics.

THE OPTIMUM TARIFF TO CAPTURE MORE OF THE GAINS

The reciprocal demand or offer curves employed in expositions
of the determination of the terms of trade were thought to represent the countries' supply-and-demand conditions in competitive situations. The imposition of tariffs can change the effective
curves and affect their intersection. Thus, an artful set of tariff
rates could, through clever exploitation of monopolistic or
monopsonistic positions of one of the countries *vis-à-vis* its trading partner, improve that country's terms of trade, that is, enable
it to squeeze or gouge the partner and thereby gain for itself a
larger share of the combined increase in total output, although
that total may be reduced in the process. Thus the theory of the
'optimum tariff' was worked out and it gave protectionists a
new argument.

Its use in the theory of the customs union added some fascinating facets to an intellectually challenging analysis. Whether it is
operationally significant in the sense that it may be helpful in
actual tariff setting and tariff bargaining is very doubtful. In its
pure form it makes the assumption that the victimised country,
the country 'robbed' by the 'scientific' tariff of the aggressive
party, will not retaliate. In a sophisticated form, the theory of
games may be applied to a model of tariff bargaining. Apart
from the doubtful practicality of the theory, pure or sophisticated, one may question the moral acceptability of schemes of
national enrichment at the clear expense of one's trading partners.

MARKET FAILURE AS REASON FOR PROTECTION

Since the assumptions that support the laws of comparative advantage and reciprocal demand and their application to the
theory of free trade include some that are evidently in the nature
of heuristic fictions rather than of real facts of economic life, it
was imperative to examine whether the maintenance of the
counterfactual assumptions vitiated the conclusions so badly
that protection rather than free trade would be the more rational policy recommendation. This examination was made quite
systematically for most types of 'market failure', that is, for con-
stellations in which the market prices for goods and services fail

to reflect the social marginal costs of their production and the social marginal benefits of their use.

Decreasing cost due to external economies of increased production has often been regarded as one of the most serious case of market failure. This 'externality' — being outside (external t the calculations of private producers, traders, or consumers — i difficult to deal with in theoretical analysis and impossible to take account of in sound commercial policy. It has to be conceded that free-market prices disregard any external economies and, hence, that free trade guided by free-market prices does not result in the most efficient structure of production and trade. However, since it is clearly impossible for policy-makers or advisers to know the locus and extent of all potential extern lities, they cannot possibly hit upon a set of customs duties tha would make the right corrections in the structure of market prices. Indeed, a tariff intended to correct some prices for expected externalities, while leaving others, with perhaps more substantial external costs or benefits, uncorrected, may result i greater deviations from the ideal optimum position.

The case of rigidity in the prices of productive services, particularly labour, has yielded to analysis and to clear precepts fo policy makers. If wage rates are unalterable in real terms, any change in supply, demand, technology, foreign prices, or anything else in the economy may lead to unemployment. The sam is true of complete immobility of labour, geographical and occu pational. Is it possible to avoid or reduce such unemployment by a clever set of tariffs or import restrictions? This is conceivable, but not very likely in actual practice. Incidentally, immobility of labour may still be consistent with free trade as the 'best' possible situation, provided that other factors — say, capital — are mobile and that factor prices, including wages, are flex ible. Only if factors are entirely immobile and their prices unalterable could free trade make matters worse. Perhaps, though, free trade may loosen up a structure of factor prices that would otherwise be rigid.

INFANT INDUSTRIES AND DEVELOPING COUNTRIES

The strongest argument for temporary and selective protection through tariffs or subsidies is the case of the infant industry. First clumsily suggested by opponents of free trade, it was later developed and formulated in theoretically tenable propositions by staunch free-traders. The essence of the argument is that the cost of experimenting and learning should be borne by present

consumers or by society at large because the benefits are likely
to accrue to others than those who take the risk of pioneering
the new industry. In actual practice the scheme is likely to be a
racket for the benefit of a few: the protection is usually not
temporary but long-lasting and the selection is arbitrary and
without even a pretence of using objective criteria.

The argument has been generalised to advocate tariff protection to promote the industrialisation of poor, developing countries, and also for blocs of less developed countries trying to
achieve closer integration in customs unions or free-trade areas
surrounded by high tariff walls. According to one of the earlier
phrases used in the advocacy of protection for the sake of industrialisation, a nation ought not to be distracted by attention
to the 'values of material goods' from the really important
national goal of 'developing its productive powers' [List, 1841].

SELF-SUFFICIENCY, INDEPENDENCE, POWER

The use of tariff walls surrounding a block of integrating economies is also advocated for reasons other than faster development; for example, to achieve greater independence from economically more advanced countries or those that monopolise
strategic supplies; to gain economic and, with it, political power
vis-à-vis some supposedly stronger or hostile countries; or more
generally, to achieve more self-sufficiency or autarky. (Incidentally, autarky and autarchy are different words, though some
dictionaries contain only the latter, meaning 'self-rule'.) These
issues have long held firm places in the discussion of trade and
economic integration. The economic significance of independence from foreign sources of supply lies chiefly in the danger
of extortion or blackmailing through exclusion or withholding
of economically or militarily strategic goods. As far as the
economic advantages of a customs union are concerned, they
lie in the *reduction* of self-sufficiency in each member country
of the union, not in any supposed *increase* in self-sufficiency
of the entire union in relation to the rest of the world.

INFLUENCING THE DISTRIBUTION OF INCOME

Yet another purpose has been seen in the imposition of a system
of protective tariffs: to influence the distribution of national or
regional income among economic sectors, classes, or ethnic
groups. That tariffs on imports can shift incomes from the export sector, or from factors specific to the production of export

goods, to the import-competing sector, or to factors specificall suited to work on the production of goods competing with im- ports, is self-evident. The issue, however, was whether, if the same kind of labour was employed in both sectors and could freely move between them, tariffs could protect the higher wag of more advanced countries against the competition from abro: that was bearing down through cheap imports produced with cheap labour in backward countries.

The case for protection of the living standard of workers in high-wage countries against the (badly misnamed) 'wage dump- ing' by producers in low-wage countries had much popular sup- port and therefore, of course, strong political support; the bett economists, however, regarded the argument as untenable, ever naive. They admitted that protective tariffs might increase the workers' *relative* share in total income, but they held that this 'larger slice of a small cake' would mean an absolute reduction, because total income would surely be diminished by cutting down international trade and leaving opportunities for efficient division of labour unused. Economists also admitted that *mone* wages might be raised as a result of the increase in domestic pro duction, but they held that real wages would surely be lowered because of diminished productivity and correspondingly higher commodity prices. Finally, economists admitted that some *specialised* types of labour employed in the protected industry might obtain higher real wages, but only at the expense of othe workers and with average and total real wages of the entire labour force undoubtedly reduced.

These negative judgements have been revised. On the basis of a reconsideration of the argument for tariff protection of high- wage labour, it was granted that under certain assumptions the real income of labour as a whole could be higher when inter- national trade is cut back through tariffs or other restrictions. Are the assumptions on which this conclusion rests extraordina ily strong (that is, difficult to satisfy) or are they no stronger than what is usually accepted? The usual idealisations — unlimi ed competition, zero cost of transportation, mobility of labour within but not between the (two) countries, perfect homogenei of labour both within and between the countries, absence of economies of scale — had been traditionally accepted for pur- poses of theorising and need not unduly disturb us. A few othe assumptions, however, seem to be harder to take: that the pro- duction functions were exactly the same in the two countries although they included only two productive factors; that the ratios in which these factors were combined in the production of the two goods differed in a consistent fashion so that one product would require a relatively greater ratio of labour to the second factor of production — land? capital? — no matter how the ratio of factor prices were altered; and finally, that the factor endowments and the relative demands for the products would not be so different in the two countries as to allow one of the countries to give up producing one of the goods and to specialise completely in producing the other.

That production functions should be precisely the same in two countries would be a very plausible assumption if really everything needed for production, including soil and climate (temperature, wind, precipitation, etc.) were part of the functions; but if only two factors — uniform labour and one other homogeneous factor — are allowed to determine output, the assumption of identical production functions in the two countries is too fantastic. That the ratios of factor inputs should be permitted to vary as the ratios of factor prices change, but never so much as to reverse the preponderance of one factor input over the other (transforming a product made chiefly of labour when wages are low into one that uses only relatively little labour when wages are high) is another condition not easy to accept.[2]

Thus, it is one thing to formulate a theorem to explain that under specified conditions certain effects would result from a particular course of action, but quite another thing to prescribe this course of action as practical policy under conditions radically at variance with those spelt out in the theorem. In the particular case, in the argument for tariff protection for industries that employ dear labour, it happens that another assumption, additional to all those listed, is quite essential and may, like some of the others, restrict the applicability of the argument in question: it was assumed that the imposition of the import tariffs would not affect the terms of trade at which the country was trading exports for imports.

RAISING LABOUR INCOME AND IMPROVING THE TERMS OF TRADE

Import tariffs were proposed as a means of raising the income share of labour in countries where labour was the relatively

---

[2] Note that the expression 'labour-intensive product' is not used in the formulation above. The reasons for avoiding it will be given in further notes below.

scarce (dear) factor of production, of which, of course, relatively
little is used in producing exports and relatively much in producing import substitutes. The stated objective can be attained only
if the tariffs do not improve the terms of trade so much that imports become actually cheaper (relative to exports) instead of
more expensive as a result of the duties.

It may be difficult to comprehend how imported goods can
become cheaper when import duties are imposed or raised. In
order to understand we must distinguish between the price or
terms at which the importing country acquires a good from
abroad and the price, including the duty, which the buyer has
to pay for it; and between price expressed in money and price as
the ratio at which goods are exchanged against each other. The
proposition in question relates entirely to exchange ratios
between export goods and import goods, that is, the terms of
trade.

We have seen before that under certain conditions a country
can, by imposing or raising an import tariff, change the terms of
trade in its favour (the major condition being that the foreign
supply of the goods imported by the tariff-raising country and/or
the foreign demand for the exports of that country are relatively
inelastic). The effected change of the terms of trade in favour of the
tariff-raising country implies that it can acquire its import goods in
exchange for smaller quantities of its export goods; that is, its
imports become cheaper (relative to its exports) as a result of
the tariff. This result, however welcomed by those who rejoice
in exploiting 'the foreigner' and in thus capturing a larger share
of the gains from foreign trade, militates against the presumably
protective purposes of the tariff. For, it should be clear, if imports become cheaper relative to exportable goods, it will be less
profitable, rather than more profitable, to produce domestic
substitutes for imports. Tariffs that substantially improve a
country's terms of trade cannot be effective in protecting the
industries that compete with imports.

There is a question of how the treasury of the tariff-raising
country will use its revenues from the import duties. The simple
assumption is that the tariff revenues will replace other tax
revenues; in this case the only point to consider is how the
people will use their increased real income, especially how great
their marginal propensity to import will be. The propensities to
spend (on imports, on exportables, on non-tradables) will, together with the foreign elasticities in offering exports in exchange
for imports, determine the outcome, in particular whether the
new tariff will help or harm the import-competing industries.

If the tariff does not help the import-competing industries, it cannot help their workers either: labour employed in producing import-substitutes will not become dearer, indeed it may become less dear, in the process. Thus, the two objectives of import tariffs conflict with each other: the purpose of imposing tariffs to improve the terms of trade may be in conflict with the purpose of imposing tariffs to improve the income shares of dear labour (the scarce factor) employed in the domestic production of a good that must compete with imports from abroad. The greater the success of the tariff in improving the terms of trade, the more likely its failure to protect the dear (scarce) factor of production from the foreign competition of cheaper imports.

EQUALISING THE EARNINGS OF EQUAL FACTORS THROUGH FREE TRADE

Several times we have referred to the fact that most of the established propositions in the theory of international trade were derived from assumptions many of which are quite unrealistic — some idealised but still acceptable as approximations to real-world conditions, some downright counterfactual. They were nevertheless accepted as heuristic fictions because they yielded interesting conclusions which were judged to remain relevant even if some of the assumptions were relaxed or entirely dropped. It takes judgement to decide which conclusions from the same set of questionable assumptions remain relevant for applications to real-world situations and which of them cannot be so regarded and ought to be set aside.

The conclusion that free trade — without any international movements of labour or capital — would make the real price of equal and homogeneous factors of production equal in the different trading countries — so that the real wage per labour hour would be the same everywhere — has seemed so unbelievable that theorists resisted it when it first suggested itself, and continued to resist it even after it was proved to be logically cogent. The same set of assumptions had yielded a number of conclusions that were deemed relevant for real-world situations, for example, to explain the pattern of trade and some effects of trade restrictions on income distribution. The logical inference, however, that real wages of labour would become equal in the freely trading countries seems palpably contradicted by all observation. This forces the theorists to consider whether any one or two of their assumptions can be singled out as particularly responsible for the variance or whether it is the conjuncture of all the unrealistic assumptions which leads to the logically cogen but empirically incredible inference.

Although the theorem of the equalisation of the prices of the same productive factors in the different countries[3] is always demonstrated by way of mathematical argument, it can be mad intuitively clear by purely verbal reasoning, at least for the case of two factors, two goods, and two countries. Assume two countries are differently endowed with productive resources; before they begin to trade, labour is relatively cheaper in one country, Laboria, and relatively dearer in the other, Terrania, where land is more plentiful. When trade is freed, Laboria will export that of its two products for which relatively more labour is used per unit of output, and Terrania will export the product for which relatively more land services are used per unit of output. With export demand added to the home demand for the more-labour-using good in Laboria and for the more-land-using good in Terrania, labour will become less abundant (less cheap) in Laboria, and land less abundant (less cheap) in Terrania. With out tariffs and transport costs, the prices of the two goods must become equalised in the two countries, as imports depress the price of the more-land-using good in Laboria and of the more-labour-using good in Terrania.[4] In each country the proportions in which the two goods are produced must change until the increase in the production of the good that uses more of the originally cheaper factor completely takes up (absorbs) what was, before trade was opened, an abundance relative to the situation in the other country. ('Absorption of relative abundance' does not mean more employment, or previous unemployment, but rather reallocation at a higher price.) When free-trade equilibrium is reached, the original (pre-trade) abundances and scarcities will have disappeared[5] and, hence, the two countries will have the

[3] In Germanic English, with its long rows of nouns linked together without prepositions (and often even without hyphens), the above expression of sixteen words (including four prepositions and four articles) is compressed into a jargon expression of only four words: 'factor price equalisation theorem'.

[4] Most writers speak of 'the land-intensive good' where I say either 'the good for which relatively more land services are used per unit of output' or in a short-cut expression, 'the more-land-using good'. I prefer my expressions because (1) they are self-explanatory, (2) they are more euphonious, and (3) they avoid the confusion between 'intensive' and 'extensive' (since *extending* the use of land is the logical opposite of using land more *intensively*). For more on the third reason see note 6 below, p. 60.

[5] Note the implications of this statement: since equilibrium with trade

same ratios of factors, the same input/output ratios for each product, and the same price ratios of factors — provided that the process of equalisation was not prematurely stopped.

STOPPING THE EQUALISATION PROCESS

One reason why the process may be stopped before factor prices become equal in the two countries is that one of the countries may reach a limit in shifting its production to its exportable product simply because it has already switched all resources previously used for producing the other good; having ceased making this good (and now satisfying its home demand for it entirely by imports) and thus being completely specialised in making the exportable good, no further increase in production and export is possible. As a result, the other country will not be able to continue its resource reallocation though not all of the original relative abundance of one of its factors will have disappeared. The greater the original differences between the factor endowments in the two countries (as reflected in the pre-trade price ratios of the factors in the two countries) and the smaller the differences in the factor-use ratios for the two commodities, the more difficult will it be to 'absorb' (eliminate) the relative abundances in both countries before one country has reached the limit through complete specialisation in producing only its exportable good.

Another reason for the ordained outcome to be frustrated can be found in some particular shapes of the production functions for the two goods. While these functions allow (continuous or non-continuous) adjustments in the use-ratios of factors per unit of output as the factor-price ratios change, the adjustments must not be too drastic. 'Too drastic' refers here to a possible reversal in the relative predominance of one of the factors in the production of one of the products. If, at a given ratio of factor

---

completely free from restrictions or other obstacles, and with several other conditions fully satisfied, will have eliminated the relative abundances and scarcities of productive factors, to speak of an abundant factor or a scarce factor will no longer make sense — unless the hypothetical character of the statement is made clear. That is to say, a factor *would be* cheaper or dearer in one country relative to the other country *if* trade were restricted or prohibited. (Thus, the theory of tariff protection designed to increase the income of the 'scarce' factor can legitimately regard the factor as scarce only if it refers to a position short of a free-trade equilibrium with factor prices equalised.)

prices, one product is produced with relatively much labour, the other with relatively much land services, changes in the ratio of factor prices — say, higher prices of labour relative to land — will cause adjustments in the factor-use ratios, land services being substituted for labour in both productions. Despite these adjustments, the good originally made with 'relatively little labour' *may* still be the one made with 'relatively less labour' than the other good. On the other hand, there may be a drastic change in one or both of the factor-use ratios with the result that, at very high prices of labour relative to land services, the more-labour-using good may become the more-land-using good. (Some economists call this a 'reversal of factor intensities', though they would do better to speak of a 'reversal of the relative predominance of one of the factors in the production of one of the products' or, in a short-cut expression, a 'reversal of the factor-use ratios.')[6] In such cases the theorem of 'factor-price equalisation' does not apply. The reason is that, with such a reversal, the product that used to be made with relatively more labour and was exported from the labour-rich country has now become the product made with relatively more land — the dear factor — and can no longer be exported. The other product, however, does not really become exportable, as a result of the flip-flop in the factor use ratios, — since it has been the export product of the other country, and they will surely not export to each other the same good. The relative abundance of labour in the one country, and of land in the other, will therefore not be removed ('absorbed') by producing for export; the price of labour in the one country will remain lower than in the other.

Having stated these exceptions, should we conclude that they explain to our satisfaction the empirical irrelevance of the theorem? Or should we look for other, more general reasons why the theorem does not teach us much about the real world?

THE THEOREM EXPANDED AND REFINED

Before we try to answer these questions, we ought to point out that the theorem, in order to acquire any claim to empirical rele-

[6] Students of Ricardian rent theory will remember that 'intensive use of land' means to use plenty of *other* factors in order to *economise* in the use of land, or using less land per unit of output. Thus, when a writer talks about a 'land-intensive product' he really means to refer to a land-*ex*tensive product (and, likewise, when he refers to a 'labour-intensive good' he really means a labour-*ex*tensive one). A deplorable case of 'reversal in terminology'.

vance, needed to be expanded to include more than two goods, two factors, two countries. The assumption of different countries having identical production functions for their products if these functions are made up of only two productive factors is too absurd to be taken seriously (except as a teaching device). It was shown, however, that the equalisation theorem remained valid for additional factors and products, provided the number of factors did not exceed the number of goods actually produced. This proviso should not cause excessive trouble since both products and factors can be subdivided on the basis of differences in quality, and it is reasonable to hold that products are more finely differentiated than factors — although the contrary assertion has been made too. As to the inclusion of more than two countries, it was shown that any number of countries could be subdivided into a 'chain of pairs', with the general result unimpaired.

The algebraic arguments presented in the literature with respect to the extension of the theorem to models with more than two countries, two goods, and two factors usually pass too rapidly over some awkward conceptual problems — problems that can be troublesome to those of us who want to understand them intuitively and verbally. What, for example, does it mean if one speaks of a 'more-labour-using good' and of a 'more-land-using good' if there are three goods? A good may require relatively more labour than one of the other goods but relatively more land than the third. Hence, the expression 'a relatively much-labour-using good' (and even worse, the misnomer 'labour-intensive good') has no immediately obvious meaning except in comparison with only *one* of the other products. These expressions, if more than two products are involved, can be replaced by labour/land ratios, or factor-use ratios, which permit ordering (ranking). Such ranking, however, may become difficult or impossible when there are also more than two factors. Even the simple case of three products made of three factors may defy the desire to give a verbal description of the character of the relative input requirements.

Whether this is just a question of verbal exposition and linguistic clumsiness or whether it may have also substantive significance for the economic relevance of the theorem under discussion, has not been unanimously resolved in the literature. Some writers have concluded their algebraic argument with specifications of certain assumptions concerning factor-input ratios (or 'factor intensities', as they persisted in calling them) that have to be satisfied if the process of international equalisation of

factor prices is to be successfully completed; and there have bee
writers who added that 'it is difficult to find realistic situations'
in which these assumptions are met. On the other hand, many
economists, relying on their mathematical reasoning, have remained confident regarding the relevance of the theorem for an₃
number of countries, products, and factors, provided only that
the number of different factors employed does not exceed the
number of different goods produced.

Among the extensions of the theory is the inclusion of non-
traded goods. It was clear from the outset that complete specialisation of one of the trading countries would stop the process
of factor-price equalisation prematurely; and hence, that, for
the process to be carried to its end, some production of the
traded goods had to be going on in the trading countries. This
requirement, at first, seemed to exclude the production of non-
traded goods, that is, products that are neither exported nor imported. This limitation was found to be invalid; the allocation of
resources to non-traded goods need not interfere with the operation of the process of factor-price equalisation. It is possible,
however, that the presence of a large home-goods sector makes
it more likely that a country will not have sufficiently large endowments of one or more of the productive factors to continue
domestic production of all import-competing goods.

A necessary refinement concerns the inclusion of capital as
one of the productive factors; this promised severe troubles because of the variability of capital values with variations in the
price of capital funds, the rate of interest. By means of a sophisticated argument it was shown that capital goods could be de-
composed into all that went into making them, and that capital
theory, therefore, need not interfere with the equalisation
theorem.

Economists who admitted only two factors into their theoretical models had two choices: either labour and capital, or labour
and land. Those more familiar with capital theory suspected
difficulties regarding the process of simultaneous equalisation of
prices of goods and of factors through free trade between the
countries involved; these economists avoided trouble by selectin
land as their second factor. On the other hand, those who wante
to contrast movements of goods with movements of factors preferred both factors to be movable; land did not qualify for this
role, and so it was assigned to capital.

The theorem seems to have survived all expansions and refine
ments; but its lack of empirical relevance becomes thereby even
more embarrassing. The question *which* of the deviations of re-

ality from assumptions are likely to be *chiefly* responsible for the empirical irrelevance of the theorem cries out for an answer.

THE ASSUMPTIONS RECONSIDERED

Traditional candidates for rejection are the assumptions (1) of pure and perfect competition in perfect markets — a combination of three separate and independent assumptions; and (2) of perfect mobility of factors within each economy. To be sure, these assumptions are unrealistic in a world of oligopolies, of all sorts of monopolistic restraints by private organisations and governmental agencies, of trade-union rules and collective bargaining. Still, the tendencies deduced from employing the idealised assumptions in theoretical arguments seem to be real enough in many capitalist and mixed economies. They may not achieve all the 'adjustments' deduced by means of the abstract model, but they go quite some way, sufficiently far to make the unrealistic assumptions helpful in explaining many observed changes in observed reality. The assumption of zero transport cost is completely harmless; that transport costs are positive would qualify but not suspend the operation of the deduced consequences of expanded trade. That free trade does not exist in reality, that some obstacles to trade remain even within customs unions and free-trade areas, is unquestioned, but we have been able to observe substantial trade liberalisation and several rounds of tariff reductions, which should allow us to consider the assumption of free trade as an approximation to real-world conditions.

The most vulnerable assumption of the entire set is the one I have previously singled out as difficult to accept: that any two countries trading with each other continue domestic production of some quantities of the goods which they import and have identical production functions for them; the idea is that, with the same factor-price ratios, they must use the factors in exactly the same proportions. That the production function is the same in all countries is perfectly acceptable and even plausible if, but only if, it contains *all* the inputs needed for making the product in question, no matter whether these inputs are free, scarce, or unobtainable, whether they are available in the market at a price, provided as a free gift of nature, or furnished without charge by the community. Such a *complete* production function would include air and water, sunshine and wind, and other requirements of production which may be abundant in one place, scarce in another, and unobtainable in a third. The effective price of an unobtainable factor is, of course, infinite; and the effective price of a scarce factor is high even when no payment has to be made for it by the producer.

For example, wine is a much-sunshine-using product even if the wine-grower makes no money payments for sunshine. In a country with little sunshine, wine will not be grown (although it may be technically possible, in greenhouses). The 'shadow prices' of the factor sunshine will of course be very different in the different countries, and no equalisation can be expected. Economists who prefer to work with *incomplete* production functions — as many do — will in consistency have to say that the production functions for wine are not the same everywhere. In any case it is clear that many imported goods are *not* produced at home.

HETEROGENEOUS FACTORS

We now know several sufficient reasons for the theorem of international equalisation of factor prices not to be empirically relevant. The most fundamental reason, however, lies in the fact that the theorem is supposed to apply to *equal* factors whereas most factors are quite *unequal* within and between countries. No one would expect the prices of land of different fertility and in different locations to be the same; and there is no good economic reason for prices of labour of different quality to be even approximately equal. The work of farmers, opera singers, welders, violinists, carpenters, painters, dentists, stenographers, stevedores, computer programmers, machinists, hod carriers, and schoolteachers calls for rather different talents, skills, physical strength, mental agility, investment, and dedication.

There is, of course, some occupational mobility which prevents differences in earnings from becoming — and staying for ever — astronomically large, but one cannot expect the differences to disappear, at least not for economic reasons. Within the large customs union called the United States of America, the price of 'labour' has not become equal. Even in the same occupations large differences in earnings have continued to exist in different parts of the country and also in the same places. To expect the theorem of the international equalisation of factor prices to be confirmed by statistically observable equalisation of labour income in different countries as they expand their trade, is to misunderstand the meaning and significance of economic abstraction. The homogeneous factor L in pure economic theory is a mental construct designed for purposes of abstract reasoning; it has no empirical counterpart in the world of operational concepts with recorded data. In the real world we would have to distinguish thousands of different kinds of work to make the expression 'equal pay for equal work' economically meaningful.

EQUALISING THE EARNINGS OF LABOUR THROUGH INTERNATIONAL MOBILITY OF FACTORS

The theorem of international equalisation of factor prices demonstrates that trade in products can under specified conditions substitute for international movements of factors. If trade alone, without factor movements across the frontiers, can reduce international differences in factor prices, how much faster can these differences be reduced if factors can move freely from countries where they are in relative surplus to countries where they are scarce? Much faster, to be sure; but one must not expect any such tendencies for equalisation to operate really fast in calendar time. Even with complete freedom to migrate, many obstacles and inhibitions would slow down the reduction, let alone elimination, of differences in the earnings of comparable labour.

International differences in earnings of 'comparable' capital funds are relatively smaller if due account is taken of differences in risk. Within the same nation or city, the interest rates on loans, the effective yields on securities, and the rates of return on fixed investments of various kinds show wide disparities, depending on maturities, liquidity, credit-worthiness, specific risks, and general uncertainty. Short loans secured by good collateral, and long-term investments in business ventures are quite different uses of capital funds, and the existence of wide differences in rates of return is easily understood. Several additional risks exist for international capital transactions: differences in legal institutions, affecting the ease with which a lender or investor can get help in the enforcement of his claims; exchange risks, partly regarding possible changes in foreign-exchange rates, partly regarding possible impositions of payments restrictions in the future; the probability of price inflation and differences in the inflation rates in different countries — these are only a few of the elements preventing complete equalisation in the returns on capital in different countries, even if there may be freedom of capital movements at the time the contracts are made.

International differences in the earnings of labour, like differences within the same country, are in the first place a matter of differences in quality and efficiency. Assuming, however, that

we are talking only of 'comparable' labour, and assuming complete freedom of travel and migration, enough obstacles and inhibitions to movement exist to explain substantial differences.
Fully integrated labour markets rarely exist even *within* countries; can one conceive of fully integrated labour markets for
different countries? High costs of moving, high psychic costs of
getting uprooted and re-acclimatised, obstacles due to ethnic
and cultural differences and to differences in learning abilities
and, finally, restrictions, if not exclusion, through rules and
practices of labour unions, would keep the international mobility
of labour far below perfection, even if governments were prepared to open the frontiers and guarantee unrestricted migration.
But apart from any obstacles to the movement of labour across
national frontiers, there is another element in the persistent inequality of labour incomes: the natural additions to the labour
supply in countries with high rates of population growth. If the
accretion to the supply of labour in low-wage countries exceeds
the volume of emigration, the surplus of labour cannot be alleviated and the gap between the earnings of labour in poor countries
and those in countries of high productivity is liable to persist.

INCREASING INEQUALITY THROUGH FACTOR MOVE-
MENTS

According to one view, neither free trade nor free mobility of
capital nor freedom to migrate would contribute to the reduction of differences in factor incomes; on the contrary, trade,
capital movements, and migration may actually increase the
existing inequalities, especially where areas on different levels of
development are involved.

This theory points to 'backwash effects' increasing the 'natural
tendency to regional inequality'. The regions that promise bigger
returns attract the best workers and most capital, leaving other
regions in a backwater with the less efficient workers, with less
ability to save and less opportunities for attractive investment.

The policy implications of this theory are, so we are told,
very different from classical and neoclassical precepts: underdeveloped countries are advised to stick to protectionism, capital
controls, and all sorts of nationalist policies. Whether this policy
advice is really implied in the theory may be questioned. The
theory itself, however, is quite plausible and depicts at least a
possible course of events, though not an inevitable one. As a
matter of fact, the weaver of this strand of ideas on integration
and disintegration admits that the 'backwash effects' may be off

set or overcompensated by 'spread effects' which have the opposite consequences of letting poorer sectors, areas, or countries benefit from the expansion of trade and investment.

While we are on the subject of international movements of factors, we ought to recall that early writers on international trade had assumed that neither labour nor capital was able to move abroad — a realistic assumption for their time. The modern theorist knows full well that international migration of labour and international movements of capital have become facts of life. However, he also knows that the effects of trade and the effects of factor movements have to be studied separately before one can proceed to study them in combination. Thus, trade integration without international movements of factors remains a subject of analysis.

INTERNATIONAL TRANSFER OF TECHNOLOGY AND ENTERPRISE

We find in the classical literature numerous, though casual, references to international transfer of skills and technical arts. The subject of transfer of technology and enterprise became more topical in discussions of patents of invention. In recent years it has become closely connected with the problems of multinational corporations and of governmentally organised co-operation in industrial projects.

With respect to its transferability technology may be of three kinds: that which can be adequately described in words, numbers, and drawings, intelligible to any trained technician; that which could be so described but is, instead, kept secret by the few who know it; and that which can be learned only by observing its practitioners in action and by working with them. The third type is what is commonly called 'know-how'; it is often supplementary to the describable types of technology and sometimes indispensable for their use in practice. The role of know-how in industrial production has probably increased over the years; it may have given a strong impetus to the development of multinational corporations and international co-operation in various industries.

The direct sale of technical know-how — through receiving teams of learners or sending teams of performers, for a fee — is not widespread. The transfer of know-how is more often associated with the transfer of capital or a transfer of enterprise or both. It takes the form of corporate mergers, take-overs, or substantial participation in the ownership of equity capital. The

problems of joint ventures and similar forms of co-operation
have recently received much attention in the economic literature

TRANSPORT AND COMMUNICATION

That cheap transportation and speedy communication are amor
the most fundamental conditions of economic integration is one
of the oldest insights. It was known to princes, governors, trade
and economists, in fact to every one concerned with commerce.

The degree of integration — within a given geographic area as
well as the extension of integration over larger areas — was seen
to depend on cheap and reliable transportation. No wonder that
historians, both those reporting on the economic integration of
nation states and those reporting on the expansion of world
trade, have assigned to the successive revolutions of transport
technology a major role. No wonder, also, that theorists analysing the effects of tariffs were wont to simplify their models for
purposes of comparative statics by assuming transport costs to
be zero. No wonder, too, that at least one economist tried to
elucidate the effects of tariffs on prices and production by spea
ing of them as 'negative railways' [Bastiat, 1847].

There has been less discussion or analysis of the role of telecommunication in the progress of economic integration, perhap
because it is far too obvious to attract the curiosity of scholarly
researchers. One of the major effects of speedy and reliable
systems of telecommunication is manifest in the integration of
international markets for staple commodities and financial asset
It would not be easy to conceive of organised commodity exchanges, stock exchanges, and currency markets functioning, in
the manner to which we have become accustomed, without the
present means of telecommunication.

TRANSFERS OF MONEY

Equal to cheap transport as a precondition of economic integration ranks cheapness and reliability of transfers of money. It
requires a monetary system that allows importers to make payments to their foreign suppliers with a minimum of bother, risk,
and other costs; handlers of capital to remit funds to their forei
borrowers or correspondents; and debtors to pay interest and
principal to their foreign creditors.

Needless to say, the oldest literature dealt chiefly with easy
payments in foreign trade; the freedom and ease of capital move
ments entered the discussion only later. The importance of easy

payments has been extensively discussed in mercantilist writings about unification of the nation state, when large numbers of different coins, made of gold and silver of different weight and different fineness, circulated within the provinces, principalities and splinter states. After the establishment of nation states, the formation of monetary unions to guarantee the interconvertibility of national currencies became an object of public discussion, governmental negotiations and actual agreements, none of which has proved a lasting success.

The discussion continues. No economist will question that a higher degree of monetary integration may make a significant contribution to general economic integration, but many will disagree on the best sequence of steps to bring it about. Questions such as the stability or rigidity of foreign-exchange rates, the autonomy of national monetary authorities, the co-ordination of national monetary policies, the use of governmental restrictions and controls of foreign payments and transfers of capital, and the eventual replacement of national currencies by a uniform money for the entire economic union, all these questions have remained controversial.

The essence of money as a general medium of exchange is that it can be used freely without constraints. If within a country every money transaction required a licence or permit from a control authority, one could hardly speak of monetary integration within that national economy, and the degree of its general economic integration would probably be minimal. International monetary integration means that anybody is free to use his money for any kind of purchase or payment abroad. If countries have different currencies, interconvertibility of these currencies is the essence of international monetary integration.[7] The guarantee of fixed exchange rates may add a great deal to this integration; but if controls or restrictions of international money transactions are imposed, the question is whether integration is increased or reduced on balance. If exchange rates are fixed, but the exchanges for which payments are to be made are restricted, the net addition to integration may well be negative. This is the crux of the argument. Without an accepted technique of measuring the disintegrating effects of restrictions and the integrating

[7] Many writers distinguish between 'market convertibility' and 'official convertibility'. The former means freedom of individuals and firms to convert currencies in unlimited amounts at whatever exchange rates they agree to accept. Official convertibility means the obligation and preparedness of the monetary authorities to convert unlimited amounts of the national currency into some specified foreign currency or other asset at fixed rates.

effects of fixed rates in international transactions, one cannot
entertain much hope for the controversy being resolved.

OPTIMUM CURRENCY AREA

One other point regarding currencies and exchange rates should
be emphatically restated, because it has confused the discussion
about monetary integration almost beyond repair: contrary to
the contention of virtually all experts, maintenance of unalterably fixed exchange rates is *not* equivalent to the exclusive use
of a single common currency in the entire area of the monetary
union.

If a single currency is used for an 'integrated' region, it will be
almost impossible to impose workable controls and restrictions
on money transactions; and, secondly, net flows of currency
from one part of the region to another will not change the total
stock of money in circulation. If, however, different currencies
are used in the various member countries of the monetary union,
their interconvertibility at unalterably fixed exchange rates can
be secured only by two devices, used separately or in combination: any excess supply of one currency relative to others —
which is equivalent to a flow of funds to other parts of the
region — would either have to be absorbed by monetary authorities exchanging the offered currency into the currencies demanded; or it would have to be made ineffective by governments sup-
pressing the demand for the desired currencies by prohibiting or
restricting the intended transactions (purchases of goods, services
land, capital assets, securities). The first technique involves
monetary expansion through the issue of the currencies demanded in exchange for the currencies in excess supply, without
assurance that the authorities issuing the latter would allow the
stock of their currency to be reduced. The second technique
would constitute economic disintegration.

How has it been possible for competent and respected economists to assert the equivalence, for a given region, of a multiple-
currency system with fixed exchange rates and a single-currency
system? Simply by assuming that separate national central banks
would behave as if they were branches, without autonomy or
decision-making power, of a supranational regional central bank.
Such an assumption, however, is quite unreasonable, at least in
our time. If the member countries of a community or monetary
union were willing to give up their monetary autonomy, they
would agree on surrendering the right to issue their own national
currencies and would accept a common currency as the sole cir-

culating medium. Their insistence on retaining their sovereignty
in matters of currency and credit indicates that they would not
give up the possibility of using their money-creating machinery
for national objectives, such as providing cheap credit to their
fiscal authorities or to their industries and 'creating' additional
jobs in periods of unemployment.

There have been a good many attempts to define the concept
of an 'optimum currency area'. The originally proposed definition was in terms of internal mobility and external immobility
of productive factors — perfect intraregional mobility of resources,
including uninhibited emigration and immigration of labour,
and unrestrained outflow and inflow of capital funds. Other
definitions have been in terms of mutual compatibilities of the
member countries in matters of political or economic ideology,
in terms of harmonisation of economic institutions and co-
ordination of national policies, in the complementarity of their
trade patterns, and similar criteria. What ultimately counts, however, is that all members are willing to give up their independence
in matters of money, credit, and interest. Pragmatically, therefore, an optimum currency area is a region no part of which in-
sists on creating money and having a monetary policy of its
own.[8]

INTEGRATION OF CAPITAL MARKETS

The discussion of free mobility of capital funds within an integrated region or community has been complicated by inconsistent terminologies. Most theorists spoke about loanable funds or
investible funds without regard to the practitioners' habit of distinguishing between 'capital markets', where long-term securities
are traded, and 'money markets', where short-term promises to
pay are exchanged for liquid funds. The capital markets are
chiefly stock exchanges and bond markets, but also various supplementary markets in which a variety of financial assets of
deferred maturity are exchanged against money. Money markets
deal in 'money-market instruments', including promissory notes,
bills, certificates of deposits, acceptances, loans of maturities
ranging from overnight money to six-month credits, and too
many other kinds of paper to enumerate. The difficulty of rela-

[8] I admit to a deviation from my expository design. On almost all other
issues of economic integration I confined myself to a report on the views
or theories presented in the literature; on the present issue I allowed myself to be carried away and give special emphasis to my own views.

ting the nominal durations expressed in the maturities of loans
and securities to the duration of actual or expected availabilities
of the loanable or investible funds constitutes a serious source of
misunderstanding in economic analysis. Repeated 'rolling over'
of short-term loans and quick resales of long-term securities may
reverse the contractual terms and make the money market into
a source of supply of long-term capital funds, and the capital
market into a source of hot money, subject to withdrawal without any notice and used for speculative transactions effectively
closed within a few days.

These difficulties matter little within an economy, chiefly because we know so little about what is going on — and what we
do not know does not bother us. For international flows of
capital, however, the fiscal and monetary authorities have
arranged for a central intelligence system, with all kinds of
recording and reporting obligations, ranging from supervision
and surveillance of banking, via compilations of foreign transactions in detailed balances of payments on capital account, to
tight controls of capital transactions or even all foreign-exchange
transactions. It is not possible to identify 'real' or 'intentional'
short-term and long-term capital transactions, because the operational concepts of short-term and long-term instruments or
securities do not really correspond to the theoretically significant concepts in question. In other words, they are poor proxies
for the 'real thing' — or for what we think is the really significant (theoretically meaningful) mental construction.

The trouble is that some economists have concluded that international long-term capital movements are 'good' and short-
term flows are 'bad'. There is a speck of insight in this, because
long-term availability of capital allows a country to use it for
long-term investment, which will increase the productivity of
the economy, while availability for only short periods would
make the use of the funds for investment in fixed assets (that
can pay for themselves only over a long period of years) inappropriate. This 'insight' is not generally valid. But even if it were,
the impossibility of identifying long-term and short-term availability of capital by the outward appearances (or guises) of the
instruments or securities against which the loanable or investible
funds are exchanged would make it rather foolish to apply it to
real-world decisions about legal or administrative provisions or
policies.

A national economy would be crippled if internal flows of
capital were subjected to strict controls. The economic integration of a regional community would be seriously obstructed by

a disintegrated capital market. Thus, perfect mobility of capital funds was given high priority by the early architects of regional economic union. By some strange quirk in official thinking, capital movements into and out of countries in the European Economic Community have been regarded with great suspicion and apprehension, and consequently have been subjected to governmental controls of many sorts. These measures have usually been explained by the argument that the stability of foreign-exchange rates ought to be defended against speculative movements of funds because fluctuations in exchange rates would be disturbing to a healthy progress in 'trade integration'. This may be so, but the prohibitions and restrictions imposed to avoid movements of capital funds are surely negating 'factor integration'.

CAPITAL MOVEMENTS AND ADJUSTMENT MECHANISM

Advocates of controls and restrictions of capital movements, including intraregional ones, see these movements chiefly as destabilising, disequilibrating, disturbing, and possibly injurious to production and trade. Most economists analysing these problems first distinguish autonomous from induced movements, and stress that flows of capital funds across national frontiers may be stabilising, equilibrating, instrumental in short-term adjustment and, in general, helpful to the economies concerned.

Autonomous flows of capital, that is, those not induced by other transactions that figure in the international balance of payments, are disequilibrating by definition. This does not mean that they are a nuisance or a calamity: under a methodological convention, one calls disequilibrating (a disturbance of equilibrium) anything that one decides to examine as a cause of subsequent developments, good or bad. Obversely, that a capital flow is regarded as an equilibrating one, means merely that one has decided to treat it as a consequence of some antecedent event or change of conditions.

Certain international flows of capital are attributed to changes in differentials in interest rates or profit rates, which in turn may be attributed to changes in the economy that may have also some other bearing on international transactions. Induced capital movements of this sort play a significant role in the adjustment process, possibly helping to restore balance in international payments in the short run. Of special importance are accommodating capital movements, that is, those by which the banking

system — commercial banks and central banks — accommodates
an excess supply or excess demand in the foreign-exchange market. Close integration of capital markets promotes the creation
of internationally acceptable financial claims, which enable the
banking system to provide this accommodation with a minimum
of cost and friction.

Most frequent are accommodating capital movements that
balance, in the short run, some surpluses or deficits either on
current account or on long-term capital account. Sometimes the
trade balance and the autonomous capital balance change in the
same direction; this calls for accommodating movements of
capital to compensate for the change in the 'basic balance'. The
number of possible combinations is large, and the literature is
full of special cases. There is, for example, the 'common-cause
hypothesis' for open economies: some favourable development
in the export sector of an economy may result in increases in
exports of goods as well as in imports of capital. The consequen
excess supply of foreign funds places a double burden on the
cushioning mechanism of compensatory, accommodating capita
outflows. Only with closely integrated capital markets (money
markets, in this case) will the mechanism function in a reliable
and enduring fashion. Governmental controls, or fears of such
controls, will impair or destroy it.

TAX INCENTIVES AND DISINCENTIVES FOR FOREIGN INVESTMENT

Capital movements of all kinds are subjected to controls and restrictions of various types, mostly through measures which the
government or the monetary authorities execute through banks;
but some types of control engage also other financial intermedi-
aries and, quite often, brokers in securities markets. All these
controls focus on individual transactions, such as foreign payments, sales and purchases of securities, but also exports and imports of goods and services (since one can export capital by
exporting goods at low prices or without insisting on payment).
In a separate category, different from controls of transactions,
are measures designed to affect foreign investment through the
tax treatment of the returns which it yields over the years. Incentives and disincentives for capital investment abroad or
received from abroad have long existed and have been analysed
by economists.

On the most general level of analysis, it has been argued that all private investment by individual firms investing abroad disregards the marginal social product of foreign investment. Each individual investor considering loans and investments abroad will reckon with the returns he can expect on his particular undertaking, but he cannot take into account the resulting reduction of the returns accruing to all his fellow investors. This reduction is dictated by the decline of the marginal efficiency of investment abroad — a decline steeper than that visualised by the individual, competitive investor. The conclusion is that a country rich in investible funds is inclined to lend and invest too much abroad and, in order to avoid this overinvestment, ought to tax the returns on such loans and investments more heavily than the returns on domestic loans and investments.

As an additional consideration in favour of domestic lending and investing, and against lending and investing abroad, at least one writer pointed to the possibility of default and capital losses. The real capital created at home may retain some social usefulness even if the lender or original investor should lose his principal or equity; any usefulness of real capital that was built up in foreign lands will, if the lender or investor has lost his principal or equity, not be of any value to his country.

Various analyses have been made of the 'optimum tax' on foreign investment, where the optimum was always conceived as the maximum of income accruing either to the country supplying capital to foreign countries or to the country receiving capital from abroad. (In other words, it was not the revenue collected by the tax authorities that was to be maximised but the net income to the nation supplying or receiving the capital funds.) In all these studies the social marginal returns were distinguished from the private ones, because the latter were based on considerations of competing lenders, investors, or borrowers. The external effects of the additional lending, investing, or borrowing are supposed to be internalised by the tax on the returns, in order to enable the nation in question to exploit whatever monopolistic position it has as supplier of capital or whatever monopsonistic position it has as employer of foreign capital. Such exploitation, of course, implies restraints, in the form of tax disincentives, on the flow of capital funds, and net reductions in foreign investment. Some investment opportunities, efficient from a cosmopolitan point of view, are kept from being utilised in order to allow one nation to gain a little at the expense of the other. The 'optimum tax' on the returns to foreign investment is an instrument of disintegration — just like the 'optimum tariff' on imports.

THE OPTIMAL COMBINATION OF INVESTMENT TAX AND IMPORT TARIFF

That the effects of a tax on foreign investment — no matter whether it is levied by the country supplying the funds or by the country employing them — may be compared to the effects of a tariff on imports has not eluded the problem-seekers and problem-solvers in the economic profession. The optimum tariff is designed to turn the terms of trade in favour of the country imposing the tariff; the optimum tax on foreign lending and borrowing is designed to alter the terms on foreign capital in favour of the country imposing the tax. What a lovely set of problems is presented by combining the two techniques of exploiting the foreigners and finding the optimum combination of investment tax and import tariff!

This exercise in double optimisation is readily manageable by any theorist who is equipped with an arsenal of elasticities. He needs all the elasticities: of supply of all import goods and demand for all export goods as well as those of supply of loanable and investible capital and of the demand for such funds as determined by the elasticities of marginal efficiencies of investment. Of course, the importance of the gains from trade relative to that of the gains from foreign investment is a significant variable. If earnings from investment abroad bulk large in a country's balance of payments, it may be optimal strategy for it to subsidise exports, instead of levying duties on imports to improve the terms of trade. Special cases can make for fascinating exercises. For example, tariffs may be 'fixed' at a ceiling under some agreement and the net rates of return on investment may be 'given' because of vigorous competition from alternative sources of capital funds; in such circumstances it may be optimal to subsidise investment abroad or to have negative import duties.

For the case of a customs union, in which duties on imports from member countries are zero but taxes on returns from foreign investment can be changed, the problem is reduced to partial optimisation. It is rather doubtful, however, whether any of the 'solutions' are of practical significance for questions of policy, in countries belonging to a customs union or in any country whatever.

FISCAL INTEGRATION

In the last pages the subject of special taxes was broached, suggested by a preceding discussion of capital movements, which, more or less logically, had followed discussions of monetary integration and integration of capital markets. Raising the question of taxes on the returns on capital may have served as a transition to the broad problem of fiscal integration.

We must, however, avoid the suggestion that fiscal integration involves chiefly harmonisation of tax systems and tax rates. Too many advocates of economic integration have made the mistake of overemphasising tax harmonisation and slighting other, far more important, aspects of fiscal integration. Perhaps a simple enumeration of some of its various aspects can help in correcting the bias of the enthusiasts for tax harmonisation.

The very concept of a customs union implies a fiscal problem: the revenues collected from the tariffs on imports from non-member countries have to be divided among the member countries or spent for jointly agreed purposes. (There may be additional common sources of funds for which this holds true.) While this is an unavoidable fiscal aspect of a customs union, it may be a relatively insignificant one. Of major importance is the general harmonisation of public expenditures by the member countries, regarding the relative magnitude as well as the composition and direction of public spending.

As a third aspect of fiscal integration we may refer to the general harmonisation of the tax system — general, that is, with respect to the type of direct and indirect taxes raised, the shares of national product collected in taxes by the national authorities, the use of tax incentives employed by them to affect the competitive positions of industrial enterprises (and thereby to compete with member countries in attracting industries by means of tax advantage and exemptions). A fourth aspect is that of specific harmonisation of tax rates, particularly the height of certain indirect taxes, such as the value-added tax or various excises and sales taxes. It is this aspect of harmonisation that has found the most vocal advocacy, probably because producers were indignant when their competitors in another union-country enjoyed lower tax rates.

The importance of practitioners' and scholars' squabbles and controversies regarding alleged distortions and inequities involved in the non-uniformity of tax rates in different countries has been vastly exaggerated. One factor that greatly reduces the significance of rates of taxation is the serious inequality in tax effectiveness in different countries. Differences in administrative and judiciary systems, in business practices, and in the taxpayers' compliance with the law are so great and so deep-seated that they present a separate aspect of tax harmonisation. An income

tax rate of 60 per cent in a country with a tradition of tax
evasion may in effect be lower than a conscientiously observed
and enforced rate of 25 per cent in another country. With the
'tax morale' or 'tax effectiveness' a function of the height of
the legal tax rates, tax harmonisation as a part of economic integration may become an almost irrelevant issue.

An entirely different aspect of fiscal integration is the co-
ordination of the fiscal policies of all member countries — their
policies of altering the national budgets in their total expenditures and revenues, their deficits and surpluses — for the purpos
of affecting aggregate spending and (supposedly) aggregate
employment. The intraregional co-ordination of fiscal policies,
with their short-term or medium-term objectives, is really part
and parcel of monetary co-ordination, even if it is conceived as
a fiscal instrument of expansion or contraction.

A genuine aspect of fiscal integration can be seen in transfers
among the bloc members, no matter whether these transfers are
made out of national revenues or out of common revenues. Intr
regional transfers as fiscal aid to member countries in temporary
straits or permanent poverty, with overpopulation or under-
development, are almost essential accessories of regional integra
tion, at least if the regional arrangements are to endure, to sur-
vive the strains and stresses of co-operation among unequal part
ners and the pains and hardships of structural adjustment in
member countries in response to imbalances in foreign payment
and changes in production, investment, and trade. Such fiscal
transfers are quite common within countries: the use of taxes
raised in some sections for expenditures in other sections. Without analogous transfers among the members of a group resolved
to become an economically integrated region the coherence of
the group may prove rather precarious.

The last two aspects of fiscal integration — they are the eightl
and ninth in this enumeration — are a common budget and a
common system of taxation for the community. Instead of mer
aspects, we may see them as the highest forms of fiscal integration. A common system of taxation for the economically integr
ted community of nations need not mean that all state taxes,
provincial taxes, and local taxes are abolished; it does mean,
however, that a substantial part of all tax revenues is raised by
supranational fiscal authorities. A common budget of the community can exist also in the absence of a common system of
taxation, provided substantial fiscal contributions of the member countries to the common budget are secured. However, con
tinuous dependence of the community on financial contributio

from national treasuries raises serious questions regarding the viability of the regional arrangements. Their permanence is more safely secured by a common tax system, with the supranational authority as the primary collector of the taxes, perhaps with a system of sharing the revenues with the national treasuries.

BORDER TAX ADJUSTMENTS TO COMPENSATE FOR TAX-RATE INEQUALITIES

One of the worst consequences of differences in tax rates among the member countries of a customs union is the belief that equity and efficiency require that the differences be compensated for by a system of border tax adjustments. If, for example, the value-added tax in one country is higher than in another, the authorities feel obliged to refund the difference for all exports lest the exporters suffer a competitive disadvantage; and to levy a compensating tax on imports lest the domestic producers suffer from the competition from foreign producers subject to lower taxes. This sounds plausible — though economists have known for over 150 years that it is a fallacy. 'The rise of wages, a tax on income, or a proportional tax on all commodities, all operate in the same way; they do not alter the relative values of goods, and therefore they do not subject us to any disadvantage in our commerce.' [Ricardo, 1822.] It is assumed, of course, that the tax rates within each country are non-discriminatory; that the value-added tax, for example, is the same for all products without exemptions. Differences in the tax rates in different countries, however, are irrelevant and no valid economic argument can be made for their harmonisation.

The system of border-tax adjustments necessitates checkpoints on all frontiers between union-member countries, the most effective institutions for the perpetuation of disintegration.

THE FORMS OF REGIONAL ARRANGEMENTS

That arrangements to promote economic integration can be intranational (to create an integrated national economy), multinational (to create an integrated regional economy), or worldwide (to create an integrated world economy) has often been said. There has been disagreement on the question whether regional integration would be a help or a hindrance in the progress toward worldwide integration. The answers depended often on tacit assumptions regarding the forms of regional arrangements. With respect to trade, it will make a difference (a) whether

it is a customs union or a free-trade area which is being established, (*b*) whether the tariffs of the countries before they enter into these arrangements were high or low, and (*c*) whether the common external tariff of a customs union is high or low.
Assume that some of the countries had very low tariffs whereas the external tariff of the union is high, the new regional integration would involve economic disintegration from the point of view of the world as a whole. If, on the other hand, the pre-union tariffs of the countries had been high whereas the external tariff of the union is low, the new arrangement would promote regional and worldwide integration at the same time.

With regard to the comparison between a customs union and a free-trade area, it is often said that, because in a free-trade area the member countries retain their own, possibly quite different, tariffs on imports from non-member countries, it constitutes a lower form of integration. Whether this verdict is correct depend on the height of the tariffs; if the separate and different tariffs on imports from outside the area are low whereas the common external tariff of an alternatively established customs union would be high, the free-trade area would be more favourable to worldwide integration than the customs union.

THE HEIGHT OF TARIFFS, IMPOSED, ABOLISHED, OR ALTERED

Discussions of the effects of different forms of trade integration presuppose that the height of tariff walls can be measured or estimated in some meaningful way. This is not an easy problem, especially if tariffs are not the only man-made obstacles to trade Import prohibitions, quotas, or other explicit quantitative restrictions have to be translated into equivalent tariffs, that is, import duties that would have the same effects upon trade; however, since any changes in supply and demand in the respective markets may change the hypothetical import duty that would be equivalent to a given quantative restriction, its translation into equivalent tariffs is unlikely to remain valid for any length time.

Even more problematic is the method of expressing thousand or tens of thousands of tariff rates of very different magnitudes by a single average or central value. How would all the zeros for duty-free imports affect an unweighted average? How would a weighted average be affected by zero imports under some prohibitive tariff rates? Clearly, to weight the tariff rates by actual imports would be an unsatisfactory procedure, since these weights would be so strongly affected by the height of the duties to be averaged. If the purpose of the measurement is to get an indication of the volume of trade suppressed (rather than that of trade allowed), the duties should really be weighted by the 'potential' imports under free trade. Such a hypothetical weighting procedure, however, would be ruled out if consideration were given to the interdependence of all variables involved. In partial-equilibrium analysis, the question of potential imports at a zero duty, with all other duties, prices, and quantities assumed to be unchanged, makes sense. In general-equilibrium analysis, where all repercussions throughout the economies concerned have to be considered, the solution of the problem is relegated to the domain of pure fiction.

The traditional precept 'if you can't measure, measure anyhow' is often obeyed by economic statisticians, and in many instances we are grateful to them. Their estimates may be questionable and objectionable in many respects and yet better than nothing. Thus, in the matter of the heights of tariff walls, we know that they really cannot be measured, but we know that the numerical values estimated and presented as some sort of average tariff make enough sense to permit us to say that one particular tariff wall is higher or lower than another.

Such comparisons, however, make little or no sense where trade is directed by central trading bureaus or agencies ('state trading') on principles other than the use of either market-price guides or shadow-price guides calculated on the basis of conscientiously estimated opportunity costs. To say that an *ad valorem* tariff of x per cent restricts the imports of a particular commodity by q units, has a clear meaning; but by how much the quantity of imports which a state purchasing agent decides to purchase falls short of the hypothetical quantity which competitively bidding importers — traders, processors, or distributors — would buy at competitive market prices from mutually competing exporters cannot be stated — except perhaps with a well-developed system of shadow prices. Neither trade/income ratios nor time series showing the annual growth rates of intraregional and interregional trade can indicate the degree of trade integration achieved — simply because actual trade is no proof of the potential being fully realised. The question is whether all opportunities for efficient division of labour are taken advantage of, or how much closer to this state of affairs the process of integration has progressed. There is probably no way to answer this question except for some clues derived from analyses on the basis of market prices or shadow prices.

IMPERFECT COMPETITION, MONOPOLY, AND OLIGOPOI

Market prices are not always reliable guides in selecting the 'right' products and the 'right' quantities for export or import. Many writers who emphasised this observation regarded it as a reservation to the validity of the free-trade argument, and some even as a justification of tariff protection. The classical writers were fully aware of the existence and effects of monopoly, but their response was different. Indeed, exactly 200 years before the publication of this monograph, it was said that it was the 'spirit of monopoly' that was behind the invention of import barriers to protect domestic producers. Thus, not that the existence of monopoly was used in an argument against free trade but, on the contrary, protection from imports was seen as one of the means by which monopolies entrenched themselves in their positions.[9]

Many economists, at all times, recognising the imperfections of competition in domestic markets, have seen one of the greatest benefits of free or freer trade in the competition from foreign producers. Unrestrained competition from abroad can end the oligopolistic sinecures of domestic firms and force them to wor with greater efficiency. That it may open the economy to duty-free imports and thereby introduce more vigorous competition is for many economists the strongest argument for the extensio of the area of economic integration through the formation of large customs unions. After all, it does not take the whole worl it may be enough to have the producers of five or ten other countries compete in the markets of the union, to make them competitive.

FORCED EFFICIENCY

The probability that the formation of a customs union or a free trade area would increase the number of producers producing the same or similar products, who would then compete with one another in a common market, has for some writers been the Number One reason for advocating such regional arrangements. The increase in effective competition would not only result in lower selling prices for goods produced at given costs, but woul

[9] Adam Smith, *An Inquiry into the Nature and Causes of the Wealth of Nations* (1st ed., 1776). Smith, consistent with his pleas for competitive markets, advocated also the freeing of the 'colony trade' from the trading monopolies granted by the state; he wanted to open it 'to the competition of all other nations'. Ibid. (New York: Modern Library, 1937) p. 574.

force most of the competing producers to increase efficiency and thus to produce at lower costs. It is this hope for 'forced efficiency' in production and distribution which persuaded a good many advocates of worldwide free trade to give up their reservations concerning regional schemes which provided regional free trade and regional protection at the same time. 'Half a loaf is better than none', they reasoned when they realised that the vested interests that would block any move toward global free trade were willing to accept regional free trade.

CARTELS AND MERGERS

The explanation for the willingness of producers hitherto protected from foreign competition by national tariff walls to cope with some competition in a regional common market lies partly in their hope for friendly arrangements with their potential competitors in the other parts of the region. Many politically influential industrial groups have promoted or accepted the establishment of the Common Market only in the clearly expressed expectation that cartels or mergers would succeed in averting the outbreak of unlimited competition among the producers in the Community.

Several plans for European customs union in the first half of the twentieth century, especially in the period between the two world wars, were based on the explicit presupposition that combinations could be arranged among the producers in the member countries. Recommended combinations included territorial divisions of the "common" market and other market-sharing schemes, price cartels and selling syndicates, and trusts and mergers securing joint control over the policies of the combining firms.[10] Even after several years of the European Economic Community in action, some economists have been voicing conjectures to the effect that in a good many industries competition is rather temperate, probably limited by friendly understandings if not downright agreements among the potential competitors. These suspicions are usually denied, not only by the members of the industries concerned, but also by disinterested observers. However, the tradition of European economists in matters of market

---

[10] As a matter of fact, the first formally agreed and ratified step in the formation of the European Community — the treaty establishing the European Coal and Steel Community — provided for a system of pricing and production controls that would have been illegal in the United States as agreements 'in restraint of trade', for which (without special legislative exemptions) the guilty parties could have been sent to prison.

competition is in general quite different from the austere anti-
monopoly attitudes cultivated in the United States. Thus, state
ments about the vigour and rigour of competition among producers in Europe may be difficult to interpret. In any event, fe
economists doubt that the degree of competition in the Comm
Market is higher than it was in the separate countries or than it
would be if they had remained separate and sheltered by natior
al tariffs.

UNION BETWEEN WEAKER AND STRONGER NATIONS

An issue repeatedly raised concerns the possible consequences
which a union between partners of unequal size or economic
strength would have for the future development of the weaker
party. The discussions are reminiscent of the old dispute on
whether the total gains derived from an expansion of trade —
and integration implies trade expansion — are likely to be divid
inequitably: favouring either the 'strong' or the 'small' country
The former thesis was suggested by the supposition that a stror
country would be able to influence the terms of trade to its advantage; the latter thesis was supported by the argument that a
small country would more easily be able to specialise than a
large country and hence benefit from the ensuing larger change
in the terms of trade. (See the section on 'Dividing the Gains
from Trade' p. 49 above.)

This dispute was to some extent at cross-purposes, since stro
and small need not be opposites. Moreover, the question now
raised is not concerned with the division of gains from trade expansion in the near future, but rather with the possibilities of
economic development in the very long run. A less developed
country may possibly obtain the lion's share of the gains from
the more efficient division of labour achieved through integration with a more developed country and yet may find that its
long-run development is hampered by the new partnership. The
trouble with thinking and talking about such possibilities is that
everything is conceivable and nothing can be said with any degr
of certainty. The presence and strength of conditions for faster
economic development are difficult to ascertain and still more
difficult to predict. One can without undue imagination conceiv
of circumstances in which the development of a backward
country would be helped and accelerated by its association with
more advanced areas. But one can just as easily conceive of circumstances in which the backward country would be held back
by such an integration, and its economic development retarded.

One theory of retarded development through trade-and-factor integration was briefly described above (in the section on 'Equalising the Earnings of Labour through International Mobility of Factors', p. 65). It featured the 'backwash effect' of faster development in the richer areas, draining the poorer areas of their best workers and attracting all the capital funds. Another theory of retardation through integration highlights the possibility that industrialisation may be concentrated in places and areas already most industrialised. To avoid such concentration, positive measures for regional development within the integrated community have been prescribed.

There is also a school of thought which combines the theory of terms of trade tending to be adverse to weaker countries with the theory of retarded development of backward countries. This school claims the existence of secular forces operating to change the terms of trade between advanced and backward countries, always to the disadvantage of the latter. The analytical support is seen in differences in income elasticities of demand (high for industrial products and low for primary products) combined with differences in competitive positions (more monopolistic in markets for industrial products and for organised industrial labour, more competitive in markets for primary products and unorganised labour). Thus, as world income increases, the producers in more industrialised countries would capture increasing shares of the gains derived from any increases in productivity in the production of industrial as well as primary products. Apart from this theoretical argument, the school has pointed to findings of statistical research which supposedly showed continuous deterioration in the terms of trade of countries exporting chiefly primary products. These findings were spurious. Nevertheless, the theory, despite the criticism from empirical researchers and theoretical analysts, has still many followers, especially among students of economic development.

NON-DISCRIMINATORY PROTECTION VERSUS DISCRIMINATORY LIBERALISATION

Protection and discrimination were the two chief heresies in the eyes of free-trade economists; liberalisation and non-discrimination were the policies they urged upon governments. What a dilemma for them to find governments sometimes prepared to consider liberalisation, but limited to only a few countries and hence with discrimination against all other nations; or to observe the rule of non-discrimination, but only with strong pro-

tection against imports from anywhere! Confronted with this
choice, for which alternative should the free-trade advocates ca
their vote? Which was less damaging to the welfare of their own
country, of the group of countries considering mutual trade pre
ferences, or of the world at large?

Given a propensity of governments to protect domestic producers from competitive imports, the policy of non-discrimination through the widest possible use of the most-favoured-natic
(MFN) clause had come to be regarded as a liberalising influenc
For it did occur from time to time that two governments found
it mutually advantageous to agree on some tariff concessions,
and the existence of trade agreements with the MFN clause led
then to generalised tariff reductions. On the other hand, would
not a discriminatory preferential abolition of tariffs for a limite
number of countries eventually increase the pressures, from
within the bloc and outside, either to extend the free-trade
group by admitting additional countries or to reduce the tariffs
on imports from non-member countries? These were questions
of long-term strategy, where the economic adviser might couns
a short-run loss of welfare in the hope of attaining a long-run
gain as future developments ran their course in the desired dire
tion. It surely was not safe for specialists in economic theory to
count on political developments in future years. Their expertise
as forecasters of future government policies may be questioned
they may well be asked to 'stick to their last' and analyse the
benefits and costs of a proposed arrangement on the assumptio
that it would remain unchanged.

Thus, the economists were back to the challenging task of
evaluating the comparative net benefits (or net costs) of a discriminatory reduction or abolition of the tariff, on the one han
and the non-discriminatory maintenance of the tariff, on the
other.[11] Classical economic theory had no analytical apparatus
for such an exercise in welfare economics, and had bequeathed
to its successors only a broad prejudgement to the effect that
tariff preferences can conceivably cause greater divergencies
from the ideal free-trade model than uniform protection.

TRADE CREATION AND TRADE DIVERSION

The distinction between trade creation and trade diversion was

---

[11] Customs unions and free-trade areas, with all duties on trade among
the members abolished, represent the highest degree of tariff preference –
though international law has exempted this maximum preference from th
application of the most-favoured-nation clause.

an important step in constructing an analytical apparatus for the analysis of preferential trade arrangements. After some casual appearances in the writings of earlier economists, the distinction had its formal début in 1950. It was the beginning of the modern theory of customs union. The first issue centered on the effects of the formation of customs union upon the utilisation of comparative advantages in production.

If countries A and B form a union by removing the tariffs on imports from each other but retain a tariff on imports from C, it is possible that a new import from B, no longer subject to duty, will displace in A either a home-made product of A or an import from C. If it displaces A's domestic product, new foreign trade (though it is intra-union trade) is created. If it displaces a previous import from C, no new trade is created, but trade is diverted from a cheaper source of supply to a more expensive one, which (thanks only to the tariff discrimination) becomes more competitive. From the point of view of greatest possible economy in production, the customs union will increase economic welfare only to the extent that the effects of trade creation outweigh those of trade diversion.

Perhaps the welfare effects of trade creation can be made clearer if one is quite explicit about the fact that the new international trade created by the customs union involves a decline or cessation of domestic production of commodities that have previously been (thanks to the tariff) successfully competing with imports. Trade is created by the substitution of imports for domestic production. Welfare is increased if the productive factors released by the decline or cessation of the inefficient production are put to other uses, ordinarily the production of exports.

ECONOMIES OF SCALE

Economy and efficiency in the use of productive resources are the first considerations in evaluating the effects of customs unions through the relocation of production. Cost conditions are assumed as given and the relocation is partly from higher-cost to lower-cost facilities and partly the reverse. The statement in this simple form abstracts from the possibility of changing the given cost conditions, particularly with possibly existing economies of scale.

The theory of economies by producing larger volumes of output for which particularly large plants can yield much greater efficiency is not a novel invention or discovery; it has been in the literature for a long time — at least for 128 years, probably longer. That economies of large-scale production could be exploited only where markets were sufficiently wide was recognised long before technological developments gave serious practical relevance to the conception. The extension of markets through the removal of tariffs among the numbers of a customs union or free-trade area would permit potential economies of scale to be realised. Larger plants and larger firms could produc at lower unit cost where national markets had been too small fc 'optimum-sized' plants or most efficient types of organisation t be used.

Should one, or may one, attribute to the formation of a customs union effects that could be realised equally well or better by generally freer trade? It is, after all, the abolition of tariffs o intra-union trade, not the maintenance of tariffs on imports from other countries, which affords the benefits in question. Only if one argues that governments could never be persuaded to adopt substantially free-trade in general, and would at best agree to a scheme limited to a small number of countries, can one reasonably credit the establishment of the customs union with the extension of the market and the rise in productivity through larger-scale production.

Ingenious attempts have been made recently to measure the economies of scale that were attained with the enlargement of markets for industrial products through the formation of the European Economic Community. Some analysts find the result of the research impressive, but others find it inconclusive, since too many determinants of costs and sales have been changing (for example, total demand has increased with the general growth of incomes).

Incidentally, if scale economies exist and are actually attaine after a customs union is formed, they can give rise to the phenc enon of 'trade suppression'. Assume that in three countries, each surrounded by a tariff wall, a commodity is produced chiefly in C; little or nothing of it is produced in A and B, whic import it from C. After A and B establish a common market large enough for producing the commodity in A with substantiε economies of scale, the demand in B is met by imports from A instead of C, and the demand in A is met entirely by domestic production. The substitution in B of imports from the union partner A for imports from the previous supplier constitutes trade diversion, but this time not from a more efficient to a less efficient source, since the economies of scale have made A more efficient. (The price in B is reduced on two counts: imports are from a cheaper source as well as free of duty.) The substitution in A of domestic production for imports from C constitutes trade suppression.

CONSUMPTION EFFECTS OF PRICE REDUCTION

It would be erroneous to judge the net benefits (or net costs) of the formation of a customs union only by its 'production effects', that is, by the increased or reduced costs at which given quantities of commodities can be produced after the tariff is abolished on imports from member countries and left standing on imports from non-member countries. The next step in the evaluation of the effects on welfare is the analysis of the 'consumption effects' of the price reductions that are associated with the removal of duties on imports from member countries. Even with no shifts to make better or worse uses of opportunities for comparatively more advantageous production — indeed even if production remained unchanged everywhere — the changes in relative prices charged to consumers would induce them to rearrange the pattern of their consumption in line with their preferences. If the taxes on imports had caused worse distortions of the price structure relative to the cost structure of the goods and services produced than will be caused by any new taxes which the governments will have to raise in order to replace the lost revenues from import duties, consumer welfare will have increased by the formation of the customs union. Favourable consumption effects of this sort may conceivably outweigh any adverse production effects of trade diversion from lower-cost to higher-cost sources of supply.

It was in the analysis of comparisons of this sort that the 'theory of second-best' was developed.

THE TWO EFFECTS TOGETHER

Instead of comparing the separate magnitudes of production effects and consumption effects in order to appraise the net effect upon welfare, a novel way has recently been proposed to look at the two effects together. It specifies that trade diversion be defined as the substitution of an unchanged physical volume of tax-free imports from the favoured trade partner for taxed imports from the previous (lower-cost) source of supply. If the definition thus limits trade diversion to the physical quantities of goods previously imported from countries now excluded by the discriminatory tariff, any increase in consumption induced by the price reduction effected by the removal of the duty on imports from the favoured source constitutes new trade — that is, trade creation — as consumers substitute imports for some domestic products.

Looking at the results in this fashion one comes back to the simple verdict that trade diversion reduces, and trade creation raises, economic welfare of integrated countries.[12]

ANOTHER TWO-STEP ANALYSIS

To facilitate appraisals of the effects of the creation of customs unions, free-trade areas, or other preferential trade schemes, another two-step analysis has been proposed. Instead of sorting out the various positive and negative effects of the discrimina-tory reduction or removal of import tariffs while the tariffs on imports from non-member countries are left unchanged or unified at agreed levels, one can analyse the results in two simple steps: the first step is a general abolition of tariffs on all imports from anywhere, the second step is the selective and discrimina-tory imposition of duties on imports from particular countries (with a uniform tariff in the case of a customs union, different tariffs in the case of a free-trade area, and more complicated arrangements in the case of other preferential schemes). All trade creation will be the result of the tariff abolition, and all trade diversion (plus some trade suppression) will be attributable to the discriminatory re-imposition of tariffs.

It hardly needs saying that the merit of this two-step analysis lies only in the theoretic-analytic domain, not in that of empiri-cal-statistical research. Both steps are purely hypothetical, and no statistical data are obtainable to make them operational. However, the aid of the two-step fiction for comprehending the effects of the trade to be analysed is unquestioned.

INVESTMENT CREATION AND INVESTMENT DIVERSION

The distinction between trade creation and trade diversion as the two possible consequences of the establishment of a customs

---

[12] It certainly simplifies matters if the consumption effects can be merged with trade creation; but the assumption that all the effects of lower prices for imported goods that are no longer taxed will show up in increased volumes of these cheapened imports is questionable. The assumption would imply that the price elasticities of demand for these goods are unity or higher. Otherwise some of the consumption effects of the price reduction may involve some increased demand for domestic goods, and hence not be realised in new trade (in the sense of international trade).

union has proved extraordinarily fruitful. But this conceptual framework was designed only for one purpose: to examine and evaluate the effects which the discriminatory removal (or reduction) of tariffs within the union would have upon production, consumption, and trade; the original conception did not include any explicit references to induced changes in investment, although the expansion of production any product in any of the parts of the customs union would undoubtedly involve increased investment in enlarged production facilities. An analogous distinction between investment creation and investment diversion suggested itself, but the use of this pair of concepts occurred in a different context and with somewhat different connotations. In the cases of trade creation as well as of trade diversion, production at one place is increased at the expense of production elsewhere.[13] Regarding investment induced by the establishment of a customs union, the question is whether total investment within and without the union is increased or is left unchanged. In the latter case the induced investment in one or more member countries is diverted from somewhere else; on the other hand, if the induced investment (attracted to the larger area without internal customs barriers but with tariffs against imports from the outside) is a net addition to total investment, one can speak of 'investment creation'.

Whereas trade creation and trade diversion have strong connotations of respectively increasing and reducing total welfare, this is not so in the case of investment creation and investment diversion. To divert investment from one country to another may be to employ capital more efficiently — where its marginal efficiency is greater — with a resulting increase in the combined income of the countries concerned (though labour and landowners' incomes may suffer in the country from which capital is diverted). To increase investment is likely to increase total product if saving potentials exceed investment opportunities or if higher saving rates can be induced and sustained; however, if this is not the case, investment creation may invite subsequent recessions and losses of capital. Thus, investment creation is not always 'good', and investment diversion may not be 'bad' at all.

Additional distinctions are made with respect to foreign direct investment, especially if the analysts are interested not only in

---

[13] International trade is *created* if production is increased in one of the member countries at the expense of production in another member country after the removal of the import duty. Trade is *diverted* if production in one of the union countries is increased at the expense of a country outside the union.

the total volume of investment but also or foremost in the question whether ownership and control of the new production facilities are domestic or foreign, and whether jobs are destroyed in the country from which investible funds and investment opportunities are exported. Starting from the fact that a firm in Homeland has made a direct investment in Hostland, to ascertain the effects is to assume that we know what would have happened if this particular investment had not been made. There are several possibilities. If the firm had not invested in Hostland, it might instead have invested in another foreign country or at home in Homeland or not at all; and the investment in Hostland might have been made by a foreign investor from another country or by a domestic Hostlander or not at all. To evaluate the comparative probabilities of all these non-realised, hypothetical potentialities is a rather bold undertaking — but this is what people expect economists to do.

The trouble with most economists is that they try so hard to answer questions for which neither a theoretical model nor historical experience nor observation of present conditions can furnish any reliable clues, at least not at the present state of knowledge. The question about foreign and domestic investment, as it was formulated above, offered nine possible combinations to choose from, but we could easily have added more possibilities. We might have included, for example, the possibility that firms in Homeland, having been barred from investing in Hostland, would reduce also their domestic investments; or that firms in Hostland, not having received the Homelander's investment, would reduce their domestic investments — and this modest addition of two more alternatives would increase the number of possible outcomes to fourteen, multiplied by the number of possible results due to other variables associated with the effects of changes in investment. The only way to give seemingly confident answers to such questions about the effects of this or that is to exclude many of the possible outcomes by slyly inserting some inconspicuous but plausible assumptions that restrict more or less arbitrarily the degrees of freedom of the entire set.

Questions of the sort just discussed have been raised especially in connection with activities of multinational corporations. These companies have drawn much attention to themselves and their doings largely because their size impresses laymen as well as experts. Statements such as those about the sales volume of ABC corporation exceeding the gross national product of all countries in black Africa taken together have startled people who did not understand that these comparisons are irrelevant for almost all issues economic or political, apart from their capacity to shock the innocent. This does not prevent scholars from embarking on the most ambitious research projects — which, however, need not be bad in view of the serendipity that may turn any search into a success.

THE DEGREE OF INTEGRATION

Although several writers on economic integration have made use of the term 'degree' of integration, they used it in different meanings, and thus no consistent body of thought exists on this conception. In Chapter 2 I devoted several pages to what I think may be a useful way to employ it. To repeat the main point: since 'complete' integration of any geographic area means that 'all' opportunities for efficient division of labour among the resources available in the area are being utilised, anything less than full use of the potential signifies that only a certain degree of integration has been attained.

This makes good sense, conceptually, for a closed economy, but it involves difficulties in economies that have some trade with the outside world: taking account of the opportunities for efficient division of labour with any part of the world outside the area on which something is to be predicated, will almost certainly change the original set of opportunities; the comparative advantages of various productive activities will be altered with each inclusion of productive resources available outside the original area. The inherent conceptual difficulties are as yet insufficiently explored. One might construct a few simple models with a small number of factors, goods, and countries, with given production functions and given preference systems, and then try to compare different combinations of 'integrated' areas. Such an exercise might yield some elucidation of what is implied in 'higher' and 'lower' degrees of integration when the extension of the area in question is varied in a variety of ways.

INTERNAL VERSUS EXTERNAL INTEGRATION

Pending the solution of the problem of how degrees of integration may be conceived — let alone measured — it seems rather daring to pronounce on the possible welfare effects obtainable by the two modes of utilising opportunities of efficient division of labour: more intensive exchange within the area in question or outward extension of the area. Yet, pronouncements on this

question have been made and, I must admit, with a ring of plausi-
bility. The question was formulated as a comparison between
two possible policies: toward a *partial* approach to a *wider* union
and, alternatively, toward a *more complete* approach to a
narrower union. The answer suggested an application of the law
of diminishing returns; if there has been a good deal of integration achieved within the given area, it would seem more promis-
ing to look for extending trade with the outside world. That is
to say, larger net additions to the economic welfare of the inhabitants of the original area may be expected from extended
than from intensified integration.

This view obviously took it for granted that the degree of internal integration in the original area was reasonably high. If one
assumes, however, that serious obstacles have existed to economic integration within the area — say, that strong trade unions
have effectively closed entry into some of the most productive
activities, or that industries with entrenched positions of monopoly or oligopoly have restricted the production of important
materials — the removal of these obstacles and, hence, the attainment of a higher degree of internal integration of the economy
(national or regional) may well make a greater contribution to
economic welfare than could be expected from an extension of
division of labour with other countries. It happens that the conflict in judging the merits of the alternative policies may be
more apparent than real, since the extension of external trade
may at the same time reduce the power of the disintegrating
elements within the economy (nation or region). For example,
competition through imports may reduce the restrictions imposed by organised labour and monopolistic industry. In this
case the outward-looking policy, securing a higher degree of
economic integration with the outside world, would at the same
time raise the degree of internal integration.

That this happy result of more extensive (international) integration aiding internal integration — a chance of killing two birds
with one stone — cannot reasonably be generalised may readily
be seen if one assumes that the obstacle to internal integration is
not a monopoly situation that can be overcome by foreign competition but, instead, a condition that will not yield to it. Take,
for example, a case of government regulation restricting domestic transport through distorted freight charges that bear no relation to the cost of hauling goods by rail, road, barge, or ship.
This kind of disintegrating regulation will not be alleviated by an
increase in foreign trade, and benefits derived from an increase
in international division of labour may well be smaller than

those obtainable from allowing a higher degree of domestic integration by replacing the bureaucratic follies of public regulation of transport with the anonymous forces of competition among truckers and rival haulers of goods.

The point made by these examples is, again, to warn against facile generalisations. It may be safe to pronounce a judgement to the effect that a nation (or region), starting from a high degree of internal economic integration and a low degree of international (interregional) economic integration, may expect a larger increase in its economic welfare from extending its division of labour with the outside world than from trying to intensify its internal integration. To go beyond this judgement would not be safe; where internal economic integration has been hindered (or obstructed) by obstacles to the movement of factors and products, by institutional rigidities, and by administrative bungling, removal of these disintegrating roadblocks may deserve highest priority on the nation's (or region's) agenda.

However, the comparison of the welfare effects obtainable from stepping up the degree of internal integration and those from an extension of external trade would make good sense only where the two policies were disjunctive alternatives, each excluding the other. Where this is not the case, where the nation or region does not have to choose between the two courses of action but can proceed with both, the benefits it can obtain need not be measured against each other. Economic integration can reach higher degrees internally, interregionally and internationally at the same time.

INTERPRETING THE CHANGES IN TRADE RATIOS

In statistical descriptions of developments in international trade certain ratios of trade to other magnitudes have been assigned significant roles, particularly with regard to what is purported to indicate 'progress' in economic integration. The ratio of a country's trade with other *members* of its trading bloc, customs union, or free-trade area to its *total* international trade, and the changes in that ratio over the years, have been regarded as highly significant. Other widely advertised ratios have been those of intraregional, interregional, and world trade, to the gross national product of the country or group of countries concerned. Unfortunately, the theoretical support for the inferences drawn from the statistical observations was often lacking; and if the ratios, and any trends shown by their changes, were said to be significant, one can hardly help asking: 'significant for what?'

A simple example may explain why this rude question had to be asked. If, for any reason (say, because of the removal of obstacles or because of some 'positive' actions of government), a country's trade increases both with other bloc members and with non-member countries, it depends on which increase happens to be greater relative to the previous trade volumes, whether the ratio of intraregional trade to total trade will be higher or lower than it had been. A decrease in that ratio, in the face of an increase in the absolute volume (physical or by value) of intra-regional trade, would surely *not* indicate a decline in the degree of regional integration. (See also my comments on this point in Chapter 2.) Even if intra-bloc trade remained unchanged and only the trade with non-member countries were increased, the fall in the ratio of intraregional trade to total trade need not be indicative of a decline in regional integration.

More relevant to the problem of integration are changes in the basic shares of a country's expenditure (absorption, intake). These basic shares are for domestic production, imports from member countries, and imports from non-member countries. Other things remaining equal, the reduction or abolition of intra-bloc tariffs and increase in regional integration can be expected to raise the relative share of imports from member countries at the expense of the shares of domestic production and of imports from non-member countries. A reduction in the share of expenditure on domestic products would indicate trade creation, and a reduction in the share of expenditure on imports from non-member countries would indicate trade diversion. Since other things may have changed, besides the preferential treatment of imports from bloc countries, actual expenditures would, for purposes of empirical estimation, have to be corrected for the effects of these other changes, so that the residual changes in the three basic shares could be attributed to the deliberate promotion of regional integration.

Such an approach, however, can at best give some clues regarding the progress of regional integration, but usually not even that, because the increase in the share of expenditures for imports from bloc countries may be due to disintegrating changes within the national economy and/or to disintegrating obstacles to imports from non-bloc countries. Of course, the econometrician may have 'caught' all these other changes and corrected the observed data for their presumed effects. (Many changes in the country's wage structure brought about by collective bargaining may have disintegrating effects in the national economy. They are difficult to catch and even more difficult to

take into account in correcting the recorded expenditure data.)
Equally difficult to deal with are the effects of changes in commercial policy *vis-à-vis* non-bloc countries; for example, reductions of duties on imports from these countries may have occurred together with the abolition of the duties on intra-bloc trade.
Simultaneous progress in regional and worldwide integration
could, however, be ascertained only by hypothetically elimina-
ting in turn the effects of the changes promoting first the one
and then the other; otherwise the relative share of expenditures
on imports from non-bloc countries might rise at the expense,
not only of the domestic share, but also of that of imports from
bloc countries, and wrongly indicate a decline in regional integration.

Some economic analysts, trying to assess the degree or progress of trade integration, have focused on trade/income ratios
and their changes. Before one can see the relevance or irrelevance
of these ratios, one must first understand the implications of the
relative size of the countries for their trade ratios. If by 'size'
one means a country's total (national or domestic) product, and
by 'trade' the value of its exports plus its imports — and if one
assumes, for the sake of simplicity, that countries are approximately equal in every respect that matters in this context (chiefly the stage of industrialisation, degree of economic integration,
the peoples' tastes and wants, the wealth and incomes per head)
— it follows that the trade/income ratio will vary inversely with
the countries' size.[14]

[14] If this is not immediately obvious to the reader, let him imagine a
world of only three countries of equal size (national income) and equal
trade/income ratios; now let two of these countries merge into a double-
sized one. Total national income of this large country will, of course, be
twice that of each part; its total foreign trade, however, will not be
doubled, because half of what was foreign trade is now counted as domestic trade between the two halves of the united country; the actual foreign
trade of the two halves will therefore add up to an unchanged trade volume
of the enlarged country. With the national product doubled but foreign
trade unchanged, the trade ratio of the double-size country will be one-half
that of the small country.

This may be the place to explain why some relatively small but highly
industrialised countries may have trade/income ratios close to unity or even
above. If there is much trade — exports plus imports — in materials and
semi-finished products, which enter trade statistics with their full value,
foreign trade may exceed national income, which contains only the value
added by domestic activities to the values of materials and semi-finished
products. Cases in point are Belgium and the Netherlands, whose foreign
trade (exports plus imports) in the last two years exceeded their national
incomes, was about equal to their gross national products and only slightly
below their gross domestic products.

This relationship between the trade/income ratio and the relative size of countries make the ratio useless for comparisons of the degree of integration, national or worldwide, of different countries. On the other hand, changes in the trade/income ratio over the years may be significant as symptoms of progress of international economic integration. If the foreign trade of a given country, with its political frontiers unchanged, grows consistently at a faster annual rate than its national (or domestic) production, the resulting increase in the trade/income ratio may indicate that the country's economy is getting more closely interwoven with the world economy. A steady increase in the trade/income ratio for a group of countries will tell the same story for the group, as will the world-trade/world-income ratio for the entire world.

If foreign trade is divided into intraregional, interregional, and worldwide trade, on may use the changing ratios of each of these figures to the income of a country (or group of countries) as clues to the progress of the various kinds of trade integration over the years. But, to repeat for emphasis, while changes in the said ratios over time may be relevant for appraisals of trends in these respects, the ratios cannot be used for comparisons of the degree of integration attained by different countries at any par- - ticular moment of time.

One other statistical indicator may be briefly mentioned: the ratio of trade balances to the total value of trade. If a country's foreign trade is disaggregated to show its trade (exports plus imports) with all its trading partners and its balance of trade is likewise disaggregated by country, the ratios of the balance to the total may indicate the degree of bilateral balancing. Complete bilateral balancing makes the ratio infinite, since all balances are zero. For a country using all its proceeds for its exports to one group of countries to pay for its imports from another group of countries, the ratio of the sum of its trade balances (surpluses *plus* deficits) to its total trade (exports *plus* imports) will be unity and will indicate completely triangular or multilateral trade patterns. What matters, however, is less the degree of bilateralism in any given year than the changes over the years. A consistent decline over time in the ratio of a country's absolute sum of its positive and negative trade balances with its many trade partners to the volume of its total trade may indicate an increase in bilateral trade arrangement; a consistent increase in the ratio, an increase in multilateralism. Multilateralism is associated with a higher degree of worldwide integration.

METHODOLOGICAL DISTINCTIONS REGARDING THE EFFECTS OF INTEGRATION

Virtually all distinctions which economic theorists have made for their various techniques of reasoning have found a place in the literature dealing with the effects of trade liberalisation, trade discrimination, and the formation of trading blocs. There are, of course, the usual dichotomies and trichotomies of direct and indirect effects; primary, secondary, and tertiary effects; short-run, medium-run, and long-run effects; static and dynamic effects; effects inferred from partial-equilibrium analysis and those consistent with general equilibrium. All these distinctions have been applied to the analysis of effects on product prices, factor prices, resource allocation, production, employment, trade, gains from trade, movements of productive factors, distribution of income and wealth, investment, economic development and growth, and all the rest.

In some instances the distinctions were more confusing than helpful, and often they were rather arbitrary and idiosyncratic. It made good sense, however, to designate the effects of establishing a customs union as primary in so far as they bore on the changes in imports resulting directly from the reduction or removal of import duties; as secondary in so far as they modified the prices and quantities of substitutes and complements of the products primarily affected; and as tertiary in so far as they were repercussions of adjustment processes necessary to restore balance in international payments. It was quite evident that any limitation of the analysis to the primary effects involved partial equilibrium only and left the processes associated with general equilibrium unexplored. On the other hand, effects derived from partial-equilibrium analysis are, as a rule, more fully determinate than those derived from general-equilibrium analysis, which calls for an infinitely greater number of specifications of conditions (and policy decisions) if the degrees of freedom are to be reduced sufficiently to make the problem manageable and the outcome more 'predictable'.

The least helpful distinction proposed in the analysis under consideration was that between static and dynamic effects. The use of this pair of adjectives has had a long and spotty history, but in recent years economic theorists had more or less agreed to associate the terms with the use of dated and lagged variables in their models or systems of relationships. It was then entirely in contravention to this usage if some economists decided to speak of dynamic effects of the removal of tariffs, not in order to characterise the type of analysis employed in explaining the effects, but in order to separate realisation of economies of scale, increase in competition, and diversion of investment from all other induced changes of resource reallocation. Any and all of these changes can be explained by means of static or of dynamic analysis, and there just is no sense in which a particular change is a 'dynamic effect'. Of course, as in most terminological and methodological discourses, no harm to the validity of the analysis of the investigated problems follows necessarily from the inappropriate use of language.

ECONOMIC WELFARE, SOCIAL WELFARE, PRIDE AND ENVY

There is wide agreement on the pronouncement that the analysis of economic integration constitutes only a bare skeleton of positive economics and that virtually all its meaty substance is welfare economics. (See Chapter 2.) This is so for at least two reasons: (1) The chief problem of economic integration is the division of the gain in material output among different regions, different countries, and different groups of people; and any statement about net benefits from integration involves, therefore, an evaluation of gains enjoyed and losses suffered by different persons. (2) It is not only the distribution of material products that is involved, but also that of satisfactions and dissatisfactions of a merely 'psychic' nature, including the pleasures and displeasures associated with non-tangible changes which may induce feelings of pride and envy.

Considerations of the distributional aspects of changes in economic welfare and of the sentimental aspects of changes in social welfare are entirely in the domain of evaluative (normative) economics. This does not relegate matters into the dustbin of metaphysical speculations; for better or for worse, the value judgements about the effects and side-effects of economic integration are crucial in the policy decisions of governments acting for their constituencies. Their actions may include such things as the gratification of national pride at the expense of efficient production for increased material consumption; or their actions may be motivated by envy and resentment and imply the acceptance of sacrifices of potential gains just in order to avoid larger gains accruing to others. These are, therefore, very pragmatic questions about national choices. Perhaps the magnitude of the costs and sacrifices is not always known to the nations clamouring for such decisions but, apart from this incomplete knowledge, one cannot contend that the basic considerations are irrational — even if other people, with more accurate knowledge of the benefits and costs or with different preferences and appreciation of social welfare, might advocate very different policies.

THE INCLUSION OF PUBLIC GOODS

Among the most frequently 'demanded' intangibles are the gratifications of national pride in being able to produce something within the country instead of importing it from abroad. While economists acknowledge that such satisfactions are 'public goods' that are part of total welfare, they question whether the choices in favour of the merely psychic incomes are made in full awareness of the cost, that is, of the material goods sacrificed by producing at home what could be had much more cheaply from abroad.

Similar doubts may be raised in connection with other public goods which can be produced more efficiently for smaller communities than for large ones. There is a real conflict — a contradiction, in Marxian jargon — between the optimal scale of production for most private, material goods and that for many collective intangible goods. If it were established that private, material goods are most efficiently produced on a scale so large that only a very large integrated region, if not the whole world, can fully utilise the appropriate productive capacity, while on the other hand the services that are rated as public, collective goods are most efficiently provided in the small and cozier, more culturally coherent, environment of a small community, a serious question of the 'optimum area of integration' would arise. Almost fifty years ago, a highly respected economist raised it and tentatively concluded that, since services were becoming more important than material goods, free trade was becoming less and less significant for total welfare. This argument, downgrading free trade, would by implication downgrade international division of labour and economic integration of extended areas. A counterargument suggests, however, that most nations can afford to devote increasing portions of their incomes to the provision of the types of services regarded as public goods only because private material goods, the necessities of life, have become so much less expensive thanks to international division of labour.

A COMPROMISE BETWEEN FREE-TRADERS AND PROTECTIONISTS

A customs union or any regional trade bloc may be seen as a compromise between two groups of antagonists promoting seemingly irreconcilable principles of policy: free-traders and protectionists. Having made the compromise, the former are happy about the abolition of barriers in intra-bloc trade, the latter about the continuation of barriers against extra-bloc imports. Does it make sense to ask who has made the greater concession in reaching the compromise?

The question makes sense indeed, and the answer depends on the height of the trade barriers abolished and that of the barriers retained. But, as a matter of fact, a good many free-traders (with a 'more realistic' world-outlook) had not been seriously concerned about the tariff walls retained around the region and about the trade discrimination which it implied, because (as eternal optimists) they counted on both a gradual lowering of the walls and a gradual pushing outward of the walls: more countries would join the union and a continuing growth of world trade would not only be admitted but actually desired and promoted.

This optimistic prognosis has often been made, sometimes founded on a strange faith in the basic rationality of human action, including political action, sometimes on nothing but wishful thinking. More recently, rigorous mathematical proofs have been furnished, using set-theoretical methods, demonstrating that an incentive to form and enlarge customs unions persists until the world is one big customs union, that is, until universal free trade prevails. That this process is so slow is explained by game-theoretic problems (choosing partners, dividing spoils, enforcing agreements), non-economic national objectives, inertia and ignorance. With goodwill and luck, these obstacles on the path of economic rationality may eventually be overcome.

POLITICAL INTEGRATION

The two groups of friends of trade blocs and customs unions, those aiming at regional protection and those aiming at eventual worldwide trade integration, were greatly aided by a third group, those who cared far less about economic integration as an objective, but saw it as a catalyst of political integration. They were hoping that closer economic relations among the members of a customs union would lead to closer political ties and eventually to political unification.

Part Three
The Contributors

I propose five labels for my files of contributors:

(1) *historians* reporting on the formation of nation states, customs unions, and unification projects (Chapter 5);

(2) *political economists* proposing, promoting, or opposing various integration projects (Chapter 6);

(3) *statesmen, men of affairs, and men of letters* promoting (or rejecting) customs unions and other projects for economic integration, regional or worldwide (Chapter 7);

(4) *committee members and organisation staff* studying, promoting, and reporting on integration projects (Chapter 8);

(5) *economic theorists* analysing essential issues of international trade and economic integration (Chapter 9).

These classes may be overlapping in many instances. An economist writing on the history of the making of a nation-state or on the history of customs unions would be classified here as a historian; he may at the same time be a theorist, classified in Group 5, if he has contributed to the economic analysis of the effects of customs unions. And he may also belong to Group 4 as one of the (mostly anonymous) members of the staff of an international organisation who collaborated in drafting a public statement or report issued by that organisation. The distinction between Groups 2 and 3 may be somewhat arbitrary, since a statesman, a man of affairs, or a man of letters may on the basis of his studies or insights qualify as a political economist. The decision in a doubtful case will be guided by the character of the man's main activities or major publications.

As a matter of fact, I shall make several double entries. For example, Eli Heckscher, Jean Marchal, and Jacob Viner will appear as historians and as theorists; Friedrich List, Lionel Robbins, Gottfried Haberler, Charles Kindleberger, Maurice Allais, and Nicholas Kaldor will be entered both as political and as theoretical economists. Many more double entries could be justified, especially in the categories of economists arguing for or against a particular cause or programme and of those engaged in theoretical analysis. Indeed, I may with good reason make a few triple entries — for economists who did historical research on economic integration, advocated or opposed some particular scheme, and contributed to analysis. I shall, however, make no effort in this direction.

5 Historians of Customs Unions and Integration Projects

Perhaps I should justify my including historians in a history of thought on the subjects on which they report. Historians select the events and circumstances which they research according to the importance they attach to them; and these implicit valuations of relative importance are necessarily based on some general thoughts and insights. If historians report, for example, on Colbert's efforts to remove interprovincial trade barriers in France, they evidently imply that such a policy has had some significance for the economic and political development of France and that Colbert may have been aware of that significance, although perhaps — as some have actually tried to show — for reasons not tenable on the ground of present economic theory. If historians report on the free-trade and protectionist debates among the American colonies before the Confederation, on the development of the British system of Imperial Preference, on the creation of the European Economic Community or the Council for Mutual Economic Assistance, they cannot help having some point of view — sometimes perhaps a little vague or even naive, but sometimes very clear and explicitly stated — from which they judge the course of events. The views of historians, or their concealed value judgements, may be as important for a history of thought on economic integration as the views of 'pure' economic theorists. Representatives of the historical school of economics may attach even more importance to the historians' accounts than to the theorists' speculations.

I shall first present a list of the subjects of historical research that are likely to have elicited relevant thoughts on economic integration. Afterwards I shall name the books and articles which I came across or consulted as I prepared this survey. I shall conclude the chapter with a few comments on 'Historians' Predictions and Explanations'.

105

THE ERAS AND THE AREAS

A CUSTOMS ASSOCIATIONS AND DISCRIMINATIONS IMPORT PROHIBITIONS IN THE HOLY ROMAN EMPIRE (OF THE GERMAN NATION) FROM THE 16TH CENTURY UNTIL ITS END IN 1806

Proposal for commercial union between Austria, Spain, Bavaria, and some German principalities, 1665.

Edict by Emperor Leopold I prohibiting all French imports into any part of the Empire, 1676; a second edict with stricter import prohibitions, 1689; a third edict, promulgated by the Emperor Joseph, 1705.

B UNIFICATION OF GREAT BRITAIN

Proposals of unions between England and Scotland, 1547—8; union of the crowns, 1603; King James I (VI of Scotland) decree equalisation of import duties for goods imported into Scotland and England but, after negotiations for commercial union fail, the decree is cancelled; in 1668 new negotiations for a treaty of commercial union fail; the Act of Union of England and Scotland, 1703 (ratified by Scots parliament in 1707), establishes political as well as economic union.

Act of Union of England and Ireland, 1801, produces partial commercial union, with tariffs on coal and important industrial products remaining; customs union completed, 1826.

C UNIFICATION OF FRANCE

Colbert's plan to unite all provinces of the Kingdom into a customs union with internal free trade, 1664, fails except for some uniform duties established for the 'Five Big Farms' (Northern France); a royal edict establishes a national tariff on some 60 products, 1667, but this still leaves over 5000 internal tolls, duties, and other imposts within France; abolition of all internal barriers by the Revolutionary government, 1789—90.

D BRITISH COLONIES AND COMMONWEALTH

Canadian colonies — Ontario, Quebec, Nova Scotia, and New Brunswick — agree on free trade in foodstuffs and raw materials, 1850; as a single union they conclude Reciprocity Treaty with the United States of America, removing all import tariffs on natural products of both nations, 1854; Canadian Confederation establishes free internal trade, 1867.

South African Federation proposed in 1871 and 1888; arrangements between Cape of Good Hope and the Orange Free State in 1889; between these two and Natal in 1898; South African colonies and protectorates south of the Zambezi agree on a customs union in 1903 and complete it in 1906; Union of South Africa, 1910.

Six Australian colonies establish the Commonwealth of Australia, 1900.

Preferential tariff systems adopted by Canada, 1897—8; New Zealand, 1903; South Africa, 1904; Australia, 1907; Great Britain on most products of the British Empire, 1919; Ottawa Economic Conference of self-governing members of the British Empire and India, 1932, leading to a series of preferential treaties.

E UNITED STATES OF AMERICA

American colonies maintained separate tariff systems with moderate numbers of duties; debates among protectionist and free-trade colonies; Confederation, 1783—9, exempts American goods generally from state imposts.

Constitution of the United States, 1789, bars the individual States from levying 'any imposts or duties on imports or exports'.

F GERMAN ZOLLVEREIN

German splinter states with customs duties at 38 frontiers; plans for customs union, 1813—15; Prussia abolishes internal tariffs, 1818; bilateral and multilateral customs treaties, 1818—28, establishing three customs unions, (i) Württemberg-Bavaria, (ii) Prussia-Hesse-Darmstadt, and (iii) Central-German Union; treaty establishes single German *Zollverein*, 1833, in effect from 1834 to 1871.

G OTHER EUROPEAN CUSTOMS UNIONS

Austrian Crown States: Austria with Bohemia, 1775; Austria with Modena and Parma, 1849; Austria with Hungary-Croatia-Slavonia-Siebenbürgen, 1850; Austria with Hungary, 1851, renewals in 1867, 1878, 1887, 1907; Austria with Bosnia and the Herzegowina, 1879.

Cantons of Switzerland: abolition of internal trade barriers,

1798, not accepted; Rossi Pact, abolishing internal tariffs, 1830 rejected; Swiss Confederation established with economic union, 1848.

Italian states united, with customs union, 1860—6.

East-European countries: Moldavia and Wallachia, still under Turkish suzerainty, form a customs union in 1847 (followed by political union only in 1878); Russia with Poland, 1850.

Scandinavian countries: after earlier unsuccessful attempts, Sweden and Norway establish a customs union, 1874—5.

The Low Countries: Belgium and Luxembourg form a customs union in 1921; Belgium, Luxembourg, and the Netherlands establish the customs union BENELUX in 1944, effective in 1947.

H TRADE AGREEMENTS AND MOST-FAVOURED-NATION CLAUSE

German Zollverein with Netherlands, 1839; Great Britain, 1842, Belgium, 1844; Portugal, 1844; Sardinia, 1845; Denmark, 1846; France, 1862 (1865); Great Britain, 1865; Austria, 1865.

France with Great Britain, 1859; Belgium, 1861; Italy, 1863; Switzerland, 1864; German Zollverein, 1865; Sweden, 1865; Netherlands, 1865; Spain, 1865; Austria, 1866; Portugal, 1866.

Switzerland with Sardinia, 1851; Great Britain, 1855; Italy, 1860; Belgium, 1863; France, 1864; Austria, 1868; German Zollverein and Luxembourg, 1869.

Belgium with Netherlands, 1868.

I EUROPEAN PROJECTS THAT FAILED TO COME OFF

Motions, in the Darmstadt conferences, to include Switzerland, Piedmont, and the Netherlands in the German Zollverein are lost, 1830—6.

Customs union between France and Belgium is opposed by Great Britain, Prussia, and Austria, 1835—42.

Attempts to create a Scandinavian Customs Union are unsuccessful in 1846 and again in 1888.

Plans for a customs union of the separate Italian states, promoted by Lord Palmerston, come to nothing, 1848—50.

Austrian proposals of a customs union comprising Austria, Hungary, Northern Italy, and the entire German Zollverein, recurrently negotiated but opposed by Prussia, are finally rejected 1849—53; they lead, however, to preferential tariffs between Austria and the German states, 1853.

Plans for a customs union between Germany and Austria, or

among all countries of Central Europe, are vigorously debated but find little political support, 1878—1906.

Negotiations between Belgium and the Netherlands fail in 1878; a new plan, opposed by Germany, fails in 1907.

Political and economic union of 'German Austria' with Germany is vetoed by the victorious allies in 1919; a customs union between Austria and Germany is effectively opposed by France, Italy, and Czechoslavakia in 1931.

A World Economic Conference, summoned by the League of Nations in 1927, is slow in reaching any agreements; the League's Economic Consultative Committee, meeting in Geneva in 1929, reports 'little progress'.

Belgium, the Netherlands, and Luxembourg conclude the Ouchy Convention, 1932, for gradual reduction of tariffs; opposed by Great Britain and other countries, it never went into effect.

France and Italy agree on an economic union, 1947—9, which, however, fails to be ratified by their parliaments.

J   WORLDWIDE ARRANGEMENTS ON PAYMENTS, CREDIT, AND TRADE

The Bretton Woods Agreements of 1944 set up the International Monetary Fund (IMF) and the International Bank for Reconstruction and Development (IBRD, also called World Bank), the former to supply foreign currencies to countries in payments deficit, the latter to make long-term loans to developing countries.

Drafts for a Charter of an International Trade Organization (ITO) were prepared, 1946—8, for a conference in Havana, in March 1948. The Charter, embodying six agreements on international economic relations, was signed by 53 countries, but failed to become effective. One of the agreements to be included in the Charter, the General Agreement on Tariffs and Trade (GATT) was adopted in Geneva in October 1947 and became effective in 1948, as another specialised agency of the United Nations, to promote systematic liberalisation of international trade.

Two affiliates of IBRD are established to provide more liberal loans to poor countries, the International Finance Corporation (IFC) in 1956 and the International Development Association (IDA) in 1960.

In order to supplement the facilities available through IMF, a

General Arrangement to Borrow (GAB) is made in 1962, under which countries in surplus may through swaps provide short-term finance to countries in need of reserves.

In order to accelerate the economic development of poor countries, the United Nations Conference on Trade and Development (UNCTAD) is launched in 1965.

K   WEST-EUROPEAN ECONOMIC CO-OPERATION SINCE 1948

The plan for European recovery, co-operation, and eventual integration is launched by an address of the US Secretary of State in June 1947 [Marshall Plan].

In a conference in Paris in July 1947, sixteen West European countries establish the Committee for European Economic Co-operation (CEEC) to work out a European recovery programme.

The Bermuda agreement between the United States and the United Kingdom, in 1947, the Treaty of Dunkirk in the same year between the United Kingdom and France, and the Treaty of Brussels of these two countries with the BENELUX countries in March 1948, prepare for their co-operation in creating a Common Market.

In April 1948, President Truman signs the Economic Co-operation Act, establishing the US Economic Co-operation Administration (ECA).

A convention setting up the Organization of European Economic Co-operation (OEEC) in Paris is signed in 1948 by 17 countries, all but one receiving aid under the Marshall Plan: Austria, Belgium, Denmark, France, Germany, Greece, Iceland, Ireland, Italy, Luxembourg, the Netherlands, Norway, Portugal, Sweden, Switzerland, Turkey, and the United Kingdom.

Ten countries, Belgium, Denmark, France, Iceland, Italy, Luxembourg, the Netherlands, Norway, Sweden, and the United Kingdom, join in 1949 in creating the Council of Europe, with a Consultative Assembly, and a Council of Ministers to recommend policies of mutual concern to member countries. Greece, Turkey, Western Germany, and Austria join at later dates.

In November 1949 the member countries of OEEC agree to liberalise imports by cutting within six weeks all duties to 50 per cent of their 1948 level. In 1950 they establish the European Payments Union (EPU) as a central clearing house for payments and settlements to promote multilateral transactions, with credit facilities provided by the United States. This multilateral payments system is linked with a Code of Liberalization, providing for successive steps towards complete abolition of quantitative restrictions (quotas) on imports from member countries.

In the Treaty of Paris in April 1951, the European Coal and Steel Community (ECSC) with a supranational High Authority is established by six countries, France, Western Germany, Italy, Belgium, Luxembourg, and the Netherlands, to come into effect in 1952, removing import quotas and tariffs on coal, iron ore, scrap, and steel.

The same six countries, after more ambitious plans for a European Defence Community were scuttled by French opposition, form in 1954 the Western European Union (WEU) with the objective of promoting the unity and encouraging the progressive integration of Europe.

Again the same six countries, in 1957, set up EURATOM, to exercise control over the supply of nuclear fuels, to regulate the production of nuclear energy, and to operate joint enterprises in this area.

The Treaty of Rome, signed in March 1957 and ratified subsequently by the same six countries, establishes the European Economic Community (EEC), providing for the gradual reduction and abolition of all tariffs on trade among the member countries, a common tariff on imports from other countries, and free movements of labour and capital within the Community.

The Treaty of Stockholm is signed in 1959 by seven countries, Austria, Denmark, Norway, Portugal, Sweden, Switzerland, and the United Kingdom, establishing the European Free Trade Area (EFTA); it provides for gradual reduction and eventual abolition of quotas and tariffs on imports from member countries, but leaves their tariffs on imports from other countries unaffected.

The EPU is liquidated in 1958 after countries had effectively restored the interconvertibility of their currencies; it is replaced by a European Monetary Agreement (EMA) among 16 of the previous member countries plus Spain, with a European Fund (EF) to help members in payments deficits with short-term credits.

The amalgamation of ECSC, EURATOM, and EEC in 1965 is shown by adoption of the new name 'European Community' (EC).

In July 1968, the EC, with all internal tariffs and other non-agricultural trade restrictions abolished, becomes a complete customs union. In two conferences, the first in December 1969, in The Hague, the second in March 1971, the members of the EC resolve to establish in several steps, over a period of about ten years, an 'economic and monetary union', with the first phase devoted to a narrowing of the band of permissible fluctuations of exchange rates around fixed parities. The plan is later suspen ed when floating rates seem unavoidable.

EEC, which in 1963, because of a French veto, had failed to admit the British to membership, at last admits the United Kin; dom, Ireland, and Denmark as of January 1973.

L EAST-EUROPEAN ECONOMIC CO-OPERATION SINCE 1948

At a conference in Moscow in 1949, Bulgaria, Czechoslovakia, Hungary, Poland, Rumania, and the Soviet Union sign a treaty establishing the Council for Mutual Economic Assistance (CME also COMECON); Albania, East Germany, and Mongolia join later. It provides for mutual economic and technical assistance and specialisation of production.

An International Bank for Economic Co-operation (IBEC) was established in 1964 to finance joint undertakings of the members of CMEA.

M LATIN AMERICAN AND CARIBBEAN REGIONAL ARRANGE-MENTS SINCE 1948

An agreement on establishing a Greater Colombia Economic an Customs Union ('Quito Charter') was concluded in 1948, but has not been executed.

In 1950 Costa Rica, Guatemala, Honduras, and Nicaragua sig an 'Agreement on the Regime for Central American Integrated Industries' and a 'Multinational Treaty on Central American Free Trade and Economic Integration' as a first step to a custon union. [Costa Rica did not ratify.] Between 1952 and 1957 Central American countries conclude seven bilateral free-trade agreements. In December 1960 at a conference in Managua, Guatemala, El Salvador, and Honduras — joined later by Costa Rica and Nicaragua — create a free-trade area in a Treaty of Economic Association. A Central American Common Market (CACM) was to come into effect within five years. In 1963 the members of CACM agree on the Uniform Central American Customs Code (CAUCA), with most customs barriers among these countries eliminated.

In 1956 the United Nations Economic Commission for Latin America (ECLA) sets up a committee to study the problems of creating a Latin American Common Market. In February 1960 the Montevideo Treaty is signed by Argentina, Bolivia, Brazil, Chile, Mexico, Peru, and Uruguay, establishing a Latin America

Free Trade Association (LAFTA), with a timetable of gradual
reduction of tariffs. Colombia, Ecuador, Paraguay, and Venezu-
ela sign the Treaty at later dates, but the timetable was not
honoured by performance.

With LAFTA arrangements ineffective, the Andean Subregion-
al Group is formed by the Agreement of Cartagena in 1969, providing for completion of a customs union within eleven years.
The group includes Bolivia, Chile, Colombia, Ecuador, and Peru.
The five member countries agree also on a common policy on
foreign investments, royalties, and industrial property.

In 1966 the Caribbean Free Trade Area (CARIFTA) is established, including Antigua, Barbados, and Guyana, with other
countries joining subsequently. In July 1973 it is transformed
into the Caribbean Community, comprising twelve (mostly
English-speaking) countries and territories.

In 1975, an organisation called the Latin American Economic
System (SELA), was founded by 25 countries to aid 'organization for consultation, co-ordination, and joint economic and
social promotion'.

N AFRICAN REGIONAL ARRANGEMENTS

The Union of South Africa and Southern Rhodesia agree in
1948 to establish a customs union. The South African Customs
Union, formed in 1910 by the Union of South Africa, Bechuana-
land, Basutoland, and Swaziland is revised but continued in
1969.

A customs union of the British colonies of Kenya and Uganda,
formed in 1917, was extended in 1927 to include Tanganyika.
In 1964 the governments of the now independent countries —
Kenya, Uganda, and Tanzania — sign the Kampala Agreement,
modifying the original customs union. In 1967 they sign a new
treaty of East African Co-operation, adding to the customs
union various federal institutions, an East African Development
Bank and an agreement to co-ordinate their industrial policies.
(Some of the agreed co-operation and co-ordination seems to
have been suspended in recent years.)

The West African Customs Union is created in 1959 to preserve the previous economic links established under the former
Federation of French West Africa; Dahomey, the Ivory Coast,
Mali, Mauritania, Niger, Senegal, Togo, and Upper Volta become
members of this Union. The treaty is revised in 1966, but without much success. To replace the Union, the same countries
establish in 1970 the Economic Community of West Africa.

The Central African Republic, the Congo (Brazzaville), Gabon and Cameroun form the Central African Common Market (UDEAC) in 1964. In 1968 the Congo (Kinshasa) [now Zaire], Chad, and the Central African Republic sign a treaty creating the Union of Central African States, to provide for a common market and for co-ordination of industrialisation policies.

Algeria, Morocco, Tunisia, and Libya, in 1964, set up the Maghreb Permanent Consultative Committee to secure the abolition of tariffs on internal trade in certain industrial product the establishment of a uniform tariff on imports from other countries, and an institution to facilitate multinational payment Little progress has been made toward any of these objectives.

Q ASIAN REGIONAL ARRANGEMENTS

Japan-Manchuria: in 1931 Japan occupies the Chinese province Manchuria and, in 1932, recognises the new state of 'Manchukuo An economic construction programme is promulgated in 1933 and a Joint Economic Commission established in 1935 to achiev 'co-ordination of the economies of the two countries'. A fixed parity is set between the two currencies and, in 1936, a Five-Year Industrial Development Plan announced, chiefly to establish industries and control primary production from a military point of view. A revision in 1938 merges the Five-Year Plans for Japan and Manchukuo with a view to achieving self-sufficiency of the 'yen bloc' in several strategic products (including coal, iron and steel, and foodstuffs) by 1942. (During the war Japan extends its economic integration by conquest to other parts of China, Southeast Asia, and Indonesia.)

In 1961 the Association of Southeast Asia is established, with Malaysia, the Philippines, and Thailand as members; Indonesia and Singapore join later.

Eight Asian countries, Bangladesh, India, Laos, Pakistan, the Philippines, South Korea, Sri Lanka, and Thailand agree in 1975 on multilateral tariff concessions as the first step toward the formation of an Asian free-trade zone.

P AUSTRALIAN REGIONAL ARRANGEMENTS

A New Zealand—Australia Free Trade Agreement (NAFTA) is concluded in 1965, providing for gradual reduction or removal of duties on selected imports from the other country within eight years, assuring, however, virtual avoidance of any trade creation or even of effective competition and, hence, hardly any progress toward freer trade.

BIBLIOGRAPHY OF HISTORICAL WRITINGS

The books and articles in which the events in the history of economic integration have been reported, interpreted, and discussed will be shown here under the same headings that we used in the historical survey to specify the eras and areas covered. Where authors dealt with more than one specific class of events, so that their writings would have to be listed under several headings, they will be entered in a 'polyhistoric' group, with letters added in brackets to indicate the headings under which the materials treated would fall. This arrangement avoids duplication; some works would have to be listed under six, seven, or even nine headings had I not chosen this device of a mixed group for publications on more than one era and area. Readers who look for references to works on a particular era and area are warned not to overlook the relevant entries in the group of miscellanea.

RELATING TO TWO OR MORE SUBJECTS [indicated by letters A to P in brackets after the entry]

Allais, Maurice, 'Customs Unions and Trade Agreements', in *Encyclopedia Britannica*, 15th ed. (Chicago: Helen Hemingway Benton, 1974) Vol. 5, pp. 376—85. [D,E,F,G,H,J,K,L,M]

Allen, James Jay, *The European Common Market and the GATT* (Washington: Georgetown University Press, 1960). [J,K]

Bosc, Louis, *Unions douanières et projets d'unions douanières* (Aix, Marseilles, Paris: Arthur Rousseau, 1904). [B,C,F,G,H,I]

Bosc, Louis, *Zollallianzen und Zollunionen in ihrer Bedeutung für die Handelspolitik der Vergangenheit und Zukunft*, translated from the French by Schilder (Berlin: Elwin Staude, 1907). [B,C,F,G,H,I]

Ghai, Dharam P., *Current Problems of Economic Integration: State Trading and Regional Economic Integration among Developing Countries* (New York: United Nations Conference on Trade and Development, 1973). [M,N]

Heckscher, Eli F., *Mercantilism*, translated from the Swedish by Mendel Shapiro (London: Allen & Unwin, 1935; rev. ed., 1955). [A,B,C,D,F]

Henderson, William Otto, *The Genesis of the Common Market* (Chicago: Quadrangle Books, 1962). [H,I,K]

Henderson, William Otto, 'A Nineteenth Century Approach to a West European Common Market', *Kyklos*, Vol. 10, No. 4 (1957) pp. 448—56. [F,H]

Hylkema, Edgar, *Bénélux: Le chemin vers l'unité économique* (Paris: A. Pedone, 1948). [G,H,I,K]

Ledermann, László, *Féderation Internationale: Idées d'hier — Possibilités de demain* (Neuchâtel: de la Baconnière, 1950). [A,F,G]

Levasseur, Emile, *Histoire du commerce de la France*, 2 vols. (Paris: Arthur Rousseau, 1911, 1912). [C,H]

Marchal, Jean, *Union douanière et organisation européenne* (Paris: Recueil Sirey, 1929). [A,B,C,F,G,H,I]

Pentmann, Juda, *Die Zollunionsidee und ihre Wandlungen im Rahmen der wirtschaftspolitischen Ideen und der Wirtschaftspolitik des 19. Jahrhunderts bis zur Gegenwart* (Jena: Gustav Fischer, 1917). [B,C,D,F]

Renouvin, Pierre, *L'idée de féderation européenne dans la pensée politique du XIXe siècle* [Tabaroff Lecture] (Oxford: Clarendon Press, 1949). [F,G]

Schmitt, Hans A., *The Path to European Union: From the Marshall Plan to the Common Market* (Baton Rouge: Louisiana State University Press, 1962). [I,K]

Schmoller, Gustav Friedrich von, 'Die Handels- und Zollannäherung Mitteleuropas', *Jahrbuch für Gesetzgebung, Verwaltung und Volkswirtschaft im Deutschen Reich*, Vol. 40, No. 2 (1916) pp. 529—50. [G,H,I]

Viner, Jacob, *The Customs Union Issue* (New York: Carnegie Endowment for International Peace, 1950). [A,B,C,D,E,F,G, H,I]

Viner, Jacob, 'Power versus Plenty as Objectives of Foreign Policy in the Seventeenth and Eighteenth Centuries', *World Politics*, Vol. I (1948) pp. 1—29. [B,C,D]

Viner, Jacob, *Studies in the Theory of International Trade* (New York: Harper, 1937). [B,C]

Wionczek, Miguel S., ed., *Economic Co-operation in Latin America, Africa, and Asia: A Handbook of Documents* (Cambridge, Mass.: MIT Press, 1969). [M,N,O]

SUBJECT A: HOLY ROMAN [GERMAN] EMPIRE

Beer, Adolf, *Die Zollpolitik und die Schaffung eines einheitlichen Zollgebietes unter Maria Theresia*, in *Mitteilungen des Instituts für Österreichische Geschichtsforschung*, Vol. 14 (Innsbruck: 1880).

Bog, Ingomar, *Der Reichsmerkantilismus: Studien zur Wirtschafts-politik des Heiligen Romischen Reiches im 17. und 18. Jahrhundert* (Stuttgart: Gustav Fischer, 1959).

Döberl, Michael, 'Das Projekt einer Einigung Deutschlands auf wirtschaftlicher Grundlage aus dem Jahre 1665', *Forschungen zur Geschichte Bayerns,* Vol. 6 (1898) pp. 163—205.

Humpert, Magdalene, *Bibliographie der Kameralwissenschaften* (Cologne: K. Schroeder, 1937).

Seckendorff, Veit Ludwig von, *Teutscher Fürsten-Staat* (1656).

Small, Albion W., *The Cameralists, The Pioneers of German Social Policy* (Chicago: University of Chicago Press, 1909).

Walb, Ernst, 'Die Reichsidee bei den deutschen Kameralisten', *Schmollers Jahrbuch für Gesetzgebung, Verwaltung und Volkswirtschaft im Deutschen Reich,* Vol. 65 (Dec 1941) pp. 683—704.

SUBJECT B: GREAT BRITAIN

A Breviate of the Proposals Made to the Honourable Council of State by the Commissioners from Scotland', in *The Acts of the Parliaments of Scotland and Government during the Commonwealth, 1124—1707,* Vol. 6, pt. 2, p. 779a (Edinburgh: Cmd. 1814—44).

Cornwallis, Sir William, *The Miraculous and Happie Union of England and Scotland* (London: Blount, 1604).

Hughes, Edward, 'The Negotiations for a Commercial Treaty between England and Scotland in 1668', *The Scottish Historical Review,* Vol. 24 (October 1926) pp. 30—47.

Keith, Theodora, *Commercial Relations of England and Scotland, 1603—1707* (Cambridge: Cambridge University Press, 1910).

Keith, Theodora, 'The Economic Causes for the Scottish Union', *English Historical Review,* Vol. 24 (1909) pp. 44—60.

Lythe, Samuel G. E., 'The Union of the Crowns in 1603 and the Debate on Economic Integration', *Scottish Journal of Political Economy,* Vol. 5 (February 1958) pp. 219—28.

Murray, Alice Effie, *A History of the Commercial and Financial Relations between England and Ireland from the Period of the Restoration* (London: P. S. King and Son, 1903).

SUBJECT C: FRANCE

Bosher, John Francis, *The Single Duty Project: A Study of the Movement for a French Customs Union in the Eighteenth Century* (London: The Athlone Press, 1964).

Cole, Charles W., *Colbert and a Century of French Mercantilism*, 2 vols (New York: Columbia University Press, 1939).

Cole, Charles W., *French Mercantilism, 1683—1700* (New York: Columbia University Press, 1943).

Hauser, Henri, *La pensée et l'action économiques du Cardinal de Richelieu* (Paris: Presses Universitaires de France, 1944).

Léon, Pierre, and Carrière, Charles, 'L'appel des marchés', in Ernest Labrousse and Fernand Braudel, eds, *Des derniers temps de l'âge seigneural aux préludes de l'âge industriel (1660—1789)*, Vol. 2 of *Histoire économique et sociale de la France* (Paris: Presses Universitaires de France, 1970) pp. 161—215.

SUBJECT D: BRITISH COLONIES AND COMMONWEALTH

Davidson, John, *Commercial Federation and Colonial Trade Policy* (London: Swan Sonnenschein & Co.; New York: Charles Scribner's Sons, 1900).

Knorr, Klaus Eugen, *British Colonial Theories: 1570—1850* (Toronto: Toronto University Press, 1944).

McDiarmid, Orville John, *Commercial Policy in the Canadian Economy* (Cambridge, Mass.: Harvard University Press, 1946).

McGuire, Edward B., *The British Tariff System* (London: Methuen, 1939).

McLean, Simon J., *The Tariff History of Canada* (Toronto: Warwick Bros. & Rutter, 1895).

Patterson, Gordon D., *The Tariff in the Australian Colonies, 1856—1900* (Melbourne: F. W. Cheshire, 1968).

Perry, J. Harvey, *Taxes, Tariffs and Subsidies: A History of Canadian Fiscal Development*, Vol. 1 (Toronto: University of Toronto Press, 1955).

Russel, Ronald S., *Imperial Preference: Its Development and Effects* (London: Empire Economic Union, 1947).

Semmel, Bernard, *The Rise of Free Trade Imperialism* (Cambridge: Cambridge University Press, 1970).

Thompson, Leonard Monteath, *The Unification of South Africa 1902—1910* (Oxford: Clarendon Press, 1960).

SUBJECT E: UNITED STATES OF AMERICA

Hamilton, Alexander, Madison, James, and Jay, John, *The Federalist Papers* (New York: M'Lean, 1788).

Hill, William, *The First Stages of the Tariff Policy of the United States* (Baltimore: Guggenheimer, Weil & Co., 1893).

ensen, Merrill, *The New Nation: A History of the United States during the Confederation, 1781—1789* (New York: Alfred A. Knopf, 1967).

taples, William R., *Rhode Island in the Continental Congress*, edited by Reuben Aldridge Guild (Providence, R. I.: Providence Press Company, 1870).

aussig, Frank W., *The Tariff History of the United States* (New York and London: G. P. Putnam's Sons, 1905).

UBJECT F: GERMAN ZOLLVEREIN

egidi, Ludwig Karl, *Aus der Vorzeit des Zollvereins* (Hamburg: Noyes & Geisler, 1865).

Dieterici, [Karl Friedrich] Wilhelm, *Der Volkswohlstand im Preussischen Staate: In Vergleichungen aus den Jahren vor 1806 und von 1828 bis 1832, so wie aus der neuesten Zeit, nach statistischen Ermittelungen und dem Gange der Gesetzgebung aus amtlichen Quellen dargestellt* (Berlin: E. S. Mittler, 1846).

ckert, Christian, 'Zur Vorgeschichte des deutschen Zollvereins: Die preussisch-hessische Zollunion vom 14. Februar 1828', *Schmollers Jahrbuch für Gesetzgebung, Verwaltung und Volkswirtschaft in Deutschen Reich*, Vol. 26 (1902), Part 2, pp. 51—102.

isenhart Rothe, Wilfried von, and Ritthaler, Anton, eds, *Vorgeschichte und Begründung des deutschen Zollvereins, 1815—34: Akten der Staaten des Deutschen Bundes und der Europäischen Mächte* (Veröffentlichungen der Friedrich List-Gesellschaft), Vols. 8—10 (Berlin: Reimar Hobbing, 1934).

aertner, Alfred, *Der Kampf um den Zollverein zwischen Österreich und Preussen von 1849 bis 1853* (Strassburg: Herder, 1911).

enderson, William O., *The Zollverein* (Cambridge: Cambridge University Press, 1939).

ebenius, Carl Friedrich, *Der deutsche Zollverein, sein System und seine Zukunft* (Carlsruhe: Chr. Fr. Müller, 1835).

ebenius, Carl Friedrich, 'Über die Entstehung und Erweiterung des grossen deutschen Zollvereines', *Deutsche Viertel-Jahrschrift*, 1838, Part 2, pp. 319—59.

rice, Arnold H., *The Evolution of the Zollverein: A Study of the Ideas and Institutions Leading to German Economic Unification between 1815 and 1833* (Ann Arbor: University of Michigan Press, 1949).

Roscher, Wilhelm, 'Zur Gründungsgeschichte des deutschen Zollvereins', *Deutschland*, 1870, pp. 143—211; also as a book (Berlin: van Muyden, 1870).

Schmölders, Günter, 'Der deutsche Zollverein als historisches Vorbild einer wirtschaftlichen Integration in Europa', in *Aspects financiers et fiscaux de l'intégration économique internationale*, Travaux de l'Institut International de Finances Publiques, Neuvième Session, Frankfort, 1953 (The Hague: W. P. van Stockum & Fils, 1953) pp. 137—48.

Treitschke, Heinrich Gotthard von, 'Die Anfänge des deutschen Zollvereins', *Preussische Jahrbücher*, Vol. 30 (1872) pp. 397ff., 479ff., 648ff.

Treitschke, Heinrich Gotthard von, 'Der letzte Akt der Zollvereinsgeschichte', *Preussische Jahrbücher*, Vol. 45 (1880) pp. 626—42. [Reprinted separately in 1880 and 1913.]

Treitschke, Heinrich Gotthard von, *Die Gründung des deutscher Zollvereins*, ed. Horst Kohl (Leipzig: R. Voigtländer, 1913).

Weber, W., *Der deutsche Zollverein: Geschichte seiner Entstehung und Entwicklung* (Leipzig: Veit & Comp., 1869; 2nd ed 1871).

Zollverein, Central-Büreau, ed., *Verträge und Verhandlungen aus dem Zeitraume von 1833 bis einschliesslich 1836 über die Bildung und Ausführung des deutschen Zoll- und Handels-Vereins*, Vol. 1 (Berlin, 1845).

SUBJECT G: OTHER EUROPEAN CUSTOMS UNIONS

Dérobert, E., *La politique douanière de la Conféderation suisse. Etude sur la politique douanière suisse, depuis la constitution de l'Etat fédéral jusqu'à nos jours, et exposé du problème douanier actuel* (Geneva: Imprimerie Jent, 1926).

East, William Gordon, *The Union of Moldavia and Wallachia, 1859: An Episode in Diplomatic History* (Cambridge: Cambridge University Press, 1929).

Eisenmann, Louis, *Le compromis austro-hongrois de 1867; Etude sur le dualisme* (Paris: Bellais, 1904).

Hommel, Luc, *Une expérience d'union économique: Bilan de dix années d'union économique Belgo-Luxembourgeoise* (Louvain: Edition de la Société d'études morales, 1933).

Ito, Nobufumi, *La clause de la nation la plus favorisée* (Paris: les Editions Internationales, 1930).

Majerus, Emil, *Das Wirtschaftsbündnis des Grossherzogtums Luxemburg mit Belgien* (Zürich: inaugural dissertation, 192·

Meade, James E., *The Belgium—Luxembourg Economic Union,*
1921—1939: Lessons from an Early Experiment, Essays in
International Finance, No. 25 (Princeton: International
Finance Section, 1956).

Meade, James E., 'Benelux: The Formation of the Common
Customs', *Economica,* n.s. Vol. 23 (August 1956) pp. 201—13.

Meade, James E., *Negotiations for Benelux: An Annotated*
Chronicle, 1943—1956, Princeton Studies in International
Finance, No. 6 (Princeton: International Finance Section,
1957).

Michelis, Eduard, 'Die Zolltrennung Österreich-Ungarns in ihren
mutmasslichen Rückwirkungen auf die deutsch-österreichisch-
ungarischen Handelsbeziehungen, *Jahrbuch für Gesetzgebung,*
Verwaltung und Volkswirtschaft im Deutschen Reich, Vol. 32
(1908) pp. 557—620.

Protocol between the Netherlands on the one hand and Belgium
and Luxemburg on the other, signed at The Hague, March 14,
1947', in *Staatsblad van het Koninkrijk der Nederlanden,* No.
H 282 (1947) pp. 6—9. [Clarified and interpreted.]

Robertson, W., 'Benelux and Problems of European Integration',
Oxford Economic Papers, n.s. Vol. 8 (Feb 1956) pp. 35—50.

Rubin, Marcus, 'En Nordisk Toldunion', *Tilskuren* (Copenhagen,
1888) pp. 13—60.

Sardá, Juan, *Uniones aduaneras y uniones economicas* (Madrid:
Aguilar, 1953).

Sieghart, Rudolf, *Zolltrennung und Zolleinheit: Die Geschichte*
der österreichisch-ungarischen Zwischenzollinie (Vienna: Manz,
1915).

Treinen, J., *L'économie luxembourgeoise sous le régime de*
l'union douanière belgo—luxembourgeoise (Luxembourg:
Impr. de la Cour, J. Beffort, 1934).

SUBJECT H: TRADE AGREEMENTS AND M.F.N. CLAUSE

Rist, Marcel, 'Une expérience française de libération des échanges
au XIXe siècle: Le traité de 1860', *Revue d'Economie Politi-*
que, Vol. 66, part 2 (Nov—Dec 1956) pp. 908—57.

Schmoller, Gustav, 'Der italienisch-deutsche (1883) und der
spanisch-deutsche Handelsvertrag im Vergleich mit den deutschen Handelsverträgen der sechziger Jahre, *Jahrbuch für*
Gesetzgebung, Verwaltung und Volkswirtschaft im Deutschen
Reich, Vol. 7, No. 4 (1883) pp. 1373—82.

Schmoller, Gustav, 'Neue Litteratur über unsere handelspolitische

Zukunft', *Jahrbuch für Gesetzgebung, Verwaltung und Volks-wirtschaft im Deutschen Reich*, Vol. 15 No. 1 (1891) pp. 275—82.

Schumacher, Hermann, 'Meistbegünstigung und Zollunterschei-dung', *Die wirtschaftliche Annäherung zwischen dem Deut-schen Reiche und seinen Verbundeten, Schriften des Vereins für Sozialpolitik*, Vol. 155, Part 1, pp. 61—132.

Sombart, Werner, 'Die neuen Handelsverträge, insbesondere Deutschlands', *Jahrbuch für Gesetzgebung, Verwaltung und Volkswirtschaft im Deutschen Reich*, Vol. 16, No. 2 (1892) pp. 547—611.

SUBJECT I: UNSUCCESSFUL EUROPEAN PROJECTS

'Agreement regarding the Guiding Principles for an Economic Union between the Two States, Signed at Salzburg, October 11, 1918', in Gustav Gratz and Richard Schüller, *Die Äussere Wirtschaftspolitik Österreich-Ungarns, Mitteleuropäische Pläne* (Vienna: Hölder-Pichler-Tempsky, 1925) p. 93.

Alauro, Orlando d', 'Le "Unione Economiche" et l'Unione Italo Francese', *Economia Internazionale*, Vol. 1 (Genoa, August 1948) pp. 786—99.

Alphand, Hervé, 'Les recommandations de la conférence de Stresa [for the economic restoration of central and eastern Europe]', *Revue de droit international*, Vol. 10 (1932) pp. 555—78, 652—69.

The American Foundation, Inc., *The World Court's Advisory Opinion on the Austro-German Customs Union Case* (New York: American Foundation, 1931).

Argus (pseud.) [Stepán Osusky], *The Economic Aspect of the Austro-German Customs Union* (Prague: Orbis, 1931).

Armstrong, Hamilton F., 'Danubia: Relief or Ruin', *Foreign Affairs*, Vol. 10 (July 1932) pp. 600—16.

Ball, M. Margaret, *Post-War German-Austrian Relations: The Anschluss Movement, 1918—1936* (Stanford, California: Stanford University Press, 1937).

Beer, Adolf, 'Die Zollpolitik und die Schaffung eines einheit-lichen Zollgebietes unter Maria Theresia', *Mittheilungen des Instituts für österreichische Geschichtsforschung*, Bd. 14 (Vienna: Universitas Viennensis, 1882; or Innsbruck: 1894)

Beneš, Edvard, *The Austro-German Customs Union Project* (Prague: Orbis, 1931).

Bethlen, István, 'The Danube States and the Tardieu Plan',

Political Science Quarterly, Vol. 47 (September 1932) pp. 352—62.

Bitterman, M., *Austria and the Customs Union* (Prague: Orbis, 1931).

Commission Mixte Franco-Italienne pour l'Etude d'une Union Douanière entre la France et l'Italie, *Compte rendu de la Commission Mixte Franco-Italienne d'Union Douanière, Paris, January 22, 1949* (Paris: Imprimèrie Nationale, 1949).

Dechamps, A., 'Une page d'histoire: Negociations commerciales avec la France; Union douanière' *Revue générale* (Brussels) Dec 1922.

'Declaration regarding the Establishment of a Customs Union, Signed at Paris, September 13, 1947', 'Protocol regarding the Formation of a Customs Union, Made at Turin, March 20, 1948', 'Decision Taken by France and Italy at the First Session, Havana, March 20, 1948', and 'Treaty for the Establishment of a Customs Union between France and Italy, Signed at Paris, March 26, 1949', US Department of State *Bulletin*, 1949, Aug 22, pp. 243—6.

De Launoy, 'Les projets d'union douanière franco-belge en 1841—42', *Revue catholique des idées et des faits* (Brussels), Dec 1922.

Diehl, Karl, *Zur Frage eines Zollbündnisses zwischen Deutschland und Österreich-Ungarn* (Jena: Gustav Fischer, 1914: 2nd. ed., 1915).

Elissalde, L., 'Union douanière Austro-Allemande', *Revue de droit international*, Vol. 9 (Jan—Mar 1931) pp. 14—32.

Fisk, George M., *Continental Opinion regarding a Proposed Middle European Tariff Union*, Johns Hopkins University Studies in Historical and Political Science, Series 20, Nos. 11—12 (Nov—Dec 1902), (Baltimore: Johns Hopkins Press, 1902).

France, Conseil Economique, *Union douanière France-Italie: Rapport sur le traité d'union douanière entre la France et l'Italie du 26 mars 1949*, No. 7 of Conseil Economique, *Etudes et Travaux* (Paris: Presses Universitaires de France, 1949).

Francke, Ernst, 'Zollpolitische Einigungsbestrebungen in Mitteleuropa während des letzten Jahrzehnts', in *Beiträge zur neuesten Handelspolitik Deutschlands*, Vol. 1, *Schriften des Vereins für Socialpolitik*, Vol. 90 (1900) pp. 187—272.

Gedye, George E. R., 'The French Schemes for Danubian Europe', *Contemporary Review*, Vol. 141 (May 1932) pp. 561—8.

Gerloff, Wilhelm, *Der wirtschaftliche Imperialismus und die Frage der Zolleinigung zwischen Deutschland und Österreich-Ungarn*, No. 45 in the series *Der Deutsche Krieg* (Stuttgart and Berlin: Deutsche Verlags-Anstalt, 1915).

Gratz, Gustav and Schüller, Richard, *Die Äussere Wirtschaftspolitik Österreich-Ungarns: Mitteleuropäische Pläne* (Vienna: Hölder-Pichler-Tempsky, 1925).

Grazzi, Umberto, 'Some Aspects of the Franco-Italian Customs Union in Regard to the Gradual Manner of Its Achievement', *Banca Nazionale del Lavoro Quarterly Review*, No. 5 (July 1948) pp. 365—8.

Guthmann, Oskar, *Ein Zollbündnis zwischen Belgien und den Niederlanden: Untersuchungen über die Handelsbeziehungen zwischen Belgien und den Niederlanden seit der Mitte des 19. Jahrhunderts* (Tübingen: H. Laupp, 1907).

Henderson, William O., 'A Nineteenth Century Approach to a West European Common Market', *Kyklos*, Vol. 10, No. 4 (1957) pp. 448—59.

Kautsky, Karl, *Die Vereinigten Staaten Mitteleuropas* (Stuttgart: I. H. W. Dietz, 1916).

Mamroth, Karl, 'Das Projekt eines österreichisch-deutschen Zollvereins', *Annalen des deutschen Reiches*, 1886, pp. 508—15.

Philippovich, Eugen von, *Ein Wirtschafts-und Zollverband zwischen Deutschland und Österreich-Ungarn* (Leipzig: S. Hirzel, 1915).

Ridder, Alfred de, *Les projets d'union douanière franco-belge et les puissances européennes (1836—1843)* (Brussels: Maurice Lamertin, 1932).

Riedl, Richard, *Exceptions to the Most-Favoured-Nation Treatment: Report Presented to the International Chamber of Commerce*, Papers Presented to the Washington Congress, 1931, No. 8 (London: P. S. King & Son, 1931).

Rochebrochard, Guy de la, *L'Union douanière Austro-Allemand* (Paris: A. Pedone, 1934).

Salter, Sir Arthur, *The United States of Europe and Other Paper* (London: Allen & Unwin, 1933).

Sartorius von Waltershausen, August, 'Beiträge zur Beurteilung einer wirtschaftspolitischen Foederation von Mitteleuropa', *Zeitschrift für Sozialwissenschaft*, Vol. 5 (1902) pp. 557—70, 674—704, 765—86, and 860—94.

Spiethoff, Arthur, 'Gründe für und wider einen deutsch-österreichisch-ungarischen Zollverband', *Die wirtschaftliche Annäherung zwischen dem Deutschen Reiche und seinen Verbün-*

deten, *Schriften des Vereins für Socialpolitik*, Vol. 155, Part 1 (1916) pp. 1—60.

Stolper, Gustav, 'Uber die Formen eines Wirtschaftsverbandes zwischen Deutschland und Österreich-Ungarn', *Die wirtschaftliche Annäherung zwischen dem Deutschen Reiche und seinen Verbündeten, Schriften des Vereins für Socialpolitik*, Vol. 155, Part 1 (1916) pp. 1553—82.

Truchy, Henry, 'Les ententes douanières', *Revue d'Economie Politique*, Vol. 47 (Mar—Apr 1933) pp. 455—65.

Wolf, Julius, 'Vorläufer und Parallelen einer europäischen Zollunion', in Heiman, Hans, ed., *Europäische Zollunion: Beiträge zu Problem und Lösung* (Berlin: Reimar Hobbing, 1926) pp. 9—22.

SUBJECT J: WORLDWIDE ARRANGEMENTS

Bergsten, C. Fred, *Completing the GATT: Toward New International Rules to Govern Export Controls* (Washington: The Brookings Institution, 1975).

Cairncross, Alec, *The International Bank for Reconstruction and Development*, Essays in International Finance, No. 33 (Princeton: International Finance Section, 1959).

Committee on Reform of the International Monetary System and Related Issues (Committee of Twenty), *International Monetary Reform: Documents of the Committee of Twenty* (Washington: International Monetary Fund, 1974).

Diebold, Jr., William, *The End of the I.T.O.*, Essays in International Finance, No. 16 (Princeton: International Finance Section, 1952).

Fleming, J. Marcus, *The International Monetary Fund: Its Form and Functions* (Washington: IMF, 1964).

General Agreement on Tariffs and Trade, *Analytical Index: Notes on the Drafting, Interpretation and Application of the Articles of the General Agreement* (Geneva: the Contracting Parties to the GATT, February 1966).

General Agreement on Tariffs and Trade, *Basic Instruments and Selected Documents*, 2 vols (Geneva: The Contracting Parties to the General Agreement on Tariffs and Trade, May 1952). Also annual supplements.

General Agreement on Tariffs and Trade, *The Role of GATT in Relation to Trade and Development* (Geneva: The Contracting Parties to the GATT, Mar 1964).

Gold, Joseph, *Membership and Nonmembership in the Inter-*

national Monetary Fund: A Study in International Law and Organization (Washington: IMF, 1974).

Gold, Joseph, *Voting and Decisions in the IMF: An Essay on the Law and Practice of the Fund* (Washington: IMF, 1972).

Halm, George N., *International Monetary Co-operation* (Chapel Hill: University of North Carolina Press, 1945).

Hawtrey, Ralph George, *Bretton Woods: For Better or Worse* (London: Longmans, Green & Co., 1946).

Horie, Shigeo, *The International Monetary Fund: Retrospect and Prospect* (New York: St. Martin's Press, 1964).

Horsefield, J. Keith, and others, *The IMF, 1945—1965: Twenty Years of International Monetary Co-operation*, 3 vols (Washington: IMF, 1969).

International Bank for Reconstruction and Development, *The World Bank: Policies and Operation* (Washington: IBRD, 1957).

International Development Association, *Articles of Agreement and Accompanying Report of the Executive Directors of the International Bank for Reconstruction and Development* (Washington: IDA, 1960).

International Development Association, *IDA: 50 Questions and Answers* (Washington: IDA, May 1970).

International Monetary Fund, *Articles of Agreement of the International Monetary Fund as Modified by the Proposed Amendment* (Washington: IMF, 1968).

International Monetary Fund, *The First Ten Years of the International Monetary Fund* (Washington: IMF, 1956).

International Monetary Fund, 'Fund Policies and Procedures in Relation to the Compensatory Financing of Commodity Fluctuations', *International Monetary Fund Staff Papers*, Vol. 8 (Nov 1960) pp. 1—76.

International Monetary Fund, *Outline of a Facility Based on Special Drawing Rights in the International Monetary Fund* (Washington: IMF, 1967).

International Monetary Fund, *Selected Decisions of the International Monetary Fund and Selected Documents*, seventh issue (Washington: International Monetary Fund, 1 Jan 1975).

Lutz, Friedrich A., *International Monetary Mechanisms: The Keynes and White Proposals*, Essays in International Finance, No. 1 (Princeton: International Finance Section, 1943).

Machlup, Fritz, *Remaking the International Monetary System: The Rio Agreement and Beyond* (Baltimore: Johns Hopkins University, 1968).

Oliver, Robert W., *Early Plans for a World Bank*, Princeton

Studies in International Finance, No. 29 (Princeton: International Finance Section, 1971).

Mason, Edward S., and Asher, Robert E., *The World Bank since Bretton Woods* (Washington: The Brookings Institution, 1973).

Tew, Brian, *The International Monetary Fund: Its Present Role and Future Prospects*, Essays in International Finance, No. 36 (Princeton: International Finance Section, 1961).

United States, Congress, House of Representatives, *Bretton Woods Agreements Act*, Hearings before the Committee on Banking and Currency on H.R. 2221 (Washington: Government Printing Office, 1945).

United States, Congress, Senate, *Bretton Woods Agreements Act*, Hearings before the Committee on Banking and Currency on H.R. 2221, 2 vols; Hearings on H.R. 3314, 1 vol. (Washington: Government Printing Office, 1945).

United States, Department of State, *Proceedings and Documents of the United Nations Monetary and Financial Conference, Bretton Woods, NH, July 1—22, 1944*, 2 vols (Washington: Government Printing Office, 1948).

United States, Congress, House of Representatives, *International Development Association Act*, Hearings before Subcommittee No. 1 of the Committee on Banking and Currency (Washington: Government Printing Office, 1960).

Viner, Jacob, 'Two Plans for International Monetary Stabilization', *The Yale Review*, Vol. 33 (September 1943) pp. 77—107.

Weaver, James H., *The International Development Association: A New Approach to Foreign Aid* (New York: Praeger, 1965).

Wilcox, Clair, *A Charter for World Trade* (New York: Macmillan, 1949).

SUBJECT K: WEST-EUROPEAN CO-OPERATION SINCE 1948

Bailey, Richard, *Tarifs et commerce en Europe occidentale; les six et les sept* (Turin: G. Giappichelli, 1961).

Balassa, Bela, ed., *European Economic Integration* (Amsterdam: North Holland Publishing Co., 1975).

Biclet, Yves, 'From the European Payments Union to the European Monetary Agreement', in Organisation for European Economic Co-operation, *At Work for Europe* (Paris: OEEC, 5th ed., 1960) pp. 39—54.

Bok, Derek Curtis, *The First Three Years of the Schuman Plan*,

Studies in International Finance, No. 5 (Princeton: International Finance Section, 1955).

Cairncross, Sir Alec; Giersch, Herbert; Lamfalussy, Alexandre; Petrilli, Giuseppe; and Uri, Pierre, *Economic Policy for the European Community: The Way Forward* (New York: Holmes & Meier, 1975).

Camps, Miriam, *Britain and the European Community, 1955—1963* (Princeton: Princeton University Press, 1964).

Diebold, Jr., William, *Trade and Payments in Western Europe: A Study in Economic Cooperation, 1947—1951* (New York: Harper, published for the Council on Foreign Relations, 1952).

Diebold, Jr., William, *The Schuman Plan: A Study in Economic Cooperation*, 1950—1959 (New York: Praeger, published for the Council on Foreign Relations, 1959). [With critical bibliography.]

European Communities, Commission, *Stocktaking of the Common Agricultural Policy*, Supplement No. 2/75, *Bulletin of the European Communities*, (Brussels, 1975).

European Communities, Commission, *Community Measures for the Approximation of Laws (1972—1974)*, Supplement No. 3/75, *Bulletin of the European Communities* (Brussels, 1975).

Haas, Ernst B., *The Uniting of Europe: Political, Social and Economic Forces, 1950—1957* (Stanford: Stanford University Press, 1958). [Includes bibliography.]

Hilbert, Lothar, *The Stockholm Convention Establishing the European Free Trade Association (EFTA) 1960* (Luxembourg: Faculté Internationale de Droit Comparé, 1962).

Imbert, Armand, *L'union de l'Europe occidentale* (Paris: R. Pichon et R. Durand-Auzias, 1968).

Jensen, Finn B., and Walter, Ingo, *The Common Market: Economic Integration in Europe* (Philadelphia: Lippincott, 1965).

Jürgensen, Harold, *Die westeuropäische Montanindustrie und ihr gemeinsamer Markt* (Göttingen: Vandenhoeck & Ruprecht, 1955).

Lambrinidis, John S., *The Structure, Function, and Law of a Free Trade Area: The European Free Trade Association* (London: Stevens, 1965).

Lerner, Daniel, and Aron, Raymond, *France Defeats EDC* (New York: Praeger, 1957).

Lindsay, Kenneth, *European Assemblies: The Experimental Period, 1949—1959* (New York: Praeger, 1960).

Lister, Louis, *Europe's Coal and Steel Community: An Experiment in Economic Union* (New York: Twentieth Century Fund, 1960).

Marjolin, Robert, 'Economic and Monetary Policy in the Common Market', *Progress* [London], Vol. 54 (Oct—Dec 1970) pp. 38—101.

Marjolin, Robert, *Europe and the United States in the World Economy* (Durham, N.C.: Duke University Press, 1953).

Marjolin, Robert, 'The European Trade and Payments System: A Study in Co-operation', *Lloyds Bank Review*, n.s. No. 31 (Jan 1954) pp. 1—15.

Mason, Henry L., *The European Coal and Steel Community* (The Hague: Nijhoff, 1955).

Mathijsen, Pierre, 'Problems Connected with the Creation of Euratom', in Melvin G. Shimm, Hans W. Baade, and Robinson O. Everett, eds, *European Regional Communities: A New Era on the Old Continent* (Dobbs Ferry, N.Y.: Oceana Publications, 1962) pp. 92—107.

Maury, René, *L'intégration européenne* (Paris: Sirey, 1958).

Mayne, Richard, *The Community of Europe* (London: V. Gollancz, 1962; New York: Norton, 1963).

Meyer, Frederick V., *The European Free-Trade Association: An Analysis of 'The Outer Seven'* (New York: Praeger, 1960).

Oppenheimer, Peter M., 'Monetary Union: A Survey of the Main Issues', *De Economist*, Vol. 122, No. 1 (1974) pp. 23—48.

Organisation for European Economic Co-operation, *European Economic Co-operation: A Survey for the Council of Europe* (Paris: OEEC, annually 1951 to 1956).

Organisation for European Economic Co-operation, *A Decade of Cooperation* (Paris, OEEC, 1958).

Ouin, Marc, *The OEEC and the Common Market: Why Europe Needs an Economic Union of 17 Countries* (Paris: Organisation for European Economic Co-operation, 15 Apr 1958).

Ouin, Marc, 'Liberalisation of Trade', in Organisation for European Economic Co-operation, *At Work for Europe* (Paris: OEEC, 5th ed., 1960) pp. 27—38.

Palmer, Michael; Lambert, John, *et al.*, *European Unity: A Survey of the European Organisations* (London: Allen & Unwin for PEP [Political and Economic Planning], 1968). [With classified bibliography.]

Phillip, André, *The Schuman Plan: Nucleus of a European Community* (Brussels: International Secretariat, European Movement, 1951).

Pinder, John, 'The Community and the Developing Countries: Associates and Outsiders', *Journal of Common Market Studies*, Vol. 12 (Sept 1973) pp. 53—77.

Riley, Reynold C., and Ashworth, Gregory John, *Benelux: An*

Economic Geography of Belgium, the Netherlands, and Luxembourg (New York: Holmes & Meier, 1975).

Robertson, Arthur H., *The Council of Europe: Its Structure, Functions and Achievements* (New York: Praeger, 1956).

Robertson, Arthur H., *European Institutions: Cooperation, Integration, Unification* (New York: Praeger, 1959; 2nd ed., London: Stevens, 1966).

Schlepegrell, Adolf, 'Liberalisation of Invisibles and Capital Movements', In Organisation for European Economic Co-operation, *At Work for Europe* (Paris: OEEC, 5th ed., 1960) pp. 55—62.

Schuman, Robert, 'Origine et Elaboration du "Plan Schuman",' *Cahiers de Bruges*, No. 4 (Dec 1952).

Stikker, Dirk U., 'The Functional Approach to European Integration', *Foreign Affairs*, Vol. 29 (April 1951) pp. 436—44.

Stikker, Dirk U., *Bausteine für eine neue Welt* (Düsseldorf and Vienna: Econ Verlag, 1969).

Strauss, Emil, *Common Sense about the Common Market* (London: Allen & Unwin, 1958).

Wightman, David, *Economic Cooperation in Europe: A Study of the United Nations Economic Commission for Europe* (London: Stevens, 1956).

SUBJECT L: EAST-EUROPEAN CO-OPERATION SINCE 1948

Ágoston, István, *Le marché commun communiste: Principes et pratique du COMECON* (Geneva: Droz, 1965).

Ausch, Sandor, and Bartha, F., 'Theoretical Problems of CMEA Intratrade Prices', in Földi, Tamás, and Kiss, Tibor, *Socialist World Market Prices* (Budapest: Akadémiai Kiadó, and Leyden: A. W. Sijthoff, 1969) pp. 101—27.

Ausch, Sandor, *Theory and Practice of CMEA Cooperation* (Budapest: Akadémiai Kiadó, 1972).

Berend, Ivan T., 'The Problem of Eastern-European Economic Integration in a Historical Perspective', in Vajda, Imre, and Simai, Mihaly, eds, *Foreign Trade in a Planned Economy* (Cambridge: Cambridge University Press, 1971) pp. 1—28.

van Brabant, Jozef M., *Bilateralism and Structural Bilateralism in Intra-CMEA Trade* (Rotterdam: Rotterdam University Press, 1973).

Diachenko, Vasili Petrovich, 'Main Trends in Improving Prices in Trade among CMEA Members', *Problems of Economics*, Vol. 11 (June 1968) pp. 40—9.

Hewett, Edward A., *Foreign Trade Prices in the Council for Mutual Economic Assistance* (London: Cambridge University Press, 1974).

Kaser, Michael, *COMECON: Integration Problems of the Planned Economies* (London: Oxford University Press, 1965; 2nd. ed., 1967). [Nine appendixes on conventions, meetings, and principles.]

Kiss, Tibor, *International Division of Labour in Open Economies, with Special Regard to the CMEA* (Budapest: Akadémiai Kiadó, 1971).

Köhler, Heinz, *Economic Integration in the Soviet Bloc, with an East German Case Study* (New York: Praeger, 1965).

Lavigne, Marie, *Le COMECON: Le programme du COMECON et l'intégration socialiste* (Paris: Cujas, 1973).

Pryor, Frederic L., *The Communist Foreign Trade System: The Other Common Market* (Cambridge: M.I.T. Press, 1963).

Schaefer, Henry Wilcox, *Comecon and the Politics of Integration* (New York: Praeger, 1972).

Uschakow, Alexander, ed., *Der Ostmarkt im COMECON: Eine Dokumentation* (Baden-Baden: Nomos, 1972).

SUBJECT M: LATIN AMERICAN AND CARIBBEAN ISLANDS SINCE 1948

Aitken, Norman D., and Lowry, William R., 'A Cross-Sectional Study of the Effects of LAFTA and CACM on Latin American Trade', *Journal of Common Market Studies*, Vol. 11 (June 1973) pp. 326—36.

Andic, Fuat M., 'Fiscal Aspects of Economic Integration with Special Reference to Selected Caribbean Countries', in Sybil Lewis and Thomas G. Mathews, eds, *Caribbean Integration: Papers on Social, Political, and Economic Integration*, Third Caribbean Scholars Conference, Georgetown, Guyana, 4—9 April 1966 (Rio Piedras, Puerto Rico: University of Puerto Rico, 1967) pp. 38—57.

Andic, Fuat M.; Andic, Suphan; Dosser, Douglas, *A Theory of Economic Integration for Developing Countries: Illustrated by Caribbean Countries* (London: Allen & Unwin, 1971).

Balassa, Bela, 'Regional Integration and Trade Liberalization in Latin America', *Journal of Common Market Studies*, Vol. 10 (Sept 1971) pp. 58—77.

Best, Lloyd, 'Current Development Strategy and Economic Integration in the Caribbean', in Sybil Lewis and Thomas G. Mathews, eds, *Caribbean Integration: Papers on Social, Politi-*

cal, and Economic Integration, Third Caribbean Scholars Conference, Georgetown, Guyana, 4—9 April 1966 (Rio Piedras, Puerto Rico: University of Puerto Rico, 1967) pp. 58—76.

Blough, Roy and Behrman, Jack N., *Problems of Regional Integration in Latin America*, Committee for Economic Development, Supplementary Paper No. 22 (New York: Committee for Economic Development, 1968).

Cochrane, James D., and Sloan, John W., 'LAFTA and the CACM: A Comparative Analysis of Integration in Latin America', *Journal of Developing Areas*, Vol. 8 (Oct 1973) pp. 13—37.

Dell, Sidney, *A Latin American Common Market?* (London, New York, Toronto: Oxford University Press, 1967).

Haas, Ernst B., and Schmitter, Philippe C., *The Politics of Economics in Latin American Regionalism: The Latin American Free Trade Association after Four Years of Operation* (Denver: University of Denver Social Science Foundation, 1965—6).

Hilton, Ronald, ed., *The Movement toward Latin American Unity* (New York and London: Praeger, 1969).

Lleras, Alberto, 'Report on the Ninth International Conference of American States', *Annals of the Organization of American States*, Vol. 1 (No. 1, 1949) pp. 1—75.

Maritano, Nino, *A Latin American Economic Community: History, Policies and Problems* (Notre Dame, Indiana: University of Notre Dame Press, 1970).

Mathis, John F., *Economic Integration in Latin America: The Progress and Problems of LAFTA*, Studies in Latin American Business Series, No. 8 (Austin: Bureau of Business Research, University of Texas at Austin, 1969).

Mikesell, Raymond F., *Liberalization of Inter-Latin American Trade* (Washington: Pan American Union, 1957).

Mikesell, Raymond F., 'The Movement Toward Regional Trading Groups in Latin America', in Albert O. Hirschman, ed., *Latin American Issues: Essays and Comments* (New York: The Twentieth Century Fund, 1961) pp. 125—51.

Milenky, Edward S., *The Politics of Regional Organization in Latin America: The Latin American Free Trade Association* (New York: Praeger, 1973).

Morawetz, David, 'Harmonization of Economic Policies in Customs Unions: The Andean Group', *Journal of Common Market Studies*, Vol. 11 (June 1973) pp. 294—313. [The same article, with a slight change in its title — substituting 'in a Free-Trade Area' for 'in Customs Unions' — appeared in *Welt-*

wirtschaftliches Archiv, Vol. 109, No. 4 (1973) pp. 579—600).]

Organization of American States, 'The Economic Agreement of Bogotá, *Annals of the Organization of American States*, Vol. 1, No. 1 (Washington: Pan American Union, 1949) pp. 99—108.

Perusse, Roland I., *A Strategy for Caribbean Economic Integration* (San Juan, Puerto Rico: North-South Press, 1971).

Schmitter, Philippe C., 'Central American Integration: Spill-Over, Spill-Around or Encapsulation?', *Journal of Common Market Studies*, Vol. 9 (Sep 1970) pp. 1—66.

Sloan, John W., 'Dilemmas of the Latin American Free Trade Association', *Journal of Economic Issues*, Vol. 5 (Dec 1971) pp. 92—108.

Urquidi, Victor L., *Free Trade and Economic Integration in Latin America: The Evolution of a Common Market Policy* (Berkeley: University of California Press, 1962).

Wilford, Walton T., 'The Central American Common Market: Trade Patterns after a Decade of Union', *Nebraska Journal of Economics and Business*, Vol. 12 (Summer 1973) pp. 3—22.

Wionczek, Miguel S., ed., *Latin American Economic Integration: Experiences and Prospects* (New York: Praeger, 1966).

SUBJECT N: AFRICA

Bechtold, Peter K., 'New Attempts at Arab Cooperation: The Federation of Arab Republics, 1971', *Middle East Journal*, Vol. 27 (Spring 1973) pp. 152—72.

Directory of Cooperative Organisations: Africa South of the Sahara, Supplement No. 3 to *Cooperative Information*, International Labour Office Publications (Geneva, 1975).

East African Protectorate, 'Notice regarding the Amalgamation of the Customs Departments of the East Africa and Uganda Protectorates', *Official Gazette of the East African Protectorate* (Nairobi, 1917) p. 314.

El-Agraa, Ali M., 'The Sudan and the Arab Customs Union: a Conflict', *Eastern Africa Economic Review*, Vol. 1 (Dec 1969) pp. 39—51.

Ghai, Dharam P., 'The Association Agreement between the European Economic Community and the Partner States of the East African Community', *Journal of Common Market Studies*, Vol. 12 (Sep 1973) pp. 78—103.

Girgis, Maurice, 'Development and Trade Patterns in the Arab World', *Weltwirtschaftliches Archiv*, Vol. 109, No. 1 (1973) pp. 121—68.

134   *A History of Thought on Economic Integration*

Gitelson, Susan Aurelia, 'Can the UN Be an Effective Catalyst for Regional Integration? The Case of the East African Community', *Journal of Developing Areas*, Vol. 8 (Oct 1973) pp. 65—82.

Great Britain, Colonial Office, *Papers relating to the Question of Closer Union*, Imperial Government Publications (Colonial No. 57, 1931).

Green, Reginald Herbold, *Economic Co-operation in Africa: Retrospect and Prospect* (Nairobi: Oxford University Press, 1967).

Green, Reginald Herbold, and Seidman, Ann, *Unity or Poverty? The Economics of Pan-Africanism* (Harmondsworth: Penguin, 1968).

Hazlewood, Arthur, ed., *African Integration and Disintegration: Case Studies in Economic and Political Union* (London and New York: Oxford University Press, 1962).

Hazlewood, Arthur, 'The Kampala Treaty and the Accession of New Members to the East African Community', *East African Economic Review*, n.s. Vol. 4 (Dec 1968) pp. 49—63.

Massell, Benton F., *East African Economic Union: An Evaluation and Some Implications for Policy* (Santa Monica, California: Rand Corporation, 1963).

Musrey, Alfred G., *An Arab Common Market: A Study in Inter-Arab Trade Relations, 1920—1967* (New York: Praeger, 1969).

Mutharika, B. W. T., *Toward Multinational Economic Cooperation in Africa* (New York: Praeger, 1972).

Ndegwa, Philip, *The Common Market and Development in East Africa*, East African Studies No. 22 (Nairobi: East Africa Publishing House, 1965).

Newton, Arthur Percival, ed., *Select Documents relating to the Unification of South Africa* (London: Longmans, Green & Co., 1924).

Ngoudi, Ngom, *La réussite de l'intégration économique en Afrique* (Paris: Présence africaine, 1971).

Nowzad, Bahram, 'Economic Integration in Central and West Africa', *International Monetary Fund Staff Papers*, Vol. 16 (Mar 1969) pp. 103—39.

Ouattara, A.D., 'Trade Effects of the Association of African Countries with the European Economic Community', *International Monetary Fund Staff Papers*, Vol. 20 (July 1973) pp. 499—543.

Report of the Joint Select Committee on Closer Union in East Africa (3 vols), Imperial Government Publications (London: H.C. 156, 1931).

Reports of the Commission on Closer Union of the Dependencies in Eastern and Central Africa, Imperial Government Publications (London: Cmd. 3234, 1929).

Robson, Peter, *Economic Integration in Africa* (Evanston, Illinois: Northwestern University Press, 1968).

Statement of the Conclusions of HM Government in the United Kingdom as Regards Closer Union in East Africa, Imperial Government Publications (London: Cmd. 3574, 1930).

Tanganyika Territory, 'Customs Agreement [with Kenya, July 8; with Uganda, July 11]', *Tanganyika Territory Gazette Supplement* (Nairobi, 1927) pp. 130, 132.

Union of South Africa, 'Customs Union (Interim Agreement)', *Union of South Africa Government Gazette Extraordinary* (No. 2059, 1948).

RELATING TO SUBJECT O: ASIA

Bienstock, Gregory, *Struggle for the Pacific* (New York: Macmillan, 1937).

Chamberlin, William Henry, *Japan over Asia* (Boston: Little, Brown, 1937).

Clark, Grover, *Place in the Sun* (New York: Macmillan, 1936).

Clyde, Paul Hibbert, *History of the Modern and Contemporary Far East* (New York: Prentice-Hall, 1937).

Greve, Ingo, 'The Paddy Grows in Silence' [on the attempts to build a South East Asian Community of the countries in ASEAN, the Association of South East Asian Nations], *Intereconomics*, Vol. 6 (June 1974) pp. 178–81.

Hudson, Gregory Francis, *Far East in World Politics* (Oxford: Clarendon Press, 1937).

Koo, Vi Kyuiu Wellington, *Memoranda Presented to the Lytton Commission* (New York: The Chinese Cultural Society, 1932–3).

Kramer, Irving I., *Japan in Manchuria* (Tokyo: Foreign Affairs Association of Japan, 1954).

Lederer, Emil, and Lederer-Seidler, Emy, *Japan in Transition* (New Haven: Yale University Press, 1938).

Manchuria, Foreign Office, *Economic Conditions in Manchukuo* (Hsinking, 1940).

Matsuoka, Yosuko, *Economic Cooperation of Japan in Manchuria and Mongolia: Its Motives and Basic Significance* (Dairen, Manchuria, 1929).

Report of the Commission of Enquiry of the League of Nations,

Signed at Peiping September 4, 1932 (Nanking, Waichiaopu, 1932). [Lytton Report.]

Royal Institute of International Affairs, *China and Japan*, Information Department Papers, No. 21 (New York: Oxford University Press, 1938).

Schumpeter, Elizabeth Boody, ed., *The Industrialization of Japan and Manchukuo: 1930—1940* (New York: Macmillan, 1940).

Stewart, John R., 'Japanese Enterprises in North China', *Far Eastern Survey*, Vol. 7, no. 9 (1938) pp. 99—107.

Stimson, Henry L., *Far Eastern Crisis* (New York: Harper, 1936)

Tandon, Rameshwar, 'Regional Trade Co-operation in South-East Asia', *Journal of World Trade Law*, Vol. 8 (Jul—Aug 1974) pp. 388—400.

United States, Library of Congress, Division of Bibliography; Florence S. Hellman, compiler, *The Japanese Empire: Industries and Transportation. A Selected List of References* (Washington: Library of Congress, 1943).

Wightman, David, *Toward Economic Cooperation in Asia: The UN Economic Commission for Asia and the Far East*, published for the Carnegie Endowment for International Peace (New Haven: Yale University Press, 1963).

SUBJECT P: AUSTRALIA

Bentick, Brian, *Prospects of an Australia—New Zealand Economic Union*, Committee for Economic Development of Australia, Study No. 4 (Canberra: Committee for Economic Development of Australia, May 1962).

Crawford, Sir John Grenfell, *Australian Trade Policy, 1942—66* (Canberra: Australian National University Press; and Toronto University of Toronto Press, 1968).

Elkan, Peter G., 'Blueprint for an Area of Quantitatively and Structurally Balanced Free Trade', *Journal of Common Market Studies*, Vol. 5 (Sept 1966) pp. 1—12.

Lloyd, Peter J., *Economic Relationships between Australia and New Zealand* (Canberra: Research School of Pacific Studies, Australian National University, 1976).

Lloyd, Peter J., *New Zealand Manufacturing Production and Trade with Australia*, Research Paper No. 17 (Wellington: New Zealand Institute of Economic Research, 1971).

Perkins, James O. N., *Australia in the World Economy* (Melbourne: Sun Books, 1968).

HISTORIANS' PREDICTIONS AND EXPLANATIONS

Some of the historians of customs unions have entertained very firm ideas on economic or political prerequisites or consequences, and some of these ideas sound a bit odd to us with the hindsight now available. In a fine study (by Pentmann, published in 1917) we can read that any customs union beyond that of a single nation-state — for example, a European customs union — would be impossible as well as undesirable. At least one half of his assertion, and probably all of it, has proved false. Why should a historian stick his neck out on statements of this sort, especially in an otherwise excellent piece of historical research?

More than a few of the historians were infected with the mercantilistic belief in the blessings of exports and, especially, an export surplus. In the papers left by the late Jacob Viner I found a little handwritten note with a delightful quotation. No reference or author, unfortunately, was written on the note, so that I do not know whether it was an authentic quotation or perhaps Viner's invention. (Viner may have composed the fictitious quotation as an examination question.) Here is the statement, which may be given the title 'Beware of Worldwide Integration': 'There is a story told of a German professor, who is said to have explained the decline of the Roman Empire by the fact that, as the Empire grew and grew, in the end it comprised all the known world — and therefore its foreign trade shrank to nothing.'

6 Political Economists as Proponents, Promoters, and Opponents

From my files of contributors to the history of thought on economic integration I shall select for presentation in this chapter those who may appropriately be listed as political economists. Most of them were proponents, promoters, or architects of various schemes of economic integration; some were opponents or dissenters; and a few were neutral observers commenting on possible consequences or on the chances for success.

Some of those included in the survey were great economists, respected for their contributions to economic theory, others were chiefly advocates of a particular cause or project. I shall not tell whom I reckon among the somes and whom among the others, but I may note that double membership in the group of political economists and in the group of theorists (included in Chapter 9) does not reveal my rating. Not every great economist needs to have contributed to the theory of economic integration, although he may have expressed himself on some policy aspect or taken sides in a discussion of a particular proposal. Conversely, to have contributed both to practical-political and to abstract-theoretical thought on economic integration need not make the contributor a great economist.

A few writers who are often classified as economists — say, Bentham and Saint-Simon — will be found in Chapter 7 with the men of letters, because their pleas or plans were chiefly for political integration with hardly any reference to economic relations. The economists selected for the present chapter, and the causes for or against which they argued, will be presented in roughly chronological order — only roughly because some of them acted or published repeatedly over a period of years.

PROPOSALS FOR ECONOMIC INTEGRATION BEFORE 18(

Only three early advocates of national economic integration wi

be included in this section: one arguing for a United Kingdom
of Great Britain, another for German Imperial Integration, and
a third for an economically integrated United States of America.
Not that there were not many more such plans proposed before
1800, but the major activities and achievements of their promoters were in other areas. These men will therefore be regarded
as statesmen, or men of affairs, or men of letters, for whom chapter 7 is reserved. (I may be charged with arbitrary discrimination
for admitting Alexander Hamilton to the ranks of political
economists, but I was anxious to increase the population in this
first section.)

John Digby, Earl of Bristol (1580—1654), argued for reunifi-
cation of England and Scotland into Great Britain. See his pamphlet *A Discourse shewing the Great Happinesse, that hath, and
may still accrue to his Majesties Kingdomes of England and
Scotland, by Re-uniting them into one Great Britain* (London:
1641).

Johann Joachim Becher (1635—82), Austrian mercantilist
and Imperial Commissar for Confiscations, argued for a stronger
currency, for industrialisation and protectionism, for colonisation of the New World, and for what has been called German
Imperial Mercantilism, including the proposal of Bishop Royas
to create a customs union of Austria with Bavaria and Spain. See
his *Politische Discurs* (Frankfurt: J. D. Zunner, 1st ed. 1668,
2nd ed. 1673, 3rd ed. 1688.)

Alexander Hamilton (1757—1804) argued for a full economic
union of the thirteen States of the Confederation, because 'the
commerce of the United States would . . . be much more favourable than that of the thirteen States without union or with partial
union'. (*The Federalist Papers*, New York: Mentor edition, p.
90). In the Constitutional Convention and in the pages of *The
Federalist* (for which he wrote 85 essays) he defended the articles
of the Constitution, particularly the safeguards they provided
against internal trade barriers and for a common tariff on the
external trade of the United States. See *The Federalist* [with
John Jay and James Madison] (New York: 1778; complete
edition, New York: J. and A. M'Lean, 1863); also *Papers on
Public Credit, Commerce and Finance* (New York, 1790—2;
complete edition, New York: Columbia University Press, 1934).

PROPOSALS FOR VARIOUS EUROPEAN ARRANGEMENTS, 1814—1918

This period, from the end of the Napoleonic wars to the end of

World War I, included the formation of the German *Zollverein*, the establishment of the second German Empire, repeated attempts to achieve economic integration of Austria-Hungary with Germany, proposals of alternative economic blocs among various countries of Europe, and a movement for a British Imperial Customs Union. Many economists participated in the discussion of these proposals either as advocates or as opponents. I selected 27 writers for presentation in this group, sixteen of them German or Austrian, five British, four French, one Hungarian and one Italian.

Michael Alexander Lips (1779—1838) argued for a German customs union. See his pamphlet *Der Wiener Congress oder was muss geschehen um Deutschland vor seinem Untergang zu retten* (Erlangen: Chr. Fr. Müller, 1814) and later publications (Nürnberg, 1825; and a long book, Giessen 1833).

Carl Friedrich Nebenius (1784—1857) argued for a German customs union, possibly including Austria. See his memorandum of 1819, reprinted as Appendix of a pamphlet published 1833; also his book *Der deutsche Zollverein, sein System und seine Zukunft* (Carlsruhe: Chr. F. Müller, 1835).

Friedrich List (1789—1846) argued for German economic unification, but also for various other plans; urged placing emphasis on the nation as an ethnic group (as opposed to individuals, on the one hand, and entire humanity on the other), yet wanted to force Holland with its colonies to join the German *Zollverein*; opposed 'cosmopolitical economy' but favoured free trade in agricultural and other primary products. Among his most quotable statements is that 'commercial union and political union are twins; the one cannot come to birth without the other following' (1846). See his memoranda 1819 and many later writings, particularly *Das nationale System der politischen Oekonomie* (Stuttgart: Cossa, 1841), his editorials in his influential review, *Das Zollvereinsblatt*, published from 1843 on, and the essay 'Über den Wert und die Bedingungen einer Allianz zwischen Grossbritannien und Deutschland' (1846, reprinted in *Schriften, Reden, Briefe* (Berlin: Hobbing, 1931) Vol. 7, pp. 267—96.

Karl Heinrich Rau (1792—1870) argued the case of economic integration within the territory of the badly fragmented Germany; he proposed free internal trade, better roads and waterways, free movement of journeymen throughout the federation, and a common tariff on imports from abroad. See 'Anhang' [Appendix] to Rau's German translation, *Malthus und Say über die Ursachen der jetzigen Handelsstockung* (Hamburg: Perthes & Besser, 1821) pp. 298—9. In later years Rau argued against the proposed customs union between the German Zollverein and the Austrian-Hungarian monarchy. See his article 'Die Krisis der Zollunion', *Archiv für politische Ökonomie*, n.s. Vol. 10 (1853).

Adam Heinrich Müller (1779—1829) argued for and against various schemes of German economic union, sometimes favouring multinational unions (including Austria, Hungary, etc.). See his *Vermischte Schriften über Staat, Philosophie und Kunst* (Vienna: Heubner, 1812; 2nd ed., 1817), *Gesammelte Schriften* (Munich: Franz, 1839).

Johannes Scharrer (1785—1844) argued for freer trade beyond customs union. See his pamphlet *Bemerkungen über den deutschen Zollverein und über die Wirkung hoher Zölle in nationalökonomischer Hinsicht* (Nürnberg: Riegel & Wiessner, 1828).

Léon J. Faucher (1803—54) argued for a customs union of France, Belgium, Spain, and Switzerland — because 'nations become productive only through a unification of their capacities' — but he conceived the customs union largely as a step in the direction of worldwide free trade. See his 'Union du Midi', *Revue des Deux Mondes* (1837), republished as a book, *Union du Midi* (Paris: Paulin, 1842).

Robert Torrens (1780—1864) argued for reciprocity in commercial policy and against unilateral abolition of tariffs, because countries could turn the terms of trade against the unprotected country. He also argued for extending 'territorial division of labour' to the widest possible area, and proposed 'a British Commercial league — a colonial Zollverein' with internal free trade. See his collection *The Budget: A Series of Letters on Financial, Commercial and Colonial Policy* (London: Smith Elder & Co., 1841—3).

Richard Cobden (1804—65) argued for universal and also unilateral free trade; campaigned for abolition of the British Corn Laws and the Navigation Act; founded the Anti-Corn-Law League in 1838 and the League for Promotion of Free Trade in 1848; negotiated (with Michel Chevalier) a commercial treaty with France, 1860. See his *Speeches on Questions of Public Policy* (John Bright and J. E. Thorold Rogers, eds, new edition 1878). [For John Bright see Chapter 7.]

Michel Chevalier (1806—79) argued for free trade and agreements for freer trade; negotiated (with Cobden) a trade treaty with Britain, 1860. See his *Cours d'économie politique* (3 vols, Paris: Capelle, 1842—4) and 'Introduction', *Rapports du jury international de l'Exposition Universelle de 1867* (Paris: Paul Dupont, 1868).

John Prince-Smith (1809—74), German economist, argued for free trade and urged agreements for tariff reductions; he opposed the admission of Austria to the German Zollverein, partly because he preferred general use of the most-favoured-nation clause, partly because the inclusion of Austria would presuppose higher external tariffs. He advised the Prussian Government (Delbrück) on commercial policy. See his *Handelsfeindseligkeit und Zollschutz* (Königsberg, 1843); and *Für und wider Schutz- und Differenzialzölle* (Berlin, 1848); also his *Gesammelte Schriften* (Berlin: F. A. Herbig, 1877—80).

Gustave Comte de Molinari (1819—1912) argued for successive geographic extension of customs unions to include all Central Europe (Germany, France, Belgium, Netherlands, Denmark, Switzerland, and Austria-Hungary) as the best way to universal free trade. See his 'L'Union douanière de l'Europe centrale', *Journal des Economistes*, 4e série, Vol. 5 (Jan—Mar 1879) pp. 309—18; also discussion, pp. 337 and 341; again, 5e série, Vol. 28 (Nov 1896) pp. 161ff.

Pierre Paul Leroy-Beaulieu (1843—1916) argued for a less ambitious project of a customs union of France, Belgium, Netherlands, and Switzerland. See his discussion of the 'projet d'union douanière de l'Europe centrale', *Journal des Economistes*, 4e série, Vol. 5 (Jan—Mar 1879) pp. 338ff.

Alexander von Peez (1829—1912), Austrian economist, argued for a European customs union protected against British and American competition. Though he had first doubted whether the countries could ever agree, he became convinced that a Central-European customs union would be established sooner or later. See his *Die amerikanische Konkurrenz* (Wien: Konegen, 1881) and *Englands Vorherrschaft aus der Zeit der Kontinentalsperre* (Leipzig: Duncker & Humblot, 1912).

Lujo Brentano (1844—1931) argued for a Central-European Customs Union of Germany, Austria-Hungary, and Christian parts of the Balkans (definitely excluding France). See his 'Über eine zukünftige Handelspolitik des deutschen Reiches', *Schmollers Jahrbuch für Gesetzgebung, Verwaltung und Volkswirtshaft im deutschen Reich*, Vol. 9 (1885) pp. 1—29.

Albert Eberhard Friedrich Schäffle (1831—1903) argued for a European free-trade area with separate and different tariffs against imports from outside. He promoted a Central-European customs union when he served in 1871 as Minister of Commerce of Austria. Later he proposed a Continental Union [*Festland-*

verein] among the three imperial powers, Germany, Austria-Hungary, and Russia, with access open to all continental European countries. See his 'Abschluss von kombinierten Währungs- und Differentialzollverträgen zwischen den drei Kaiserreichen mit offenem Beitritt für alle festländischen Mächte', and other papers, in his *Gesammelte Aufsätze* (Tübingen: H. Laupp, Vol. 1, 1885; Vol. 2, 1886); and his books *Ein Votum gegen den neuesten Zolltarifentwurf* (Tübingen: H. Laupp, 1901) and *Aus meinem Leben* (Berlin: Hofmann, 1905, 2 Vols).

Vilfredo Pareto (1848—1923) argued for customs unions and other systems of closer commercial relations as means to the improvement of political relations and the maintenance of peace. See his contribution to the *Atti del Congresso di Roma per la pace e per l'arbitrato internazionale* (Città di Castello, 1889). This preceded Pareto's appointment to the University of Lausanne (1893) and the publication of his major works in economics and sociology.

Sandor [Alexander] von Matlekovits (1842—1925) argued for freer trade and, especially, for a European customs union with more effective protection of agriculture against overseas imports; he regarded a customs union between Austria, Hungary, and Germany as an economic necessity. See his book, *Die Zollpolitik der österreichisch-ungarischen Monarchie und des deutschen Reichs seit 1868 und deren nächste Zukunft* (Leipzig: Duncker & Humblot, 1891) and his paper 'Die handelspolitischen Interessen Ungarns', in *Beiträge zur neuesten Handelspolitik Österreichs, Schriften des Vereins für Socialpolitik*, Vol. 93 (1901) pp. 1—60.

August Sartorius Freiherr von Waltershausen (1852—1938) argued the general case of the superiority of large market areas, but warned of the existence of political obstacles in the way to a realisation of the plans for a Central-European customs union or even for a customs union between Germany and the Netherlands. See his articles 'Ein deutsch-niederländischer Zollverein', *Zeitschrift für Sozialwissenschaft*, Vol. 3 (1900) pp. 494—518, and 'Beiträge zur Beurteilung einer wirtschaftspolitischen Foederation von Mitteleuropa', *Zeitschrift für Sozialwissenschaft*, Vol. 5 (1902) pp. 557—70, 674—704, 765—86, and 860—94.

Josef Gruntzel (1866—1934) argued for trade agreements in preference to customs unions and proposed a 'tariff alliance' between Austria and Germany. See his papers 'Ein Zoll-und Handelsbündnis mit Deutschland', *Vorträge der Gesellschaft österreichischer Volkswirte* (Wien: Gesellschaft Österreichischer Volkswirte, 1900), and 'Die handelspolitischen Beziehungen

Deutschlands and Österreich-Ungarns', in *Beiträge zur neuesten Handelspolitik Österreichs, Schriften des Vereins für Social-politik*, Vol. 93 (1901) pp. 61—101; also his book *Handelspolitik und Ausgleich in Österreich-Ungarn* (Wien: Alfred Hölder, 1912).

Sir Robert Giffen (1837—1910) argued against proposals of a 'British Zollverein', chiefly on grounds of overwhelming practical difficulties, and against the movement for Imperial Preference arrangements, chiefly on grounds of economic disadvantages, especially the disruption of Britain's foreign trade that would result from such a protectionist policy. See his article 'The Dream of a British Zollverein', *Nineteenth Century*, May 1902; reprinted as Chapter XXX in his *Economic Inquiries and Studies* (London: G. Bell & Sons, 1904) Vol. II, pp. 387—404.

Charles F. Bastable (1855—1945) argued against the plan for an Imperial Customs Union or Customs Preference. It would 'divert two-thirds of the foreign . . . trade of the United Kingdom into the Colonial direction'; it would be 'thoroughly bad', because 'the cheapest sources of supply for many articles of prime necessity are outside, not within the empire'. The scheme 'rests on the false economic idea that trade between members of the same political body is better than trade with foreigners . . . The true line of progress lies in greater freedom of commerce for and with all countries.' See his note 'An Imperial Zollverein with Preferential Tariffs', *Economic Journal*, Vol. 12 (Dec 1902) pp. 507—13.

Arthur Cecil Pigou (1877—1959) argued against Imperial Preference, after he had carefully analysed the conceivable benefits and the likely costs of a preferential tariff favouring the British colonies. If there were some political and moral benefits to be expected from Imperial Preference — which he considered to be unlikely — bounties would be a better means to that end than preferential duties. See his book *Protective and Preferential Import Duties* (London: Macmillan, 1906).

Gerhard Hildebrand (18??—19??) argued for a Western European customs union, to prevent excessive industrialisation and monopolisation of European countries under national tariff protection. See his book *Die Erschütterung der Industrieherrschaft und des Industriesozialismus* (Jena: G. Fischer, 1910).

Wilhelm Gerloff (1880—1954) argued for an economic union between Austria-Hungary and an expanded Germany (including the Low Countries) as a sufficiently large area for internal free trade with protection from outside competition. See his pamphlet, *Der wirtschaftliche Imperialismus und die Frage der Zolleinigung zwischen Deutschland und Österreich-Ungarn* (No. 45 of

the series *Der Deutsche Krieg*, Stuttgart and Berlin: Deutsche
Verlags-Anstalt, 1915).

Gustav Schmoller (1838–1917) argued for a 'common market
of 120 million people' through a customs union between Germany and Austria-Hungary to be achieved gradually, beginning
immediately [during World War I] with a system of preferential
tariffs, which, however, he would also accept as a permanent
solution if the fear of excessive competition were too great and
could not be sufficiently reduced through the hope for restraints
through cartels. Schmoller went even beyond the two large
countries of the Entente and proposed that Belgium and Poland
(to become independent after the war) join the customs union.
He made this plea despite his conviction that it was 'a historical
rule'[1] that political union has to precede commercial union, and
that the German Zollverein had been 'the one considerable
exception'. See his article 'Die Handels- und Zollannäherung
Mitteleuropas', *Schmollers Jahrbuch für Gesetzgebung, Verwaltung und Volkswirtschaft im Deutschen Reich*, Vol. 40, No. 2
(1916) pp. 529–50, especially pp. 529, 538–9, 543, 548. In
earlier writings he had argued against the most-favoured-nation
clause and for a system of differential tariffs: a general tariff on
imports from countries with which there is no trade agreement,
a preferential tariff for imports under trade agreements, and a
concessionary tariff for neighbouring countries with close ties of
friendship. See his review of a book by Alexander Peez in the
*Jahrbuch für Gesetzgebung, Verwaltung und Volkswirtschaft im
Deutschen Reich*, Vol. XIX (1895) p. 1053. In another paper,
he had argued that the twentieth century must bring close co-
hesion [*Zusammenhalten*] of the countries of Central Europe
against the competition from the economic world powers. See
'Die Wandlungen in der europäischen Handelspolitik des 19.
Jahrhunderts', *Jahrbuch für Gesetzgebung, Verwaltung und
Volkswirtschaft im Deutschen Reich*, Vol. 24 (1900) p. 382.

Karl Kautsky (1854–1938) argued, in a booklet on *Die
Vereinigten Staaten Mitteleuropas* (Stuttgart: H. W. Dietz,
1916), that the idea of a Federation of Central Europe was inspired by nationalistic and imperialistic sentiments. His argument
was chiefly a critique of Naumann's *Mitteleuropa* [see Chapter 7
below, p. 165], where it had been said, among other things, that
'Central Europe would in essence be German'. Kautsky distinguished between the nation-state and the multi-nationalities

---

[1] In some references this dictum was rendered in English as 'historical
law', though Schmoller had written *Regel*.

state (*Nationalitätenstaat*) and expected serious conflicts in the latter. Kautsky, rejecting a Central European Federation, would favour a United States of Europe, both for economic and for political reasons, and possibly at a time when the proletariat had become so powerful that its triumph was assured (p. 48).

PROPOSALS FOR EUROPEAN CUSTOMS UNION, 1918—39

After World War I a strong movement for European economic union was launched, chiefly by statesmen and men of affairs, though some of the latter were more interested in industrial integration (in the sense of international cartellisation) than in economic integration (in the sense of more extensive international division of labour. Economists, with a few exceptions, were cool to such proposals. Thus we find few economists who endorsed the economic schemes designed by the political integrationists of the time. We should bear in mind that the period between the two world wars was characterised by disastrous economic disintegration engineered by restrictive and protectionist governmental policies.

Wladimir S. Woytinsky (1885—1960) argued for a United States of Europe, with socialist features, to include Great Britain and the Soviet Union. See his *Die Vereinigten Staaten von Europa* (Berlin: J. H. W. Dietz Nachfolger, 1926).

Franz Eulenburg (1867—1943) argued against the idea of a European customs union for several reasons: to exclude Britain would be against German and French interests, but to include the British empire would be quite impossible; the customs union would undoubtedly be highly protectionistic; the problems of monetary stability and fiscal order would have to be solved first; the interests of the weaker members would have to be protected at the expense of the stronger members, with the result that an inefficient organisation of the division of labour would be perpetuated or the union would be dissolved; Germany had more to gain from closer relations with Britain and the United States. See his paper 'Gegen die Idee einer europäischen Zollunion' in Hanns Heiman, ed., *Europäische Zollunion* (Berlin: Hobbing, 1926) pp. 109—21; also his book *Aussenhandel und Aussenhandelspolitik*, Grundriss der Sozialökonomik, Vol. VIII (Tübingen: Mohr (Siebeck), 1929).

Gustav Stolper (1888—1947) argued that a European customs union was either useless — since the economic benefits would be attained faster and more simply by means of a policy of free

trade — or it would have to be a supranational federation of the
European nations. See his paper 'Staat — Nation — Wirtschaft:
Zur Problematik der Europäischen Zollunion', in Hanns Heiman,
ed., *Europäische Zollunion* (Berlin: Hobbing, 1926), pp. 45—60,
esp. pp. 59—60.

Alfred Weber (1868—1958) argued for parallel and successive
reductions of all European tariffs on external as well as intra-
European trade. Protection of European producers was unhelp-
ful, even for infant industries; protection against dumping might
be needed, with antidumping duties determined by an international commission. See his paper 'Europa als Weltindustriezen-
trum und die Idee der Zollunion', in Hanns Heiman, ed., *Europäische Zollunion* (Berlin: Hobbing, 1926) pp. 122—32.

Elemer Hantos (1881—1942) argued for a European customs
union with a strong admixture of industrial combinations. See
his 'Der europäische Zollverein', *Weltwirtschaftliches Archiv*,
Vol. XXIII (1926) pp. 229—38, and his books *Europäischer
Zollverein und mitteleuropäische Wirtschaftsgemeinschaft*
(Berlin: Organisation Verlagsgesellschaft, 1928) and *L'Europe
centrale: une nouvelle organisation economique* (Paris: Alcan,
1932).

William E. Rappard (1883—1958) argued for 'economic peace'
and 'co-operation' at a time of complete disunity and economic
warfare through restrictive, discriminatory, and unpredictable
policies; he hoped that 'from the progressive realisation of the
inevitably increasing interdependence of all nations' eventually
some 'progress of international co-operation' could be expected.
See his book, *Uniting Europe* (New Haven: Yale University
Press, 1930), especially pp. 148 and 302.

Paul van Zeeland (born 1893) argued consistently, over a
period of more than forty years, for European economic co-
operation and federation; as Belgian Prime Minister and as President of the Economic League for European Co-operation he
acted as a steadfast 'European'. See, among his many writings,
A View of Europe, 1932 (Baltimore: Johns Hopkins Press, 1933);
*Report Presented to the Governments of the United Kingdom
and France on the Possibility of Obtaining a General Reduction
of the Obstacles to International Trade (January 1938)* (London:
HM Stationery Office, 1938); *and International Economic Reconstruction* (New York: Garland Publ., 1972).

Sir [James] Arthur Salter (1881—1974) argued for a gradual
economic rapprochement in Europe. See his book, *United States
of Europe and Other Papers* (London: Allen & Unwin, 1933).

Barbara Wootton (born 1897) argued that all plans for an

economic union of European countries be abandoned as hopelessly unrealistic 'textbook economics'. 'The first effect of a
complete abolition of all trade restrictions throughout the Union
would unquestionably be to fling millions out of employment.'
See her article 'Economic Problems of Federal Union', *The New
Commonwealth Quarterly*, Vol. V (September 1939) pp. 152—3.

PROPOSALS FOR ECONOMIC AND MONETARY INTEGRA-TION, 1943—74

In this period of only a little more than thirty years many proposals for regional and worldwide integration were debated by
economists and several of the proposals were actually put into
effect. The European Common Market, at first promoted most
strongly by economic advisers to the Government of the United
States, became a reality, though with serious exceptions for
agriculture and restrictions on competition in coal and steel. The
majority of the 26 economists presented in this section are
British and American. Several of them were rather sceptical in
the beginning, and some have never become convinced of the
blessings claimed by others as having resulted, or going to result,
from the adoption of particular schemes. Plans for monetary
integration seemed at first less controversial than those for trade
and factor movements; in the end, however, economists became
hopelessly divided on international or regional monetary arrange
ments.

   Gottfried Haberler (born 1900) argued in favour of general
free (or freer) trade and against customs unions and any other
form of regional integration, the only exception being a complete customs union without any restrictions on internal trade —
preferably even without checkpoints on the common frontiers
of member countries — and with very low tariffs on imports
from non-member countries. He warned against a customs unior
becoming an instrument of protectionism in countries which
previously have had low tariffs. Among Haberler's many publications on these questions, see especially his essays 'The Politica
Economy of Regional or Continental Blocs', in Seymour E.
Harris, ed., *Postwar Economic Problems* (New York: McGraw-
Hill, 1943) pp. 325—44; 'Die wirtschaftliche Integration Europas
in Erwin von Beckerath *et al.*, eds, *Wirtschaftsfragen der freien
Welt* [Festschrift for Chancellor Ludwig Erhard] (Frankfurt
a.M.: Fritz Knapp, 1957) pp. 521—30; 'Bemerkungen zum Prob
lem des wirtschaftlichen Regionalismus', in Franz Greiss and

'ritz W. Meyer, eds, *Wirtschaft, Gesellschaft und Kultur* [Fest-chrift for Alfred Müller-Armack] (Berlin: Dunker & Humblot, 961) pp. 415—24; and 'Probleme der wirtschaftlichen Integra-ion Europas', in Herbert Giersch, ed., *Bernhard-Harms Vorles-ngen* No. 5/6 (Kiel: Institut für Weltwirtschaft, 1974) pp. 13—6.

Harry Dexter White (1892—1948), Director of Monetary Research in the US Department of the Treasury, argued for an nternational Stabilization Fund to help countries in payments leficits maintain fixed exchange rates at gold par values; he was nstrumental, in collaboration with John Maynard Keynes, in etting up the International Monetary Fund at the Bretton Voods Conference in July 1944. See his article 'Postwar Currency tabilization', *American Economic Review*, Supplement, Vol. XXIII (March 1943) pp. 382—7, and the *Preliminary Draft Outline of a Proposal for an International Stabilization Fund of he United and Associated Nations* (Washington: Treasury Department, 7 April 1943).

John Maynard Keynes (1883—1946), later Lord Keynes, peaking for the British Treasury, argued for an International 'learing Union to aid countries in payments deficit, but with utomatic adjustments of exchange rates to restore equilibrium oth for surplus countries accumulating excessive balances and or deficit countries accumulating excessive debt to the Union. Ie regarded the International Monetary Fund, which he helped o establish at the Bretton Woods Conference, as an instrument or greater flexibility of exchange rates. See his *Proposals for an nternational Clearing Union* (London: HM Stationery Office, md. 6437, 8 April 1943); also his speeches in *Parliamentary Debates* (Hansard), Fifth Series, Vol. 127, House of Lords, Third Volume of Session of 1942—43 (London: HM Stationery Office, 943), cols 527—37, and Vol. 131, House of Lords, Second Volume of Session of 1943—44 (London: HM Stationery Office, 944) cols 838—49.

Willard Long Thorp (born 1899) argued that European ecovery required an integrated programme involving the mutual owering of trade barriers, the creation of multilateral payments ystem, and an organisation for the review of each European ountry's requirements and prospects. As Assistant Secretary of tate for Economic Affairs from 1946 to 1954, administering he post-UNRRA Relief Act and the Interim Aid programmes, e collaborated with Acheson, Clayton, Benjamin Cohen and ther officials (see Chapter 7) in developing and promoting the Marshall Plan for assistance to, and greatly increased economic

co-operation among, the participating countries. See his testimony at various hearings of the US Congress, and *Trade, Aid, (
What?* (Baltimore: Johns Hopkins Press, 1954).

Harold Van Buren Cleveland (born 1916) argued for 'rapid a
dramatic progress toward the economic and political unificatio
of continental Western Europe' and, in particular, for assistanc
to European countries combined with pressures leading to thei
economic integration; as an economist in the Economic Develc
ment Division of the US Department of State, he wrote in 194
(jointly with Ben T. Moore and Charles P. Kindleberger) an influential memorandum, which became one of the inputs for th
Marshall Plan. See also his pamphlet (jointly with Theodore
Geiger) *Making Western Europe Defensible* (Washington:
National Planning Association, August 1951) and his book *The
Atlantic Idea and Its European Rivals* (New York: McGraw-Hil
1966).

Charles P. Kindleberger (born 1910) argued for European
economic integration; as Executive Secretary of the Committe
on European Recovery Program, organised in the US Departmc
of State on 25 June 1947 to study the projected aid programn
— the Marshall Plan — he prepared a substantial body of 'background and operating materials'. See US Department of State,
Foreign Relations of the United States, 1947, Vol. III (Washin,
ton: Government Printing Office, 1972) p. 370.

Robert Marjolin (born 1911) argued for fast progress of
economic integration in the European Common Market and fo
a linking of commercial and financial rules through an intra-
European trade-and-payments system. He was influential both
as a negotiator for France and as an international civil servant.
He participated in the organisation of the Conference for Euro
pean Economic Co-operation in 1947; a year later he became
Secretary General of the Organization for European Economic
Co-operation (OEEC), serving until 1955; he had a hand in setting up the European Payments Union (EPU) in 1950; from
1955 to 1957 he was French negotiator of the Treaty of Rome
and finally Vice-President of the Commission of the European
Economic Community (EEC) from 1958 to 1967. Among his
publications see especially his *Urgent Economic Problems:
Memorandum of the Secretary General* (Paris: OEEC, 1950),
and his book *Europe and the United States in the World
Economy* (Durham, N.C.: Duke University Press, 1953).

Adam Denzil Marris (born 1906) argued, after the Committ
of European Economic Co-operation had been established in
accordance with the Marshall Plan, that 'none of the governmen

or peoples of Western Europe is prepared to face the economic, financial, and social consequences of any real measures of integration'. See his book *Prospects for Closer European Economic Integration* (London: Royal Institute of International Affairs, 1948) p. 17.

Sir Roy Harrod (born 1900) argued against a European Customs Union[2] and for a European Free-Trade Area; against European 'unification of currencies' and for worldwide inter-convertibility of currencies; against intra-European exchange-rate fixing and for 'intra-union flexibility'; against attempts to achieve uniform tax systems, social-security systems, etc., and for leaving countries free to do their own thing as long as they avoid 'unneighbourly policies'; against restrictions on capital movements and for 'agreed specialisation' in developing countries with investment by previous agreement directed 'in each separate country'. See his articles 'European Union', *Lloyds Bank Review*, n.s. No. 9 (July 1948) pp. 1—20; 'European Economic Co-operation: A British Viewpoint', *Public Finance*, Vol. 5, No. 4 (1950) pp. 538—47; and 'Economic Development and Asian Regional Co-operation', *Pakistan Development Review*, Vol. 2, No. 1 (1962) pp. 1—22.

Ralph G. Hawtrey (1879—1975) argued for an economic union of Western Europe, but with warnings that it might become a prelude to a 'formal Federation', subject to 'the incompatibility of British political practices and habits with those of the Continent'; however, a 'joint council representing Governments' might be workable, and the United Kingdom 'would play its part in both the union and the Commonwealth'. See his book *Western European Union: Implications for the United Kingdom* (London: Royal Institute of International Affairs, 1949), especially pp. 79 and 118—19.

Richard F. Kahn (born 1905), later Lord Kahn, argued in 1949 for the establishment of a European payments scheme, setting up a multilateral clearing house for current transactions, with semi-annual or annual balances to be settled in gold or dollars, not at par values, but with a 'European Discount' periodically adjusted to reflect the combined balance *vis-à-vis* non-member countries. See his articles, 'A Possible Intra-European Payments Scheme', *Economica*, n.s. Vol. 16 (Nov 1949)

[2]'. . . a Customs Union in the traditional meaning of an area with no internal tariff obstructions and one identical tariff wall against all those outside the area would be unacceptable to Britain. The difficulties are insuperable, and wishful thinking which hopes to overcome them is doomed to disappointment.' *Lloyds Bank Review*, n.s. No. 9 (July 1948) p. 11.

pp. 293—304, and 'The European Payments Union', *Economica*, n.s. Vol. 17 (Aug 1950) pp. 306—16.

Lionel Robbins (born 1898), later Lord Robbins, argued for an Atlantic rather than a European or Western European Community, because the latter would tend towards restrictive regionalism. See his 'Towards the Atlantic Community', *Lloyds Bank Review*, New Series, No. 17 (July 1950) pp. 1—24; reprinted in his book *The Economist in the Twentieth Century* (London: Macmillan, 1954) pp. 170—97. Much earlier he had stated that 'there must be neither [mere] alliance nor complete unification, neither *Staatenbund* [confederation] nor *Einheitsstaat* [centralisation] but *Bundesstaat* [federation] . . .' See his book *Economic Planning and International Order* (London: Macmillan, 1937) p. 245

Maurice Allais (born 1911) argued for an Atlantic Community, which however could be established by extension of the European Common Market to the British Isles and the North American countries. See, among several other publications, his *Manifesto for an Atlantic Union*, which was adopted by the Committee for an Atlantic Community in April 1951, and his book *L'Europe Unie: Route de la Prospérité* (Paris: Calmann-Levy: 1960).

Robert Triffin (born 1911) argued for the simultaneous dismantling of bilateral arrangements and elimination of all quantitative restrictions on trade and payments; he was among the architects of the European Payments Union (July 1950) with its automatic credits to cushion imbalances of payments. See his article 'Aspects de la reconstruction monétaire de l'Europe', *Revue d'Economie Politique*, Vol. 60 (Jan—Feb 1950) pp. 5—36; his essay 'Institutional Developments in the Intra-European Monetary System', in *Money, Trade, and Economic Growth*, in honour of John H. Williams (New York: Macmillan, 1951) pp. 33—57; and his book *Europe and the Money Muddle: From Bilateralism to Near-Convertibility, 1947—1956* (New Haven: Yale University Press, 1957).

Jan Tinbergen (born 1903) argued for 'positive' [dirigist], not merely 'negative' [liberalising] measures of integration, and held that economic integration presupposes that countries centralise at a supranational level numerous instruments of economic policy, including those designed to achieve greater equalisation of incomes within and among countries. See his *International Economic Integration* (Amsterdam: Elsevier, 1954, revised edition 1965).

Wilhelm Röpke (1899—1966) argued for worldwide economic integration based on free trade and competitive markets without

dirigiste governmental interventions. He considered functional
and sectoral integration as hindrances to real integration. See his
essay 'Integration und Desintegration der internationalen Wirtschaft', in Erwin von Beckerath *et al.*, eds, *Wirtschaftsfragen
der freien Welt* [Festschrift for Chancellor Ludwig Erhard]
(Frankfurt a.M.: Fritz Knapp, 1957) pp. 493—501; and his book
International Order and Economic Integration (Dordrecht:
Reisel Publ. Co., 1959).

Pierre Uri (born 1911), as Director of Economic Affairs of
the Coal and Steel Community and as one of the drafters of the
Treaty of Rome (1957), argued for the realisation of European
economic integration. See his article 'Europäische Gemeinschaft
für Kohle und Stahl', *Handwörterbuch der Sozialwissenschaften*
(Stuttgart-Tübingen-Göttingen: Fischer-Mohr-Vandenhoeck &
Ruprecht, 1965) Vol. 3, pp. 364—71. Later he worked for the
Atlantic Institute and produced his book *Dialogue des Conti-
nents* (Paris: Plon, 1965) and its English version, *Partnership for
Progress: A Program for Transatlantic Action* (New York:
Harper & Row, 1963), in which he discussed various aspects of
the simultaneous operation of 'European Community and
Atlantic Partnership'.

Alfred Müller-Armack (born 1901) argued for an accommodation between EEC and EFTA through harmonisation of their
tariffs *vis-à-vis* third countries and free trade with one another
for all goods for which such tariff harmonisation was achieved
(1960—1); he had for several years been State Secretary in the
Ministry of Economics, negotiating for Germany and trying to
liberalise the EEC arrangements. See his book *Auf dem Weg
nach Europa: Erinnerungen und Ausblicke* (Tübingen: R. Wun-
derlich, 1971).

James E. Meade (born 1907) argued against the regime of
fixed exchange rates, and in favour of flexibility in the form of
sliding rates, adjusted in small but frequent steps, determined
preferably by an international monetary authority; he also
argued against European monetary integration if it involves fixed
exchange rates among the currencies of the member countries,
and in favour of the creation of a European currency defined as
a bag of national currencies in a constant or (preferably) adjustable combination. See his articles 'The International Monetary
Mechanism', *Three Banks Review*, No. 63 (Sept 1964), pp.
3—25; 'Exchange Rate Flexibility', *Three Banks Review*, No. 70
(June 1966), pp. 3—27; and his paper 'European Monetary
Union' in *Study Group on Economic and Monetary Union:
European Economic Integration and Monetary Unification*

(Brussels: Commission of the European Communities, 1973) pp. 89—105.

John H. Williamson (born 1937) argued for an exchange-rate system with the kind of flexibility proposed by Meade in 1944 but based on par values which, however, are adjusted frequently by minute amounts. The 'crawling peg' would change at a maximum rate of 1/26th of 1 per cent per week, and thus not much more than 2 per cent a year. See The Crawling Peg (Princeton: International Finance Section, 1965) p. 2. Later, Williamson argued that the inability of the United States to devalue the dollar in terms of other currencies be removed by choosing another 'pivot for parities', for example the Special Drawing Right. See The Choice of a Pivot for Parities (Princeton: International Finance Section, 1971). By properly regulating the creation of SDRs, their value can be kept stable in terms of a weighted average of currencies (p. 26). As rapporteur, jointly with Giovanni Magnifico, for a working group on European Monetary Integration (London: Federal Trust for Education and Research, February 1972), Williamson argued for the establishment of a European Bank issuing a new monetary unit, the 'Europa', in the form of deposit liabilities to central and commercial banks. In the beginning, Europa deposits would circulate in parallel with existing European currencies; parity changes, and also exchange-rate fluctuations within a band around parity, would be permissible. Eventually, when perfect harmonisation of institutions and co-ordination of policies are achieved, internal exchange-rate changes can be dispensed with; when ultimately economic union provides the necessary conditions, the national currencies can be withdrawn and replaced by the Europa as the common currency.

Kiyoshi Kojima (born 1920) argued for the establishment of a Pacific Free Trade Area, comprising the United States, Canada, Japan, Australia, and New Zealand, and also for a Pacific Currency Area with all exchange rates fixed in relation to the US dollar. See his articles 'A Pacific Economic Community and Asian Developing Countries' and 'Japan's Interest in Pacific Trade Expansion: PAFTA Reconsidered', Hitotsubashi Journal of Economics, Vol. 7 (June 1966) pp. 17—37, and Vol. 9 (June 1968) pp. 1—31, respectively; his book Japan and a Pacific Free Trade Area (London: Macmillan, 1971); and his article 'A Pacific Currency Area: A New Approach to International Monetary Reform', Hitotsubashi Journal of Economics, Vol. 10 (Feb 1970), pp. 1—17.

Heinz W. Arndt (born 1915) argues against Kojima's proposals for a Pacific Free Trade and Currency Area. See his articles 'PAFTA: An Austrialian Assessment', *Intereconomics* (Hamburg, October 1967), and 'A Pacific Currency Area: Comment', *Hitotsubashi Journal of Economics*, Vol. 11 (Feb 1971) pp. 67—72.

Raymond Barre (born 1924) argued for monetary integration and unification in the European Community, which he served as Vice President of the Commission from 1967 to 1972; he argued against flexibility of exchange rates and for the narrowest possible band for deviations from fixed parities. He advocated the 'snake', the narrow band within which the dollar-exchange rates of European currencies should move. See his *Memorandum de la Commission au Conseil sur la coordination des politiques économiques et la coopération monétaire au sein de la Communauté* (February 1969); his *Communication de la Commission au Conseil au sujet de l'élaboration d'un plan par étapes vers une union économique et monétaire* (March 1970); and his essay 'L'integration économique et monétaire européenne: problèmes et perspectives', in the volume edited by Ramond Barre, *La Monnaie et l'economie de notre temps: melanges en l'honneur de Professeur Emile James* (Paris: Cujas, 1974) pp. 1—13.

Pierre Werner (born 1913), Prime Minister of Luxembourg and Chairman of a monetary committee of the Commission of the European Communities, argued for the establishment of a European Monetary Union in several stages, beginning with a narrowing of the band of permissible fluctuations of exchange rates around fixed parities, proceeding to closer co-ordination of the fiscal and monetary policies of the member countries, then to a fusion of their national banks and eventually to the issuance of a common European currency. See *Report to the Council and the Commission on the Realisation by Stages of Economic and Monetary Union in the Community* (Brussels and Luxembourg: European Communities, 1970).

Giovanni Magnifico (born 1931) argued against the approach to monetary union recommended by the Werner Report, and for early establishment of a European bank of issue, creating a 'dual monetary system' with 'partial internal flexibility of exchange rates in the process of integration'. See his Princeton Essay No. 88, *European Monetary Unification for Balanced Growth: A New Approach* (Princeton: International Finance Section, 1971); his report (jointly with John Williamson) on *European Monetary Integration* (London: Federal Trust for Education and Research, February 1972); and his book *European Monetary Unification* (London: Macmillan, 1973).

Nicholas Kaldor (born 1908), later Lord Kaldor, argued against the British entry into the European Economic Community, both because of the heavy initial cost (higher prices of agricultural products, large payments into the agricultural fund, and a high burden of required adjustments of the balance of payments) and because of adverse long-term effects on British trade. See his 'The Truth about the "Dynamic Effects"', *New Statesman*, 12 March 1971; reproduced as 'The Dynamic Effects of the Common Market' in Douglas Evans, ed., *Destiny or Delusion: Britain and the Common Market* (London: Victor Gollancz, 1971) pp. 59—91.

Robert Mundell (born 1932) argued for years that exchange rates between currencies of large nations with limited international factor mobility should be flexible, and that only the currencies of countries within a region of perfect mobility of labour and capital should be linked by fixed exchange rates. Later, however, he argued for rigid rates even on an interregional scale. He proposed schemes for a European Currency Unit (ECU) with fixed parities maintained in the exchange markets through interventions of the national authorities buying the ECU and the European authority buying national currencies. See his memorandum 'Why Europa' in *Study Group on Economic and Monetary Union: European Economic Integration and Monetary Unification* (Brussels: European Communities, Oct 1973) Part II, pp. 110—19.

Herbert Giersch (born 1921) argued for regional policies in the European Community to offset over-congestion in urban industrialised areas. Excessive build-up of industrial sites is unduly promoted by the customs union and especially by equal-pay policies raising wages in backward areas. To counteract urban congestion, Giersch proposed that rents should not be kept from rising and commuting cost should not be subsidised; that taxes be levied on increments in land values and on public services, with the revenues used for subsidies to less developed areas. See, besides earlier articles of 1949 and 1957, his memorandum 'The Case for European Regional Policy', in *Study Group on Economic and Monetary Union: European Economic Integration and Monetary Unification* (Brussels: European Communities, Oct 1973) Part II, pp. 67—73.

7 Statesmen, Men of Affairs, and Men of Letters

As I proceed to the third group of men whose names should not be omitted in a history of thought on economic unification or integration, two brief reminders may be permitted: one, that the economic integration proposed or opposed may be national, regional, or worldwide; the other, that the inclusion of a name in this group of men need not imply a judgement that the person here named cannot be regarded as a political economist. Persons are listed as statesmen, men of affairs, or men of letters because it is chiefly in these capacities or for achievements in these fields that they have become known to the world.

It would be possible to separate men of letters, statesmen, and men of affairs; but an attempt to make such fine distinctions would surely be too arbitrary. If, for example, a successful industrialist becomes a member of a legislative body or a delegate to an international organisation, it would be captious to decide where he has made his name or where he has been more successful.

What kind of ordering would be most expedient? A strictly chronological order would present the difficulty of choosing between years of births, appointments, or pertinent events, perhaps of several political proposals, actions, or publications in different years. An ordering by nationality would be inconvenient in numerous instances in which the person's career was in more than one country. An alphabetical ordering would be almost nonsensical for our purposes. Let us decide in favour of an approximately chronological order of the most pertinent actions or publications.

KINGS, COURTIERS, AND PHILOSOPHERS, 1459—1814

Our chronological survey has rather distinguished beginnings: two heads of state and a great scholar of the fifteenth and six-

teenth centuries. Their ambitions for territorial integration wer
of diverse scope: a united Europe, a united Germany, the unioi
of England and Scotland. The seventeenth century is represente
by four statesmen and two churchmen — one, however, in botr
categories — three of them French, one Spanish-Austrian, and
one English-American. From the eighteenth century and the
early years of the nineteenth (always counting the years of
action or publication, not the years of birth) we shall meet
exclusively men of letters — philosophers and publicists — three
French, three German, and one English. Pacification and political integration were the primary concern of most of the fifteen
advocates covered in this section, but economic integration was
a major consideration of some. In a few instances national unifi
cation was the objective, but several of the plans aimed at mult
national association or federation.

George of Podiebrad (1420—71), elected King of Bohemia in
1458, proposed in 1459, on the advice of his French counsellor
Antoine Marini, a European federation, chiefly as a means of
uniting Christendom against the threat of the Muslim Turks. Th
plan provided for mutual defence against outside aggression,
arbitration of conflicts among member countries, a Federal
Assembly of heads of state with majority vote, a Federal budge
financed by contributions from all member countries, Federal
(international) civil servants, and a Federal army. No provisions
were made regarding trade among the members.[1] See the text o
his *Compactata*, in Lenglet du Fresnoy, ed., *Mémoires de Philip
de Commines* (London and Paris, 1747).

Desiderius Erasmus of Rotterdam (1466—1536), Dutch
humanist and theologian, published in his *Institutio principiis
Christiani* (1521) a plan for the economic unification of
Germany.

Edward Seymour, Duke of Somerset (c. 1506—52), Lord
Protector of England in the reign of Edward VI, proposed in
1548 a union with Scotland. Ignoring the claim to suzerainty
(revived by Henry VIII), he promised Scots autonomy with free
trade and equal privileges with England. See 'Somerset's Epistle
to the Nobility of Scotland', in *The Complaynt of Scotland*
(London, 1549; republished London: N. Trübner & Co., for the
Early English Text Society, 1872) pp. 238—46.

[1] For more information on George of Podiebrad see László Ledermann
Les précurseurs de l'organisation internationale (Neuchâtel: de la Baconni
1945) pp. 58—68.

Emeric Crucé, alias *Emery Lacroix* (c. 1590—1648), a French monk and writer, a true pacifist, tolerant of religious and ethnic diversity, pleaded for a worldwide, not merely European, con- federation — including Turkey, Morocco, Persia, China, Japan, and Mongolia. His chief aim was world peace, but he explicitly included freedom of movement for people and goods. He pointed to an interdependence between free trade and peace among nations. He also called for a uniform world currency and for uniformity of weights and measures. See his *Le nouveau Cynée, ou Discours des Occasions et Moyens d'establir une Paix Génér- ale, et la Liberté du Commerce Par Tout le Monde* (Paris 1623), reproduced in Thomas Willing Balch, *Emeric Crucé* (Philadelphia: Allen, Lane & Scott, 1900).[2]

Maximilien de Bethune, Duc de Sully (1560—1641), French statesman, secretary of state under King Henry IV, published in 1634 a Plan for Eternal Peace based on political and economic unification of Europe on a federal basis with a council presided over by France. He falsely attributed his project to a 'Grand Design' of the King.

Jean Baptiste Colbert (1619—83), Minister of Finance under King Louis XIV of France, concerned about the economic disadvantages of the economic particularism of the country (divided by several thousands of river tolls, road tolls, octrois, excises, customs duties and other imposts on intranational trade) planned to unite the provinces of the kingdom into a single customs union. A uniform tariff was published in 1664, but not accepted by all provinces. In 1667 a single tariff on some 60 industrial products was adopted. His plans for economic unifica- tion of the country were eventually carried out in the revolution which created the First Republic.

Bishop Christoph Royas y Spinola (1626—95), a Spanish[3] noble in the service of the Austrian Hapsburg Emperor Leopold I, proposed in 1665 a customs union of Austria, Bavaria, Spain, and some German principalities. His main idea was to establish an economic union as a means for bringing about political union. He greatly influenced the advocates of Imperial German Mercan- tilism, including Johann Joachim Becher.

William Penn (1644—1718), British-born statesman, Quaker,

[2] For more information on Crucé see László Ledermann, op. cit., pp. 9—81.

[3] He is sometimes referred to as 'a Hungarian', probably because he be- came Bishop of St Stephan. Moreover, his name was mutilated (an x sub- tituted for a y). See, for example, Jacob Viner, *The Customs Union Issue* New York: Carnegie Endowment, 1950) p. 93.

founder of the colony of Pennsylvania and chiefly responsible
for its Constitution of 1682, proposed in 1696 a federal 'union
of the colonies in America'. As a religiously inspired champion
of world peace, he searched for appropriate principles of international organisation. See his *Essay towards the Present and
Future Peace of Europe, through the Establishment of a Parliament or State of Europe* (London: 1693).

Abbé Charles Irénée Castel de Saint-Pierre (1658—1743),
French political thinker and author of many plans and projects,
presented his *Projet pour rendre la paix perpétuelle en Europe*
in three volumes (Utrecht: Antoine Schouten, 1713—17). It
suggested the foundation of a permanent association of European states, politically as well as economically.

Jean-Jacques Rousseau (1712—78), French political philosopher and writer on many subjects, extended the work of the
Abbé de Saint-Pierre in two books, *Extrait du projet de paix
perpétuelle de Monsieur l'Abbé de Saint-Pierre* (Geneva: 1761)
and *Jugement sur le projet de paix perpétuelle* (Geneva: 1761),
proposing a political association of European states. Both books
are included in *Oeuvres complétes de J.-J. Rousseau* (Paris: P.
Dupont, 1823—6).

Justus Möser (1720—94), German publicist, published in 177
his *Patriotische Phantasien*, in which he argued for an economic
unification of Germany.

Jeremy Bentham (1748—1832), British social philosopher,
jurist, and political economist, who is credited with having
coined the word 'international', argued for an international
organisation, comprising the countries of the entire world,
designed to achieve the greatest happiness for the greatest number. His principal objective was to stamp out wars; among his
major instruments were codification and development of international law, disarmament, emancipation of colonies, free trade
and freedom of the press. See his *Plea for an Universal and Perpetual Peace* (1789), republished as 'A Plan for an Universal and
Perpetual Peace' in *Jeremy Bentham's Plan for an Universal and
Perpetual Peace* (The Grotius Society Publications, No. 6, London: Sweet & Maxwell, 1927).

Immanuel Kant (1724—1804), German philosopher, in one c
his smaller tracts, entitled *Zum ewigen Frieden: Ein philosophi
scher Entwurf*, published in 1795, suggested a supranational
federation of sovereign states that would have power to regulat
international relations and prevent war.

Johann Gottlieb Fichte (1762—1814), German philosopher,
argued forcefully in favour of the nation state, economically

unified internally, but closed to the outside world. He published *Der geschlossene Handelsstaat* (Tübingen: Cotta, 1800) and *Reden an die deutsche Nation* (Berlin: Realschulbuchhandlung, 1808), both relevant to his ideal of a large but closed economy, which he believed would be conducive to both internal and external peace.

[Claude] Henri [de Rouvroy], Comte de Saint-Simon (1760–1825) argued for a European Federation, a 'veritable community' of independent states united by a European parliament and other common institutions independent of the national governments. See his *De la réorganisation de la societé européenne ou de la nécessité et des moyens de rassembler les peuples de l'Europe en un seul corps politique en conservant à chacun son indépendance nationale* (Paris: 1814; republished Paris: Les Presses Françaises, 1925).

FROM NAPOLEON TO WORLD WAR I, 1812–1914

This period of just about a hundred years began with an attempt of uniting Europe by conquest; and it includes, near its end, a dream of extending and transforming the British empire into an economic union of a large part of the world. Since the German *Zollverein*, an arrangement for the economic integration of 38 separate states and splinter states, was one of the achievements of the nineteenth century, the reader will not be surprised to find no less than six German and Austrian statesmen and publicists covered by this *Who Was Who*. But he will also find six Englishmen, four Frenchmen (besides Napoleon), an Italian, an American and another German mentioned in connection with a variety of schemes and issues.

Napoleon Bonaparte (1769–1821), Emperor of the French, described himself as a champion of Continental European unity. In captivity on St Helena he justified his war of 1812 against Russia as having been in the 'true interest' of tranquillity and security, attempting to 'establish a new society', an 'agglomeration', 'concentration' and 'confederation' of the peoples of Europe, 'the grand European family'.[4] See *Oeuvres de Napoléon 1er à Sainte-Hélène* (Vols 29–32 of *Correspondance de Napo-*

---

[4] I am indebted to John M. Letiche for calling my attention to Napoleon's reminiscences reproduced in Leo Tolstoy, *War and Peace* (translated by Louise and Aylmer Maude, London: Oxford University Press, 1922–3) p. 541. Wary of quoting from a secondary source, I tried to find Tolstoy's quotations in the Works of Napoleon. Tolstoy had pieced them together

léon 1ᵉʳ (Paris: H. Plon, J. Dumaine, 1858—70) Vol. 32, pp. 28 296, 304, and 306.

Heinrich Friedrich Karl Freiherr von Stein (1757—1831), German statesman, from 1804 Minister of Commerce under King Friedrich Wilhelm III of Prussia, abolished in 1818 all int nal duties within Prussia. In 1814—15 he opposed the tariff barriers around the separate German states and principalities and submitted a plan for uniform external customs duties und central control.

Johannes Joseph von Görres (1776—1848), editor of *Der Rheinische Merkur*, the most important political journal of its time in Germany, wrote, from 1814 on, in favour of an econon unification of Germany.

Johann Friedrich Benzenberg (1777—1846), physicist and publicist, authored an influential essay on 'Teutschlands Gewer und Teutschlands Zölle' in *Der Rheinische Merkur*, October 1814 (No. 126). He argued for unification of the internal revenues of all German states, but warned of the difficulty of persuading the states to give up this sovereignty.

Klemens Lothar Wenzel Prince von Metternich (1773—1859) Austrian statesman, Minister of Foreign Affairs and later Chancellor under the Hapsburg emperors Franz I and Ferdinand I of Austria, leader of the Germanic Confederation (1815), took various positions, always politically inspired, for and against Austria's participation in partial and complete German customs unions. Typical of his views was his criticism of the mobility of capital and his complaint that 'the merchant firm does not belong to one but rather to all German states' and thus serves the 'revolutionary ideals of political union'.

Tanneguy Duchatel (1803—67), French Minister of Commerc (and later Minister of Finance) under Louis Philippe, proposed in 1835 a customs union between France and Belgium. His plan was objected to by Great Britain as incompatible with Belgium' neutrality.

Sir Robert Peel (1788—1850), British statesman, Prime Minis ter under Queen Victoria, led the Tory party towards free trade and to the repeal of the corn laws in 1846.

---

from a variety of accounts of separate conversations of Napoleon with his associates at St Helena. I quoted above only what I found in the *Oeuvres*, but I may add from the Tolstoy translation: 'Europe would . . . soon have been, in fact, but one people, and anyone who travelled anywhere would have found himself always in the common fatherland. I should have demanded the freedom of all the navigable rivers for everybody, that the seas should be common to all . . .' (Tolstoy, p. 541).

John Bright (1811—89), British industrialist and statesman, joined Cobden as leader of the Manchester school, championing free trade, the repeal of the corn laws and the navigation acts. An effective orator, he fought for the causes of liberalism as member of Parliament and as member of Gladstone's cabinets. [For Richard Cobden see Chapter 6.]

Lord [Henry John Temple] Palmerston (1784—1865), English statesman, proposed and promoted, in his capacity as British secretary for foreign affairs after 1848, the formation of a customs union among the separate states of Italy.

Victor Hugo (1802—85), French author, novelist and dramatist, addressed an international conference on 22 August 1849, on the establishment of the 'Etats-Unies d'Europe', with the optimistic opening 'Un jour viendra . . .'

Carl Ludwig Freiherr von Bruck (1798—1860), Minister of Commerce and Finance under Emperor Francis Joseph of Austria, proposed, in the *Wiener Zeitung* of 26 October 1849, a customs union comprising Austria-Hungary, Northern Italy, and the entire German Zollverein; the union was to become effective in four stages with reductions of internal tariffs by steps but with high duties on imports from the outside. Bruck negotiated commercial agreements with Prussia (1853), but his plan was rejected by Prussia and finally ruled out in 1860 by the conclusion of a Franco-Prussian trade agreement that was to give most-favoured-nation treatment to France.

Prince Otto E. L. von Bismarck (1815—98), Prussian statesman and later the first Chancellor of Germany (1871—1890), opposed all plans, of Bruck and others, for Austria's entry into the German *Zollverein*, evidently because he was determined to maintain Prussia's hegemony in the group. His alleged reasons were the existence of differences in the people's consumption habits, and the difficulties of a fair distribution of common tariff revenues. Bismarck rejected also a project of a customs union that would include France, on the theory that such a union could work only for racially kindred nations.

Count Camillo Benso Cavour (1810—61), Italian statesman, Prime Minister of the Kingdom of Piedmont from 1850 to his death, speaking for Sardinia protested against a commercial treaty between Austria and Modena concluded in 1857, because, by downgrading a 1852 treaty for a complete customs union to a less complete tariff unification, it violated the most-favoured-nations agreement between Sardinia and Austria. He stated that a customs union is 'complete' only if it provides for (1) uniformity of export and transit tariffs, (2) free trade for the products of the united countries, (3) uniformity of the external import tariffs of the participating countries and suppression of any internal tariff lines, and (4) pooling of customs revenues and their partition among the participating states in accordance with a formula established in advance. Without all of these provisions the arrangements involve preferential tariff practices, which must be extended to all countries that have unconditional most-favoured-nations rights.

Emile de Girardin (1806—81), French deputy and man of affairs and letters, founder of *La Presse* and other journals, favoured an economic union of Western Europe, especially in his collections *Questions de mon temps* (1858) and in his book *Force ou Richesse* (1864).

Martin Friedrich Rudolf von Delbrück (1817—1903), Prussian statesman in the Ministry of Commerce in Bismarck's cabinet, strengthened the German Zollverein on several occasions between 1851 and 1866. In 1862 he concluded a commercial treaty with France on mutual reductions of import tariffs, which became effective in 1866, when the German Zollverein agreed to the lowered customs duties.

Sir William Ewart Gladstone (1809—98), British statesman, four times Prime Minister under Queen Victoria, impressed with liberal ideas for free trade, authorised in 1860 the economist Richard Cobden to negotiate a liberal trade agreement with France, represented by the French economist Michel Chevalier.

Comte Paul de Leusse (1835—1906), French politician, proposed in 1888 a central-European customs union, partly as a defensive bloc against agricultural competition from Russia and overseas, partly as a means to secure peace between France and Germany. See his pamphlet *La paix par l'union douanière franco-allemande* (Strasbourg: J. Bussenius, 1888).

James Gillespie Blaine (1830—93), Secretary of State of the United States of America under President James Garfield and again under President Benjamin Harrison, proposed and organised a Pan-American Conference in Washington in 1889 to discuss the possible formation of a Pan-American Customs Union. The conference rejected even the principle of reciprocity, and established the Pan-American Union only as a bureau of information.

Cecil Rhodes (1853—1902), successful man of affairs and British colonial statesman, made a fortune as discoverer of diamond mines in South Africa. He controlled the British South Africa Company, de Beers Consolidated Mines, and Gold Fields of South Africa. Was Prime Minister of the Cape from 1890 to 1896; settled a new province of the British empire, named

Rhodesia; and hoped to make Africa 'British from the Cape to Cairo'. His dream was to have the whole world united under a scheme of federation under British rule.

Joseph Chamberlain (1836—1914), British statesman, President of the Board of Trade in Gladstone's Liberal Cabinet, 1880—5, and Colonial Secretary, between 1895 and 1900, argued for an Imperial Customs Union, linking all British colonies with Britain, seeing in a commercial union a non-political foundation for the reinforcement of the British Empire. His plans for a preferential tariff found support among some industrial interests in England who hoped to obtain protection under such a scheme, but the project, heavily attacked by the most respected economists, was put aside.

Graf Hans von Schwerin-Löwitz (1847—1918), a leader of the German conservative agricultural party, pleaded at the International Agricultural Congress in Rome in 1903 for a 'United States of Europe' with protective tariffs against imports from overseas.

BETWEEN TWO WORLD WARS, 1915—39

This period begins with World War I and ends with the outbreak of World War II. My list begins with the author of *Mitteleuropa* (Central Europe), includes the author of *Pan-Europa*, and ends with the author of *Union Now* (calling for a North Atlantic Union). The rest is made up chiefly of French and German statesmen of the inter-war period.

Friedrich Naumann (1860—1919), German writer on social and political questions, advocated the formation of a Central European Union — that is, chiefly Germany and Austria-Hungary — as a step to freer trade, not for protective purposes, but with much leeway for cartelisation. The exclusion of England and Russia seemed to be essential to his plan. See his book *Mitteleuropa*, (Berlin: Reimer, 1915). [In earlier years he had championed different causes, for example, a reconciliation between proletarian socialism and German nationalism and had founded the 'Nationalsozialer Verein' to promote this idea.]

Aristide Briand (1862—1932), French statesman and Prime Minister, an indefatigable champion of European economic and political union, undertook several forceful initiatives toward this end. In 1919, soon after the end of the First World War, he sent a memorandum to 26 nations, recommending a Federal Union of Europe. He took similar actions in 1924, 1929, and 1930. In his memorandum of May 1930, to all European government members of the League of Nations, he stressed the desirability of

the 'establishment of a common market' for the products of all
European countries, but he criticised the protectionist motives
of other plans for Customs Unions in Europe 'tending to abolish
internal Customs barriers in order to erect on the boundary of
the whole community a stiffer barrier — that is to say, in order
to create, in practice, a weapon against the States situated outside these unions'.[5] The Assembly of the League unanimously
adopted the French proposal, which was endorsed by 45 states,
to pursue the objectives outlined by Briand, and a Commission
of Enquiry for European Union was constituted. This Commission held six sessions between September 1930 and September
1932 and a formal meeting in October 1937. [Quoted from
Department of Economic Affairs, *Customs Unions* (New York:
United Nations, 1947).]

   Edouard Herriot (1872—1957), French statesman, Prime
Minister (1924—5 and 1932) and President of the Chamber of
Deputies, gave strong support to Briand's initiatives, especially
in 1924. He published a book on *The United States of Europe*
(New York: Viking Press, 1930).

   Walther Rathenau (1867—1922), German industrialist and
statesman, proposed industrial combinations, including mergers,
among industrial firms in the member countries of a projected
European Customs Union, which would have a larger 'internal'
market similar to that of an enlarged national economy.

   Georg Gothein (1857—1940), German statesman, treasury
minister in 1919, member of parliament in the Weimar Republic
treated the question *Ist eine pan-europäische Zollunion möglich*
in a memorandum published by the Deutsche Liga für den Völ-
kerbund (No. 22) (Berlin: Liga, 1925); as another memorandum
for the same organisation (No. 26) he published a *Denkschrift
über den administrativen Protektionismus* (Berlin: Liga, 1930).
Later he contributed a paper 'Deutsch-französische Zollunion
als Vorstufe der Europäischen Zollunion' in Hanns Heiman, ed.,
Europäische Zollunion (Berlin: Hobbing, 1926) pp. 70—82. He
argued that a German-French customs union would be a first
step to a European union, since virtually all other countries of
Europe would soon want to join.

   Richard N. Count Coudenhove-Kalergi (1894—1972) organised the Pan-Europa movement, published a book under the title

---

[5] 'Memorandum on the Organization of a Regime of European Federal
Union, addressed to twenty-six governments of Europe, by M. Briand,
Foreign Minister of France, May 17, 1930', Carnegie Endowment for Inter
national Peace (Washington, D.C.).

Pan-Europa (Vienna: Paneuropa Verlag, 1923) and issued a periodical under the same name. Among his supporters were Herriot, Stresemann, and Briand. In September 1948 the European Parliamentary Union was established, with him as Secretary General.

Louis Loucheur (1908—52), French industrialist and statesman (Minister of Commerce), promoted horizontal combinations — mergers and cartels — among industries in Western and Central Europe. In 1927, as a member of the French delegation to the League of Nations, he proposed a World Economic Conference, at which he supported plans for European economic collaboration on the basis of publicly sponsored private agreements among industrialists in the various countries to rationalise production and regulate competition. According to the *Final Report of the World Economic Conference*, published by the League of Nations (1927), his proposals for continental solidarity and industrial cartelisation found the support of Elemer Hantos, Arnold Rechberg, and other advocates of industrial combinations.

Gustav Stresemann (1878—1929), German Chancellor (1923) and Minister of Foreign Affairs (1923—9), negotiated the Locarno Pact and Germany's admission to the League of Nations. He joined Briand in his proposal to the Assembly of the League of Nations in 1929 for the establishment of a United States of Europe. He shared the Nobel Prize for Peace with Briand in 1926.

André Pierre Gabrièl Amédé Tardieu (1876—1945), French Prime Minister, proposed the establishment of a Danubian Federation, partly as a substitute for a customs union between Austria and Germany. The plan was considered by the International Chamber of Commerce in 1932, but rejected after it had been opposed by many of the powers, especially by Germany and Italy.

William Ivor Jennings (born 1903), British constitutional lawyer, held that the establishment of a Western European Federation was necessary in order to avoid war. He drafted a 'Constitution' for such a federation. He favoured 'inter-State free trade' on principle, but believed that political reasons might dictate the imposition of controls and restrictions of various sorts, including controls on 'currency and inter-State payments and the transfer of securities' (p. 134). His draft constitution, however, would give to the Federal Legislature the 'power to make laws relating to . . . currency, . . . banking, inter-State payments . . . ' (p. 198). See his book, *A Federation for Western Europe* (New

York: Macmillan, and London: Cambridge University Press, 1940).

Clarence K. Streit (born 1896), American publicist, in a book entitled *Union Now: A Proposal for a Federal Union of the Democracies of the North Atlantic* (New York: Harper, 1939), proposed a world federation, first limited to 15 democracies but open for later extension, encompassing union citizenship, common defence force, a customs-free economy, uniform money, and a common postal and communications system. Several revised and enlarged editions appeared in later years, e.g., *Freedom's Frontier: Atlantic Union Now* (New York: Harper, 1961). The movement for an Atlantic Union found strong support in Europe as well as in the United States.

WORLD WAR II AND AFTER, 1940–70

Beginning with the pleas and plans for the post-war world, by Churchill and Roosevelt, this period includes the statesmen who prepared, promoted, or administered the Marshall Plan, the Common Market, and the other schemes for regional economic integration.[6]

Winston Leonard Spencer Churchill (1874–1965), British statesman and strong leader of his country during the Second World War, offered an 'indissoluble Union' with France in June 1940, when the German army had occupied most of France, and proposed in March 1943 that a United States of Europe be formed after the war. He repeated his call for European unity in widely quoted speeches in September 1946 in Zurich and in May 1947 in the Hague.

Franklin Delano Roosevelt (1882–1945), President of the United States of America from 1933 until his death in 1945, signed in August 1941 with Winston Churchill the 'Atlantic Charter' and concluded in February 1942 a Mutual Aid Agreement (Lend-Lease Agreement). These undertakings were later extended to other countries, including China, the USSR, Poland, Czechoslovakia, Yugoslovia, Belgium, The Netherlands, Greece, Norway, Canada, Australia, and New Zealand. The Charter and the agreements called for worldwide economic relations with

---

[6] Some of the statesmen have made it difficult for me to place them correctly; Paul Reynaud, for example, was an active champion of integration before the First World War, between the wars, and after the Second World War. The publication dates of his books made me decide to include him in the last of these periods.

reductions of trade barriers after the war and for elimination of all forms of discrimination and bilateral deals.

Cordell Hull (1871—1955), American statesman, US Secretary of State from 1933 to 1944, was the most important influence in changing commercial policy from a protectionist stance to one of freer trade. He negotiated many reciprocal trade agreements, especially with Latin American countries, and was the initiator of President Roosevelt's policies expressed in the Atlantic Charter and in Mutual Aid Agreements.

Paul Reynaud (1878—1966), French statesman, Finance Minister in the Government of Daladier, 1938—40, and Premier in 1940, was one of the most persistent advocates of European integration. Early in 1914, before World War I, he proposed in the French parliament the 'linking up' of French heavy industry with that of Germany. Between the wars he supported similar proposals, and after World War II he strongly advocated European integration, economic, political, and military. He is generally regarded, together with Churchill and Spaak, as one of the founders of the European Movement. From 1949 to 1955 he was President of the Commission on Economic Affairs of the Consultative Assembly of the Council of Europe. See his *La France a sauvé l'Europe* (Paris: Flammarion, 1947); *Au coeur de la mêlée: 1930—1945* (Paris: Flammarion, 1951); *Unite or Perish* (New York: Simon, 1951); and *The Foreign Policy of Charles de Gaulle: A Critical Assessment* (New York: Odyssey Press, 1964).

Léon Blum (1872—1950), leader of the French Socialist party, French Premier, 1936—7 and again in 1938, became later a leader of the European Movement. While a prisoner in Nazi Germany during World War II, he wrote a book *A l'échelle humaine* (Paris: Gallimard, 1945), translated into English as *For All Mankind* (London: Gollancz, 1946), in which he called for the creation of an integrated European political and economic order 'as the only satisfactory' solution of the problems arising from the war and as the only permanent basis for peace. In 1948 Blum was named an Honorary President of the European Movement.

Raoul Dautry (1880—1951), President of the French Council for a United Europe, one of the five organisations merged in December 1947 into the International Committee of the Movement for European Unity. He had been Minister in the governments of Daladier, Paul Reynaud, and Paul Ramadier.

Alcide de Gasperi (1881—1954), Italian statesman, Minister of Foreign Affairs, 1944—6 and 1951—3, and also Prime Minister from 1945 to 1953, championed European unity, including the Defence Community. In 1948 he was named, along with Blum, Churchill, and Spaak, an Honorary President of the International Committee of the Movement for European Unity.

Hendrik Brugmans (born 1906), Dutch humanist, resistance fighter during the German occupation, leader of European Federalists, and since 1950 President of the Collège d'Europe in Bruges, Belgium, was in 1946 the first President of the European Union of Federalists and later Vice-President of the European Movement. Among his writings are *L'Europe au-delà de l'Economie*, Conférences de Congres de l'Union Européenne at Lausanne 1960 (Neuchâtel: de La Baconnière, 1961); *L'Idee Européenne 1918—1965* (Bruges: de Tempel, 1965); and *Vingt Ans d'Europe* (Bruges: de Tempel, 1966).

Harry S. Truman (1884—1972), President of the United States of America from 1945 to 1952, promoted European Economic Co-operation in a succession of actions: in December 1947, after receiving the reports of various commissions and committees, he presented to the Congress a long-range European Recovery Program, which led to the Foreign Aid Act of 1947, the Foreign Assistance Act of 1948, the Economic Cooperation Act of 1948, and the amended Economic Cooperation Act of 1949. The Act of 1948 was designed to help Europe enjoy 'the advantages which the United States has enjoyed through the existence of a large domestic market with no internal trade barriers'. The Act of 1949 declared it to be 'the policy of the people of the United States to encourage the unification of Europe'.

George Catlett Marshall (1880—1959), US Chief of General Staff from 1940 to 1945 and Secretary of State from 1947 to 1949, inaugurated the European Recovery Program of the United States (the 'Marshall Plan') with an address at Harvard University on 5 June 1947. He called on the countries of Europe to take the steps leading to effective economic co-operation, and declared that the United States was prepared to give the necessary assistance for the reconstruction of the economy of Europe. Marshall received the Nobel Peace Prize in 1953.

Dean G. Acheson (1893—1971), US Under-Secretary of State, 1945 to June 1947, and Secretary of State, 1949—53, influenced the policy of the United States in the promotion of European political and economic integration. He officially praised in 1948 the proposed creation of the Council of Europe as 'a welcome step forward toward the political integration of Europe'. See his book *Present at the Creation*, (New York: W. W. Norton, 1969).

William L. Clayton (1880—1966), US Under-Secretary of

State for Economic Affairs from 1946 to October 1947, was an ardent supporter of American aid to Europe and of European economic integration. In May 1947 he stated that only 'full economic federation of Europe and massive US aid in its support' could save the situation. In September 1947 he criticised OEEC for its slow and half-hearted progress towards effective co-operation.

Benjamin Victor Cohen (born 1894), lawyer, Counselor of the US Department of State from July 1945 to July 1947, was influential in the discussions leading to the Marshall Plan. In May 1947 he argued, together with Willard Thorp (see Chapter 6), that the United States should not shrink from taking the initiative as well as the responsibility, because the European nations might be unable to agree or might agree on unsound schemes. (See *Foreign Relations, 1947*, Vol. III, p. 235.)

Charles E. Bohlen (1904–74), Special Assistant to the US Secretary of State from November 1946 to July 1947, and afterwards Counselor of the Department of State, was one of the early instigators of American action to assist European countries and to put pressure on them to develop a plan for economic co-operation and, if possible, an economic federation.

Walter Lippmann (1889–1974), American writer and influential columnist, contributed substantially to the public acceptance and endorsement of American aid for European co-operation and integration. His persuasive arguments during the discussions in 1947 and 1948 helped create the broad public support for the Congressional actions. A sample: 'the measures will have to be very large — in Europe no less than an economic union, and over here no less than the equivalent to a revival of Lend-Lease' (5 Apr 1947).

Arthur H. Vandenberg (1884–1951), US Senator, senior Republican member of the Foreign Relations Committee, skilfully and forcefully steered the proposals for the European Recovery Plan toward adoption by the Congress. The support of this statesman, formerly known for his isolationist position, was indispensable for the acceptance of the plan.

Ernest Bevin (1881–1951), British Secretary of State for Foreign Affairs, was instrumental in bringing the countries of Europe together in responding to the Marshall Plan for European co-operation. He and Georges Bidault of France agreed on 3 July 1947 to invite 22 countries (all except Russia and Spain) to an early conference. In January 1948 he stated that the United Kingdom would join a consolidated Western Europe.

Georges Bidault (born 1899) French Minister for Foreign

Affairs, in July 1947 joined Ernest Bevin of the United Kingdom
in an invitation to 22 European countries to respond immediately to the American initiative for a European Recovery Plan that
would call for close economic co-operation. In January 1948 he
made a strong plea for a European Union. In March 1948 he
and Count Sforza signed a protocol at Turin, setting up a commission to draft an action plan for full economic union between
France and Italy.

Paul Ramadier (1888—1961), French Premier from January
to November 1947, strongly supported Bidault, his Minister for
Foreign Affairs, in the initial steps toward the implementation
of the Marshall Plan for European Recovery and Cooperation.

Count Carlo Sforza (1872—1952), Italian Minister for Foreign
Affairs in 1920—1 and from 1947 to 1951, responded favourably
to the call for European co-operation. In 1948 he negotiated
with Bidault a plan for full economic union between France and
Italy. He had for many years been an enthusiastic champion of a
European economic union.

Paul Gray Hoffman (1891—1975), American business executive and statesman, became in 1948 the chief executive officer
of the Marshall Plan as Administrator of the Economic Cooperation Administration (ECA). In October 1949 he urged the governments of the Western European countries to 'have ready early in
1950' a far-reaching programme of economic integration. The
programme should include 'the formation of a single large market within which quantitative restrictions on the movement of
goods, monetary barriers to the flow of payments and, eventually,
all tariffs are permanently swept away'.

Paul-Henri Spaak (born 1899), Prime Minister and Minister of
Foreign Affairs of Belgium, Honorary President of the International Committee of the Movement for European Unity
(1947), became in 1949 First President of the Council of Europe
from which he resigned in December 1951 (partly in protest
against the lack of British support); in 1952 he became President
of the Consultative Assembly of the European Coal and Steel
Community. In March 1953 he presented a draft statute for a
European Political Community with a bicameral parliament. At
the Messina Conference of the Six (May—June 1955) he was
partly responsible for the proposals of the Benelux countries for
an expansion of the common market from coal and steel to
transport (including civil aviation) and power production
(including atomic energy), and largely responsible for the Messina
Resolution on a common market for all goods and services and
on a 'United Europe' as ultimate aim; the 'Spaak Report' was

published in Brussels in April 1956. In 1958 he became Secretary General of the North Atlantic Treaty Organization (NATO).

Robert Schuman (1888–1963), French Foreign Minister from 1948 to 1952, announced in May 1949 his plan for 'pooling French and German coal and steel production' (the Schuman Plan). A treaty creating the European Coal and Steel Community (ECSC) of France, Germany, Italy, Belgium, Luxembourg, and the Netherlands was signed in April 1951, to become effective in the summer of 1952. It established a Council of Ministers, a High Authority, an Assembly, a High Court and a Consultative Committee. See his book, *Pour l'Europe* (Paris: Nagel, 1963).

Jean Monnet (born 1888), former *Commissaire au Plan* in France, commonly regarded as the most dedicated 'European', became the first President of the High Authority of the European Coal and Steel Community in August 1952. In November 1954 he refused to stand for re-election for a second term, and subsequently resigned as a member of the Authority, in order to have full freedom of action in his work for the establishment of a United States of Europe. He became President of the 'Action Committee' for this objective. See his book *Les états-unis d'Europe ont commencé: La Communauté Européenne du Charbon et de l'Acier. Discours et allocutions, 1952–1954* (Paris: Laffont, 1955) and his article 'A Ferment of Change', *Journal of Common Market Studies*, Vol. 1 (1962–3) pp. 203–11.

Duncan Sandys (born 1908), British diplomat and cabinet minister, became Secretary General of the International Committee of the European Movement in December 1947 and was Chairman of its International Executive from 1947 to 1950. He served as a member of the European Consultative Assembly at Strasbourg from 1950 to 1951 and again since 1965. Between 1951 and 1964 he was a cabinet minister (Minister for Commonwealth Relations among other posts) in the Macmillan government. He presented the British initiative for converting the Brussels Treaty Organization into a Western European Union (WEU) and, in February 1955, saw the Treaty of Association between the United Kingdom and the European Coal and Steel Community ratified.

Edmond Giscard d'Estaing (born 1894), French industrialist [father of the President of France], favoured a European economic union. See his book, *La France et l'unification de l'Europe* (Paris: Librairie de Medicis, 1953). He argued against the fallacies of protection and dirigism (p. 73), held that 'equalization of living standards was equally Utopian among the different nations

of Europe as within one and the same nation' (p. 75), and he
warned against extending unification into 'uniformization'
(p. 264).

Walter Hallstein (born 1901), German jurist and State Secretary, was the principal negotiator for Germany on economic an
political integration during 1955—7. He became President of th
Commission of the European Economic Community from 1958
to 1967. He was one of the most determined champions of Eur
pean unity. Customs union, economic union, monetary union,
and all other institutions serving the economic integration of
Europe, had for Hallstein one ultimate objective: political unio
See his book, *Der unvollendete Bundesstaat* (Düsseldorf and
Vienna: Econ Verlag, 1969).

Charles de Gaulle (1890—1970), President of France from
1959 to 1969, who (in 1952) had been opposed to the Europe
Defence Community and (in 1957) to the Treaty of Rome
(creating the EEC), prevented in the autumn of 1958 an associ
tion of Britain and the European Free Trade Area with the EEC
In 1963 he vetoed Britain's entry into the EEC; in 1967 he too
France out of NATO, and in general he succeeded in halting th
European Federalist movement.

Groups, Committees, and Organisation Staffs

his chapter is reserved for group contributions to the history
f thought on economic integration, following two chapters
hich reported on individual contributors and preceding one
hich will again report on individuals. But since joint authors of
ooks or articles are also 'groups', I must qualify my declaration
f intent by stating another criterion: joint authors whose names
ppear with the titles of their publications are considered as
dividual contributors; group authorship in the present context
ould be taken as referring to writers who remain unnamed or
re named only in the text or in the prefaces or letters of trans-
ittal of the publications included here.

The groups in point are committees, conferences, legislative
odies, and organisation staff who have produced reports,
emoranda, or other statements relevant to the subject of this
istory of thought. In some instances the executive secretary or
erhaps the chairman of the group may have done the actual
riting; but what he wrote was supposed to reflect the thinking
f the group responsible for the ideas published. In a few cases a
eport has been linked, in later references, with a particular
erson, usually the chairman of the group, but even then it has
ot been claimed that the person whose name became attached
o his committee was actually the sole writer of the statement
nally published. I refer here to such publications as the Marshall
lan, the Mansholt Report, the Werner Report, and similar docu-
ents. The collective character of a published document can, of
ourse, never be questioned if it is a *compte rendu*, a transcript
f the proceedings of a conference, discussion group, or legisla-
ve body.

One special category of group statement has given me some
eadaches: intergovernmental (bilateral or multilateral) agree-
ents. Documents such as the Treaty of Rome, setting up the
uropean Economic Community, and the Treaty of Stockholm,

175

setting up the European Free-Trade Area, are surely importan
group statements on economic integration. In earlier drafts of
this chapter I had included many official documents recordin
national legislation and international agreements, treaties and
conventions relating to customs unions or similar undertaking
To be consistent, I had to include the treaties among the Gern
states and principalities forming the Zollverein between 1818
and 1834; however, since this customs union had evolved thro
piecemeal accession of states and splinter states, the number o
treaties and subsequent amendments became forbiddingly larg
To select only the most important ones for inclusion in this
account did not seem useful unless I could supply annotation
based on careful analysis. I finally decided against embarking
such an ambitious research project and, consequently, against
including here this category of collective statement. For the
German Zollverein, enumerations of the treaties and agreemer
can be found in various monographs; for customs unions ever
where, a list of documents of this nature can be found in the
appendixes to Jacob Viner's *The Customs Union Issue* (New
York: Carnegie Endowment for Peace, 1950).

CHOOSING THE ORDER OF PRESENTATION

The question of the most useful ordering arises again. The sim
lest procedure would be to elect a chronological listing, but it
would be less than satisfactory to find documents on a Pan-
American Union, on a South African Union, on a German-
Austrian Union, and on the European Economic Community
in the same list. A separation by continent will help; a reader,
for example, who has a special interest in regional arrangemen
in Latin America or in Asia, will save time if he is spared the
task of picking the few documents which he needs from a long
geographically unstructured list. For the large number of docu
ments on European arrangements a separation by eras may als
be useful.

The documents will thus be grouped according to whether
they relate to the World at Large; Europe, 1925—37; Western
Europe, 1943—9; Western Europe, 1949—58; Western Europe
1959—75; Eastern Europe, 1945—75; the Americas; Africa; A
and the Far East. Most of the titles will be followed by a brief
annotation indicating the contents or character of the publica
tion or providing a brief explanation of its purpose. No annot
tion will be supplied where the title of the document is self-
explanatory or where I was unable to examine the text.

*HE WORLD AT LARGE

*ongrès International d'Expansion Economique Mondiale, held
t Mons [Belgium], 24—8 Sep 1905, *Documents préliminaires
t compte rendu des séances* (Brussels, 1905).
The documents and minutes for an early international con-
*ess on closer economic relations in the world economy.]
*eague of Nations, *Report and Proceedings of the World Eco-
nomic Conference held at Geneva, May 4th to 23rd, 1927*
(Geneva: League of Nations, Dec 1927; C 356 M 129) Vol. 1,
246 pp.; Vol. 2, 250 pp.
[Volume 1 contains a full report of the Conference, verbatim
records of the eleven plenary meetings, and summary of proceedings of the Co-ordinating Committee. Volume 2 contains
summaries of the proceedings of the three subcommittees and
an index to both volumes.]
*eague of Nations, *The World Economic Conference, Geneva,
May 1927: Final Report* (Geneva: League of Nations, Dec
1927) 52 pp.
[Contains a general survey and summary by the president,
Georges Theunis, and the general resolutions adopted by the
Conference.]
*eague of Nations, Monetary and Economic Conference, London
1933, *Journal of the Monetary and Economic Conference,
London, 1933* (Geneva: League of Nations, 1933) 248 pp.
[A Preparatory Commission of Experts drew up a 'Draft
Annotated Agenda' in January 1933 for the conference in
June and July 1933. A final resolution was passed on 27 July
on some general principles.]
*eague of Nations, Monetary and Economic Conference, London
1933, *An Account of the Preparatory Work for the Conference*
(Geneva: League of Nations, May 1933) 94 pp.
[Contains an analysis of the 'Draft Annotated Agenda' and a
summary of the League's earlier economic and financial
activities from 1920 to 1933.]
Joint Committee, Carnegie Endowment—International Chamber
of Commerce, *The Improvement of Commercial Relations
between Nations, and The Problem of Monetary Stabilization*
(Paris: International Chamber of Commerce, 1936) 417 pp.
[Contains 30 memoranda prepared by seventeen economists —
including Robbins, Viner, Mises, Predöhl, Rist, Gregory, Mor-
tara, and Hammarskjöld — and 'Practical Conclusions' signed
by Gregory, Rist, Ohlin and Boehler.]
*oint Committee, Carnegie Endowment—International Chamber

of Commerce, *International Economic Reconstruction: A Survey of the Main Problems of Today* (Paris: Internationa Chamber of Commerce, Aug 1936) 225 pp.
[The survey was commissioned by an International Confere at Chatham House, London, in March 1935; a Joint Commit of the Sponsoring Organisations selected the Committee of Experts in October 1935. This Committee included sixteen economists as investigators and consultants. The two comp hensive reports were prepared by Bertil Ohlin and Theodor E. Gregory. The conclusions were signed also by Eugen Boe ler and Charles Rist.]

Royal Institute of International Affairs, *The Colonial Problem A Report by a Study Group of Members of the Royal Insti of International Affairs* (London: Oxford University Press, 1937) 448 pp.
[The Chatham House study group was chaired by Harold Nicholson. Part 1 deals with the international aspect, Part 2 with the colonial aspect, Part 3 with investment, trade, fina and settlement.]

League of Nations, Economic, Financial and Transit Depart *Commercial Policy in the Interwar Period: International Pr posals and National Policies* (Geneva: League of Nations, 1942) 164 pp.
[Part 1, 'An Historical Survey', includes chapters on the re- moval of economic barriers, 1918—21 (including the Brusse Conference of 1920); on the Genoa Conference of 1922 an the early work of the League; on later international efforts secure the removal of restrictions; and on the World Econo Conference of May 1927; on the European conferences dur the Great Depression, 1929—32 (including the establishmen of the Commission of Enquiry for European Union); the London Monetary and Economic Conference of 1933; the new protectionism, 1933—6; and the subsequent proposals trade liberalisation. Part 2, 'An Analysis of the Reasons for the Success or Failure of International Proposals', covers co mercial policy from 1919 to 1939.]

United States, Treasury Department, *Preliminary Draft Outlin of a Proposal for an International Stabilization Fund of the United and Associated Nations*, Washington, 7 April 1943, revised 10 July 1943 [White Plan] (Washington: Governme Printing Office, 1943) 19 pp.
[The 'White Plan' proposed an International Stabilization Fund as a permanent institution for international monetary co-operation, financed by the members' subscriptions of

quotas in gold, currencies, and government securities, creating a monetary unit called the 'Unitas' as the denominator for par values.]

United Kingdom, British Information Services, *International Clearing Union: Text of a Paper Containing Proposals by British Experts for an International Clearing Union*, 8 April 1943 [Keynes Plan] (London: HM Stationery Office, Cmd. 6437, 1943) 23 pp.

[The 'Keynes Plan' proposed an International Clearing Union, based on international bank-money called the 'Bancor', with borrowing quotas of the members and automatic adjustment through increases or reductions in the values of their currencies when their balances with the Union rose or fell excessively.]

Canada, Treasury Department, *Tentative Draft Proposals of Canadian Experts for an International Exchange Union*, Ottawa, 9 June 1943 (Ottawa: Treasury Department, June 1943) 19 pp.

[The Canadian proposal for an International Exchange Union was a counterpart of the White and Keynes plans. Several of its suggestions were used in the final agreement.]

United States, United Kingdom, Canada, *et al.*, *Joint Statement by Experts on the Establishment of an International Monetary Fund*, 21 April 1944, reproduced in *Federal Reserve Bulletin*, Vol. 30 (May 1944) pp. 438—41.

[The Joint Statement was based chiefly on the White Plan, with amendments by Canadian and British suggestions. The Articles of Agreement for the International Monetary Fund were approved in final form at Bretton Woods on 22 July 1944.]

United States, Department of State, *Proceedings and Documents of United Nations Monetary and Financial Conference, Bretton Woods, New Hampshire, July 1—22, 1944*, 2 vols (Washington: Government Printing Office, 1948) 1808 pp.

[Vol. 1, 'Proceedings and Documents Issued at the Conference', contains the proceedings of the conference from 1 to 22 July 1944, and all documents issued in the course of the proceedings. Vol. 2, 'Appendices', contains miscellaneous conference documents, a list of documents, a key to the symbols used, and six related papers.]

United States, Department of State, *Proposals for Expansion of World Trade and Employment* (Washington: Department of State, Publication No. 2411, Nov 1945) 28 pp.

[After an introductory analysis dealing with restrictions on world trade, this paper, developed by a technical staff, submits proposals for consideration by an international conference, especially on international economic co-operation and the establishment of an International Trade Organization.]

United States, Congress, *International Trade Organization*: Hearings before the Committee on Finance, United States Senate, 80th Congress, 1st Session, on Trade Agreements System and Proposed International Trade Organization Charter, Part 1: Testimony (Mar and Apr 1947) 676 pp; Part 2: Exhibits, pp 677—1425.
[The Exhibits contain the American draft charter for ITO on pp. 697—794 and the 'London Draft' (by the Preparatory Committee of the International Conference on Trade and Employment, Oct and Nov 1946) on pp. 795—865.]

United States, Department of State, *Draft Charter for an International Trade Organization of the United Nations* (Washington: Government Printing Office [Department of State Publication No. 2928], 1947) xiv and 70 pp.
[The purposes of the proposed organisation were to include the general applications of the most-favoured-nation principle, multilateral reductions in tariffs, elimination of preferential trade arrangements, and abolition of all non-tariff barriers to trade.]

United Nations, Conference on Trade and Employment, *Havana Charter for an International Trade Organization, Signed at Habana, Mar 24, 1948*, in US Department of State, *Commercial Policy Series*, 114 (Washington: Government Printing Office, 1948) 155 pp.
[The Charter for the ITO was not ratified and the plans had to be dropped. The General Agreement on Tariffs and Trade (GATT), which had been negotiated during the preparatory conferences for the Havana Charter, may be said to meet some of the most urgent objectives sought by the proposed ITO.]

Congrès International de Parlementaires et d'Experts pour le Développement des Echanges Commerciaux, held at Genoa, 14—17 Sep 1948, *Actes Officielles*, Vol. 2, Part 2, 'Unions économiques et douanières' (Genoa: Fratelli Pagano, 1948) pp. 60—1 and 191 ff.

The Brookings Institution, *Major Problems of United States Foreign Policy: A Study Guide* (Washington: The Brookings Institution, annually, 1947—53).
[Beginning in 1947, the Brookings Institution published annual collections of papers produced by study groups of non-governmental experts. The series was terminated with the 1953—54 volume.]

Communauté Atlantique, Conférence sur la Communauté Atlantique, held at Bruges, 9—14 Sep 1957; in *Cahiers de Bruges*, Nos. 3 and 4 (1957) 208 pp.
[Among the various subjects dealt with were religion, education, problems of economic co-operation, and future plans for the Atlantic Community.]

General Agreement on Tariffs and Trade, *Trends in International Trade: A Report by a Panel of Experts* [Haberler Report] (Geneva: GATT, 1958) 138 pp.
[The panel, consisting of Roberto Campos, Gottfried Haberler, James Meade, and Jan Tinbergen, concluded, among other things, that free movement of goods within the European Common Market should apply not only to industrial but also to agricultural products.]

Rockefeller Brothers Fund, *Foreign Economic Policy for the Twentieth Century: Report of the Rockefeller Brothers Fund Special Studies Project* [the 'Rockefeller Report' on US international economic policy] (Garden City, New York: Doubleday, 1958) 82 pp.
[The panel included Milton Katz, Harlan Cleveland, and David Rockefeller; the whole project was directed by Henry A. Kissinger.]

International Study Group of 32 Economists, *International Monetary Arrangements: The Problem of Choice*, Report on the deliberations of an international study group of 32 economists (Princeton: International Finance Section, 1964) 121 pp.
[This report, formulated by Fritz Machlup and Burton G. Malkiel, is the result of discussions at four meetings of the so-called 'Bellagio Group', organised and chaired by Machlup. The 32 members came from eleven countries and discussed alternative plans for reform of the international system to cope with the problems of adjustment, liquidity, and confidence. The emphasis was on the differences in assumptions which would account for the differences in approaches to reform.]

International Monetary Fund, 'International Liquidity', in *International Monetary Fund 1964 Annual Report*, Part 2 (Washington: IMF, July 1964) pp. 25—39.
[At the Annual Meeting of the Fund in September 1963, the Executive Directors were asked to study the problems of international liquidity. The findings of this study were published as Part 2 of the Annual Report of 1964. It is usually considered as a companion piece to the report of the Group

of Ten countries and to the report of the Group of 32 econo
mists.]

Group of Ten, *Ministerial Statement of the Group of Ten and
Annex Prepared by Deputies* (Paris: Ministry of Finance and
Economic Affairs, August 1964) 23 pp.
[The Group of Ten countries participating in the General
Arrangements to Borrow had agreed in September 1963 to
review the functioning of the international monetary system
The brief Ministerial Statement is followed by the report by
the group of Deputies, under the chairmanship of Robert
V. Roosa.]

Group of Ten, *Report of the Study Group on the Creation of
Reserve Assets: Report to the Deputies of the Group of Ten*
[Ossola Report] (Rome: Bank of Italy Press, 31 May 1965)
109 pp.
[This study group of the Deputies of the Group of Ten was
under the chairmanship of Rinaldo Ossola. It examined alter
native methods and possible effects of the creation of new
monetary reserves, including the CRU, the Collective Reserv
Unit.]

Group of Ten, *Communiqué of Ministers and Governors and
Report of Deputies, July 1966* (Frankfurt am Main: Germar
Bundesbank, Aug 1966) 25 pp.
[A brief communiqué on the Ministerial meeting of the Grou
of Ten, in July 1966 in The Hague, introduces the report of
the group of Deputies, who were chaired by Otmar Emming«
The report presents the principles relating to the need for
reserves and the method of creating and allocating additiona
reserves. It describes five 'main schemes' of reserve creation.

International Monetary Fund, *The Role of Exchange Rates in
the Adjustment of International Payments: A Report by the
Executive Directors* (Washington: IMF, 1970) 78 pp.
[The report, though objective and analytic in its first part,
reflects in its second part the traditional antagonism to flexibility.]

International Monetary Fund, *Reform of the International
Monetary System: A Report by the Executive Directors to
the Board of Governors* (Washington: IMF, 1972) 57 pp.
[This report was commissioned by the Annual Meeting of th
Fund in 1971 'to study all aspects of the international mone
tary system, including the role of reserve currencies, gold anc
special drawing rights, convertibility, . . . exchange rates, anc
the problems caused by destablizing capital movements.'
The report reviews various options for reforms of the system

International Monetary Fund [Committee of Twenty], *First Outline of Reform: Report by the Chairman of the Committee on Reform of the International Monetary System and Related Issues* (Washington: *IMF Survey*, Supplement, 8 October 1973) pp. 305—8.

[This First Outline of Reform, prepared on the basis of the discussions by the Deputies of the 'Committee of Twenty' under the chairmanship of Jeremy Morse, was submitted to the Annual Meeting of the Fund in Sept 1973 at Nairobi. Its main features related to the adjustment process, the exchange-rate mechanism, and the special drawing right as primary reserve asset.]

International Monetary Fund, Committee of Twenty, 'Outline of Reform with Accompanying Annexes', in *International Monetary Reform: Documents of the Committee of Twenty* (Washington: IMF, 1974) viii and 253 pp.

[Part 1 of the Outline of Reform, 14 June 1974, is on 'The Reformed System', Part 2 on 'Immediate Steps'. The annexes, prepared by various 'Technical Groups', deal with reserve indicators, exchange margins, floating, control over official currency holdings, a Substitution Account, SDR allocations, SDR valuation, and other issues.]

EUROPE 1925—37

Reichsverband der deutschen Industrie, [Memorandum of Dec 1925 on] *Deutschlands Wirtschafts-und Finanzpolitik* (Berlin: Reichsverband der deutschen Industrie, 1925) 67 pp.

[Calling for gradual removal of tariff walls and announcing establishment of a Commission of Inquiry on a European Customs Union.]

Union Douanière Européenne, Comité Français, *Premier Congrès d'Union Douanière Européenne, Paris, 30 juin — 1er juillet 1930* (Paris: L'Europe de Demain, 1930).

International Chamber of Commerce, *Exceptions to the Most-Favoured-Nation Treatment: Replies of National Committees and Memorandum on Dr. Richard Riedl's Report*, Papers presented to a Congress held in Washington, 1931, No. 12 (Washington: ICC, 1931) 26 pp.

[Dr Riedl had argued in favour of Austrian-German tariff preference as a transition to a customs union. Most other nations objected to the scheme as in violation of the most-favoured-nation treatment.]

United States, Department of State, Interest of the United States in the Proposed Austro-German Customs Union', *Pap(Relating to the Foreign Relations of the United States, 1931* Vol. 1 (Washington: Government Printing Office, 1946) pp. 565—93.
[The papers are chiefly diplomatic dispatches, memoranda, and letters pertaining to the agreement between Austria and Germany on the creation of a customs union. Some of the views expressed are on the legal aspects, but most of them relate to questions of preferential versus most-favoured-natio treatment.]

Permanent Court of International Justice, *Customs Regime between Germany and Austria (Protocol of March 19, 1931) Advisory Opinion of Sep 5, 1931* (Leyden: A. W. Sijthoff, 1931) 103 pp.
[The Court was asked by the Council of the League of Natio whether the proposed customs regime between Austria and Germany was compatible with the provisions of the Treaty o St Germain and the Geneva Protocol of 1932. The Court came to the opinion that the regime would not be compatibl with the Geneva Protocol.]

League of Nations, Commission of Enquiry for European Union *Documents relating to the Organisation of a System of European Federal Union* (Geneva: League of Nations, 1930 [VII, 4]) 77 pp.
[The Commission attempts an 'analytical summary' of the opinions independently expressed by the participating goverr ments and to record the replies received from some of them to a British memorandum on the proposed Union.]

League of Nations, Commission of Enquiry for European Unior *Report by the Secretary-General to the Assembly on the Wor of the Commission of Enquiry for European Union* (Geneva: League of Nations, 1931 [VII, 9] 21 pp.
[Discusses resolutions from the second session, a memorandu received from the International Labour Office, and proposals from governments.]

League of Nations, Commission of Enquiry for European Unior *Minutes of the Third Session of the Commission, May 15—21 1931* (Geneva: League of Nations, 1931) 211 pp.
[The discussions, instead of focusing on the subject of the enquiry, addressed themselves to questions of the world crise and of proposed remedies.]

League of Nations, *Report of the Secretary-General to the Assembly on the Work of the Commission of Enquiry for European Union* (Geneva: League of Nations, 1932 [VII 8]) 3 pp. [Refers to the establishment of a special committee to study the possibilities for a 'Pact of Economic Non-Aggression'; includes a report of a Committee on the extension of preference to agricultural products other than cereals.]

League of Nations, *Report by the Stresa Conference for the Economic Restoration of Central and Eastern Europe*, submitted to the Commission of Enquiry for European Union (Geneva: League of Nations, 1932 [C 666 M 321]) 40 pp. [The reports of the Financial Committee and of the Economic and Agricultural Committee of the Conference deal with proposed measures for the improvement of conditions, including relaxation of existing trade restrictions. Presumably the Report addressed the proposal for a Danube Economic Union and similar projects.]

Commission Economique de la Troisième Conférence Balkanique, 1932, Report, 'Union douanière partielle, collaboration économique', *Les Balkans* [Athens], Vol. 3, Nos. 1 and 2 (1932) pp. 141—3. [The first conference of Balkan countries had been held in Athens in 1930, the second in Istanbul in 1931, and the third in Bucharest in 1932. This report is a summary of those reports submitted by the Greek and Yugoslav delegations proposing preferential treatments on intra-Balkan trade and other methods of co-operation.]

League of Nations, Commission of Enquiry for European Union, *Report by the Committee of Experts Appointed to Examine the Monetary Normalisation Fund Scheme* (Geneva: League of Nations, 1932 [II A 23]) 32 pp. [The Committee recommends that assistance should be granted only for the purpose of aiding countries in abolishing exchange restrictions and moving towards monetary stability.]

League of Nations, *Recommendations of the Economic Committee Relating to Tariff Policy and the Most-Favored-Nation Clause* (Geneva: League of Nations, 1933 [II E 805]).

Mitteleuropa Institut [Vienna], Union Douanière Européenne, Cobden Club, *Memorandum on the Economic Problems of the Danube States* (Budapest, 1933).

Congrès d'Union Economique at Douanière Européenne (IIIe), *Texte officiel des voeux et résolutions du IIIe Congrès d'Union Economique et Douanière Européenne* (Paris: Ministère des Affaires Etrangères, 1937).

WESTERN EUROPE 1943—9

Pan-European Conference, *Report of the Pan-European Conference* at New York University, Mar 25—27, 1943] (New York
Pan-European Conference and New York University, 1943)
22 pp., mimeographed.
[The conference, the fifth of a series, was addressed by sixte-
speakers, including Coudenhove-Kalergi and Louis Marlio. It
called for 'the creation of a free and united Europe'. A 'Declaration of Aims and Principles of European Federation' was
released separately on 5 June 1943.]

Congrès d'Hertenstein, *Programme d'Hertenstein* [Charter of
Hertenstein], *21 Sep 1946*, reprinted Henri [Hendrik] Brugmans, *L'idée européenne 1918—1965* (Bruges: De Tempel,
1965) pp. 267—8.
[A proposal for a European Union created as a federal community.]

United States, Department of State, 'Report of the Special 'Ad
Hoc' Committee of the State-War-Navy Coordinating Committee' [Top Secret, Washington, 21 April 1947], published
in United States Department of State, *Foreign Relations of
the United States, 1947*, Vol. 3 (Washington: Government
Printing Office, 1972) 1131 pp.
[Secret papers are published after 25 years. This interdepart-
mental committee had submitted plans for European econon
co-operation.]

Union Européenne des Fédéralistes, *Rapports au 1er Congrès
annuel de l'UEF*, Montreux, 27—31 août 1947 (Geneva: Pala
Wilson, 1947) 141 pp.
[This non-governmental international association advocated
European Federation.]

Committee of European Economic Co-operation [Ernest Bevin
Chairman, representing sixteen participating countries],
General Report (Vol. 1) and *Technical Reports* (Vol. 2) *to
the United States Department of State, Sep 21, 1947*
(Washington: US Department of State, Publication Nos. 293
and 2952) Vol. 1, 138 pp.; Vol. 2, 552 pp.
[This intergovernmental committee was established by a con
ference of 16 countries in Paris on 12 July 1947. A preliminary report was considered unsatisfactory by the United State
because it failed to make a definite undertaking to form an
eventual customs union. A declaration of the French government held 'that the present division of Europe into small
economic units does not correspond to the needs of modern

competition; and that it will be possible with the help of customs unions to construct larger units on the strictly economic plane' (§ 98). The Committee agreed that '. . . the advantages . . . through the existence of a large domestic market with no internal trade barriers are manifest', and it endorsed 'the idea of a Customs Union including as many European countries as possible' (§ § 90—2). Vol. 2 contains the report of the Committee on Payments Agreements.]

United States, Department of the Interior, *National Resources and Foreign Aid*, Report of J. A. Krug, 9 Oct 1947 (Washington: Government Printing Office, 1947) 97 pp. [Four official reports aided in the formulation of the policies of the United States in carrying out the Marshall Plan. The 'Krug Report' of the Department of the Interior was the first of the four.]

United States, Council of Economic Advisers, *The Impact of Foreign Aid upon the Domestic Economy*, A report to the President [Nourse Report] (Washington: Council of Economic Advisers, 28 Oct 1947) 112 pp.
[The 'Nourse Report' was the second of the four reports preliminary to the formulation of the policies regarding European recovery and co-operation.]

United States, The President's Committee on Foreign Aid [Harriman Committee], *European Recovery and American Aid* (Washington: Nov 1947), Part 1: *Summary*, 13 pp.; Part 2: *General Report*, 149 pp.; *Special Reports*, 207 pp.
[The 'Harriman Committee' was asked to determine the limits within which the United States could safely and wisely extend aid to Western Europe. The Committee proposed that 'it should be made a condition of continual assistance . . . that the participating countries take all practicable steps to achieve the production and monetary goals which they have set for themselves in the Paris report'.]

United States, Congress, House Select Committee on Foreign Aid, *Final Report on Foreign Aid*, 1 May 1948 [Herter Report], Eightieth Congress, Second Session, House of Representatives Report No. 1845 (Washington: Government Printing Office, 1948) 883 pp.
[The 'Herter Report' is the Congressional report preliminary to legislation on the European Recovery Program.]

United States, Department of State, 'A Program for United States Aid to European Recovery', President Truman's Message to Congress, 19 December 1947, *The Department of State Bulletin*, Vol. 17 (28 Dec 1947) pp. 1233—43; also House

Document No. 478, 80th Congress, 1st Session (Washington
Government Printing Office, 1947) 16 pp.
[In his Message to Congress, President Truman proposed legi
lation implementing the Marshall Plan and establishing the
Economic Cooperation Administration.]

United Nations, Department of Economic Affairs, Subcommitt
of Economic Experts, *Customs Unions: A League of Nations
Contribution to the Study of Customs Union Problems* (New
York: UN, 1947) 98 pp.
[The Subcommittee of Experts, set up by the League's Commission of Enquiry for European Union in 1931, made it cle
that the ultimate goal must be the widest possible collaboration of the nations of Europe in the sense of making Europe
a 'single market' for the products of any and every country i
it.]

United States, Congress, Senate Committee on Foreign Relatio
*Hearings on United States Assistance to European Economic
Recovery*, 80th Congress, 2nd Session, Jan and Feb 1948
(Washington: Government Printing Office, 1948), in three
parts, 1466 pp.
[The Senate Committee hearings on the implementation of
the Marshall Plan.]

United Nations, Economic Commission for Europe, *A Survey c
the Economic Situation and Prospects of Europe* (Geneva:
ECE, 1948) 206 pp.
[This is the first report of ECE. It deals with economic recov
ery following the cessation of hostilities in Europe and discusses problems of European reconstruction. The report was
reproduced by the United States Senate Committee on Forei
Affairs, Committee Print, 1948, 216 pp.]

European Customs Union Study Group, *First Report* [on meet
ings on 10—14 Nov 1947, 2—6 Feb 1948, 18—23 Mar 1948]
(Brussels, March 1948) 92 pp., mimeographed.
[A study group of 16 participating countries on the possibilities of a European customs union. It considered technical
problems and measures for a transitional period.]

United States, Congress, House Select Committee on Foreign A
Subcommittee on France and the Low Countries, *Preliminar
Report Twenty-Four: The Belgian-Luxemburg-Netherlands
Customs and Economic Union*, Apr 1948 (Washington:
Government Printing Office, 1948) 3 vols.
[In its discussions of economic aid to Europe and economic
co-operation among European countries, this Congressional
Committee informed itself about the Benelux Customs Union.

Committee of European Economic Cooperation, *Convention of European Economic Cooperation, with Related Documents, April 1948* (Paris, 1948). [The Convention sets up the Organization for European Economic Co-operation (OEEC). It records that the members 'will continue the study of Customs Unions or analogous arrangements such as free trade areas . . . Those Contracting Parties which have already agreed in principle to the creation of Customs Unions will further the establishment of such Unions as rapidly as conditions permit'.]

Benelux-Studieconferentie, Amsterdam 1948, *Benelux: Rapports Soumis à la Conférence d'Amsterdam*, 19—24 Apr 1948, [organised by Nederlands Verbond van Vakvereigingen and the Confédération Génerale du Travail du Luxembourg (Antwerp: Imprimerie Moderne Excelsior, 1948) 607 pp., with tables. [Contains contributions by various participants on such matters as economic structure and trends, monetary policy, social security, and the organisation of the economies.]

International Committee of the Movements for European Unity, *Congress of Europe at The Hague, May 1948*, reported in *Europe Unites* (London: Hollis & Carter, 1949) 120 pp. [Chaired by Winston Churchill, this Congress — a non-governmental undertaking — called for the establishment of a European Assembly. Among the speakers, besides Churchill, were Ramadier, Coudenhove-Kalergi, Brugmans, van Zeeland, Macmillan, and Reynaud.]

Organisation for European Economic Co-operation, *Report to the Economic Co-operation Administration on the First Annual Programme, 1948—1949* (Paris: OEEC, Oct 1948) 69 pp., and 8 tables. [This is the first report of the OEEC, approved six months after its creation and forwarded to the ECA of the United States on Oct 16, 1948, after many difficulties had been overcome and unanimous agreement on all points was reached.]

United States, Economic Cooperation Administration, *First Report to Congress*, Oct 4, 1948, (Washington: Government Printing Office, 1948) 229 pp. [This is the first report of the ECA, established by the Foreign Assistance Act of 1948 to administer Marshall Plan aid to European countries. It contains also a chapter on the China Aid Program. A voluminous supplement contains documents, protocols, and reports on particular countries.]

Commission Mixte Franco-Italienne pour l'Etude d'Une Union Douanière entre la France et l'Italie, *Rapport final*, Rome, 22 Dec 1947 (Paris: Imprimerie Nationale, 1948).

[The report recommends a customs union of the two countr
to be achieved in steps over a period of six years, to reach
'economic fusion' in that time.]

Commission Mixte Franco-Italienne pour l'Etude d'une Union
Douanière entre la France et l'Italie, *Compte rendu de la
Commission Mixte Franco-Italienne d'une Union Douanière*,
Paris, 22 Jan 1949 (Paris: Imprimerie Nationale, 1949).
[After the Final Report of Dec 1947, the minutes of anothe
meeting are published in this document.]

United States, Economic Cooperation Administration, *A Repo
on Recovery Progress and United States Aid* (Washington:
Government Printing Office, 1949) 269 pp.
[This is the second report on ERP (European Recovery Program) by ECA. It includes discussion of the programs for the
first two years, and the beginnings of economic co-operation
by the countries receiving Marshall Aid.]

United Nations, Economic Commission for Europe, *Economic
Survey of Europe in 1948* (Geneva: ECE, 1949; annually
thereafter) 288 pp.
[This is the second report of ECE. Though not dealing direct
ly with economic integration, the reports on production,
trade, and payments in the European countries shed light on
the problems involved.]

Customs Convention of the Netherlands, Belgium and Luxemburg, *Report on the Conference of Cabinet Ministers of the
Netherlands, Belgium and Luxemburg, held at The Hague on
Mar 10th to 13th, 1949* [unofficial translation] (The Hague,
May 1949) 71 pp.
[Contains a historical survey of the monetary and commerci
agreements signed in 1943, 1944 and 1946—1949. The Proto
col of Mar 1949 concerns the removal of controls and subsidies, and actions regarding monetary, commercial and agricultural policy.]

Organisation for European Economic Co-operation, *Report to
the Economic Co-operation Administration on the 1949—
1950 Programme* (Paris: OEEC, May 1949), Vol. 1, 141 pp;
Vol. 2, 365 pp.
[Volume 1, in five chapters and two annexes, discusses the
national programmes by country and by economic branches.
Vol. 2 consists of the original memoranda submitted by the
countries.]

Organisation for European Economic Co-operation, Council,
*Agreement for Intra-European Payments and Compensations
for 1949—1950* (Paris: OEEC, Sept 1949) 44 pp.

[The first agreement for Intra-European Payments and Compensation had been accepted in Oct 1948. This is the second agreement. It was superseded in Sept 1950 by the European Payments Union.]

WESTERN EUROPE 1949–58

United Nations, Economic Commission for Europe, *European Steel Trends in the Setting of the World Market* (Geneva: ECE, 1949) 147 pp.
[The main purpose of this study was to identify future problems of the European iron and steel industry and to plan co-operative action for meeting these problems.]

Council of Europe, Consultative Assembly, *Official Reports of Debates* (Strasbourg: Council of Europe, beginning August 1949).
[These are the official minutes of the sessions of the Consultative Assembly.]

United Nations, Economic Commission for Europe, 'The Coal and Steel Industries of Western Europe', *Economic Bulletin for Europe*, Vol. 2, No. 2 (1950) pp. 16–52.
[Indicates some of the directions in which important economies may be achieved by the establishment of a unified coal and steel market in Western Europe; and draws attention to some difficulties, such as finding adequate raw materials.]

Organisation for European Economic Co-operation, *General Memorandum on the 1950–51 and 1951–52 Programmes* (Paris: OEEC, 1950), in 16 vols.
[A collection of reports covering the nations and territories which participate in the European Recovery Program, arranged alphabetically.]

Organisation for European Economic Co-operation, *Report on the Progress of Western European Recovery*, Second annual report (Paris: OEEC, Feb 1950) 109 pp.
[Covers the period end-of-war to 1948.]

United Kingdom, Foreign Office, *Anglo-French Discussion Regarding French Proposals for the Western European Coal, Iron and Steel Industries, May–June, 1950* (London: HM Stationery Office, Cmd. 7970, 1950) 15 pp.
[Contains seventeen documents, including statements by the Prime Minister in the House of Commons, discussions between the Foreign Secretary and the French Foreign Minister, a series of French and British memoranda, and several official communiqués.]

Organisation for European Economic Co-operation, *A Europea*
Payments Union and the Rules of Commercial Policy to be
Followed by Member Countries (Paris: OEEC, July 1950) 24
[The European Payments Union took the place of two annu;
agreements on Intra-European Payments and Compensations
the first accepted in Oct 1948, the second in Sept 1949. The
agreement on EPU was signed in Sept 1950.]

France, Ministry of Defence, *Déclaration de Gouvernement*
Français, le 24 octobre 1950 [Pleven Plan], reprinted in
Henri [Hendrik] Brugmans, *L'idée européenne 1918—1965*
(Bruges: De Tempel, 1965) pp. 274—9.
[A plan proposing a common European military establishme;
for the defense of Europe.]

Organisation for European Economic Co-operation, *Economic*
Progress and Problems of Western Europe, Third Annual
Report (Paris: OEEC, June 1951) 158 pp.
[The report deals with the course of economic recovery,
1947—50, describes internal financial policies, changes in
world trade, and trade and payments policy.]

Organisation for European Economic Co-operation, *European*
Payments Union: First Annual Report of the Managing Boar;
1 July 1950—30 June 1951 (Paris: OEEC, Aug 1951) 41 pp.
and 3 tables.
[Describes the operation of the Union during the first year,
and presents, in Chapter 3, 'Conclusions' drawn by the Boarc

République Française, Ministère des Affaires Etrangères, *Rappo*
de la Délégation Française sur le Traité instituant la Commu-
nauté Européenne du Charbon et de l'Acier (Paris: Oct 1951
187 pp.
[The official report on the Treaty establishing the ECSC
stresses the French initiative of the idea of a supranational
authority with institutional, monetary, and procedural guara;
tees of its political, economic, and social operations to create
a common market for coal and steel.]

Council of Europe, Secretariat General, *Economic Relations*
with Overseas Countries (Strasbourg: Council of Europe,
Secretariat General, 27 Aug 1952) 147 pp.
[Contains chapters on trade patterns and policies, commodities, monetary problems, overseas investment, and problems
of population and migration.]

'Actes du Congrès International pour l'Etude des Problèmes
Economiques de la Fédération Européenne (Gênes, 11—14
Sept 1952)', in *Economia Internazionale*, Vol. 6, Nos. 1 and
(1953) xii and 609 pp.

[The proceedings include 29 papers by European economists, including Allais, Carli, Hoffmann, Triffin, Zijlstra, etc., and an even larger number of communications and contributions to the discussion.]

Organisation for European Economic Co-operation, *Europe — The Way Ahead: Towards Economic Expansion and Dollar Balance*, Fourth Annual Report (Paris: OEEC, Dec 1952) 358 pp.
[This report is in three parts: Part 1 presents a programme of action calculated to bring about the solvency of Western Europe and to strengthen the economies of member countries; Parts 2 and 3 contain detailed country analyses of economic outlooks.]

United Nations, Economic Commission for Europe, *European Steel Exports and Steel Demand in Non-European Countries* (Geneva: ECE, 11 Apr 1953) 242 pp.
[The study's main purpose was to shed light on possible development of steel demand outside Europe and on the level of potential European steel exports in the period 1956—60; to call attention to the weaknesses in the policies of European steel exporters, particularly with regard to prices, and to indicate some of the measures which could be adopted to remedy them.]

United Nations, Economic Commission for Europe, *Economic Survey of Europe since the War* (Geneva: ECE, 1953) 385 pp.
[Contains a chapter on the progress of European integration.]

Committee for the Study of European Unity, Consultative Council of the Brussels Powers, *The Economic Integration of Europe* (Frankfurt a.M.: Vittorio Klosterman, for the Institut für ausländisches und internationales Wirtschaftsrecht, 1953) 21 pp.
[Chapter 1 discusses the objectives of integration; Chapter 2, the types of integration; Chapter 3, the phases of integration; and Chapter 4, the world economic problems arising from European integration.]

European Coal and Steel Community, High Authority, *Report on the Problems Raised by the Different Turnover Tax Systems Applied within the Common Market*, Mar 1953 (European Coal and Steel Community, High Authority, 1953) 38 pp, and Appendix.
[The 'Tinbergen Committee Report', written largely by W. B. Reddaway, a member of the Committee, examines the dissimilarities in turnover taxes in the member countries and the probable effects of tax exemptions for exports and compensa-

ting duties on imports or, alternatively, of taxation only in the country of origin.]

European Coal and Steel Community, High Authority, *The Activities of the European Community: General Report of the High Authority*, Aug 1952—Apr 1953 (Luxembourg: European Coal and Steel Community, May 1953; thereafter published annually) 116 pp.

[This, the first annual report of the ECSC, discusses the external relations of ECSC, the state of the markets, the decision on the establishment of the Common Market, and problems connected with it. Its supplement, entitled *Special Report: The Establishment of the Common Market for Steel* (May 1953) 57 pp., discusses in detail the establishment of the Common Market for Steel, problems of pricing, taxes, and cartels and combines.]

United States Congress, Senate, *European Coal and Steel Community*, Hearings before the Committee on Foreign Relations, United States Senate, 83rd Congress, 1st Session, Informal Meeting with Jean Monnet, Franz Etzel, Pierre Uri, and Dirk Spierenburg, June 4 and 5, 1953 (Washington: Government Printing Office, 1953) 37 pp.

[In an informal discussion with the members of the High Authority of ECSC, the members of the Senate Committee on Foreign Relations were briefed on the problems of the Community.]

Institut des Relations Internationales de Bruxelles, *La Communauté Européenne du Charbon et de l'Acier* [Report of a study group] (Paris: Armand Colin, 1953) 338 pp.

[A study group of lawyers, publicists, and economists examined the problems — chiefly legal and only tangentially economic — of the Coal and Steel Community.]

United Nations, Economic Commission for Europe, *Growth and Stagnation in the European Economy* (Geneva: ECE, 1954) 342 pp.

[A historical survey of growth and stagnation since 1913.]

European Coal and Steel Community, High Authority, *Bulletin from the European Coal and Steel Community* (Washington: ECSC, bimonthly Oct 1954—Apr 1958).

European Coal and Steel Community, Common Assembly, *Bibliographie analytique du Plan Schuman et de la CECA* (Luxembourg: ECSC, 1955) 131 pp.

[The (Schuman Plan) treaty was signed by foreign ministers on 18 Apr 1951.]

European Coal and Steel Community, High Authority, *Catalogue*

analytique du fonds Plan Schuman (Luxembourg: ECSC, 1955—9), in three volumes.
[A full bibliography arranged by subject and by author.]
Organisation for European Economic Co-operation, *Prolongation of the European Payments Union to 30th June 1956 and Adoption of a European Monetary Agreement and of Amendments to the Code of Liberalisation* (Paris: OEEC, Aug 1955) 47 pp.
[Describes the decisions of the Council of OEEC regarding the prolongation of EPU; it also explains the provisions of the European Monetary Agreement which will come into force when the EPU terminates.]
Organisation for European Economic Co-operation, *European Monetary Agreement* (Paris: OEEC, Aug 1955) 55 pp.
[The EMA did not come into force until Dec 1958, when a majority of OEEC member countries declared their currencies convertible in different degrees.]
Council of Europe, Research Directorate of the Secretariat General, *The Present State of Economic Integration in Western Europe* (Strasbourg: Council of Europe, 1955) 103 pp.
[Discusses the attempts at, methods for, and obstacles to, economic integration, and summarises the progress made.]
United Nations, *The Quest for Freer Trade* (New York: UN, 1955) 59 pp.
[Examines the obstacles to international trade that have resulted from national commercial policies and payments restrictions. Reviews national and concerted actions to reduce or remove these obstacles.]
Organisation for European Economic Co-operation, *La coopération économique européenne: Rapport établi pour le Conseil d'Europe* (Paris: OEEC, 1956).
Organisation for European Economic Co-operation, *Liberalisation of Europe's Dollar Trade* (Paris: OEEC, Mar 1956) 135 pp.
[This is the first report by the Joint Trade and Intra-European Payments Committee. It contains an analysis of measures of relaxation of quantitative restrictions on imports, and of the effects of such liberalisation; also of the relaxation of restrictions on invisible transactions and transfers relating to the dollar area.]
Comité intergouvernemental créé par la Conférence de Messine, *Rapport des Chefs des Délégations aux Ministres des Affaires Etrangères* [Spaak Report], Bruxelles, 21 avril 1956 (Brussels: Secretariat of EEC, 1956) 135 pp.
[Endorses the principle of supranational authorities and

changes the piecemeal approach adopted by the Messina
Resolution to a universal approach towards an Economic
Union of Western Europe — WEU.]

Organisation for European Economic Co-operation, *Code de la
libéralisation* (Paris: OEEC, Apr 1956) 126 pp.

Organisation for European Economic Co-operation, *The Organi
sation for European Economic Co-operation: History and
Structure* (Paris: OEEC, fifth edition, 1956) 44 pp.
[After a short chapter giving the history of OEEC, beginning
with the Paris Conference of July 1947, the booklet describe
the organisation — council, committees, boards, agencies,
working parties, etc.]

Organisation for European Economic Co-operation, *Liberalisation of Europe's Dollar Trade: Second Report, June 1957*
(Paris: OEEC, July 1957) 180 pp.
[This report deals with the measures and their effects, based
on reports from the member countries. It includes detailed
descriptions for each country, and a summary of the informa
tion received.]

WESTERN EUROPE 1959—75

International Secretariat of the NATO Parliamentarians' Conference, *Atlantic Congress: Report, London, 5—10 June 195!*
(London: International Secretariat of the NATO Parliamentarians' Conference, 1959) 95 pp.
[This Atlantic Congress, held in London in 1959, was similar
in scale to that of the Congress of Europe held in The Hague
in 1948. The Report contains the Proceedings of the Congres
and the Declaration of Principles and Proposals adopted at th
Final Session.]

Organisation for European Economic Co-operation, *Report on
the Possibility of Creating a Free Trade Area in Europe: Prepared for the Council of OEEC by a Special Working Party*
(Paris: OEEC, 1957) 57 pp.
[The Report discusses the difference between a free-trade are
and a customs union. It stresses the advantages of the former
in that it allows each member country to set its tariffs on imports from non-members according to its own needs.]

Centro Italiano di Studi Giuridici, *L'ensemble des Actes Officiel
du Congrès international d'études sur la Communauté Européenne du Charbon et de l'Acier*, Stresa, June 1957 (Milan:
Dott. A. Giuffré, 1957—8) 7 volumes: Vol. 1, Introduction,

245 pp.; Vol. 2, La Communauté Européenne du Charbon et l'Acier et des états membres, 407 pp.; Vol. 3, La Communauté, les pays tiers et les organisations internationales, 431 pp.; Vol. 4, La Communauté et les entreprises, 395 pp.; Vol. 5, Les interventions de la Haute Autorité, 293 pp.; Vol. 6, Le système des prix et la concurrence dans le Marché Commun, 647 pp.; Vol. 7, L'orientation sociale de la Communauté, 570 pp.

Organisation for Economic Co-operation and Development, *European Monetary Agreement*, Annual Reports of the Board of Management (Paris: OECD, first report, 1959; thereafter annually) between 50 and 85 pp. each.
[The reports consider changes in monetary reserves and other monetary transactions, balance-of-payments developments, work of the Board of Management, and operations under the European Monetary Agreement in Europe.]

European Free Trade Association, *First Annual Report of the European Free Trade Association*, for the period ending 1 July 1961 (Geneva: EFTA, July 1961; thereafter annually, up to and including the 1972 volume) 40 pp.
[Describes the organisation of EFTA and its operations; analyses the expansion of EFTA's total trade and intra-EFTA trade.]

United Nations, Economic Commission for Europe, *Some Factors in Economic Growth in Europe during the 1950's: Economic Survey of Europe, 1961*, Part 2 (New York: United Nations, 1961) 283 pp.
[Discusses the growth of the economy as a whole and of individual sectors, especially in four Western European countries and Hungary.]

European Economic Community, Commission, *The First Stage of the Common Market: Report on the Execution of the Treaty, January 1958—1962* (Brussels: European Economic Community, July 1962) 115 pp., and 5 Annex pages.
[This report discusses the internal development of the Common Market and its relations to the outside world.]

European Economic Community, Commission, 'General Report of the Sub-Groups A, B, and C appointed for the study of the various possibilities for the harmonization of turnover taxes', translated from the French text (Brussels: EEC, 1962) and published as Book I, pp. 1—92, in *The EEC Reports on Tax Harmonization* (Amsterdam: International Bureau of Fiscal Documentation, 1963).
[The Report examines how the regulations for turnover tax could be harmonised. The various proposals are dealt with

from a technical point of view, with choosing one system or
another as the basis for harmonisation.]

European Economic Community, Commission, 'Report of the
Fiscal and Financial Committee' [Neumark Report], translated from the German text (Brussels: EEC, 1963), and published as Books II and III, pp. 92—203, in *The EEC Reports
on Tax Harmonization* (Amsterdam: International Bureau of
Fiscal Documentation, 1963).
[Studied to what extent differences in the financial institutions of member countries hinder the establishment of conditions analogous to those of an internal market, and to what
extent it is possible to eliminate these differences.]

European Economic Community, *Report to the European Parliament on the State of Negotiations with the United Kingdom*,
Feb 1963 (Brussels: European Economic Community, 1963)
112 pp.

Organisation for Economic Co-operation and Development, *The
Balance of Payments Adjustment Process*, A Report by Working Party No. 3 of the Economic Policy Committee of the
OECD (Paris: OECD, 1966) 29 pp.
[This report, a joint product of experts from member countries
and staff of the OECD, was a result of different discussions,
which laboured under the political constraint imposed on
the group to adhere to the assumption of fixed exchange
rates.]

United Kingdom, Department of Economic Affairs, *Britain and
the EEC: The Economic Background* (London: HM Stationery
Office, 1967) 49 pp.
[This booklet provides a summary of essential facts concerning EEC. It compares Britain's trade with EFTA and EEC
countries.]

Action Committee for the United States of Europe [Monnet
Committee], *Statements and Declarations 1955—1967*
(London: Chatham House, 1969), 114 pp.
[Contains introduction, and all documents of the Action
Committee (list of members, communiqués, and Joint Declara-
tions) up to Oct 1968.]

European Economic Community, *Tax Harmonisation Programme,
Programme for the Harmonisation of Direct Taxes*, Supplement to the *Bulletin of the European Economic Community*
(No. 8, 1967) 20 pp.
[This is an 'Outline Programme' stating the reasons and objectives, and urgent problems regarding capital movements, industrial combination and depreciation allowance.]

Study Group, Graduate Institute of International Studies [Geneva], *The European Free Trade Association and the Crisis of European Integration: An Aspect of the Atlantic Crisis?* (London: Michael Joseph, for the Graduate Institute of International Studies, 1968) 321 pp.
[Part 1 is on European integration and Atlantic partnership, Part 2 on the position of EFTA states facing the crisis, Part 3 on EFTA's contribution to European integration, and Part 4 on Europe's options regarding integration.]

European Communities, Commission, *Memorandum on the Reform of Agriculture in the European Economic Community: The 'Agriculture 1980' Programme* [Mansholt Plan] (Brussels: European Communities, 18 Oct 1968; revised edition, 1969) 73 pp. and Appendix with 22 tables. An English discussion of the Plan appears in John Marsh and Christopher Ritson, *Agricultural Policy and the Common Market* (London: Chatham House, 1971) 199 pp.
[The Plan rests on the thesis that the only practical way of increasing the incomes of farmers was by a major reform of the structure of production: to increase the size of farm businesses and reduce the total number of farms. The proposed reduction amounts to about half the present farm labour force.]

Organisation for Economic Co-operation and Development, *Border Tax Adjustments and Tax Structures in OECD Member Countries* (Paris: OECD, Nov 1968) 264 pp.

European Free Trade Association, *The Effects of EFTA on the Economies of Member States* (Geneva: EFTA, Dec 1968).
[There are two accompanying annexes, in two volumes. Annex 1 is entitled 'Production, Trade, and Consumption', 72 pp.; Annex 2, 'The Results of the Calculation of the EFTA Effects', 109 pp., mimeographed.]

European Parliament, *The First Ten Years: 1958—1968* (Strasbourg: General Secretariat of the European Parliament, 1968) 180 pp.
[Describes the creation and operations of the European Parliament at Strasbourg from its beginning as 'Common Assembly' of the European Coal and Steel Community.]

European Communities, Commission, *Commission Memorandum to the Council on the Co-ordination of Economic Policies and Monetary Co-operation within the Community* [Barre Report], Supplement to the *Bulletin of the European Communities*, Vol. 2, No. 3 (1969) 15 pp.
[This is the first version of the report which Raymond Barre

did a year later, laying down the principles of monetary
union. For the final report and the subsequent Werner Repc
see below.]

Federal Trust for Education and Research [London], *Current
Agricultural Proposals for Europe: Report of a Conference,
26—27th Jan 1970* (London: Federal Trust for Education a
Research, 1970) 57 pp.

[A specialist conference was held in London in Jan 1970 to
discuss proposals for agricultural reform — the Mansholt Pla
— and a report by a French group of experts — the Vedel
Report. Two papers, by J. van Lierde and Alain Bienayme, a
followed by general discussion.]

European Communities, Commission, *A Plan for the Phased
Establishment of an Economic and Monetary Union* [Barre
Report], Supplement to the *Bulletin of the European Com-
munities*, Vol. 3, No. 3 (1970) 14 pp.

[In order to allow the maintenance of fixed exchange rates
within very narrow margins, the member countries should
reduce possible inconsistencies among their medium-term
objectives with respect to growth and inflation, co-ordinate
their current economic and financial policies to forestall shc
term external imbalances, consult with one another prior to
the final adoption of economic-policy measures, and establi:
facilities for short-term and medium-term monetary assistan
within the EEC.]

European Communities, Commission, *Interim Report on the
Establishment by Stages of Economic and Monetary Union:
'Werner Report'*, Supplement to the *Bulletin of the Europec
Communities*, Vol. 3, No. 7 (1970) 26 pp.

[This is the first report of the Werner Committee. The defin
tive report was submitted a few months later with some
revisions.]

European Communities, Commission, *Report to the Council
and the Commission on the Realisation by Stages of Econor
and Monetary Union in the Community: 'Werner Report'*
[definitive text], Supplement to the *Bulletin of the Europe*
Communities, Vol. 3, No. 11 (1970) 68 pp.

[The approach to monetary union should begin with a narrc
ing of the margins of exchange-rate fluctuations around fixe
parities. This would be followed by closer co-ordination of
the countries' fiscal and monetary policies, leading to a mer;
of central banks and, ultimately, to the issuance of a comm
European currency.]

European Communities, Commission, *Third Medium-Term*

Economic Policy Programme (Brussels: European Communities, 1971) 74 pp.

European Communities, Commission, *Regional Development in the Community: Analytical Survey* (Luxembourg: European Communities, 1971) 316 pp.
[The analysis deals with population, employment, and regional product for the six countries of the Common Market, divided into 100 smaller regions or provinces.]

Organisation for Economic Co-operation and Development, *Trade Measures and Adjustment of the Balance of Payments* (Paris: OECD, 1971) 81 pp.
[This report of the Secretary General discusses quantitative restrictions, customs duties, import surcharges, import deposits, export subsidies and credits, but contrasts them with an overall approach to adjustment of balance of payments.]

European Communities, Council, *Reports on the First Preliminary Draft Convention for a European System for the Grant of Patents*, inter-governmental conference for the setting-up of a European system for the grant of patents (Brussels/Luxembourg: European Communities, 1971) 32 pp.

European Communities, Commission, *Memorandum on a Community Policy on Development Co-operation: Synopsis and Programme for Initial Actions*, Communications of the Commission to the Council of 27 July 1971 and 2 Feb 1972 (Brussels: European Communities, 1972) 304 pp.
[On a community policy of co-operation with developing countries on matters of trade and aid.]

European Communities, Commission, *The Enlarged Community: Outcome of the Negotiations with the Applicant States*, Supplement to the *Bulletin of the European Communities*, Vol. 5, No. 1 (1972) 72 pp.

European Communities, Parliament, *L'état de l'unification européenne et le rôle des Parlements: Colloque parlementaire européen, Strasbourg, 15 et 16 mars, 1972* (Luxembourg: European Communities, 1972) 188 pp.

European Communities, *Documents Concerning the Accession to the European Communities of the Kindom of Denmark, Ireland, the Kingdom of Norway and the United Kingdom of Great Britain and Northern Ireland*, Special Edition of the *Official Journal of the European Communities*, 27 Mar 1972, 204 pp.

European Communities, Commission, *La politique monétaire dans les pays de la Communauté économique européenne:*

Institutions et instruments (Brussels/Luxembourg: Europe:
Communities, 1972) 448 pp.

Organisation for Economic Co-operation and Development,
*Policy Perspectives for International Trade and Economic
Relations*, Report by a High Level Group on Trade and
Related Problems to the Secretary General of OECD (Paris
OECD, Sep 1972) 170 pp.
[An analysis of the development of international economic
relations over the last 25 years and the role of multilateral
operation in the results achieved. The report of the High L
Group, under the chairmanship of Jean Rey, brings out the
changes which have occurred in international trade, and the
main problems now being experienced, and examines the
opportunities for further progress towards the general obje
tive of a greater liberalisation of international trade. Chapte
are devoted to the monetary system and the balance-of-pay
ments adjustment process, the industrial sector (in particul:
questions concerning customs tariffs, non-tariff barriers, an
multinational companies), the agricultural sector, services,
structural adjustments and safeguard provisions, regional in
tegration and special agreements, the developing countries,
planned-economy countries, and institutions.]

Organisation for Economic Co-operation and Development,
Aggregated Rebate Cartels, A Report of the Committee of
Experts on Restrictive Business Practices (Paris: OECD, No
1972) 60 pp.
[This report examines the importance of aggregated-rebate
cartels in member countries and describes the manner in wl
they are operated, their economic effects and the statutory
provisions adopted by member countries in relation to ther
It also stresses the problems raised by this type of cartel for
international competition.]

Organisation for Economic Co-operation and Development,
Restrictive Business Practices Relating to Patents and Licen
Report by the Committee of Experts on Restrictive Busine:
Practices (Paris: OECD, Dec 1972) 56 pp.
[This report considers the impact of competition policy an
patents policy on each other and how patent law and legisl:
tion regarding restrictive business practices apply to abuses
or restraints connected with patents and licences.]

Organisation for Economic Co-operation and Development,
Code of Liberalisation of Current Invisible Operations (Pari
OECD, Mar 1973) 82 pp.
[Liberalisation of international current invisible operations

one of the objectives of OECD. Like previous ones, this new edition of the Code records the agreements reached and the commitments accepted in this sector by member states. It sets forth conditions of liberalisation of services, enumerates the specific operations which have been freed, and lists the exceptions which some members are obliged to make.]

European Communities, Commission, *Progress Report 1958– 1972*, Information Memo (Brussels: European Communities, May 1973) 84 pp., mimeographed.

European Communities, *Treaties establishing the European Communities; Treaties amending these treaties; Documents concerning the Accession* (Luxembourg: European Communities, 1973) 1502 pp.
[Contains the texts of all the basic treaties and other documents, brought up to date as of 1 Jan 1973.]

European Communities, Commission, *The European Development Fund: From the Introduction of the Project to Its Completion* (Luxembourg: European Communities, revised edition, 1973) 25 pp.
[A brief exposition of the scope of the Fund and of its financing activities.]

European Communities, Commission, *Attainment of the Economic and Monetary Union, Supplement* to the *Bulletin of the European Communities*, Vol. 6, No. 5 (1973) 20 pp.
[A communication, presented by the Commission to the Council on 30 Apr 1973, on progress of the first stage of economic and monetary union, on allocation of powers and responsibilities among the Community institutions and the member states, and on the measures to be taken in the second stage of economic and monetary union.]

European Communities, Commission, *Report from the Commission to the Council on the Adjustment of Short-Term Monetary Support Arrangements and the Conditions for the Progressive Pooling of Reserves*, 27 June 1973 (Brussels: European Communities, 1973) 11 pp and 'Technical Annex' of 18 pp., mimeographed.

European Communities, Commission, *Study Group on Economic and Monetary Union: European Economic Integration and Monetary Unification* (Brussels: European Communities, Oct 1973) 196 pp.
[The first part is a 'Synthesis' of 44 pages by three rapporteurs of the Study Group, summarising the main view of the majority of its eleven members. The second part presents 'Individual Contributions' by ten members: Bosman, Denizet, Dosser,

Giersch, Magnifico, Meade, Mundell, Neubauer, Onida, and
Peeters.]

Organisation for Economic Co-operation and Development,
Code of Liberalisation of Capital Movements (Paris: OECD,
Oct 1973) 122 pp.
[The instrument of international law concerning capital oper
tions. The Code contains undertakings subscribed to by mem
ber countries in 1961 with a view to abolishing restrictions
and maintaining a system of freedom for long-term capital
operations such as direct investment, portfolio investment,
financial credits, etc. Annexed to it are lists of the restriction
which the member countries maintain for the present on a
variety of operations.]

Organisation for Economic Co-operation and Development,
Flow of Resources to Developing Countries, 1961—1971
(Paris: OECD, Dec 1973) 448 pp.
[Sets out in individual-country chapters the evolution of the
aid efforts of each of the members of the Development Assistance Committee; describes their current aid programmes and
provides indications on private flows from donor countries
which are not members of the Development Assistance Committee.]

European Communities, Commission, *Compendium of Community Monetary Texts* (Brussels: European Communities,
1974) 173 pp.
[Collection of legal texts relating to economic and monetary
union up to July 1974. Covers the Monetary Committee,
Committee of Governors of the Central Banks, exchange-rate
system, Monetary Co-operation Fund, co-ordination of econo
mic policies, capital markets, and unit of account.]

European Communities, Commission, *The European Community's Financial System* (Brussels: European Communities,
1975) 34 pp.
[Covers the historical development of the ECSC, EEC, and
EURATOM budgets, the transition to 'own resources' system
the new budgetary procedure, and 1975 revenue and expendi
ture.]

European Communities, Commission, *Statute for European
Companies*, Supplement to the *Bulletin of the European
Communities*, Vol. 8, No. 4 (1975) 223 pp.
[Amended proposal for a uniform statute creating a legal
structure for company organisation at the European rather
than national level, presented to the Council on 13 May 1975
Includes commentary on the text.]

European Communities, Commission, *Towards European Citizenship*, Supplement to the *Bulletin of the European Communities*, Vol. 8, No. 7 (1975) 32 pp.
[Two reports submitted by the Commission to the Council on 3 July 1975, concerning a European passport union and the granting of civil and political rights by each member state to nationals of other member states.]

European Communities, Commission, *Report on European Union*, Supplement to the *Bulletin of the European Communities*, Vol. 8, No. 9 (1975) 34 pp.
[Contains two resolutions of the European Parliament, the suggestions of the Court of Justice, and the opinion of the Economic and Social Committee on European Union.]

European Communities, Commission, *Aide-Memoire on the Multilateral Trade Negotiations in GATT*, Background Note No. 35/1975 (Washington: European Community Information Service, 12 Nov 1975) 14 pp.
[Outlines the situation of the negotiations as of the fall of 1975, from the Community point of view. Covers tariffs, non-tariff barriers, agriculture, tropical products, the sector approach, and safeguard clause.]

EASTERN EUROPE 1945—75

Council for Mutual Economic Assistance, 'Basic Principles of the International Socialist Division of Labor: Resolution of the Representatives of the Countries of the Council for Mutual Economic Aid' (Moscow, 1962), in English translation as Appendix C of Heinz Köhler, *Economic Integration in the Soviet Bloc* (New York: Praeger, 1965) pp. 377—95.
[An unofficial translation of the official statement on the community of the Socialist countries, the co-ordination of their national economic plans, specialisation of production, and commodity exchange among the members.]

United Nations, *Economic Integration and Industrial Specialization among the Member Countries of the Council for Mutual Economic Assistance* (United Nations, 1966) 34 pp.
[A study by the Center for Industrial Development reviewing activities of the CMEA regarding specialisation of, and co-operation among, industries in member countries.]

Akademie der Wissenschaften der DDR, *Probleme der sozialistischen ökonomischen Integration der Mitgliedsländer des RGW* (Berlin: Akademie-Verlag, 1974) 236 pp.
[Proceedings of a conference of the Scientific Council for

Economic Research of the Academy of Sciences of the Ger man Democratic Republic, containing papers and discussio by more than twenty economists on economic integration within the CMEA.]

Council for Mutual Economic Assistance, *The Council for Mutual Economic Assistance: 25 Years* (Moscow: CMEA, 1974) 106 pp.
[A survey prepared by the Secretariat to commemorate the twenty-fifth anniversary of CMEA. It gives a brief account the main stages, trends, and forms of co-operation and of t social and economic achievements of the member countrie

Council for Mutual Economic Assistance, *Collected Reports (Various Activities of Bodies of the CMEA in 1974* (Moscov CMEA, Mar 1975) 261 pp., mimeographed.
[Contains reports on various activities, including planning statistics, in several sectors or industries.]

THE AMERICAS

United States, Continental Congress, *Journals of the Continer Congress, 1774—1789*, edited from the original records by C. Ford and Gaillard Hunt, (Washington: Government Prin ing Office, 1904—37) Vol. 25, pp. 628—30, 661—4.
[Contains significant views on the economic integration of the United States of America.]

International American Conference, *Reports of Committees (Discussions Thereon* [Pan-American Conference in Washing ton, 1889] (Washington: Government Printing Office, 189 Vol. 1, 554 pp.; Vol. 2, 649 pp.; Vol. 3, *Excursion Appena* 343 pp.; Vol. 4, *Historical Appendix*, 375 pp.
[Vol. 1 includes, apart from preliminary and procedural matters, discussions of weights and measures, intercontiner railways, reciprocity treaties, communication, customs reg tions, and harbour fees and regulations. Vol. 2 deals with patents and trademarks, a proposal for an International American Monetary Union, and an International American Bank.]

Conference of American Associations of Commerce and Prod tion, *Final Declarations of the Conference of American Associations of Commerce and Production*, held at Monte- video, Uruguay, 28 May—3 June 1941 (Washington: Cham of Commerce of the United States, 1941) mimeographed.

Inter-American Council of Commerce and Production, *Summ of Conclusions* [of the Conference of Montevideo, 1941]

(Washington: United States Inter-American Council, 1948).
[See especially the part on 'Regional Accords and Customs Unions', p. 9.]

Camara Argentina de Comercio, *Union federal argentino-chilena, anticipación de una federación sudamericana* (Buenos Aires, 1942).
[This document on a proposed federal union between Argentina and Chile is considered as an anticipation of a Latin American common market.

United Nations, Economic Commission for Latin America, *Interim Report for the Period 10 July 1948—10 Jan 1949* (New York: UN, 1949).
[The first ECLA report on economic developments in Latin America.]

United Nations Economic Commission for Latin America, Secretariat, *Economic Survey for Latin America, 1948* (Lake Success: Department of Economic Affairs, 1949) Vol. 1, 279 pp.
[A comprehensive review of the economic situation in Latin America, with a discussion of production, overall measurements, factor movements, and foreign trade.]

United Nations Economic Commission for Latin America, *A Study of Trade between Latin America and Europe* (New York: ECLA, 1952) 117 pp.
[Examines the composition of trade, competitive factors, and the conditions for expansion of trade.]

United Nations, Economic Commission for Latin America, *Progress Report Submitted by the Executive Secretary Concerning the Program for Economic Integration and Reciprocity in Central America* (New York: UN, 1953) 167 pp.
[Reports on the first session of the Committee of Ministers of Economy on Economic Integration in Central America and on subsequent activities, technical assistance, and preliminary work on tariff standardisation.]

United Nations, Economic Commission for Latin America, *International Co-operation in a Latin American Development Policy* (New York: UN, 1954) 147 pp.
[The report, preparatory to a meeting at Rio de Janeiro, deals with policies for foreign investment, technical assistance, and trade and economic development; and with measures required to reduce the external economic vulnerability of Latin America.]

United Nations, Department of Economic and Social Affairs, *Foreign Capital in Latin America* (New York: UN, 1955) 164 pp.

[Part 1 surveys general trends and compares policies. Part 2 traces for each of the twenty countries the historical develop ment and present status of the external debt and foreign in vestments, and summarises policies affecting private foreign investment.]

United Nations, Economic Commission for Latin America, 'T Latin American Regional Market', *Economic Bulletin for Latin America*, Vol. 3, No. 1 (1958) pp. 1—8.
[Presents general principles for establishing a Latin Americ regional market, including universality of membership, development of less advanced countries, tariffs *vis-à-vis* the rest of the world, specialisation, the payments system, tem ary import restrictions, safeguards for agriculture, rules of competition, credits and technical assistance, and the role c private enterprise.]

United Nations, Economic Commission for Latin America, 'P gress Towards the Latin American Common Market', *Econo mic Bulletin for Latin America*, Vol. 4, No. 1 (1959) pp. 1-
[The report sketches a general outline of the common mark in order to provide the Secretariat with a basis for entering upon a new stage of work.]

United Nations, Economic Commission for Latin America, 'T Central American Economic Integration Programme', *Econo mic Bulletin for Latin America*, Vol. 4, No. 2 (1959) pp. 33—48.
[Outlines programmes for the mains sectors of the econom and discusses their possible contribution to general econom integration.]

United Nations, Economic Commission for Latin America, *Th Latin American Common Market* (New York: UN, 1959) 146 pp.
[Discusses the Latin American Common Market in relation the multilateral payments system, economic development i Latin America, the Free Trade Area, and includes a report the second session of the Trade Committee.]

United Nations, Economic Commission for Latin America, *Report of the Central American Economic Co-operation Co mittee, 1959—60* (New York: UN, 1960) 53 pp.
[Part 2 reports on the technical assistance given to the Inte tion Programme by the UN.]

United Nations, Economic Commission for Latin America, *Foreign Private Investment in the Latin American Free Tra Area*, Report of the Consultant Group (New York: UN, 19 30 pp.

[The consultants made recommendations concerning incentives for foreign capital, for the modernisation of domestic industries, for technological advancement, and related matters.]

United Nations, Economic Commission for Latin America, *Multilateral Economic Cooperation in Latin America*, Vol. 1, *Text and Documents* (New York: UN, 1962) 165 pp.
[A collection of official instruments, reports by the various organisations concerned with Central American Economic Integration, LAFTA, and payments and credits.]

United Nations, Economic Commission for Latin America, *Report of the Central American Economic Cooperation Committee, 1960—63* (New York: UN, 1963) 69 pp.
[Part 1 reviews the activities of the committee and of the ECLA secretariat; Part 2 describes the technical assistance provided by the UN agencies; Part 3 summarises the proceedings and conclusions of the eighth session; and Part 4 contains the resolutions adopted.]

United Nations, Economic Commission for Latin America, *Possibilities of Integrated Industrial Development in Central America* (New York: UN, 1963) 54 pp.
[Presents some preliminary market studies, intended to throw light on the feasibility of investment in the industries concerned.]

United Nations, Economic Commission for Latin America, 'The Growth and Decline of Import Substitution in Brazil', *Economic Bulletin for Latin America*, Vol. 9, No. 1 (1964) pp. 1—61.
[Summarises the economic arguments that explain why import substitution not only made such rapid headway in Brazil, but was also accompanied by growth rates exceeding those for Latin America as a whole.]

Canadian-American Committee, *A New Trade Strategy for Canada and the United States* (Washington: National Planning Association, 1966) 20 pp.
[A statement designed to outline a workable trade strategy between the two countries in the framework of existing institutions such as the GATT. The idea of a free-trade association is examined in the light of the existence of EEC and EFTA.]

United States, Congress, House of Representatives, *Inter-American Relations: A Collection of Documents, Legislation, Descriptions of Inter-American Organizations, and Other Material Pertaining to Inter-American Affairs*, 93rd Congress, 1st Session (Washington: Government Printing Office, 1973) ix and 780 pp.

[Includes chapters on the Inter-American Development Bank
and, in Chapter V, a section on 'Regional Integration' —
ODECA, CACM, LAFTA, Andean Group, and CARIFTA.]

AFRICA

'Minutes of Proceedings of the South African Customs Union
   Conference, Bloemfontein, March 1903', 17 pp., in *Account
   and Papers*, Vol. 45 Part 10 (London: HM Stationery Office,
   Cmd. 1640, 1903).
   [The conference discussed a draft for a customs union con-
   vention that superseded an earlier convention of 1898 betwe
   the Cape Colony, the Orange Free State, and the Colony of
   Natal.]
United Kingdom, Colonial Office, *Papers Relating to the Ques-
   tion of the Closer Union of Kenya, Uganda, and the Tanganyika Territory*, Colonial No. 57 (London, 1931).
United Nations, Economic Commission for Africa, *Economic
   Survey of Africa since 1950*, Vol. 1 (New York: UN Depart-
   ment of Economic and Social Affairs, 1959) 248 pp.
   [Part 1 deals with structural aspects, including population an
   sector analysis; Part 2, with growth trends; Part 3, with devel
   opment of external trade; and Part 4, with capital formation
East African Common Services Organization, *Economic and Sta
   istical Review* (Nairobi: East African Statistical Department)
   [Issued quarterly from Dec 1961. Issue No. 1 contains
   'An Index of Economic Activity' in Kenya, Tanganyika,
   Uganda, and Zanzibar. Issue No. 4 (Sept 1962) contains a
   study by Benton F. Massell on 'Trade between East Africa
   and Neighbouring Countries'.]
East African Common Services Organization, *Annual Report*
   (Nairobi: Information Division, East African Common Ser-
   vices Organization; annually 1965—7).
East African Community, *Annual Report 1968* (Arusha, Tan-
   zania: Information Division, East African Community, 1968)
   [This is the report by the East African Community, successo
   to the East African Common Services Organization.]
Institut d'Etudes Européennes [Université Libre de Bruxelles],
   Le Renouvellement de la Convention de Yaoundé (Brussels:
   Edition de l'Institut de Sociologie, 1969) 46 pp.
   [Contains the papers and discussions of a conference held in
   Dec 1968 concerning what in July 1969 became the second
   Yaoundé Convention. One of the papers contributed was by
   Jan Tinbergen.]

ASIA AND THE FAR EAST

United Nations, Economic Commission for Asia and the Far East, *Interim Report to the Economic and Social Council* (New York: UN, 1948).

United Nations, Economic Commission for Asia and the Far East, *Economic Survey of Asia and the Far East* (New York: UN, annual since 1948).
[Discusses characteristics of Asian and Far Eastern economies, population trends, salient changes since the war, production, monetary and fiscal developments, and the international balances of payments.]

United Nations, Economic Commission for Asia and the Far East, *A Study of Trade between Asia and Europe* (Bangkok: UN, 1953) 146 pp.
[Seeks to determine the contribution of trade to the economic welfare of the region.]

United Nations, Economic Commission for Asia and the Far East, *Regional Economic Cooperation in Asia and the Far East: Report of the Ministerial Conference*, Manila, 1963 (New York: UN, 1964) 77 pp.
[Discusses measures of economic co-operation in the ECAFE region, especially the UN Conference on Trade and Development and its bearing on the region.]

United Nations, Economic Commission for Asia and the Far East, *The Asian Development Bank and Trade Liberalization* (New York: UN, 1965) 137 pp.
[Concludes that an Asian Development Bank could make a useful contribution to economic co-operation and development in the region.]

Parliament of the Commonwealth of Australia, Senate Standing Committee on Industry and Trade, *Interim Report on Australia-New Zealand Trade*, Parliamentary Paper No. 179 (Canberra, 1972) 2 pp.
[The arrangements for NAFTA seem to be lip service but no actual approach to economic integration.]

Parliament of the Commonwealth of Australia, Senate Standing Committee on Industry and Trade, *Australia-New Zealand Trade* (Canberra: Australian Government Publishing Service, 1973) 183 pp.
[A report from the Standing Committee on the developments under the NAFTA agreement of 1965, showing virtually no trade creation but, instead, the institution of restrictive practices by industries in instances where competition threatened

to emerge.]

United Nations, Department of Economic and Social Affairs,
'Economic Co-operation among Member Countries of the
Association of South East Asian Nations', *Journal of Develop
ment Planning*, No. 7 (1974) 261 pp.

[A study team appointed by the United Nations reports on
general issues and techniques of economic, financial, and
monetary co-operation among the member countries of the
Association of South East Asian Nations, which was created
in Bangkok in Aug 1967. The report made use of 14 ASEAN
industrial studies. Gunal Kansu was leader and Sir Austin
Robinson senior adviser of the team.]

9   Economic Theorists

As we come to the fifth group of contributors, those among my readers who are chiefly interested in economic analysis may at last get what they have been patiently (or impatiently) waiting for. In Chapter 4 a review of the theoretical issues was offered without indication of the parentage of the ideas; now the names of the authors will be given together with some of their intellectual offspring. But first a few general principles regarding the inclusiveness, selectivity, and general arrangement of this survey should be set forth.

GENERAL GUIDELINES

We should bear in mind that virtually all economic propositions about international economic integration are part and parcel of the theory of international trade and finance and, obversely, that most of this body of theory is directly relevant to issues of economic integration. I doubt whether one can find any proposition in trade theory that has no bearing on some of the implications of economic integration. To demonstrate this for individual contributions to the theory would be too tedious and I shall therefore take it for granted.

Where an author has written a comprehensive book on international economics it would be quite arbitrary to pick out those of his contributions which may be most relevant to our present concerns. Nearly everything regarding the effects of extending or restricting trade, free trade or protection, customs unions and other forms of geographic trade discrimination, the gains from trade and their distribution, the terms of trade and their implications, the prices of productive factors and their divergencies in different countries, tendencies toward an international equalisation of factor prices, international movements of labour and

213

capital, international payments and their balance or imbalance,
mechanisms of adjustment and transitional financing of imbalances, exchange rates and monetary policy, and so on and so
forth — everything that has been said on any of these matters
bears on the analysis of the implications of general economic
integration. Only deliberate arbitrariness and ruthless selectivity
can help us keep this survey down to acceptable proportions.

This arbitrary selectivity will make the survey vulnerable to
charges of misplacement of emphasis. For example, several
authors may have made equally important contributions to the
theory of comparative advantage, but one of them may have
addressed the customs-union issue; the latter will then be cited
or quoted on his propositions on customs unions while his work
on the more general and more fundamental points may remain
unmentioned. Or some authors may have dealt with matters of
economic integration through abolition of trade restrictions, co-
ordination of monetary policies, and harmonisation of fiscal
institutions; chances are that their work on trade integration will
be cited while their contributions to other issues will be slighted
or disregarded — because I believe that the former has made
more substantive progress than the latter. (See Chapters 2 and 4
for my views regarding the relative sterility of much of the work
on monetary and fiscal integration, especially for my opinion
that the practical-political measures adopted or recommended in
the monetary and fiscal areas may actually have hindered, rather
than promoted, integration of product markets and capital markets.) Finally, many authors in the field surveyed will be left out
for no other reason than that their work has not been widely
referred to by other writers and, thus, apparently has not made
a strong impact on this discussion. The number of omissions
from this survey is probably a multiple of the number of inclusi

Where should we begin? How far back should we go in this
review? Who were the first economists to understand the econo
mic benefits obtained from trading freely with others than one'
immediate neighbours in the same locality or province? We have
learned from Jacob Viner that we cannot attribute such insights
to the physiocrats; they advocated foreign trade not for the
advantages to be derived from more extended division of labour
they saw in foreign trade the fulfilment of liberty and justice
and, before all, of divine providence, which had endowed nation
with very different natural conditions.[1] (Incidentally, I shall rel

---

[1] Jacob Viner, *Studies in the Theory of International Trade* (New York
Harpers, 1937) pp. 100—4.

on Viner's *Studies* as the major guide and principal source for almost all classical contributors to the theory of international trade.) My list of authors must begin with those who clearly saw a genuinely economic advantage in extending the area of trade.

THE ADVANTAGES OF EXTENDING THE AREA OF TRADE, 1691—1879

The authors assembled in this section examined the most fundamental of the relevant issues: the absolute and comparative advantages of extending trade over a larger area and the division of the gains from such trade among the countries concerned. The contributions of sixteen economists are reviewed, beginning with a posthumously published study by Sir William Petty; including all major British writers of the classical period; and ending with virtually definitive formulations by Mangoldt, the German mathematical economist, and by Alfred Marshall. The review will sketch the development of the theory from an intuitive understanding that the extension of the area of trade is advantageous to the partners, to a fundamental understanding that reciprocal demand determines the terms of trade and hence the division of the gains, and finally to the ultimate understanding that the process involves the simultaneous determination of wage rates, foreign-exchange rates, relative prices as well as exports and imports.

Sir William Petty (1623—87), in his *Political Anatomy of Ireland* (London: Brown & Rogers, 1691), ridiculed those who wanted 'to keep Ireland a distinct kingdom' as he asked them 'why was there ever any union between England and Wales? and why may not the entire Kingdom of England be further cantonized for the advantage of all?' (2nd ed., 1719, p. 34).

Charles Davenant (1656—1714) may have anticipated later theorists in understanding the law of comparative advantage in his *Essay on the East-India Trade* (London: J. Knapton, 1696, reprinted in 1771); but this is a matter of how his brief allusions may be interpreted.

Anonymous. An unknown but widely quoted author of a pamphlet on *Considerations on the East-India Trade* (1701, reprinted in John R. McCulloch, ed., *A Select Collection of Early English Tracts on Commerce*, 1856, pp. 541—629), showed that the fundamental advantage of acquiring cheap imports lies in the saving of domestic resources.

Isaac Gervaise (1670—1739) published a pamphlet on *The System or Theory of the Trade of the World* (London: Woodfall

& Roberts, 1720, reprinted Baltimore, Md., Johns Hopkins Press, 1954) which anticipated in several respects not only Hume but also Ricardo. His chief claim to fame is his understanding of the monetary adjustment mechanism that restores balance in international payments and trade.

Patrick Lindsay (1699—1746), in his pamphlet *The Interest of Scotland Considered* (Edinburgh: R. Fleming Co., 1733) drew the practical conclusion that Scotland ought to concentrate on making linen and buy its woollen goods from England, because Scotland was losing by using its labour for making its own woollens.

David Hume (1711—76) in his *Essays: Literary, Moral, and Political* (1741—2) gave a detailed explanation of the mechanism of adjustment of the balances of trade and payments. He surely understood the idea of absolute cost advantages in production and trade. Whether he had also grasped the idea of comparative advantage is open to question. When he wrote 'Of the Jealousy of Trade' (1758) and stated that 'Nature, by giving a diversity of geniuses, climates, and soils, to different nations, has secured their mutual intercourse and commerce' (p. 79), absolute differences in real costs would suffice to make this true. When he added that no country [nation] need fear that its trading partners 'will improve to such a degree in every art of manufacture, as to have no demand' for its products, this sounds almost like an inference from the law of comparative advantage. Yet, a conditional clause in the same sentence spoils it again. The reservation was 'so long as it [the nation] remains industrious'. [After all, even the laziest and most indolent nation would probably be less inefficient in some activities than in others, and hence have comparative advantages in the latter.]

Adam Smith (1723—90), in his *Inquiry into the Nature and Causes of the Wealth of Nations* (London: Strahan & Cadell, 1776), pronounced explicitly on the mutually useful division of labour between areas on different levels of development; like Hume before him, and like Josiah Tucker in his correspondence with Hume, Smith had no reservations about the full application of the principle of free trade in such situations.[2] This position, however, can be arrived at without support from comparative advantage; of course, the volume of mutually beneficial trade would be smaller if only absolute cost differences — that is, costs in terms of factor inputs — were exploited, but there

[2] Samuel Hollander, *The Economics of Adam Smith* (Toronto: University of Toronto Press, 1973) p. 291.

would still be foreign trade. Interpreters of what Adam Smith
really knew and really meant differ on just how the advantages
from international trade are to be explained. 'By opening a more
extensive market for whatever part of the produce of their
labour may exceed the home consumption, it [foreign trade]
encourages them to improve its productive powers, and to aug-
ment its annual produce to the utmost . . .' (Smith 1776, Modern
Library ed., 1937, p. 415). Was this improvement of productive
powers an increase in efficiency either through acquired skills or
through production on a larger scale, or was it due to a reallocation of labour from branches now cut down as a result of cheaper
imports from abroad? Or did it perhaps consist only in the
exchange of a surplus commodity for something not produced
at home? The latter was John Stuart Mill's interpretation of
Smith's thought and he called it the 'vent-for-surplus' argument
for free trade. A new interpretation has recently been offered to
the effect that 'trade economizes capital and therefore allows a
faster increase in the demand for labour as capital is released for
additional ventures'.[3] None of the several explanations of the
benefits from international trade that have here been mentioned
would be inconsistent with the later explanation of the advantageous pattern of trade among nations that arises from relative
differences in the 'scarcity' of the major productive factors.
These relative scarcities may be caused by differences in supply
(endowment) or demand (tastes) in the markets for productive
factors and may give rise to trade-inducing comparative advantages and disadvantages, even in the absence of any technological, climatological, physiological, psychological or attitudinal
differences. An anticipation of this 'modern' idea can be found
in Smith's discussion of the mutually beneficial trade with the
American colonies, where land was cheap and labour dear relative to the price ratios prevailing in the countries of Europe
(Book IV, Chapter VII). In any case, Smith's dictum that 'The
division of labour is limited by the extent of the market' (Book
I, Chapter III), together with his conviction that extensions in
the division of labour would increase its productivity, made him
infer that every extension of the market will increase the product in all countries, regions, or continents involved and thus be
advantageous to all.

   Robert Torrens (1780—1864) was the first undisputed exposi-
tor of the law of comparative advantage. Through his books,
The Economists Refuted (London: S. A. & H. Oddy, 1808), *An*

---

[3] Hollander, op. cit., p. 276.

Essay on Money and Paper Currency (London: J. Johnson Co.,
1812), and *An Essay on the External Corn Trade* (London:
Hatchard, 1815; 2nd ed. 1820), Torrens' priority is clearly established. However, in contrast to Ricardo, who made this law the
major premise for an unqualified endorsement of free trade,
Torrens, in the course of his discussion on the international
division of the gains from trade, was unwilling to concede that
unilateral reduction of tariffs would benefit the liberalising
country. Torrens was among the first to show that a tariff might
turn the terms of trade in favour of the country imposing the
tariff;[4] his advocacy of reciprocity in commercial policy, and his
opposition to unilateral free trade, followed from this insight.
[See also p. 221 below.]

David Ricardo (1772—1823) saw the explanation of the
'general benefit' to be derived from international trade almost
exclusively in the more efficient allocation of productive
resources that was associated with the extension of trade. In his
book *On the Principles of Political Economy and Taxation*
(London: John Murray, 1817) he wrote: 'Under a system of
perfectly free commerce, each country naturally devotes its
capital and labour to such employments as are most beneficial
to each. This pursuit of individual advantage is admirably connected with the universal good of the whole. By stimulating
industry, by rewarding ingenuity, and by using most efficaciously
the peculiar powers bestowed by nature, it distributes labour
most effectively and most economically: while by increasing the
general mass of productions, it diffuses general benefit, and
binds together, by one common tie of interest and intercourse,
the universal society of nations throughout the civilized world'
(Sraffa edition, 1951, Vol. I, pp. 133—4). The 'diffusion' of the
benefit was attained by commodity prices falling relative to
labour as a result of 'the better division and distribution of
labour' (p. 94). Again, as Ricardo wrote in a letter to Malthus
between 1820 and 1830, 'In proportion as the market is extended, the people of every country are enabled to make the best
division of their labour, and the most advantageous use of their
exertions' (Sraffa edition, Vol II, p. 360). [According to Edgeworth, 'the incomparable vigour of Ricardo's chapter on foreign
trade has not been approached by any of his successors.' Francis
Y. Edgeworth, 'The Pure Theory of International Values.'

[4] Lionel Robbins noted that some recent writers have been under the
impression that this theory of the 'optimum tariff' was discovered in the
1940s. See Lionel Robbins, *Robert Torrens and the Evolution of Classical
Economics* (London: Macmillan, 1958) p. 182.

in *Papers Relating to Political Economy*, (Cambridge: Cambridge University Press, 1925) Vol. 2, p. 19.] Ricardo did not miss the effects which tariffs have on the distribution of income. It was clear to him that the repeal of the corn laws would injure landlords and benefit consumers and, indirectly, capitalists (Sraffa edition, Vol. I, pp. 424—7).

James Mill (1773—1836) found that neither Ricardo nor his immediate followers had solved the problems of how the gains from trade — that is, the additional output produced thanks to the more efficient allocation of resources — would be divided among the trading countries. James Mill made a famous error when he, in his first edition of his *Elements of Political Economy* (London: Baldwin, Cradock & Joy, 1821), counted the gains twice: each of the two countries was assumed to gain the entire increment in output. He corrected this error in the third edition (1826) but naively believed that each of the two countries would gain one-half of the increment. [James Mill's idea of a fifty-fifty sharing of the gains from trade was set aside and a solution found when the principle of reciprocal demand was developed by his son, John Stuart Mill.]

John Stuart Mill (1806—73) wrote the puzzle-solving essay in 1829—30, but published it only in his *Essays on Some Unsettled Questions of Political Economy* (London: John W. Parker, 1844, p. 12). There was a letter from James Pennington to Kirkman Finlay, Esquire, 'On the Importation of Foreign Coin', which also contained the solution of the problem. It was printed in 1840, but when it was written is unknown. Thus there is a question of priority, though it may well have been an instance of multiple invention. In any case, Mill's exposition is the one from which later generations of economists have learned that the division of the gains from trade is determined by the terms of trade, which in turn are determined by the reciprocal demand for each other's product. This was only one of several important contributions John Stuart Mill made to the theory of international trade, some of them in the first edition of his *Principles of Political Economy* (London: John W. Parker, 1848), others in later editions. (See the Ashley edition, 1909, and the University of Toronto edition, 1965: subsequent page references are to the latter.) There was a clear understanding of the economies of large-scale production, as Mill said that the possibility of 'substituting the large system of production for the small, depends, of course, in the first place, on the extent of the market' (p. 140). Chapter XVII of Book III of his *Principles* treats entirely 'Of International Trade': para. 1 deals with the interna-

tional immobility of factors; para. 2 with comparative cost; para.
3 explains that the 'advantage [of trade] consists in a more efficient employment of the productive forces of the world'; para.
4 criticises Smith for his narrow view of foreign trade as a country's 'vent for its surplus'; para. 5 shows how long-run, indirect
benefits are combined with direct benefits: 'A country which
produces for a larger market than its own, can introduce a more
extended division of labour, can make greater use of machinery,
and is more likely to make inventions and improvements in the
processes of production' (p. 593). [This emphasis on development is nowadays discussed under the heading of 'dynamic' considerations and set against the alleged one-sidedness of 'classical'
and 'static' considerations.] Another indirect benefit of trade is
seen in the international transfer of technology, enterprise, and
industrial discipline, if one may thus translate Mill's statement
that a nation may borrow from others 'not merely particular
arts and practices, but essential points of character in which its
own type is inferior' (p. 594). [One may wonder how the dynamic critics of classical statics can reconcile their feelings of
superiority with this statement of Mill's.] In Chapter XVIII of
Book III, Mill treated 'Of International Values', and presented
his theory of reciprocal demand. The exposition was largely in
terms of two countries exchanging two goods only. From the
third edition (1852) onwards Mill recognised that, with only two
goods traded, it would be possible for the entire gain from trade
to accrue to only one of the two countries (p.599). In such a
case, trade would quickly be extended to a greater number of
goods and both countries could get some of the benefits. Mill
also clearly recognised that an improvement in a country's efficiency in producing an export good would worsen its terms of
trade if the 'cheapening' of this good 'would increase the deman
for it' in the importing country in not 'so great a proportion as
that of the increased cheapness' (p. 606). In Chapter XXV, Mill
dealt with 'Competition of Different Countries in the Same
Market', and in Chapter IV of Book V, with the effects which
duties on exports or imports may have on the terms of trade.
Chapter X of Book V included a section on the 'Doctrine of
Protection of Native Industry'.

   William Ellis (1800—81), a minor writer in the circle of J. S.
Mill, was among the earliest to observe that the theory could
not be kept confined to two countries and two commodities. In
an article on 'Exportation of Machinery' in *Westminster Review*
Vol. III (1825, pp. 388—9), he pointed to an extension of the
theory of comparative costs to more than two countries. [The

task was obviously beyond the technical capabilities of the time. Most teachers of international trade will admit that even now, 150 years later, we have serious difficulties with such extensions — especially if we extend the model also to three or more factors of production, something most of the classical economists avoided by sticking to labour as the sole factor.]

Samuel Mountifort Longfield (1802—84) attempted to extend the theory of comparative costs to more than two goods. In his *Three Lectures on Commerce and One on Absenteeism* (Dublin: William Curry, 1835), he was able to show that comparative money wage rates in the two countries would determine the precise line of division between exported and imported commodities. He did not correctly explain, however, how the wage differentials were determined. On the other hand, he anticipated Heckscher and Ohlin when he stated that 'independent of every difference of soil or climate, the exchange between two countries . . . will consist principally of articles produced by that species of labour which in each country is relatively cheapest' (p. 240); and again when he remarked that 'commerce which exchanges the production of human labour has the same effect as if the labourers themselves could remove from one country to another . . .' (p. 239). On a different issue, Longfield greatly advanced the understanding of the adjustment mechanism in international payments and trade as he showed the interactions of what we today call income effects and price effects. See his 'Banking and Currency', *Dublin University Magazine*, Vol. 15 (1840) p. 10.

Robert Torrens (1780—1864) should in this context again be mentioned, first for his attempt to analyse the case of trade in more than two commodities; secondly for elaborating the theory of the terms of trade being improved by import tariffs and worsened by unilateral abolition of tariffs; thirdly for advancing an incipient theory of customs union; and fourthly for stating the role of money wages in determining the pattern of trade, the international distribution of money stocks and the division of the gains from trade. The fourth of these achievements was in his book on *Colonization of South Australia* (London: Longmans, Rees, Orme, Brown, Green & Longman, 1835), where Torrens made progress toward solving the problem of the determination of the money wage rates that would, with given reciprocal demand of the countries concerned, separate the exportable goods from the importable ones in such a way that trade is balanced (pp. 148—74). The terms of trade and the division of the gains from trade would be determined in the process. The effects of import duties on the terms of trade are treated, among other places, in Letters II, III, and X in *The Budget: A Series of Letters on Financial, Commercial and Colonial Policy* (London: Smith Elder & Co, 1841–3). The allusion to the economics of a customs union are chiefly in Letter IV of *The Budget*, where he held that colonisation would create and enlarge markets in areas whose commercial policy would be determined by the central authorities, so that the danger of hostile manipulations of the terms of trade is eliminated: 'The prosperity of the country cannot be arrested by the hostile tariffs of foreign rivals if England will establish throughout her wide-spread empire a British Commercial league — a colonial Zollverein' (p. 102). Torrens coined the phrase 'territorial division of labour' and insisted that the wider this territory the better for all parties concerned.

John Elliott Cairnes (1823–75) finally provided an essentially correct solution to the problem of the pattern of trade with many commodities, in his book *Some Leading Principles of Political Economy Newly Expounded* (London and New York: Macmillan, 1874) pp. 334–41, though it was rather vague and not easy to comprehend. Cairnes' most significant contribution to the theory of international trade was his calling attention to 'non-competing groups within a nation' (p. 386).

Hans Karl Emil von Mangoldt (1824–68) had anticipated Cairnes in presenting the solution of the problem of the simultaneous determination of wage rates, exchange rates, relative prices, exports and imports, and, as a result, the division of the gains from trade. It was contained in his book *Grundriss der Volkswirtschaftslehre* (Stuttgart: Engelhorn, 1863; 2nd ed. [revised by Friedrich Kleinwächter] Stuttgart: J. Maier, 1871) as Appendix II, entitled 'Von der Gleichung der internationalen Nachfrage', but became more widely known only through an article by Francis Y. Edgeworth, 'The Pure Theory of International Values', *Economic Journal*, Vol. IV (1894) pp. 35–50, 424–43, 606–38. [In his *Papers Relating to Political Economy* (Cambridge: Cambridge University Press, 1925) Vol. II, p. 4, Edgeworth says that 'Of all the writers, classical or mathematical who are passed in review in the article of 1894, Mangoldt is the one who emerges unscathed from the critical examination.'] An English translation of Mangoldt's statement was published (edited by John S. Chipman) under the title 'On the Equation of International Demand', *Journal of International Economics*, Vol. 5 (1975) pp. 55–97.

Alfred Marshall (1842–1924), in his first published work,

The Pure Theory of Foreign Trade (privately printed, 1879, together with the *The Pure Theory of Domestic Values*; reprinted London: London School of Economics, 1930), presented a much improved and refined exposition of John Stuart Mill's theory of the reciprocal demand of two countries for each other's products. Changes in 'the rate of interchange' [commodity terms of trade and double-factor terms of trade] were explained as consequences of all sorts of conditions (inventions, fashions) in such a way that the possibilities of improving a country's terms of trade through withholding some of its supply (p. 5) or of worsening them through producing exports more cheaply on a larger scale became immediately clear (p. 13). A book published 45 years later, *Money, Credit and Commerce* (London: Macmillan, 1923), contained much of the 1879 essay, especially in Appendix J, 'Graphical Presentation of Some Problems of International Trade', pp. 330—60, but also in a verbal exposition of the possibility of a country improving its terms of trade at the expence of its trading partner by taxing imports or exports (pp. 180—4).

ELOQUENT ADVOCATES OF PROTECTION OR FREE TRADE, 1827—61

Having proceeded with this survey to 1863, 1874 and 1879, we must pause to consider three authors, a German, an American, and a Frenchman, whose publications preceded the previous three entires and who engaged more in advocacy than in analysis: List, Carey, and Bastiat. List was mentioned in Chapter 6 of this book among the political economists who proposed or promoted economic integration through customs unions, but his omission from the ranks of economic theorists would be resented by his many admirers. Carey is a well-known advocate of American protectionism. Bastiat, an ardent defender of free trade, is sometimes regarded as a journalist and, perhaps also because of his wit and penchant for satire, excluded from the ranks of serious economic analysts. What the three writers have in common is that they have taken very firm positions on free trade and protection.

Friedrich List (1789—1846) developed his protectionist ideas during his stay in the United States, where he published a book, *Outlines of American Political Economy* (Philadelphia: S. Parker, 1827). His major work appeared in German in 1841 under the title *Das nationale System der politischen Ökonomie* (Stuttgart:

J. G. Cotta, 1841). Beginning in 1843 he published *Das Zoll-vereinsblatt*, a periodical devoted to his views on issues of the German Zollverein. There were also later editions of his books, several volumes of his collected writings, speeches, and letters (Berlin: R. Hobbing, 1927—36), and English editions of his 184 volume under the title *The National System of Political Economy* (London: Longmans, Green & Co., 1885; New York: Longmans Green & Co., 1928). List's entire work was a rejection of the 'principle of absolute free trade' (1928 edition, p. 21). He even attacked the famous illustration of the mutually beneficial exchange of British cloth against Portuguese wine and argued that it was beneficial to England only, but disadvantageous to Portugal. Not that he tried to refute the law of comparative advantage — indeed, there is no indication in his book that he had comprehended it — but he believed that the 'theory of productive powers' was more important than the 'theory of value'. A country had not reached the maximum development of its productive powers until it had developed its manufacturing industries sufficiently not only to meet its own wants for industrial products but also to produce a surplus of exports. [Since it would be logically impossible for all countries to have export surpluses in manufactured products, one may assume that List would have been satisfied if every country had an export surplus in *some* kinds of manufactured products.] Countries that had not yet reached this stage of industrialisation should protect their national industries. [No hint is given as to the optimum degree of industrialisation: of how many manufactured product should a country be a net exporter?] List evidently was thinking about under-utilised potentials for industrial production; he thus championed the cause of what others called the temporary protection of infant industries, and the cause of protected industrialisation of underdeveloped countries. His arguments, however, lacked the necessary analytical support. His assertion that free competition between two nations can be mutually beneficial only if both of them are in a nearly equal position of industrial development is completely unfounded. [What about several parts of a nation with different degrees of industrialisation?]

Henry C. Carey (1793—1879), American economist and publisher, championed protectionism, using a variety of arguments against free trade. His major books in which he expounded these views were *The Past, the Present, and the Future* (Philadelphia: Carey & Hart, 1848) and *The Harmony of Interests, Agricultural Manufacturing and Commercial* (Philadelphia: Skinner, 1851). In the latter book he naively explained that protection would benefit both domestic production and consumption because 'every producer is a consumer to the whole extent of his production' and, therefore, 'the more that is produced [under protection], the more *must* be consumed' (1851, pp. 44—5). He even believed that protection would increase the commerce of a nation. 'The object of protection is to produce dear labor, that is, high-priced and valuable labor, and its effect is to cause it to increase in value from day to day, and to increase the equivalents to be exchanged, to the great increase of commerce ... Make protection perfect and permanent, and immigration will increase rapidly, for there will be more cloth and iron to be exchanged against labor' (pp. 72—3).

Frédéric Bastiat (1801—50), French writer, became famous for his simplified and popularised formulations of libertarian economic principles. Best known is his parable in which he shows the absurdity of protection: a mock petition of the candlemakers. Its full title is 'Petition from the Manufacturers of Candles, Wax-lights, Lamps, Chandeliers, Reflectors, Snuffers, Extinguishers: And from the Producers of Everything Used for Lights.' It first appeared as a pamphlet in 1845 and was later included in the volume *Sophismes Economiques* of his *Complete Works* (Paris: Guillaumin, 1863), English translation *Sophisms of the Protection Policy* (New York: Putnam, 1848). In this satire the candlemakers and allied manufacturers complain about the unfair competition from free sunlight and point to the great increase in employment and domestic production that would result if the manufacturers were protected against the free importation of sunlight.

FACTOR PRICES AND INCOMES, FACTOR ENDOWMENT AND MOBILITY, TARIFFS AND TERMS OF TRADE, 1878—1976

From the digression on writers who were somewhat outside the mainstream of trade theory we return to classical and neoclassical analysis of international division of labour. Perhaps my reference to 'classical' theory ought to be qualified (or even disqualified) in view of the different meanings attached to this designation. Karl Marx, who was the first to use it, meant to refer only to economists before John Stuart Mill, whereas John Maynard Keynes included almost all economists writing before 1936. But there are also more subtle distinctions; for example, Bertil Ohlin, whose work our survey will reach in this section, believed that his fundamental assumptions (about the conditions

which determine trade) were so different from those made by
earlier economists as to set him apart from them as a dissenter
from classical theory. Subsequent writers have not seen such a
wide gulf and have had no misgivings when they included Ohlin
among the neoclassical economists.

In this section we shall come to a few writers who addressed
themselves directly to issues raised by the establishment of
customs unions or other techniques of closer economic integration among different countries. In order to separate their more
general contributions to trade theory from their statements on
the effects of custom unions, I shall defer the latter to a separate
section; I hope that the inconvenience of having some writers —
for example Taussig, Marshall, Viner, and Haberler — appear in
two, three or more sections will not be regarded as a high cost
to pay for a more orderly exposition.

Charles F. Bastable (1855—1945), in his brief textbook, *The
Theory of International Trade: With Some of its Applications to
Economic Policy* (Dublin: Hodges, 1887; 4th ed., London: Macmillan, 1903), confirmed the conclusion of earlier writers that
large countries may fail to derive any gains from their trade with
small countries (Chapter II). In an article on 'Some Applications
of the Theory of International Trade', *Quarterly Journal of
Economics*, Vol. 4 (1889) pp. 1—17, he discussed the adjustment
mechanism of the balance of payments, and emphasised, not the
level of money wages or the rate of efficiency earnings, but
rather the 'aggregate of money incomes' as the decisive element
in restoring balance. In a later book, on *The Commerce of
Nations* (London: Methuen, 1st ed. 1892; 10th ed., revised by
T. E. Gregory, 1927), Bastable presented the arguments for and
against protection. A major advantage of Bastable's exposition
was that he did not assume constant cost of production but,
instead, costs varying with output.

Frank W. Taussig (1859—1940) exerted for many years a
wholesome and most important influence on the development of
international economics through his teaching and writing.
Among his books were *The Tariff History of the United States:
A Series of Essays* (New York: Putnam, 1892), *Some Aspects
of the Tariff Question* (Cambridge, Mass.: Harvard University
Press, 1915), *Free Trade, the Tariff and Reciprocity* (New York:
Macmillan, 1920) and *International Trade* (New York: Macmillan, 1927), a work in pure and applied theory in the classical
tradition. Taussig stressed the imperfections in the labour market and the resulting barriers to domestic mobility and efficient

allocation, but did not conclude that tariff protection could be justified on such grounds. [Some issues raised by Taussig that bear directly on the economics of customs union will be deferred to the next section.]

Francis Ysidro Edgeworth (1845—1926) published a long article, consisting of three parts, entitled 'The Theory of International Values', *Economic Journal*, Vol. 4(1894) pp. 35—50, 424—43, and 606—38. With some omissions and reorganisation, the article was reprinted as Chapter R, entitled 'The Pure Theory of International Values' in Edgeworth's *Papers Relating to Political Economy* (London: Royal Economic Society, 1925) Vol. 2, pp. 3—60. In the author's own words, it was 'a restatement of first principles, both on classical lines and in the language of mathematics; with criticisms of leading writers' (1925, p. 3). Edgeworth stressed the necessity to distinguish 'between the interests of the home country and that of the world at large'; between small and large changes; between changes originating at home and those abroad; between changes affecting primarily exports and those that affect imports; 'between the case of two countries and that of several countries; and so forth' (pp. 7—8). He recalled the case, first treated by Mill, of an improvement in the production of a country's export goods, leading to a worsening of its terms of trade and a consequent loss of income (p. 10); and the case, treated by Mill and Bastable, of a tax on imports leading to more favourable terms of trade and a net gain for the country that imposed the tariff (pp. 12—18, with a list of writers who had rejected the proposition as false). Edgeworth devoted more than half of the reorganised article to 'Mathematical Theory' (pp. 31—60). Besides developing several propositions and novel analytical techniques (including geometrical devices) of lasting importance, Edgeworth discussed, in part critically, in part approvingly, the contributions to the mathematical theory of international trade that had been made by Augustin Cournot (1838), Karl Heinrich Hagen (1844), Hans Karl Emil von Mangoldt (1863), and Rudolf Auspitz and Richard Lieben (1889). Reference may be made here to comments which Edgeworth made in the third instalment of an article called 'Appreciations of Mathematical Theories', *Economic Journal*, Vol. 18 (Sep and Dec 1908) pp. 393—403, 541—56, about an article which C. F. Bickerdike had published in 1906 [see below]. It concerned a proof of the proposition that under certain conditions a country could impose a small ('incipient') duty ('tax') on imports and make 'the foreigner' pay the tax. Edgeworth warned that, partly because of the danger of retaliation, 'the direct use of the theory is likely to be small. But it is to be feared that its abuse will be considerable'. Thus, 'Let us admire the skill of the analyst, but label the subject of his investigation POISON' (pp. 555—6).

Charles Frederick Bickerdike (1876—1961), in an article on 'The Theory of Incipient Taxes', *Economic Journal*, Vol. 16 (Dec 1906) pp. 529—35, demonstrated geometrically and verbally that a country can improve its terms of trade by imposing a small ('incipient') tax on its imports or exports, if the elasticity of the foreign reciprocal demand for its exports is less than infinite. 'The more elastic the home demand for the taxed article, the stronger is the tendency to reduction of the total bill payable to the foreigner, and, therefore, the greater (but still small) the tendency to raise price-level and improve the terms of exchange' (p. 534). Bickerdike returned to this theme in a review of Pigou's book on *Protective and Preferential Import Duties* in the *Economic Journal*, Vol. 17 (Mar 1907) pp. 98—102.

Eli Heckscher (1879—1952), Swedish economist and economic historian, published a seminal article on 'The Effect of Foreign Trade on the Distribution of Income', *Ekonomisk Tidskrift*, Vol. 21 (1919) pp. 497—512. His starting proposition was that differences in the relative scarcities (reflected in relative prices) of the same factors of production in different countries and differences in the proportions in which the factors are used in different commodities are prerequisites for international trade. If the same techniques are used and free trade equalises the prices of commodities in the trading countries, each country will import products for which relatively more of its scarcer factors are used and will export products for which relatively more of its abundant factors are used. As a result, the scarce factors become less scarce, and the abundant ones less abundant. Trade will thus affect the prices of the factors — and, hence, the distribution of income — and will expand until the relative scarcities (relative prices) of the factors in the trading countries have become equal. The original differences in comparative costs of products will have disappeared when all potentialities of profitable trade are fully utilised. Should the effects on income distribution be considered undesirable, the rational policy to avoid them would be taxation, not protection.

Gustavo del Vecchio (1883—1973), in his book *Teoria del commercio internazionale* (Padova: La Litotipo, 1923), came close to Heckscher's theory that, since each country exports goods made largely with its relatively cheap factors of production, trade will increase the demand for these factors and raise their remuneration. Del Vecchio did not, however, pursue this argument to the conclusions which Heckscher had reached.

Frank D. Graham (1890—1949), in an important article, 'The Theory of International Values Reexamined', *Quarterly Journal of Economics*, Vol. 28 (1923) pp. 54—86, corrected or qualified several conclusions of Mill's and later theorists regarding the division of the gains from trade. Generalisations from an analysis of only two countries' trade and in but two commodities were disconfirmed by analyses of models with more countries and more commodities. Graham showed that it is not always the smallest or poorest country that gains most from trade, but rather the country, large or small, whose price ratios are most drastically changed by trade. He also showed, rather surprisingly, that a country with but one export commodity stands to gain more than a country that exports a large variety of goods. As to a country's share of the total gain, 'it makes no difference whether this variation [in price ratios] is due to great superiority in the production of the goods which are exported or to great inferiority in the production . . . of the goods which are imported.' Graham developed his analyses further in his book *The Theory of International Values* (Princeton: Princeton University Press, 1948). His technique of analysis, apparently primitive in its use of arithmetical illustrations, was in fact an anticipation of linear programming.

Jacob Viner (1892—1970) is regarded as the greatest scholar in the history of preclassical and classical theory of trade and as a pioneer in the theory of customs unions. His first publication in the area was *Dumping: A Problem in International Trade* (Chicago: University of Chicago Press, 1923). In 1931, he published an article on 'The Most-Favored-Nation Clause', *Index* (Svenska Handelsbanken, Stockholm) Vol. 6 (Jan 1931) pp. 2—25, reprinted in his book *International Economics* (Glencoe, Ill.: Free Press, 1951, pp. 94—108), in which he argued that non-discrimination in tariff protection was likely to be less injurious than a discriminatory reduction of tariffs. [See next section.] His *Studies in the Theory of International Trade* (New York: Harper, 1937) became the standard history of thought in the field. His book on *The Customs Union Issue* (New York: Carnegie Endowment, 1950) will be annotated separately in the next section.

Mihail E. Manoilescu (1891—1950), Rumanian economist, published a book on *The Theory of Protection and International Trade* (London: 1931) with several reformulated arguments against free trade and in favour of protection. His chief case for protection relates to differences in marginal productivities and wage rates in different occupations or sectors of the economy.

Gottfried Haberler (born 1900) reformulated the theory of comparative advantage — which had originally been based on labour cost and later on various notions of 'real cost' — in terms of opportunity cost, which allowed its use for any number of factors of production employed in variable proportions. See his articles 'The Theory of Comparative Costs Once More', *Quarterly Journal of Economics*, Vol. 43 (1929) pp. 376—81, and 'Die Theorie der komparativen Kosten und ihre Auswertung für die Begründung des Freihandels', *Weltwirtschaftliches Archiv*, Vol. 32 (1930) pp. 349—70. His formulation of the determination of the exchange ratios among different goods on the basis of their substitution costs yielded a consistent theory of the gains from trade. Haberler published what was at the time the most up-to-date text on *Der internationale Handel* (Berlin: Springer, 1933) and its English translation *The Theory of International Trade* (Edinburgh: Hodge, 1936). In his seminal article 'Some Problems in the Pure Theory of International Trade', *Economic Journal*, Vol. 60 (June 1950) pp. 223—40, he analysed the differences which relaxations of the usual assumptions of traditional free-trade theory would make for the outcome, especially for the possible gains or losses of a small country trading in the world market. He examined the effects of immobility of labour (with capital mobile or immobile), of rigidity of wage rates (and other factor prices), of decreasing costs through economies of scale, and of other externalities (such as the potential increases in efficiency through gradual development of skills in infant industries). The findings did not support a policy of tariff protection. [Haberler's discussions of economic integration and, especially, of customs unions will be reviewed in the next section.]

Bertil Ohlin (born 1899) in his book *Interregional and International Trade* (Cambridge, Mass.: Harvard University Press, 1933), followed Eli Heckscher in taking differences in the endowment of different regions with productive factors as the chief 'cause of interregional division of labour', since 'each region is best equipped to produce the goods which require large proportions of the factors relatively abundant there' and 'least fit to produce goods requiring large proportions of factors existing within its borders in small quantities or not at all' (p. 12). Exchange-rate adjustments or demand adjustments play an indispensable role in adapting relative money costs and money prices to the task of determining which products are exportable and which importable (p. 19). However, 'the list of relative factor prices in the isolated state does not tell us how high the exchange

rate will be [when trade has been opened], and therefore we
cannot say which or how many factors will be cheaper in the
one region than in the other' (p. 21). Since exports make the
abundant factor less abundant and imports make the scarce
factor less scarce, the effect of trade is 'a tendency towards
equalization of the prices of the [same] productive factors' in
different regions or countries (p. 36). We cannot expect 'complete equalization', not only because of transport costs and
artificial impediments to trade, but also 'because the industrial
demand is always the "joint demand" for several factors' and
'their combination cannot be varied at will' (p. 38). But it 'is not
worth while to analyze in detail why full equalization does not
occur' (p. 38). 'The price differences . . . are reduced but they
do not disappear' (p. 40), as they would if factors were as
mobile as to make one region out of separate regions. But 'the
mobility of goods to some extent compensates the lack of interregional mobility of the factors' (p. 42). All regions or countries
gain from trade, since 'only if trade did not change the relative
scarcity of factors in [a country] at all is it conceivable that the
terms of exchange would be unaffected', but 'such a case is impossible' (p. 43). It 'can be taken for granted that the [average]
level of factor price [in terms of commodities] will rise in all
regions. Consequently a relative decline in the price of one of
them, say labour, compared to another, land, does not necessarily mean that the wage level is lowered in terms of goods' (p. 44).
'Wages are such a substantial part of the total income that it is
almost unthinkable that a considerable rise of the [total income]
could fail to raise total wages also, even if the percentage going
to the labourers became somewhat reduced' (p. 44). [We ought
to note that such reasoning based on a comparison between free
trade and no trade may not be conclusive for a comparison
between more trade or less trade.] In any case, 'interregional
trade serves as a substitute for . . . interregional factor movements' (p. 49).

    Abba P. Lerner (born 1903) published a series of articles on
the pure theory of international trade in *Economica*, 1932,
1934, and 1936, all reproduced in his book of *Essays in Economic Analysis* (London: Macmillan, 1953). The theme of monopolistic exploitation of the trading partner came up several times.
In his note on 'The Symmetry between Import and Export
Taxes', *Economica*, n.s. Vol. 3 (Aug 1936) pp. 306—13, Lerner
explained an interesting slip in the 1894 article by Edgeworth
that arose from a failure to make specific assumptions about the
way in which the government spends the revenues it collects.

[The relevance of this problem was later exhibited in an analysis by Lloyd Metzler, see below, p. 237.] In his book *The Economics of Control* (New York: Macmillan, 1944), Lerner offered concise formulations of several important propositions on international trade, including the one concerning trade restrictions improving the terms of trade, with the benefit to the country imposing the restrictions smaller than the loss inflicted on the foreigners (p. 356). A tax on an import good can lower the price at which foreigners will sell it, and a tax on an export good can raise the price foreigners will pay for it, according as their elasticities of supply and demand, respectively, are less than infinite (pp. 360—2). 'There is a simple formula for the optimum tax on imports and on exports . . . if it desired to exploit the foreigner', namely 'the inverse of the foreign elasticity of supply' for the tax on imports, and 'the inverse of the foreign elasticity of demand' for the tax on exports (pp. 382—3). Of course, 'this invites retaliation which would make everybody lose' (p. 362). [We shall come back to Lerner in another context.]

Frederic [Charles Courtenay] Benham (1900—62) questioned the practical-political significance of the theory that taxes on imports or exports could improve a country's terms of trade. In an article on 'The Terms of Trade', *Economica*, n.s. Vol. 7 (Nov 1940), pp. 360—76, he stressed the difficulties of measuring the terms of trade in the face of changes in taste, and of determining the kinds of goods traded and the shares of different goods in total exports and imports. As to a country's ability to force up the prices of its exports, Benham held that it could succeed only 'if it combines with other countries exporting similar goods, and the group between them provide most of the actual and potential supply' (p. 369).

Nicholas Kaldor (born 1908), in 'A Note on Tariffs and the Terms of Trade', *Economica*, n.s. Vol. 7. (Nov 1940) pp. 377—80, demonstrated, following Bickerdike and Edgeworth and using the 'Edgeworth barter diagram' and the concept of 'community indifference curves', that 'a system of import duties will always improve the position of the country imposing it, provided that the rate of duty is below a certain critical level, and provided also that the introduction of the tariff does not lead to retaliation . . . by other countries' (p. 377). He showed 'that the introduction of import duties can reproduce exactly the same effect as the introduction of monopoly' (p. 380).

Tibor Scitovsky (born 1910) advanced some highly influential ideas in an article 'A Reconsideration of the Theory of Tariffs',

Review of Economic Studies, Vol. 9 (1941—2) pp. 89—110. He
first introduced the 'double-bribe test' to ascertain whether any
change, such as the imposition or abolition of a tariff, would
increase or decrease the welfare of the community (nation). The
criteria of a net increase in total welfare obtained through such
a change are: (1) that those who gain from it could fully compensate the losers and still be better off as a result of the change;
and (2) that the losers would not be able to buy off the beneficiaries of the change (that is, they could not offer them a
sufficiently high bribe to make them give up the chance of this
benefit) with a pay-off smaller than the loss they would suffer
as a result of the change. By applying these criteria one might
judge whether a given tariff was optimal for the nation as a
whole. Scitovsky went on to show the consequences of policies
designed to optimise tariffs. Since the imposition of a tariff may
secure for a country an improvement in its terms of trade, provided other countries fail to retaliate, any 'optimum tariff' may
prove actually injurious to all as in fact the countries take turns
in trying to change the terms of trade in their favour and succeed
mainly in reducing international trade in the process (p. 100).
[Other contributions by Scitovsky will be reviewed in the next
two sections.]

Wolfgang Stolper (born 1912) and **Paul A. Samuelson** (born
1915) published an article on 'Protection and Real Wages',
Review of Economic Studies, Vol. 9 (1941—2) pp. 58—73, in
which they demonstrated that, since an extension of trade will
raise the prices of relatively abundant (cheap) factors of production and reduce the prices of relatively scarce (dear) factors, a
restriction of trade through the imposition of tariffs on imports
may benefit workers in countries where labour is the scarcer
factor. In such countries, therefore, protection may raise not
only money wages but also real wages and increase the share of
labour in national income both absolutely and relatively. [The
argument was made on the basis of assumptions of two factors
producing two goods in two countries, with no country completely specialising, that is, with both goods continuing to be
produced in both countries and with the same techniques. It
was assumed, moreover, that the imposition of tariffs would not
alter the terms of trade; if the tariffs were to improve the terms
of trade, the earnings of the relatively scarce factor might be
depressed instead of raised in the process. See Lloyd Metzler
below, p. 236.]

Joan Robinson (born 1903), in an article on 'The Pure Theory
of International Trade', *Review of Economic Studies*, Vol. 14

(1946—7) pp. 98—112, supplied a concise literal exposition of
the international adjustment mechanism working 'through movements in relative money-wage levels' (p. 99) as an alternative to
movements in exchange rates or in trade restrictions (import
tariffs). She explained the theoretical possibility, but slight probability, of perverse elasticities, as, for example, when the
income elasticities of the home demand for imports are negative
(inferior goods) and the price elasticities of foreign demand for
exports are smaller than unity. In general, 'the mechanism of
rising wages [in surplus countries] can be relied upon to wipe
out an export surplus, at some level or other' (p. 101); and in
deficit countries, 'the hidden hand will always do its work, but
it may work by strangulation' (p. 102). In her analysis of the
effects of import duties, she concluded that 'when the gain in
the terms of trade outweighs the loss of real productivity',
the country would enjoy 'a larger share of a diminished total world
real income' (p. 107) and that 'this must be the case where the
rest of the world's demand for [the country's] goods has an
elasticity not greater than unity . . . '. The net gain for the
country imposing the tariff consists in 'the additional home product of labour released from export industries. . . . If the elasticity of the foreign demand for its exports is less than unity,
their value, and consequently the value and the volume of
imports actually rises and [the country] enjoys additional
imports as well as additional home output.' Mrs Robinson
amends other economists' qualifications regarding the magnitude
of the tariff. 'So long as the elasticity of demand for [the
country's] exports is not greater than one, a tariff, however high,
will increase [its] real income.' Even if that elasticity is greater
than one, the country's real income will be increased, provided
that the tariff is not too high, because the gain in home product
is greater than the loss in the volume of imports even if world
prices of imported goods are unchanged. Hence, the elasticity of
foreign demand for the import-taxing country needs to be only
smaller than infinity (p. 108). The argument against the policy
of tariffs to improve the terms of trade — 'that it is immoral for
one country to gain an advantage at the expense of the rest' —
she judged to be of little weight for poor countries, especially if
a poor country has to choose whether it should remove a deficit
through reducing wage rates or imposing tariffs.

  Richard F. Kahn (born 1905), later Lord Kahn, in an article
on 'Tariffs and the Terms of Trade', *Review of Economic
Studies*, Vol. 15 (1948—9) pp. 14—19 — building on the earlier
contributions to the problem of the optimum tariff by Bicker-

dike, Lerner, Kaldor, and Scitovsky — aimed 'at arriving . . . at
some rough idea of what' that optimum might be 'in actual
quantitative terms'. He concluded that the optimum tariff 'will
often be far from being "small" ', as others had thought, but
might be as big as 50 per cent *ad valorem* (pp. 17—18). However, if the assumption of 'no retaliation' is dropped, the result
shows that the countries, each trying to get the better of the
others, would end up worse off; they would be well advised to
agree on free trade. In the course of his argument, Kahn questioned the use of indifference curves in the analysis; and he discarded the notion of 'making the foreigner pay the tax' as irrelevant for the problem since a prohibitive tariff would yield no tax
revenue but may still improve the terms of trade (p. 15). He also
explained the apparent paradox that the size of the optimum
tariff 'should depend only on the elasticities of foreign demand
for exports and of foreign supply of imports'; the foreign elasticities determine indeed the *height* of the optimum tariff, but
the *extent* of the benefit from it 'will depend also on the domestic elasticities' (p. 16).

Ian M. D. Little (born 1918), in his article on 'Welfare and
Tariffs', *Review of Economic Studies*, Vol. 16, No. 2 (1948—9)
pp. 65—70, found that the Kaldor-Hicks criterion of a welfare
increase could be contradicted by the Scitovsky criterion only
if the compensation is not actually paid to the losers. But since
such payment is impractical, effects on the distribution of real
income must not be disregarded, especially if the magnitude of
a change, as through tariffs imposed or removed, is considerable
and may effect income shifts between different social groups.
Thus, a change is clearly 'good' only if both criteria are satisfied
and any associated redistribution is judged beneficial. If it is not,
the so-called 'optimum' tariff does not deserve this designation,
apart from the fact that it presupposes 'a purely competitive
system of fully employed economic individuals who preferably
never die' (p. 70). In his book *A Critique of Welfare Economics*
(Oxford: Clarendon Press, 1950, 2nd ed. 1957) Little, devoting
Chapter XIII to 'Welfare Theory and International Trade',
rejected in even stronger terms the use of the usual welfare
criteria in disregard of income distribution. One cannot reasonably 'say that free trade is desirable unless one believes that the
free-trade distribution of real income between countries is best
. . .' (p. 256).

Jan de Villiers Graaff (born 1928) wrote 'On Optimum Tariff
Structures', *Review of Economic Studies*, Vol. 17, No. 1 (1949—
50) pp. 47—59. He confirmed and 'refined' Scitovsky's findings

on the subject, holding that 'the rational thing for each country, acting separately, [was] to try to turn the terms of trade in its favour by protection' (p. 57). In a later book, *Theoretical Welfare Economics* (Cambridge: Cambridge University Press, 1967) he devoted Chapter IX to an analysis of the welfare-maximising volume of trade (pp. 122—41). He argued that 'the optimum amount of trade' would not be 'the amount realized under free trade' — 'except under quite exceptional circumstances' — because a country without tariffs cannot take advantage of possibilities of improving its terms of trade. The optimum taxes on import and export goods would be determined by Lerner's formula, assuming that the cross-elasticities of supply and demand are zero, so that any restriction on imports or exports affects only the prices of the goods taxed (p. 132). But the application of the theory is complicated by the probability that the elasticities of supply and demand are not independent of the height of the tariffs and of the distribution of income. To determine the tariffs on the basis of given elasticities would imply approval of the given distribution.

Lloyd A. Metzler (born 1913), in his article, 'Tariffs, the Terms of Trade and the Distribution of National Income', *Journal of Political Economy*, Vol. 57 (Feb 1949) pp. 1—29, pointed out that a protective tariff will not always have the intended effects of raising the relative prices of the import-competing goods and of the scarce factors used in their production, as Stolper and Samuelson [see above] had concluded. Of course, the tariff will raise the domestic prices of imports and import-competing goods above the foreign prices of these goods; but whether it will raise their prices relative to the domestic prices of export goods will depend on the induced change in the terms of trade. 'Whether a tariff increases or reduces the real and relative returns of the scarce factors . . . depends upon the magnitude of the favorable movement in the terms of trade, compared with the size of the tariff' (p. 7). If the terms of trade are much improved, the industries competing with imports, and therefore the scarce (relatively dear) factors, will be hurt. That is, 'the factor relatively more important in the industries competing with imports suffers both a relative decline in its share of the real income and an absolute decline in its real return', — which is just the opposite of what the tariff is supposed to achieve (p. 8). The induced change in the terms of trade alters both the national income and its distribution. 'The real income of a country's scarce factors of production is not likely to be increased by a tariff unless world demand is such that the tariff clearly diminishes the country's total income; and, conversely, the scarce factors are not likely to be injured by a tariff unless the tariff benefits the rest of the economy' (p. 20). What actually will happen depends on the elasticity of world's demand for the exportable goods of the country imposing or raising its import tariffs, and on that country's marginal propensity to consume its own exportables. If the said elasticity is smaller than the said propensity, the tariff will harm, not help, the import-competing industries and the dear factors they employ. As a sequel to this pathbreaking study Metzler published a briefer article, 'Tariffs, International Demand, and Domestic Prices', *Journal of Political Economy*, Vol. 57 (Aug 1949) pp. 345—51, in which he furnished additional equations describing the conditions for a tariff to leave domestic price ratios unchanged as a result of countervailing changes in foreign prices. The changes in individual and government spending (due to the tariff revenues collected by the government) are essential parts of the equations. On a somewhat different issue, Metzler showed that 'Graham's Theory of International Values', *American Economic Review*, Vol. 40 (June 1950) pp. 301—22, was not so different from the classical theory as Graham had thought. It is true that in complex situations, with many commodities and many countries, adjustment to changes in supply conditions may occur through an intermediate commodity or an intermediate country without any significant movements in international price ratios. Moreover, with productive factors sufficiently mobile in all countries, international equilibrium can be achieved in the long run without serious alterations in the terms of trade. Such stability in the long run, however, is compatible with fluctuations in the short run, and both are consistent with the classical model of reciprocal demand or offer curves appropriately interpreted.

Raúl Prebisch (born 1901), noted economist from Argentina, was the author of a report on *The Economic Development of Latin America and Its Principal Problems*, published by the Economic Commission for Latin America, United Nations (1949). He rejected the application of the theory of comparative advantage to less developed countries and supported protective tariffs to promote the industrialisation of developing regions. His main reasons for rejecting the comparative-cost argument was his belief that a persistent deterioration of the terms of trade for primary products favoured the industrial countries. The latter can keep 'the whole benefit of the technical development of their industries' for themselves and, in addition, receive a share of the fruits of the increased productivity of the 'peri-

pheral' countries (p. 10). This iniquitous development, as Prebisch views it, is largely the consequence of wage increases in
industrial countries during upswings and wage rigidity during
downswings, resulting in ever-increasing prices of industrial
products (p. 13).

Paul A. Samuelson (born 1915) published, besides numerous
other contributions to the theory of international trade, the
following five papers on the equalisation of the prices of the
same productive factors in different countries: 'International
Trade and the Equalisation of Factor Prices', *Economic Journal*
Vol. 58 (June 1948) pp. 163—84; 'International Factor-Price
Equalisation Once Again', *Economic Journal*, Vol. 59 (June
1949) pp. 181—97; 'A Comment on Factor-Price Equalisation',
Review of Economic Studies, Vol. 19 (1951—2) pp. 121—2;
'Prices of Factors and Goods in General Equilibrium', *Review of*
Economic Studies, Vol. 21 (1953—4) pp. 1—20; and 'Equalizati
by Trade of the Interest Rate along with the Real Wage', in
Richard E. Caves, Harry G. Johnson and Peter B. Kenen, eds,
Trade, Growth, and the Balance of Payments (Chicago: Rand,
McNally, 1965) pp. 35—52. He demonstrated 'that free commodity trade will under certain specified conditions inevitably
lead to complete factor-price equalisation' (1949, p. 181). The
conditions specified that two countries produce two commodities
from two factors of production, with production functions
yielding constant returns to scale and diminishing marginal productivities of both factors, the factors being qualitatively identical and the production functions the same in both countries,
but the two commodities differing in the ratios in which they
use the two factors. With some quantities of both commodities
produced in both countries and moving perfectly freely in international trade, without tariffs and transport costs, and with
competition effectively equalising the market price-ratio
between them (whereas the factors cannot move between the
countries), the result — equal real prices of each factor in both
countries (p. 182) — was 'established unequivocally' (p. 187).
In his 1948 and 1949 articles Samuelson had taken labour and
land as his only inputs, because both were primary factors. In
his 1965 essay he proceeded to introduce capital as a factor
required in production. This involved the problems of depreciation, reproduction, gross and net rentals, and interest rates.
[Most writers on trade theory, as also on distribution theory,
took capital as one of the two factors, but blithely disregarded
the problems involved.] Samuelson demonstrated, among other
things, that under specified conditions the interest rate would

be equalised by (unrestricted and costless) trade of consumer goods, no matter whether we assume the existence of one all-purpose capital good or of heterogeneous capital goods for the production of different commodities (p. 49). He also formulated a 'sweeping theorem' for 'all kinds of intermediate goods', which allows exclusive attention to be given to the primary factors and the ratios in which they are used in the production of traded consumer goods (1965, p. 52).

Abba P. Lerner (born 1903) published in 1952 a paper he had written for a seminar in 1933, in which he anticipated Samuelson's demonstration of the theorem of the international equalisation of the prices of the same productive factors. The article, 'Factor Prices and International Trade', *Economica*, n.s. Vol. 19 (Feb 1952) pp. 1—15, used more geometrical than algebraic arguments. The condition that the relative factor-use ratios must not be 'reversed' when the factor-price ratios change (that is, to say, that the more-labour-using good must not become the less-labour-using good as the price of labour rises) is illustrated by the shapes of the isoquants of the two goods (pp. 77—80). Lerner extended his demonstration to the case of more than two countries.

Ivor F. Pearce (born 1916) wrote on 'The Factor Price Equalisation Myth', *Review of Economic Studies*, Vol. 19 (1951—2) pp. 111—19, contending that increased trade was more likely to result in growing disparities than in equalisation of the prices of factors in different countries. His chief reasons were (1) that production functions are likely to be different in different countries, (2) that factor-input ratios may be reversed when factor-price ratios change so as to transform the predominant factor into the relatively unimportant one, and (3) that, in a world of many goods and many factors, instances of complete specialisation become too numerous. In 'A Further Note on Factor-Commodity Price Relationships', *Economic Journal*, Vol. 69 (Dec 1959) pp. 725—32, Pearce undertook to reinforce his arguments regarding the lack of realism in the assumptions on which the 'myth' of factor-price equalisation rests.

Svend Laursen (1912—60) gave one of the most readable and lucid expositions of the theorem of international equalisation of factor prices, in his article 'Production Functions and the Theory of International Trade', *American Economic Review*, Vol. 42 (Sept 1952) pp. 540—57. He made it clear that too wide disparities in the factor endowments of the countries and too small diversities in the factor-input ratios of the commodities produced would lead to complete specialisation of one of the countries in the production of one of the commodities and, hence, would halt the process that tends to make for equal prices of the same factors in the two countries. He showed that the equalisation theorem is not affected if the number of countries is increased, or if the number of factors is increased by at least as much as the number of products, except that such increased numbers may increase the probability of complete specialisation in one or more activities. Where the number of factors exceeds that of commodities, the theorem will not apply. Laursen's verbal exposition, especially of the significance of the restrictive assumptions required for the applicability of the theorem, succeeded in making the essential points intuitively obvious.

Robert E. Baldwin (born 1924), in an article on 'The New Welfare Economics and Gains in International Trade', *Quarterly Journal of Economics*, Vol. 66 (Feb 1952) pp. 91—101, criticised the welfare criteria proposed by Scitovsky [see above] as too strong in some respects and misleading in others (pp. 93—4). He stressed that the possibility of improving the terms of trade was confined to the case of inelastic foreign offer curves and to the prevalence of pure competition among sellers as well as buyers. The idea that only tariffs or other government interventions in foreign trade can help a country to take advantage of inelastic foreign offer curves presupposes that individual producers and traders are unable to influence the prices at which they buy or sell.

Wassily Leontief (born 1905) undertook to test empirically, with the use of his input-output coefficients, the Heckscher-Ohlin theory of comparative advantage as determined by the countries' relative endowment with productive resources. In his papers on 'Domestic Production and Foreign Trade: The American Capital Position Reexamined', *Proceedings of the American Philosophical Society*, Vol. 97 (Sept 1953) pp. 332—49, and 'Factor Proportions and the Structure of American Trade: Further Theoretical and Empirical Analysis', *Review of Economics and Statistics*, Vol. 38 (Nov 1956) pp. 386—407, he showed that $1 million of American exports would require $2,550,780 of capital and 182,313 man-years of labour, while $1 million of import-competing products would require $3,091,339 of capital and 170,004 man-years of labour. Thus, the capital/labour ratio in the production of exports (14,010) was smaller than that in the production of import-substitutes (18,180). If American imports were produced abroad with the same techniques as import substitutes were produced in the United States, this would mean that imports required relatively more capital, and exports elatively more labour. How could this be reconciled with the general factual judgement that labour was relatively dear, and capital relatively cheap, in the United States? Leontief did not regard this contradiction as a refutation of the theory he had set out to test. Instead, he proposed that the factual judgement concerning relative endowments was erroneous: if labour were measured in efficiency units, it would be regarded as the relatively more plentiful resource in the United States. The 'Leontief Paradox' gave rise to sparkling discussions for many years.

Victor E. Morgan (born 1915) and **Graham L. Rees** (born 1921) joined in writing an article on 'Non-Traded Goods and International Factor Price Equalisation', *Economica*, n.s. Vol. 21 (Nov 1954) pp. 334—9, in which they strengthened the belief in the relevance of the equalisation theorem. They held that complete specialisation of one country in the production of a traded good need not halt the movement towards equalised factor prices when there is a domestic sector, that is, when the production of non-traded goods absorbs much of the relatively abundant factors.

Tadeusz Mieczyslaw Rybczynski (born 1923) examined the relationship between 'Factor Endowment and Relative Commodity Prices', *Economica*, n.s. Vol. 22 (Nov 1955) pp. 336—41, by showing, particularly, the effects of an increase in the quantity of one of the two existing factors upon the price ratio between two commodities produced with different proportions of the factors. Under the usual assumptions, the increase 'will always lead to a worsening of the terms of trade, or the relative price, of the commodity using relatively much of that factor. The marginal propensity to consume influences the degree of deterioration, but it can never reverse its direction' (p. 340). The ratio of physical quantities produced and consumed depends on whether the marginal propensity to consume the cheaper commodity is equal to, or greater or smaller than, the average propensity to consume it. If 'the commodity using relatively much of the factor, the quantity of which had been increased, is an item of export, . . . external terms of trade will deteriorate; conversely, should the commodity be an import, the terms of trade must improve' (p. 341).

James Meade (born 1907), in his book *The Theory of International Economic Policy*, Vol. II, *Trade and Welfare* (London: Oxford University Press, 1955), provided important insights into several issues of international economics. The lucidity of the exposition of 'The Distributional Argument for Trade Control', both with respect to 'The International Terms of Trade' (Chapter

17) and with respect to 'The Domestic Distribution of Income' (Chapter 18) is unsurpassed. Four chapters (20 to 23) are devoted to the theory of 'Trade as a Substitute for Factor Movements', explaining the problems with a patience hardly found in any other source. Meade's six-point summary of these chapters should be quoted here:

First, free trade is the more likely to lead to the equalisation of marginal products, the less difference there is in the original factor endowments in the trading countries. In this case the relative scarcities and so the marginal products will not differ too much in the original situation, and free trade will have less work to do in bringing about their complete equalisation — Second, the fewer are the number of factors of production in each country, the smaller will be the number of jobs which free trade will be called upon to do in equalising marginal products. — Third, the greater are the number of products produced in each country, the larger will be the potential number of channels through which free trade can do its work of equalising the marginal products of the factors. — Fourth, the larger are the number of products for which a policy of free trade is adopted in both countries, the larger will be the number of actual channels through which free trade can exert its influence. — Fifth, the larger are the differences in the proportions in which the various factors are used in the production of the various products, the greater will be the leverage which free trade can exert upon the relative demands for the various factors in the two countries. — Finally, the more consistent are the differences in the proportions in which the various factors are used in the production of the various products, the more likely is this leverage to be exerted in a way which will bring factor prices into equality in the trading countries (p. 392).

Ronald W. Jones (born 1931) wrote a helpful note on the definition of relative abundance and relative scarcity of productive factors in the resource endowment of countries before they begin to trade with each other. In 'Factor Proportions and the Heckscher-Ohlin Theorem', *Review of Economic Studies*, Vol. 24, No. 1 (1956) pp. 1—10, he distinguished between the ratios of the physical quantities of available factors and the ratios of the (real) prices of the factors. The definition in terms of physical quantities focuses on supply in disregard of demand, whereas the definition in value terms includes the effects of demand on relative scarcity. It was the latter definition which Heckscher and Ohlin had in mind. In an article on 'Comparative Advantage and the Theory of Tariffs: A Multi-country, Multi-commodity Model', *Review of Economic Studies*, Vol. 28 (June 1961) pp. 161—75, Jones, referring to the writings of Frank Graham and Lionel McKenzie, developed the necessary and sufficient conditions for efficient specialisation in a model with many commodities and many countries. A country has a comparative advantage in producing any commodity j relative to commodity k (compared with the rest of the world) if, and only if, the sacrifice of one unit of commodity k in that country can yield a greater increase in the production of commodity j than the same sacrifice would in the rest of the world. [More on Jones below, p. 248.]

Harry G. Johnson (born 1923), in his article 'Factor Endowments, International Trade and Factor Prices', *Manchester School of Economic and Social Studies*, Vol. 25 (Sept 1957) pp. 270—83, gave a concise summary of some of the essential points made in the discussion on factor prices. He characterised the theorem as a combination of two propositions: one, that differences in factor endowments are the cause of trade, the other that differences in factor prices disappear as an effect of trade. He showed, as Jones and others had before him, that differences in endowments, if interpreted in terms of physical quantities of resources, may easily be overcompensated by differences in demand. [Ohlin had conceived of relative scarcities in terms of factor prices, not of quantities.] Johnson pointed to the possibility that relative scarcities and abundances may not be relieved by trade if factor-input ratios are reversed as factor-price ratios change. Thus, the applicability of the Heckscher-Ohlin theorem depends ultimately on empirical questions regarding the nature of technology and the range of variations in the factor endowments of different countries.

Robert A. Mundell (born 1932), in an article on 'International Trade and Factor Mobility', *American Economic Review*, Vol. 47 (June 1957) pp. 320—35, examined the interdependence of the effects of restraints on the mobility of goods and of factors. Impediments on international movement of factors stimulate trade, and impediments on trade stimulate factor movements. If labour cannot move but capital can, a country with abundant labour will, by imposing trade barriers, attract capital from a country that has relatively much of it.

Subimal Mookerjee (born 1923) provided a lucid 'statement and appraisal of the Heckscher-Ohlin theory' in his book on *Factor Endowments and International Trade* (Bombay: Asia

Publishing House, 1958). He showed, more clearly than others, the problems which the assumption of more countries, more commodities, and more factors raises for the relevance of the equalisation theorem. Most significant is what Mookerjee and others call the consistency of 'factor intensities', that is, the question whether, for three or more commodities, the relative predominance of certain productive factors in particular product remains consistent regardless of substitution among various factors associated with changes in their price ratios. Relative factor predominance is consistent only if every factor can be linked with a single good as its most important input, but 'it is difficult to find realistic situations where this assumption . . . is valid' (p. 60). If factors were consistently predominant or un- important in the production of particular goods, adding more countries into the model would raise no problems, since the 'analysis can be applied to trade between *any* two of the many countries' (p. 69). One country may be linked with another 'through the common production of commodities *A* and *B*', while a third country may be linked to the second 'through the common production of two different commodities *C* and *D* which may or may not be produced' in the first country (p. 70) However, with many products and many factors, the meanings of relative factor dominance and relative factor endowment become increasingly obscure (p. 88).

Roy F. Harrod (born 1900), later Sir Roy Harrod, rejected the theory of equalisation of the prices of equal factors in free- trading countries, in an article on 'Factor-Price Relations under Free Trade', *Economic Journal*, Vol. LXVIII (June 1958) pp. 245—55, chiefly on two grounds: the number of factors may well be larger than the number of commodities if all gradations of quality and specificity are taken into account; and the factor use ratio in the production of one of the goods may vary so much with the factor-price ratio that it may in some range use more labour and in another range use more capital relative to the other good. Harrod concluded that the case 'of the alterna- tives of equal factor prices of 100% specialisation is a *curiosum* in international trade theory . . , rather than a fundamental principle, . . . an analysis of any probable development' (p. 255) In an earlier article, on less abstract grounds, on 'European Economic Co-operation: A British Viewpoint', *Public Finance*, Vol. V (No. 4, 1950) pp. 588—47, he had taken issue with the equalisation myth as applied to the Common Market:

There are ideas circulating to the effect that European unifica

tion should mean a tendency to equalisation of wages in any
given occupation throughout Europe. But surely this is quite
chimerical. The general level of wages in any country must
depend on the general level of productivity of that country.
Many factors go to make that up — past history, the scale of
existing equipment, the industry of the workers, the skill of
the management. . . . There is no reason to suppose . . . that
the improvement that is likely to take place, will constitute a
movement towards greater equality, nor is it necessarily desirable that it should' (pp. 543—4).

Warner Max Corden (born 1927), in an article on 'Tariffs,
Subsidies, and the Terms of Trade', *Economica*, n.s. Vol. XXIV
(Aug 1957) pp. 235—42, examined the question whether a
government, determined to help an industry competing with
imports, should use direct subsidies or protective tariffs. He concluded that, if the country were unable to affect its terms of
trade, tariffs, distorting both production patterns and consumption patterns, would be much more costly than subsidies. If, on
the other hand, tariffs improve the terms of trade, the best solution would be to impose the 'optimum tariff' and, if this should
be insufficient help for the industry, to supplement protection
with direct subsidy. In a later article, on 'Protection and Foreign
Investment', *Economic Record*, Vol. 43 (June 1967) pp. 209—
32, Corden discussed the relationship between tariff protection
and the inflow of foreign capital. Whether protection of import-
competing industries will increase the net inflow is uncertain in
view of adverse effects of import barriers upon export industries.
With a given structure of the tariff there exists some optimal
combination between the level of the tariff and of taxes on
returns to foreign investment. A non-optimal tariff system may
cause a social loss from the inflows of foreign capital.
    Kelvin Lancaster (born 1924) took exception to some formu-
lations by Stolper and Samuelson regarding tariffs supposed to
benefit scarce labour. In his article, 'Protection and Real Wages:
A Restatement', *Economic Journal*, Vol. 67 (June 1957) pp.
199—210, he contended 'that no general statement about which
of the factors will have its real wage raised as a result of tariff
protection can be deduced from the relative "scarcity" of the
factors in the Stolper-Samuelson sense'. He affirmed, however,
the general validity of a restatement in the form 'Protection
raises the real wage of the factor in which the imported good is
relatively intensive' [Better read: . . . 'is employed in relatively
larger quantities']. In effect, Lancaster denied that relative

scarcity of a factor in a country, either in terms of the relative
physical quantities in which they are available or in terms of
their relative prices, determines the patterns of exports and imp

Jagdish Bhagwati (born 1934) restated and amended earlier
propositions, especially by Stolper and Samuelson, Metzler, an
Lancaster, regarding 'Protection, Real Wages, and Real Income
Economic Journal, Vol. 69 (Dec 1959) pp. 733—48. 'Protectio
(prohibitive or otherwise) will raise, reduce or leave unchanged
the real wage of the factors, intensively [read, '*ex*tensively']
employed in the production of a good according as protection
raises, lowers, or leaves unchanged the internal relative price of
that good' (p. 743). Protection by a prohibitive tariff will neces
sarily raise the relative price of the import substitute; but if the
tariff is not prohibitive, the relative price of the supposedly pro
tected good will only rise (that is, the relative price of the expo
good will only fall) if foreign elasticity of demand for the
exports of the country that imposes the tariff on imports is
greater [in absolute value] than the country's domestic margin
propensity to consume its exportables. This was Metzler's conclusion, but Bhagwati expanded the formula to deal with cases
where existing import duties are increased; distinguished
between the different definitions of scarcity and abundance of
productive factors; and elaborated on the assumptions (chiefly
those regarding production functions) which are necessary if th
tariff and the resulting price-increase of import-substitutes are
to increase the real wage of the factor predominantly employed
in their production. He also examined the possible difference
between real factor price (wage) and real factor income, the
latter being affected by the way in which the government uses
its tariff revenues. The factor injured by protection may be
compensated (or rather overcompensated) for its loss by payments (or government services) financed from tariff revenues;
but overcompensation is possible only if 'the real income of the
country as a whole is improved' by the import duties (p. 744).
Bhagwati later produced a helpful guide through 'The Pure
Theory of International Trade: A Survey', *Economic Journal*,
Vol. 74 (Mar 1964) pp. 1—84. Positive theory is dealt with in
five sections: 1. The Pattern of Trade; 2. Factor Price-Equaliza-
tion; 3. Theorems in Comparative Statics; 4. Theorems in Dynamics; 5. Central Limitations of Pure Theory; Intermediate and
Capital Goods. Welfare theory is covered in the subsequent thre
sections: 6. Gains from Trade; 7. Measurement of Welfare; 8.
Trade Theory and Development Planning. No brief abstract
could do justice to such an encyclopaedic survey.

George Donald Alastair MacDougall (born 1912), later *Sir Donald MacDougall*, raised some novel questions on 'The Benefits and Costs of Private Investment from Abroad: A Theoretical Approach', *Economic Record*, Vol. 36 (Special Issue in honour of Sir Douglas Copland, Mar 1960) pp. 13—35. MacDougall saw the gains to the host country chiefly in (1) revenues from taxing the profits of foreign investors, (2) possible economies of scale, (3) acquisition of foreign know-how, technical or managerial, and (4) increased competition forcing greater efficiency upon domestic producers (p. 34). He also discussed several other possible influences of increased inflows of foreign capital — on the size of the labour force (immigration), on domestic capital formation, on the terms of trade, on the balance of payments, etc. — but did not attribute substantial benefits or costs to them (pp. 17—22, 28—32). Since the elasticity of supply of foreign capital to a particular host country, such as Australia, may be small (lack of information), tax incentives for foreign investors may not pay directly; however, a 'reduction in tax rates might still be worth while, for the other consequences might be favourable' to the income of the host country (p. 34).

Murray C. Kemp (born 1926) treated problems of foreign investment in an article, 'Foreign Investment and the National Advantage', *Economic Record*, Vol. 38 (Mar 1962) pp. 56—62, and in a note, 'The Benefits and Costs of Private Investment from Abroad: Comment', ibid., pp. 108—10. He argued that capital-rich countries tend to invest too much abroad, because individual investors as pure competitors cannot take account of what for all investors as a group is a faster decline in the marginal rate of returns on such investment. By levying higher taxes on these returns from abroad, the country could internalise the difference between marginal and average returns and thereby restrict investment abroad to the point where marginal returns collected abroad equal average returns on domestic investment. [In other words, the tax achieves optimum monopolistic exploitation for the nation, counting tax revenues and the lenders' or investors' returns.] Kemp also stressed that in the case of loss of equity or borrowers' default, domestic investment has the advantage that the fixed assets might still be of some value to the nation, whereas assets abroad would be useless to the country that had supplied the investible funds. In the note in the same volume, Kemp examined the national advantage of the country that receives capital funds from abroad. Contradicting an earlier suggestion by MacDougall regarding possible subsidies to imports of foreign capital, Kemp found that the country could maximise its income by levying taxes on all earnings of foreign-owned capital.

John S. Chipman (born 1926) contributed an elaborate and elegant 'Survey of the Theory of International Trade'—'Part 1, The Classical Theory'; 'Part 2, The Neo-Classical Theory'; 'Part 3, The Modern Theory'; — *Econometrica*, Vol. 33 (July 1965 and Oct 1965) pp. 477—519 and 685—760, and Vol. 34 (Jan 1966) pp. 18—76. The survey emphasises 'the mathematical structure of international trade theory' (p. 478) and is most thorough and vigorous in the exposition of the basic theorems and their extension and elaboration. The theory of customs unions or other aspects of commercial policy are not included. In an essay on 'The Theory of Exploitative Trade and Investment Policies: A Reformulation and Synthesis', in Luis Eugenio di Marco, ed., *International Economics and Development* [in Honor of Raúl Prebisch] (New York: Academic Press, 1972) pp. 209—44, Chipman provided a rigorous and amended restatement of the problem of joint optimisation of restrictions on foreign trade and foreign investment. Since the intended redistribution of the gains from foreign trade and investment succeed only in the absence of retaliation, Chipman substituted the word exploitative for optimal (p. 210). He showed that Kemp's result of 1962 hold only for the case in which one country completely specialises. If both countries produce both goods, and trade is unrestricted, 'movements of capital into or out of the exploited country will not affect its rate of return there' (p. 211). In this case non-interference with capital flows is the best policy for the would-be exploiting country. On the other hand, the country may succeed in exploiting its partner by taxing imports or exports. It may in the process 'raise or lower the foreign rate of return on capital', depending on whether the taxed product uses relatively more capital or more labour. It depends, of course, whether the country is a lender or a borrower. If it is an importer of capital and its export industry uses much capital, then a restriction on trade will improve both the country's terms of trade and terms of borrowing.

Ronald W. Jones (born 1931), in an article on 'International Capital Movements and the Theory of Tariffs and Trade', *Quarterly Journal of Economics*, Vol. 81 (Feb 1967) pp. 1—38, analysed the combined effects, from a national point of view, of combinations of tariff and taxation policies on the comparative returns on capital investments abroad. If earnings from foreign investment bulk large in the balance of payments, it may prove to be optimal strategy in the home country to subsidise exports, instead of levying a duty on imports to improve the terms of trade. If either tariffs are 'bound' by agreement (and hence cannot be changed) or flows of capital are unimpeded (so that net rates of return cannot be influenced) 'paradoxical' results are possible: for example, it may be optimal to subsidise investment abroad or to have negative import duties. In a note on 'Tariffs and Trade in General Equilibrium: Comment', *American Economic Review*, Vol. 59 (June 1969) pp. 418–24, Jones criticised the results of Södersten and Vind which seemed to refute Metzler's finding that a tariff levied on imports can, under certain conditions, lower the relative domestic price of the imported commodity. Södersten and Vind had assumed that an increase in the relative domestic price of good A always raises consumption of good B when income remains constant in terms of B-units. When this assumption is removed, general-equilibrium analysis confirms Metzler's finding.

James Rae Melvin (born 1938) published several articles on the pure theory of trade patterns and factor prices. In 'Production and Trade with Two Factors and Three Goods', *American Economic Review*, Vol. 58 (Dec 1968) pp. 1249–68, he showed that, with identical production functions in two trading countries and non-reversible ratios of factor predominance in producing each good, equalisation of factor prices is more likely in the case of two factors and three goods than in the case of two factors and two goods. The pattern of trade, however, may become indeterminate. In 'Increasing Returns to Scale as a Determinant of Trade', *Canadian Journal of Economics*, Vol. 2 (Aug 1969) pp. 389–402, Melvin demonstrates that, with factor endowments and factor prices equal in the two countries, and therefore not causing any trade or factor movements between them, the existence of economies of scale may result in trade. Such trade will, of course, increase the combined output, but the gain may accrue to only one of the countries. Factor prices will become unequal in the process and, if they lead to factor movements, combined output will increase further.

Franz Gehrels (born 1922), in an article on 'Optimal Restrictions on Foreign Trade and Investment', *American Economic Review*, Vol. 61 (Mar 1971) pp. 147–59, undertook to expand the rules for finding the optimal combination of tariffs on imports and taxes on returns on foreign investment, as first developed by Jones and Kemp. He extended the rules to the case of any number of importable goods and considered partial optima for conditions where either the tariff or the tax was fixed. Finally he examined the optimal restrictions on imports

and foreign investment for the case of given imperfections in th
domestic labour market.

THE EFFECTS OF CUSTOMS UNION AND OTHER FORMS OF ECONOMIC INTEGRATION, 1892—1976

The theorists' contribution surveyed thus far were all eminently
pertinent to the economics of national, regional, and worldwide
integration; but only because they helped explicate the econom
effects of trade expansion and trade restriction in general. With
out this theoretical foundation the economic effects of a customs
union, a free-trade area, or any other institutions attempting to
promote *intra*regional trade in preference to *inter*regional and
world trade could not be understood. The theories of the gains
from trade, the terms of trade, the distributional effects of trad
and all the rest, are essential in the development of the theory
of the customs union. The contributions surveyed from here or
are addressed *directly* to the economic consequences of closer
economic integration among countries previously protected by
uniform tariffs levied on imports from abroad. The essential
questions concern tariff preferences, that is, discriminatory
tariff reductions on imports from 'favoured' countries or the
complete removal of restrictions on the trade with specified
countries. Besides free trade there may be also free movements
of persons and capital funds and perhaps also harmonisation of
institutions, co-ordination of economic policies, and co-operation of several kinds among the integrating countries.

The literature on these subjects is far too extensive to permit
complete coverage in this survey. I shall do my best to review
here the most widely cited contributions to the discussions of
trade integration and factor integration. Questions of monetary
and fiscal integration will be treated in a separate section.

Frank W. Taussig (1859—1940) with his important works on
the general theory of international trade and on commercial
policy was given his due praise in the preceding section. In an
early article on 'Reciprocity', *Quarterly Journal of Economics*,
Vol. 7 (Oct 1892) pp. 26—39, he discussed the possible effects
of preferential duties and showed that they may be injurious to
the countries involved. His arguments are fully applicable to the
economics of customs unions. Among other things he demonstrated that the reduction [abolition] of duties on imports from
a favoured nation may divert trade from a non-favoured country
to the favoured one, but still leave the price in the importing

country unchanged as long as its entire import demand cannot
be met from the favoured source. In such a case the diversion of
trade would present primarily a gift from the treasury of the
importing country, sacrificing some of its tariff revenues, to
the producers in the favoured country. Taussig's article was reprinted in his book *Free Trade, the Tariff and Reciprocity* (New
York: Macmillan, 1920) pp. 120—31.

Jean Marchal (born 1905) published a book on *Union
Douanière et Organisation Européenne* (Paris: Recueil Sirey,
1929) for the Comité Français d'Etudes pour l'Union Douanière
Européenne. Probably written as a doctoral dissertation, the
study offers a valuable historical survey of customs unions and
of the relevant literature. The book gives an excessive number of
citations of pronouncements by Lucien Brocard, who apparently supervised the study, provided a Preface to the book, and
evidently influenced the author in a direction towards protection
against American competition through tariffs and towards
'regulation' of intra-European competition through agreements
among producers. (See pp. 135—48, especially p. 141.)

Gottfried Haberler (born 1900), some of whose general contributions to the theory of international trade were reviewed in
the preceding section (see p. 230) made several statements on
the problems of regional integration and discrimination in trade.
In his *Theory of International Trade* (Edinburgh: Hodge, 1936)
he held that 'Customs unions are always to be welcomed, even
when they are not between neighbouring or complementary
States. A Customs Union must be especially advantageous for
small States, since these are particularly injured if they exclude
one another's goods . . . '. On the other hand, he argued that a
customs union could not procure any advantages that could not
be attained in a still fuller measure by 'a general removal of
duties' (p. 390). In a later essay on 'The Political Economy of
Regional or Continental Blocs', in Seymour E. Harris, ed., *Post-
war Economic Problems* (New York: McGraw Hill, 1943),
Haberler repeated that 'the economic arguments for . . . regional
blocs are identical with the old classical argument for free trade',
namely 'the advantages of mass production and of full division
of labour' (p. 130). Several notable suggestions were made in
Haberler's essay 'Die wirtschaftliche Integration Europas', in
Erwin von Beckerath *et al.*, eds, *Wirtschaftsfragen der freien
Welt* [Festschrift for Chancellor Ludwig Erhard] (Frankfurt
a.M.: Fritz Knapp, 1957) pp. 521—30. There was a proposal to
distinguish 'degrees of economic integration' (p. 521). [See also
Erich Schneider, 1957, and Jean Weiller, 1958.] There was an

allusion to the possibility that the substitution effects of discriminatory duties on imports from non-member countries will be overcome by income effects due to fast growth (p. 525). Finally, there was the statement that discrimination in favour of member countries may cause both trade diversion and trade creation at the same time if the price reductions due to reduced or abolished duties cause consumption and total imports to increase (p. 527). One other of Haberler's contributions to this literature should be mentioned. In his address on 'Integration and Growth of the World Economy in Historical Perspective', *American Economic Review*, Vol. LIV (Mar 1964) pp. 1–22, Haberler asserted that the 'wave of world-wide integration [which started soon after World War II] has had more powerful and beneficial effects than the much more advertised and talked-about series of regional integrations' (p. 3). And he expressed the fear that 'attempts at regional integration in various parts of the world constitute an imminent danger to world-wide integration and further growth of multilateral trade' (p. 20).

Lionel Robbins (born 1898), later Lord Robbins, discussed the economic effects of customs unions in his book *Economic Planning and International Order* (London: Macmillan, 1937). He argued that 'the gain from regional regrouping or wider units of any kind' does not come from the increase in self-sufficiency on the part of the larger union but rather from the reduction in self-sufficiency 'on the part of the areas which are thus amalgamated. . . . From the international point of view, the tariff union is not an advantage in itself. It is an advantage only in so far as, on balance, it conduces to more extensive division of labour. It is to be justified only by arguments which would justify still more its extension to all areas capable of entering into trade relationships' (p. 121). In a later book, *The Economist in the Twentieth Century* (London: Macmillan, 1954), Robbins explained that unilateral free trade (or tariff reduction), however beneficial it would be in the long run, might in the short run cause serious problems of adjustment [unemployment, deflationary pressures]. This suggests an argument for customs union as an arrangement for simultaneous multilateral abolition of import restrictions (pp. 137–9).

Wilhelm Röpke (1899–1966) was probably the chief influence on the adoption of the term 'economic integration', especially through his book *International Economic Disintegration* (London: William Hodge, 1942). He had circulated earlier versions in German and had published in 1939 an article on the same theme in *Economisk Tidskrift*. He found that 'world economy' had been 'an interdependent and intercommunicating system', chiefly through multilateral trade almost free from obstacles and restrictions (pp. 14—17). With the outbreak of the war in 1914 a period of economic disintegration set in, characterised by nationalism and restrictionism, and associated with socio-political disintegration in the international field (p. 76). In a later essay on 'Integration and Desintegration der internationalen Wirtschaft', in Erwin von Beckerath *et. al.*, eds, *Wirtschaftsfragen der freien Welt* [Festschrift for Chancellor Ludwig Erhard] (Frankfurt a.M.: Fritz Knapp, 1957) pp. 493—501, Röpke made it clear that economic re-integration could be achieved only through universal liberalisation of trade and payments (p. 500). In two other articles in German, published in 1958 and 1959 in *Ordo* Vols 10 and 11, he discussed the schemes of regional economic integration devised through EEC and EFTA. The first of these articles appeared in English under the title 'European Free Trade — The Great Divide', *The Banker*, Vol. 108 (Sept 1958) pp. 580—8. Röpke held that 'The common market and the free trade area alike can improve the use of resources and raise productivity only to the extent that the removal of tariffs hurts producers inside, not outside, the union. . . . However, . . . the distortions of the common market are likely to be much more enduring or harmful than those of the free trade area: for they will be aggravated by the effects of its supranational economic planning' (p. 587). Finally, in his book on *International Order and Economic Integration* (Dordrecht: Reidel Publ. Co., 1959), Röpke offered additional arguments for integration by competitive market forces and against integrating efforts through dirigiste techniques. He defined economic integration as a 'state of affairs which will permit trading relations among different national economies to be as free and mutually advantageous as those which exist within a national economy' (p. 225), and held that this would be possible only with 'the free use of money, without regional limitation' (p. 226). He deplored the widespread 'misunderstanding' that 'piecemeal ('functional') integration' was likely to lead to 'real' or 'integral integration' (pp. 229—30).

John Sterling de Beers (born 1914) published an article on 'Tariff Aspects of a Federal Union', *Quarterly Journal of Economics* Vol. 56 (Nov 1941) pp. 49—92, in which he raised four of the decisive questions in an analysis of the economic effects of a tariff union between countries A and B:

1. Before the tariff reduction, did A have a revenue, protec-

tive, or prohibitive tariff? 2. Under free trade, would B suppl
ail, some or none of A's imports? 3. Is there a constant, increasing, or decreasing supply-price schedule for C's exports?
for B's exports, for A's production? 4. In a customs union,
will the external tariff (against C) be the same as, higher than
or lower than the previous tariff of A?

Kurt W. Rothschild (born 1914) in an article 'The Small
Nation and World Trade', *Economic Journal*, Vol. 54 (Apr 1944)
expressed concern that small nations would suffer from 'the
growth of a monopolistic and oligopolistic environment' even as
members of regional blocs, even indeed, under free world trade.
If a *laissez-faire* policy is pursued, the creation of a federal union
will tend to reinforce and perpetuate the economic structure of
its constituent members. The larger 'industrial countries will
become the centres of heavy and other monopolistic industries.
The smaller countries will find opportunities in the small-scale
industries and in agriculture. Backward countries will remain
backward just because they were backward before' (p. 31).
Rothschild concluded that small and/or backward countries
would need not merely temporary but permanent tariff protection.

Jan Tinbergen (born 1903) published his book on *International Economic Cooperation* (Amsterdam: Elsevier, 1945), the
revised edition of which appeared under the title *International
Economic Integration* (Amsterdam: Elsevier, 1954). In 1952 he
published an essay 'On the Theory of Economic Integration' in
Les Cahiers de Bruges (pp. 290 ff.), which was later reprinted in
his *Selected Papers* (Amsterdam: North Holland Publ. Co., 1959)
He distinguished three kinds ('phases') of integration: (i) trade
in commodities without transfers of capital or people, (ii) with
transfers of only capital, and (iii) with transfers of both capital
and people. He introduced a further distinction between 'negative' and 'positive' measures to promote economic integration,
the former being the 'elimination of institutions' [restrictions],
the latter the establishment of institutions. In the second edition
of *International Economic Integration* (Amsterdam: Elsevier,
1965), Tinbergen regards 'a customs union between a limited
number of countries' as only a 'partial form of integration'
(p. 28) and speaks of 'economic integration' only if countries
centralise 'at a supra-national level' numerous 'instruments of
economic policy' (p. 67).

Luigi Einaudi (1874—1961), professor, senator, central-bank
governor, budget minister, and finally President of Italy, pub-

lished a book *I problemi economici della federazione europea*
(Milan: La Fiacola, 1946) 112 pp. in which he discussed the
economic implications of European federation. He attempted to
dispel widespread errors and anxieties regarding the removal of
protective tariffs.

Charles P. **Kindleberger** (born 1910), an early protagonist of
European integration, authored and co-authored in various
American government positions several secret but influential
memoranda, some of which have in later years been circulated
and quoted. One, written in 1947, was among the materials pre-
pared for designing the Marshall Plan; another, of 1948, was
intended to preserve the record of the 'Origins of the Marshall
Plan' (now published in US Department of State, *Foreign
Relations of the United States 1947*, Vol. III, Washington: 1972,
pp. 241—7). In an essay on 'European Economic Integration', in
Money, Trade, and Economic Growth [in Honor of John H.
Williams] (New York: Macmillan 1951) pp. 58—75, Kindleberger observed that despite the widespread sentiment in favour of
European integration 'at no time was there in existence a single
clear idea of what is meant' (p. 59). He found that 'the problem
is essentially one of resource allocation' (p. 61) and that the
various forms — Customs Union, integrated planning, and Clearing Union — were discussed without regard to the integration of
Europe in the world economy. He argued in favour of trade preferences, specifically 'discriminatory reductions of trade barriers
and quotas on products to be affected by new investment'
(p. 74). An unpublished memorandum of 1953, entitled 'Notes
on the Integration of the Free World Economy', was written to
suggest revisions in an outline which Gunnar Myrdal had prepared for a report of the UN Economic Commission for Europe
(ECE). Kindleberger proposed that equalisation of prices of
qualitatively equal factors of production be used as a criterion
of economic integration. He emphasised that, chiefly because of
the existence of non-competing groups, such equalisation had
not occurred even within nations; with national integration sadly
incomplete in most countries, international integration was only
in its earliest stages. In an article on 'The United States and
European Regional Integration', *Social Science*, vol. 34 (Oct
1959) pp. 210—17, he held that trade creation was most likely
to outweigh trade diversion, but that little, if any, economies of
larger scale were to be expected in Europe. He warned of the
possibility of 'investment diversion' (p. 214). He was most
optimistic regarding the effects of the Common Market upon
long-term growth (p. 217). In a later survey article on 'Trends in

International Economics', *The Annals of the American Academy of Political and Social Sciences*, Vol. 358 (Mar 1965) pp. 170—9, he gave special attention to the contributions which Viner, Meade, Scitovsky, and Lipsey and Lancaster had made to the theory of tariff protection and customs unions.

Maurice Allais (born 1911) published dozens of articles on the economic unification of Europe and its importance as a first stage toward an Atlantic community. Among the articles were 'Les conditions de l'unification économique de l'Europe, *Productions Françaises*, Vol. 1 (Dec 1949) pp. 7—9; 'Les interêts des groupes sociaux et nationaux et l'union économique de l'Europe *Economia Internazionale*, Vol. IV (Feb 1951) pp. 1—14; and 'Fondements théoriques, perspectives et conditions d'un marché commun effectif.' *Revue d'Économie Politique*, Numéro special No. 1 (Jan-Feb 1958) pp. 56—99. In his book, *L'Europe Unie: Route de la prospérité*, (Paris: Calmann-Lévy, 1960), he held that a 'total liberalization' of trade and capital movements (with monetary integration) in Europe would lead to an 'immense technical progress', allowing the standard of living to double (p. 252) He regarded the eventual extension into an Atlantic community not only as imperative but as a perfectly realistic objective that might be attained within a period of some twenty years (pp. 220—2 and 254). Among his later works in his book *La libéralisa tion des relations économiques internationales, accords commerciaux ou intégration économique* (Paris: Gauthier Villars, 19'

Jean Weiller (born 1905) published several articles and books relevant to the subject surveyed. Let us mention three articles, all in the *Revue Economique*: 'Politique d'intégration régionale et libération des échanges', Vol. 1 (May 1950) pp. 101—6; 'Aspects particuliers d'une libération des échanges', Vol. 1 (Dec 1950) pp. 608—13; and 'Les degrés de l'intégration et les chances d'une "zone de co-opération" internationale', Vol. 9 (Mar 1958) pp. 233—54. In the latter he presented various taxonomic distinctions, spoke of an optimal degree of integration (p. 235) — perhaps far short of an *ideal* maximum — reminded us of the difference between national, multinational, and global integration, suggested a coefficient of dependence (on essential imports), contrasted 'spontaneous' integration (through free-market forces) with 'conscious efforts' at integration (through governmental measures and institutions), and stressed the importance of international co-ordination of national economic policies (p. 238). [The 'degrees' of integration in Weiller's sense seem to have little connection with the 'degrees' in Erich Schneider's conception or my own.]

Herbert Giersch (born 1921), in an article on 'Economic Union between Nations and the Location of Industries', *Review of Economic Studies*, Vol. XVII (1949—50), argued that the abolition of barriers to inter-European trade and movements of factors would 'strengthen the attractiveness of the highly industrialized centre both for labour and capital' and, hence, lead to agglomeration 'beyond the social and economic optimum' (pp. 91—3). He opposed Rothschild's argument for intraregional tariffs to offset locational distortions due to monopolies, but recommended a 'specific location tax which offsets the [external portion of] social costs', and also subsidies to firms in locations with potential social advantages (p. 94). In a French essay on 'Libéralisme, Dirigisme et Intégration Economique de l'Europe', in a volume arranged by Raymond Racine (for the Centre Européen de la Culture), entitled *Demain l'Europe sans Frontières*, (Paris: Librairie Plon, 1958) pp. 69—90, Giersch discussed the fundamental conflict between the ideologies of libertarianism and dirigism. He showed, however, that the representatives of both schools of thought agreed that the integrating countries would have to give up national dirigism: the dirigistes would replace it by supranational dirigism, the libertarians by no dirigism at all. For the latter, European economic integration is a minimum step toward worldwide integration, for dirigistes it is the furthest they would want to go (pp. 70—1). Giersch argued, however, that the conflict was really exaggerated, since most libertarians were recognising the need for governmental interventions, and modern socialists recognised the usefulness of the market mechanism. To achieve its goal, the Community has to do more than abolish the existing restrictions on the mobility of goods, services, people, and capital; it will have to take positive measures (p. 79). These include central planning of transport and communication, harmonisation of monetary and fiscal policies, consistent wage policies, anti-monopoly policies, demographic policies, and a system of taxes and subsidies designed to offset existing differences between private and social marginal productivity (pp. 80 ff.). In his memorandum 'The Case for European Regional Policy', in *Study Group on Economic and Monetary Union: European Economic Integration and Monetary Unification* (Brussels: European Communities, Oct 1973) Part II, pp. 67—73, Giersch stated that 'the differences in per capita income between the Six have clearly declined since the EEC was founded. To say that in the process of economic growth the rich become richer and the poor become poorer is obviously little more than a myth' (p. 69). However, deliberate policies to equalise wages throughout a country or region retard the development of poor areas and promote congestion in large over developed cities at a high social cost of providing needed infrastructure and avoiding environmental deterioration (p. 70).

Jacob Viner (1892—1970), in his article on 'The Most-Favoured-Nation Clause', *Index* (Stockholm) Vol. 6 (1931) pp. 2—25, had defended the principle of non-discrimination and shown the possibility that preferential duties could mean a greater diversion of trade from its free-trade pattern than uniform protection. In 1950 he offered his pioneering distinction between trade creation and trade diversion as essential for the analysis of the economic consequences of a discriminatory reduction or removal of tariffs. His book *The Customs Union Issue* (New York : Carnegie Endowment for International Peace, 1950) has been credited with opening up a new branch of the theory of commercial policy. [The basic distinctions had been in Taussig's article of 1892, but not the terms introduced by Viner nor the clarity of the exposition.] Trade creation occurs when a previously protected domestic product is displaced by a lower-cost product imported from a member country of the union after the previous duty is lowered or removed. Trade diversion occurs when an import of a lower-cost product of a non-union country is displaced by a higher-cost product imported from a union country after the latter is accorded preferential treatment. Free-traders will approve only of trade creation, not of trade diversion (p. 43); indeed, the combined benefits of all countries involved are increased only if trade creation is predominant. In instances in which a domestic market is too small for an industry to produce at low cost in a world with tariff walls around all countries, the extension of a market through a customs union may allow production on a larger scale within one of the union countries, and a consequent suppression of trade; the combined gain for all countries involved may be positive or negative, depending on circumstances (p. 46). Viner finally set forth the conditions under which a customs union is more likely to operate in the free-trade direction (pp. 51—52). They included large size of the enlarged economic area, lowness of external tariffs, a small degree of complementarity of the member countries with respect to their previously protected industries, large differences in unit costs for the same kind of goods in different member countries, and potentials for economies of scale.

Raymond F. Mikesell (born 1913) contributed an essay on 'Economic Integration of Foreign States: Some Fundamental

Problems' to the volume *Money, Trade, and Economic Growth* [in Honor of John H. Williams] (New York : Macmillan, 1951) pp. 76—93. Foremost among the measures which he prescribed for integrating the countries of Europe were 'a substantial freeing of intra-European trade and a system of multilateral payments with . . . a gradual approach to convertibility' (p. 93). He also advised intraregional co-ordination of investment, particularly in basic industries. In an essay on 'The Movement toward Regional Trading Groups in Latin America', in Albert O. Hirschman, ed., *Latin American Issues* (New York: Twentieth Century Fund, 1961) pp. 125—51, Mikesell presented a critical analysis of the Treaty of Montevideo (which established LAFTA, the Latin American Free Trade Area). A paper by Mikesell on 'The Theory of Common Markets as Applied to Regional Arrangements among Developing Countries', in Roy Harrod and Douglas Hague, eds, *International Trade Theory in a Developing World* (London: Macmillan, 1963) pp. 205—40), placed chief emphasis on the so-called dynamic effects of integration. Under this heading he included 'increasing opportunities for profitable foreign and domestic investment', 'broadening the export base', 'achieving balance-of-payments equilibrium', 'mobilizing unemployed resources', and 'avoiding economic dualism' (p. 205).

Helen Makower (born 1910) and **George Morton** (born 1918) published 'A Contribution towards a Theory of Customs Unions', *Economic Journal*, Vol. 63 (Mar 1953) pp. 33—49. They proceeded along the lines of Viner's analysis, showing that the gains from trade creation would be larger the more dissimilar were the cost ratios of the same commodities in the two countries. Terminological decisions have to be made: if the two countries produce the same commodities, they might be called 'competitive' economies; but, if the cost ratios are very different, the economies could be defined as 'complementary'.

James E. Meade (born 1907) published a succession of important contributions to the history and theory of integration through customs unions. The theoretical work was embodied chiefly in two books: *Problems of Economic Union* (Chicago: University of Chicago Press, 1953), and *The Theory of Customs Unions* (Amsterdam: North-Holland Publ. Co., 1955). In the 1953 book he explained why 'a *partial* movement toward a *wider* economic union' was in general preferable to 'a *more complete* movement toward a *narrower* union' (p. 9). He divided the economic benefits from integration into three categories as to their sources: 'maximization of production' (due to reallocation of resources), 'optimization of trade' (due to shifts of consump-

tion), and 'increase in competition' (due to forced efficiency
and relaxation of monopolistic restraints) (pp. 9—13). He pointed to significant differences in 'the degree of integration which
has been achieved' in the United States relative to Europe (p. 28).
In his book of 1955, Meade asked how the gains from trade
creation could be balanced against the losses from trade diversion, and suggested that both the volumes of created and diverted
trade and the sizes of the cost reductions and cost increases on
each unit of traded goods be considered (p. 35). Even if there is
a net loss through diversion of trade from cheaper to more expensive sources of supply, the reduction of the price to the consumer may expand consumption, permitting a welfare gain, offset by a loss of tax revenue to the government. If this revenue is
replaced by means of less price-distorting taxes, welfare may
still be increased on balance (p. 43). A 'customs union is more
likely to raise standards [of the combined welfare of all countries]
(i) the higher are the initial duties of the countries forming the
union, (ii) the lower are the duties in the outside countries; (iii)
the more substitutable for each other are the products of the
outside world with the products of the countries forming the
union' (p. 52). In the evaluation of gains or losses of welfare,
account must be taken of any reductions or increases in the
divergences between marginal values and costs as may be due to
monopoly positions, taxation, and external economies and dis-
economies (p. 65). However, one must not confine oneself to
the 'primary changes', the increases in imports of products from
a country which has just been granted a preferential reduction
(or removal) of import duties (p. 67); one must also consider
the 'secondary changes' in the trade in products which in the
countries concerned are substitutes or complements of the products primarily affected (p. 68); and the 'tertiary changes', the
adjustments in the trade flows that are made necessary to restore
balance in international payments (p. 83). Economies of scale
may accentuate the extent of all changes in trade as well as the
size of their effects upon combined economic welfare (p. 93). If
the interest of the policy makers is not in total world income
but rather in income distribution among all countries concerned,
or among the member countries of the union, or within a
member country, the evaluation of changes could be seriously
affected (p. 94). [This has been only a small sample of the rich
crop of insights obtained from Meade's analysis.]

Robert Marjolin (born 1911), besides making his effective
contributions to the politics of European integration, contributed interesting observations on common-market theory in his

book *Europe and the United States in the World Economy* (Durham, N.C.: Duke University Press, 1953). In describing the implications of the Schuman Plan he stressed the difference between general liberalisation of trade and 'complete integration of limited sectors' like coal and steel. He held that sectoral integration was 'quite an original combination of liberalism and planning' in that it provided 'for a controlled system of free competition' (p. 51). He recognised, however, that it was still uncertain whether the system would function 'as the protector of free enterprise or as a cartel' (p. 53).

Francois Perroux (born 1903) was rather pessimistic in his book *L'Europe sans rivage* (Paris: Presses Universitaires de France, 1954) regarding the extent to which trade would actually be freed within a European union and regarding the height of tariff barriers against imports from countries outside the union. He was also apprehensive concerning a possibly dominant position of Germany within the union. In a later article on 'L'intégration et l'échec de la théorie traditionelle des échanges extérieurs', *Economic Appliquée*, Vol. 21, No. 2 (1968) pp. 379—96, he held that 'traditional theory' was inapplicable in the economics of customs unions, chiefly because 'the mechanism of competitive markets is never of the essence in the dynamics of integration. Decisive are the choice of the rules of the game and the promotion of exchange by dominant firms and public and mixed organisation.' Integration of the European Six is 'permeated with monopolistic and oligopolistic competition, with positions of strong market power, and with policies of structural intervention by the State' (p. 386). 'Integration policy . . . consists never . . . in the elimination of obstacles. It consists of positive actions of promoting productive units and an environment' favouring their efforts. Integration 'never tends toward an optimisation of the type conceived in the static optimisation theorem and reflected in an equalisation of prices of factors and products' (p. 396).

Petrus J. Verdoorn (born 1911), in his article 'A Customs Union for Western Europe: Advantages and Feasibility', *World Politics*, Vol. 6 (July 1954) pp. 482—500, favoured liberalisation through a customs union over the use of non-discriminating agreements (p. 483) and called the retention of tariffs against non-member countries 'passive discrimination . . . only incidental to' closer co-operation among the union partners (p. 486). He observed 'a close functional relation between productivity at a given moment and total accumulated production up to that moment', from which he inferred the existence of a 'learning curve'. The learning processes in manufacturing industry may be operating on labour, management, engineering, and also on external improvements, with a joint result of a 5 per cent increase in productivity for every 10 per cent increase in the industry's [not the firm's] production. The effects of liberalisation may be largely a concentration of output toward the largest (and therefore cheapest) producers. In a later (largely econometric) study of 'The Intra-Block Trade of Benelux', published in E. A. G. Robinson, ed., *The Economic Consequences of the Size of Nations* (London: Macmillan, 1960) pp. 291—329, Verdoorn tried to assess the economic effects of the Benelux Union. He found that the share of intra-bloc trade in the countries' total foreign trade was definitely increased, with a particularly strong increase in the price per volume-unit. He explained the relative price increase (of 30 per cent), as compared with imports of the same kinds of goods from outside countries, as a result of changes in the composition of trade, the union having fostered mutual trade in products of which the value added was relatively high (p. 292). He also estimated the effects of tariff reductions on imports from the union partners and found relatively high elasticities of demand (p. 293).

Franz Gehrels (born 1922) and **Bruce F. Johnston** (born 1919), in their joint article on 'The Economic Gains from European Integration', *Journal of Political Economy*, Vol. 63 (Aug 1955), pp. 275—92, applied Viner's criteria and some of their own to the case of a European economic union and concluded that substantial benefits were to be expected for its members. A major consideration was that cost differences within Europe were quite large, so that the abolition of tariffs among union members would create trade as imports from member countries would be substituted for more expensive domestic production. Moreover, there would be beneficial long-run effects on investment, technical progress, producers' competition and efficiency, economies of scale, and economic growth.

Gehrels, in an article on 'Customs Unions from a Single Country's Viewpoint', *Review of Economic Studies*, Vol. 24 (1956—7) pp. 61—4, presented the substitution effects in consumption consequent upon the price changes which result from a reduction or removal of duties. Such consumption effects are independent of any production effects. [Gehrels came upon this thought at the same time as Meade (see p. 260 above) and Lipsey (see p. 266 below).]

Tibor Scitovsky (born 1910), in an article on 'Economies of Scale, Competition, and European Integration', *American*

Economic Review, Vol. 46 (Mar 1956), attributed the lower productivity of European industries, relative to American, to the restrained competition in the small markets of the separate countries. Plants of optimum size are 'not likely to be built in an oligopolistic situation when the industry operates with a price structure that allows each member an adequate profit, even though productive methods are suboptimal and costs are higher than they need be' (p. 83). The 'average European manufacturer', selling in a contiguous market with relatively few retail outlets, shies away from encroaching on his competitors' share of the market. Integration, 'freeing of intra-European trade', would 'increase the number and geographic coverage of the market outlets . . . and thus increase the number of firms he [the manufacturer] regards as his competitors' (p. 89). With 'less personal' competition, the producer would be 'less considerate' of his competitors' interests and would invest more enterprisingly in more efficient plans. Scitovsky elaborates on these views in his book on *Economic Theory and Western European Integration* (Stanford: Stanford University Press, 1958; revised edition, 1962). He held that in the case of Western Europe no substantial benefits could be expected from a reallocation of productive resources through better division of labour; the main results would come from 'the increase in competition which the common market is almost certain to bring about' (p. 10). Competition would bring increased pressures 'upon the economic behaviour of Governments, entrepreneurs, workers, and others'. In a paper on 'International Trade and Economic Integration as a Means of Overcoming the Disadvantages of a Small Nation', in E. A. G. Robinson, ed., *The Economic Consequences of the Size of Nations* (London: Macmillan, 1960) pp. 282—90, Scitovsky distinguished two disadvantages of smallness: a country may be too small to provide a market for the full-capacity output of the most efficient plant in a given industry — this is a 'technological' disadvantage — or it may be too small to provide the competitive conditions necessary as a spur to utmost economy and efficiency.

Gunnar Myrdal (born 1898), in his book *An International Economy: Problems and Prospects* (New York: Harper, 1956), declares that 'Economic integration is the realization of the old Western ideal of equality of opportunity' (p. 1). 'Migration, capital movements, international aid and trade are not the primary means of achieving this closer integration. In a real sense they are the products of integration, not the cause. They can help, but they cannot be relied upon to do the job. The major task is first to force economic development in the underdevel-

oped countries . . . ' (p. 3—4). [These statements are only intellig
ible if one knows what Myrdal means by integration and knows
also his theories of inequality of incomes.] As he pointed out in
his book *Rich Lands and Poor: The Road to World Prosperity*
(New York: Harper & Row, 1957), integration is, in his view, a
process of income equalisation, achieved in large part by 'egalitarian policies' (p. 51). He distinguishes between 'national
integration policies' and international ones. 'The main idea . . .
is that the play of the forces in the market normally tends to
increase, rather than to decrease, the inequalities between
regions' within a state (p. 26) as well as in the world. More
specifically the movements of labor, capital, goods and services'
have 'positive results' for the 'lucky regions' and negative results
for the unlucky ones (p. 27). The chief reason for the 'natural
tendency to regional inequality' is the operation of 'backwash
effects'. The regions that promise bigger returns attract the best
workers and most capital, leaving the other regions 'in a backwater' with the less efficient workers, with less ability to save
and less opportunities for attractive investment. There are also
some 'spread effects' of the 'expansionary momentum from the
centers of economic expansion to the other regions' (p. 31), but
they are usually too weak to offset the backwash effects. Only
together with strongly egalitarian policies can the spread effects
overcome the backwash effects. Neither trade nor capital movements nor migration can be 'relied upon to counteract international inequalities' (p. 53). In the absence of a world government that could institute international egalitarian policies, 'the
road to international integration must be sought through
national integration. The adoption of nationalist policies by the
poor countries and an increase of their bargaining power, as a
result of these policies and of increased co-operation between
them as a group, are a necessary stage in the development of
more effective world-wide international co-operation' (pp. 71—2).
Yet 'the approach to national integration in the underdeveloped
countries will . . . in the first instance increase international disintegration' (p. 72). The poor countries 'have available blackmailing powers which they will increasingly learn to use to their
own advantage' (p. 75). Since Myrdal is convinced that 'there is
no other road to economic development than a forceful rise in
the share of the national income which is withheld from consumption and devoted to investment' (p. 84), he recommends
'utmost austerity', enforced by 'an over-all, integrated national
plan' (p. 81) for which 'the criteria . . . are . . . entirely outside
the price system' but are 'determined by the political process'

(p. 91). The national plan will require the use of import restrictions and payments regulations (p. 96), used for the protection of new industries and, more generally, the implementation of the development policy adopted. [I felt it necessary to give that much space to Myrdal's views because they are so far outside the mainstream of the ideas on economic integration that a shorter comment could hardly be comprehended.]

Richard G. Lipsey (born 1928) and Kelvin J. Lancaster (born 1924) published a formulation of 'The General Theory of Second Best', *Review of Economic Studies*, Vol. 24 (1956–7) pp. 11–32, based on the traditional convention of optimality in the patterns of production and consumption under a structure of prices that equate the marginal social costs of all goods produced with the marginal valuations of all goods consumed. The existence of taxes, monopoly prices, externalities of all sorts, and customs duties makes the attainment of the best patterns practically impossible. Since some of the price distortions may offset one another, the removal of certain duties may make matters worse rather than better, that is, increase the distance from a 'second-best' position. A small variation of any tax or duty is more likely to raise welfare than a large variation would.

Fritz W. Meyer (born 1907), besides contributing several memoranda on questions of economic integration through the European common market, published an essay 'Über Auswirkungen von Zollpräferenzen', in Erwin von Beckerath *et al.*, eds, *Wirtschaftsfragen der freien Welt* [Festschrift for Ludwig Erhard] (Frankfurt a.M.: Fritz Knapp, 1957) pp. 608–18. He showed that even in manifest cases of trade diversion, as imports from a favoured source replace imports subject to a discriminatory tariff, some trade creation is likely to occur if the elasticity of the world supply of the particular product is less than infinite. Its price will decline and trade will be created.

Erich Schneider (1900–70), renowned German economist, showed in an Italian article, 'Lineamenti di una teoria economica del mercato commune', *Rivista Internazionale di Scienze Economiche e Commerciali*, Vol. 2 (Feb 1957) pp. 107–18, that an understanding of economic integration requires definitions of the two extremes — complete isolation and perfect integration — and differentiation of degrees of integration between the extremes.

Richard G. Lipsey (born 1928), in an article on 'The Theory of Customs Unions: Trade Diversion and Welfare', *Economica*, n.s. Vol. 24 (Feb 1957) pp. 40–6, presented the thesis of the

beneficial consumption effects of the changes in relative prices
due to reductions or removals of tariffs. He had shown these
effects previously in his doctoral dissertation (University of
London, 1957), which was later published as a book, *The
Theory of Customs Unions: A General Equilibrium Analaysis*
(London: Weidenfeld & Nicolson, 1970). In his brief note 'Mr.
Gehrels on Customs Unions', *Review of Economic Studies*, Vol.
24 (1956—7) pp. 211—14, Lipsey pointed to an error of reasoning on the basis of a model with only two commodities, and
corrected it by introducing a third commodity. He showed that
the asserted general presumption of a welfare gain derived from
a customs union was not valid. In his most instructive survey
article, 'The Theory of Customs Unions: A General Survey',
Economic Journal, Vol. 70 (Sept 1960) pp. 496—513, Lipsey
defined this theory as 'that branch of tariff theory which deals
with the [welfare] effects of geographically discriminatory
changes in trade barriers' (p. 496). He contrasted the older arguments, Viner's new reasoning, and the post-Viner developments,
and provided a most lucid exposition of the present state of the
theory. Some of this is repeated in Lipsey's article on 'International Integration: Economic Unions' in the *International
Encyclopedia of the Social Sciences* (New York: Macmillan,
1968) Vol. 7. Lipsey distinguished the following types (or
'degrees') of economic integration among two or more countries:
preferential tariff system (lower internal than external tariffs);
free-trade area (zero internal tariffs); customs union (common
external tariff); common market (free movements of factors);
economic union (common monetary, fiscal, and other policies);
and complete economic integration (single economic policy). Of
the economic effects of integration, he regards resource reallocation, adjustments of consumption patterns, and changes in the
terms of trade as 'static', and economies of scale, changes in
market structures (competition), and changes in growth rates as
'dynamic'.

Harry G. Johnson (born 1923) made a series of contributions
to the theory of international trade and regional integration:
'The Criteria of Economic Advantage', *Bulletin of the Oxford
University Institute of Statistics*, Vol. 19 (Feb 1957) pp. 33—8;
'The European Common Market: Risks or Opportunity', *Welt-
wirtschaftliches Archiv*, Vol. 79, No. 2 (1957) pp. 267—80; 'The
Gains from Free Trade with Europe: An Estimate', *Manchester
School*, Vol. 26 (Sept 1958) pp. 247—55; 'The Cost of Protec-
tion and the Scientific Tariff', *Journal of Political Economy*,
Vol. 68 (Aug 1960) pp. 327—45; 'The Economic Theory of

Customs Unions', *Pakistan Economic Journal*, Vol. 10 (1960)
pp. 14—32, reprinted in Johnson, *Money, Trade, and Economic
Growth* (London: Allen & Unwin, 1962) pp. 46—73; 'Optimal
Trade Intervention in the Presence of Domestic Distortions', in
Richard E. Caves, Harry G. Johnson, and Peter B. Kenen, eds,
Trade, Growth, and the Balance of Payments (Chicago: Rand,
McNally Co., 1965) pp. 3—34; and 'An Economic Theory of
Protectionism, Tariff Bargaining, and the Formation of Customs
Unions', *Journal of Political Economy*, Vol. 73 (June 1965)
pp. 256—83. Since Johnson touched on nearly every aspect of
the relevant theories, I select only a few for inclusion in this
review. In his 1958 article, he presented reasons why closer
integration between the British and West European economies
could not be expected to produce more than very modest material benefits: neither reallocation of productive resources nor
economies of larger-scale production could bring more than
minute improvements in productivity. In his 1965 article on the
'Economic Theory of Protectionism . . . ' he introduced a novel
approach to the understanding of so-called non-economic objectives of society, particularly the gratifications (pride) of the
citizens from knowing that their country was producing certain
goods at home, rather than importing them more cheaply from
abroad: 'Industrial production [within the nation or region] . . .
appears as a collective consumption good yielding a flow of
satisfaction to the electorate independent of the satisfaction
they derive directly from the consumption of industrial products'
(p. 258). Thus, if I may paraphrase him, Johnson holds that the
real income of a nation or region includes the psychic income
which its citizens derive from the pride of having 'their own'
industrial production just like the biggest nations. [Their good
feeling or happiness is comparable to that derived from having a
winning football team, a native or resident composer of world
fame, or a generally admired natural world wonder. I cannot
help raising the question whether the citizens know the cost of
protection in terms of real product forgone, that is, whether
they know how much consumption of material goods they have
to give up for the pleasure of having certain things home-made
rather than imported.] In a later contribution on 'Trade-Diverting Customs Unions: A Comment', *Economic Journal*, Vol. 84
(Sept 1974) Johnson questioned the usefulness of adding 'consumption effects' to the 'production effects' of customs union.
The separation of these effects was required only because trade
diversion was defined as referring to the quantity of trade that
prevailed before the duties on imports from the union partner

were reduced or removed. The consequent price reduction
allowed an increase in consumption and, hence, a favourable
consumption effect. If, however, trade diversion is defined as
referring to an unspecified volume of imports, it becomes clear
that the outcome will include both 'the welfare-decreasing shift
of initial trade to a higher-cost location and the welfare-increas-
ing increase in trade due to the substitution of imports for
domestic goods', and that this trade diversion may increase welfare on balance (p. 619). The outcome, however, is more easily
grasped if the increment of imports above the initial quantity is
regarded as trade creation — a substitution for domestic production — and only the substitution for the previous imports is
seen as trade diversion. Looked at in this way, trade creation
adds to welfare, trade diversion reduces it.

Sidney Dell (born 1918), in 'Economic Integration and the
American Example', *Economic Journal*, Vol. 69 (Mar 1959) pp.
39—54, noted that the American experience is often singled out
to prove the advantages of a large integrated economy in exploiting to the full the benefits of mass production and specialisation.
On the basis of that experience, Dell concluded, it does not
necessarily follow that a larger, integrated economy in Europe
will increase competition, generate higher levels of productivity,
or narrow regional differentials of income per head.

Mordechai E. Kreinin (born 1930) published numerous contributions to the economics of customs unions; among the earlier
ones were 'On the "Trade-Diversion" Effect of Trade-Preference
Areas', *Journal of Political Economy*, Vol. 67 (Aug 1959) pp.
398—401; 'The "Outer-Seven" and European Integration',
American Economic Review, Vol. 50 (June 1960) pp. 370—86;
and a note on 'Trade Creation and Diversion in a Customs-
Union: A Graphical Presentation', *Kyklos*, Vol. 16, No. 4 (1963)
pp. 660—1. In an article 'On the Dynamic Effects of a Customs
Union', *Journal of Political Economy*, Vol. 72 (Apr 1964) pp.
193—5, he made the laudable attempt to define what is meant
by 'static' and 'dynamic' effects of customs unions of free-trade
areas: static effects were 'changes in output and income resulting from reallocation of a fixed amount of productive resources'.
However, he proceeded to place 'scale economies and competitive effect' and 'investment diversion' under the heading of
'dynamic effects'. [Why should production on a larger scale or
increases of efficiency under the pressure of competition not be
matters of resource reallocation? Why should 'investment diversion' be anything but a different allocation of a given supply of
capital?] The substantive point he made concerning the

'dynamic' effects was that the damage to non-members may exceed the benefits to members. In an article on 'Effects of the EEC on Imports of Manufactures', *Economic Journal*, Vol. 82 (Sept 1972) pp. 897—920, Kreinin critically examined previous estimates of integration effects by Lamfalussy, Waelbroeck, Truman, Balassa, Clavaux, Major and Hays, Williamson and Bottrill, and the EFTA Secretariat, and produced some estimates of his own: 'To determine the effect of integration it is necessary to construct hypothetical estimates of what the trade flows would have been in the absence of integration and compare them with the actual flow' (pp. 897—8). Some of the 'heroic assumptions' which underlie these necessary constructions relate to all sorts of influences (other than those attributable to integration) upon the ratios between imports and consumption of particular goods. Kreinin concludes that trade creation in EEC countries was many times the size of trade diversion, and that this trade diversion was probably more than compensated by the growth effects of integration. This article and several of his more recent ones are reproduced in Kreinin's book *Trade Relations of the EEC: An Empirical Investigation*, (New York: Praeger Publishers, 1974).

Erik Thorbecke (born 1907) extended the empirical investigation which Folke Hilgerdt had done for the League of Nations (published in *The Network of World Trade*, Geneva, 1942). In his book on *The Tendency towards Regionalization in International Trade 1928—1956* (The Hague: Martinus Nijhoff, 1960) he found that the share of intra-bloc trade in world trade had been increasing during the period. He was referring in particular to three blocs, the Sterling Area, the Continental OEEC countries, and the Dollar Area, and stated that 'The magnitude of the trade balances in general has not kept pace with the growth in the total value of international trade. This obviously means that a greater proportion of world trade has become bilateral' (pp. 80—1). Thorbecke looks for geographical, political, economic, and monetary causes as determinants of the 'regionalization' of trade.

Bela Balassa (born 1928) has been one of the most productive contributors to the literature on our subject, beginning with his article 'Towards a Theory of Economic Integration', *Kyklos*, Vol. 14 (1961) pp. 1—17, and his book *The Theory of Economic Integration*, (Homewood, Ill.: Irwin, 1961). Differences between integration of developed and developing countries are treated in *Economic Development and Integration* (Mexico: CEMLA, 1965). Having introduced the distinction between intra-industry and inter-industry specialisation, in 'European Integration: Problems and Issues', *American Economic Review*, Vol. 53 (Proceedings, May 1963) pp. 175—84, he applied it in 'Tariff Reductions and Trade in Manufactures among the Industrial Countries', *American Economic Review*, Vol. 56 (June 1966) pp. 466—73, chiefly to explain the ease of adjustment to the elimination of tariffs within the common market. In his book *Trade Liberalization among Industrial Countries: Objectives and Alternatives* (New York: McGraw-Hill, 1967) he examined the choices among alternative trade arrangements, regional as well as multilateral. He used data on trade/income ratios to evaluate 'Trade Creation and Trade Diversion in the European Common Market', *Economic Journal*, Vol. 77 (Mar 1967) pp. 1—21, and again in *Manchester School*, Vol. 42 (June 1974) pp. 93—135. In a chapter of his own on 'Structural Policies in the European Common Market' in a recent book edited by himself, *European Economic Integration* (Amsterdam: North-Holland Publishing Co., 1975) pp. 225—74, Balassa discussed the effect of the Common Market on French planning. He concluded that 'industry-level planning' had become 'practically impossible in France' (p. 229).

Paul Streeten (born 1917) wrote a book on *Economic Integration: Aspects and Problems* (Leyden: A. W. Sijthoff, 1961), published under the auspices of the Council of Europe. He held that 'integration should not be defined in terms of the means (free trade, unified market, convertibility, liberalization, etc.) but in terms of the ends: equality, liberty, prosperity' (p. 16). Streeten is quite contemptuous of the claims of 'classical liberal theory' — such as the benefits of competition, comparative advantage and other arguments for free trade and free factor movements — and especially of the failure to respond to 'the existence of forces making for cumulative inequality'. He emphasises that 'without policies correcting the maldistribution resulting from the free play of market forces, the gains from economic progress and free trade will tend to be unevenly distributed' (p. 55). He deals extensively with the balance of the advantages of balanced and unbalanced growth (pp. 96—132), the implications of indivisibilities and complementarities in consumption, production, and investment: 'First, in some condition lack of balance promotes growth. Secondly, in order to get growth, one may have to sacrifice balance' (p. 132).

Alexandre Lamfalussy (born 1929), in 'Europe's Progress: Due to Common Market?', *Lloyds Bank Review* (Oct 1961) pp. 1—16, compared the experience of the individual European

countries before and after the formation of the Common Market
and found 'no obvious figures which would point to a causal
relationship between the establishment of the Common Market
and the rapid growth of its members' (p. 1). Noting that it is
possible to argue the reverse causal relationship, he suggested
the hypothesis that 'inherently' high growth rates of the various
European countries had stimulated trade and thus made it possible to achieve whatever progress was made in the arrangements
for a common market. He also showed that the difference in
growth trends observed between EEC and EFTA countries over
the period 1958—61 was already apparent during the five years
preceding the changes in the institutional framework of European
trade. Lamfalussy added further evidence in support of his
sceptical view in a paper on 'Intégration et croissance économique', in Henri Brugmans, ed., *Intégration européenne et réalité
économique*, Semaine de Bruges 1964 (Bruges: de Tempel,
1964) pp. 33—47.

Hans H. Liesner (born 1929) contributed to the collective
work by James E. Meade, S. J. Wells, and H. H. Liesner, *Case
Studies in European Economic Union* (London: Oxford University Press, 1962); and to the conference proceedings, Roy Harrod
and Douglas Hague, eds., *International Trade Theory in a
Developing World* (London: Macmillan, 1963). The essay included in the latter volume was on 'Regional Free Trade: Trade-
Creating and Trade-Diverting Effects of Political, Commercial
and Monetary Areas' (pp. 194—204). Liesner expected that the
most important benefits from European integration would come
through increases in 'internal economic efficiency' — the reduction of slackness and inertia — under the pressure of more vigorous competition (p. 197). He found that the shockingly low
estimates of gains through cost reductions — between 0.05 per
cent of national income (Verdoorn) and a maximum of 1.00 per
cent (Harry Johnson) were not so implausible for Britain. If
some 27 per cent of her national product were to become subject
to foreign competition; if the largest cost reduction at the margin equalled the height of the tariff removed, say, 20 per cent,
with the average only about one half, that is, 10 per cent; then
this 10 per cent of 27 per cent would account for a cost reduction of 2.7 per cent. To this, however, one would have to add
the 'consumption effects' and any external economies of scale
(p. 199).

Pierre Uri (born 1911), in his book *Partnership for Progress:
A Program for Transatlantic Action* (New York: Harper & Row,
1963) examined problems of economic integration that have

been encumbering integration in the European Community and
would be similarly vexing in the establishing of an Atlantic Partnership. His discussion, more pragmatic than theoretical, included questions of dumping and anti-dumping measures, cartels
and anti-cartel policies, distortions of competition and attempts
at harmonisation (pp. 52—67). His observations on export
credits, an 'indirect form of subsidy . . . creating artificial
trade which would not otherwise exist' were of special interest
(p. 59).

John Spraos (born 1926), in an article on 'The Conditions for
a Trade-Creating Customs Union', *Economic Journal*, Vol. 74
(Mar 1964) pp. 101—8, found it preferable to analyse the effects
of the union only in terms of production effects, since the consumption effects were relatively unimportant. He stated that
'the condition for trade creation depends on the relation
between two ratios: (*a*) the ratio of the difference between the
two members' pre-union tariff rates and the post-union common
tariff against non-members, and (*b*) the ratio of the price deriva-
tives (slopes) of the two members' supply functions' (pp. 104—5).
The condition is sufficient only on certain (not very strong)
assumptions, and it is both sufficient and necessary only for
small steps between tariff rates before and after union.

Petrus J. Verdoorn (born 1911) and Franciscus J. M. Meyer
zu Schlochtern (born 1930) contributed a paper on 'Trade
Creation and Trade Diversion in the Common Market', in Henri
Brugmans, ed., *Intégration Européenne et Réalité Economique*,
Semaine de Bruges 1964 (Bruges: de Tempel, 1964) pp. 95—137
in which they undertook to measure the effects of the tariff
reductions among the member countries of the EEC upon their
trade. The authors assumed that the observed results were a
combination of (1) the shifts in demand due to the tariff cuts,
(2) cumulative 'impulse-effects' on the national economy, and
(3) longer-run effects on productivity (through investment,
especially of labour-saving type, larger lot sizes, specialisation
within industry branches, etc.). They criticised simple projec-
tions of demand as functions of GNP and favoured 'share analysis' of the trade matrix to estimate the effects of the tariff cuts
(p. 101). They concluded that 'trade diversion was practically
"non-existent" for the period and for the products studied'
(p. 109), that 'the reduction of a country's average tariff by 1%
has been accompanied by a trade creation of at least 2%'
(p. 114), and that about 17% of the total effect on trade —
which they estimated at 26% for the period — was 'accounted
for by the direct influence of tariff reduction' (p. 115).

Jean Waelbroeck (born 1927) made several attempts to measure by econometric methods the effects of the Common Market on the pattern of international trade. In his essay 'Le commerce de la Communauté Européenne avec les pays tiers', in Henri Brugmanns, ed., *Intégration Européenne et Réalité Economique*, Semaine de Bruges 1964 (Bruges: de Tempel, 1964) pp. 139—64, he showed that any effort at measuring the effect of a particular policy implied a comparison with a hypothetical world in which nothing else had changed or in which the effects of other changes could be assumed to be ascertainable. Waelbroeck discussed a few possible solutions and proceded to compare the distribution of trade volumes by regions or countries on the basis of two different models. He concluded by confessing that, although he had previously believed that the Common Market had fundamentally changed the trade pattern, he had now become convinced that its effects on trade were quite modest.

Lawrence B. Krause (born 1929) furnished a useful survey in the 'Introduction' to a book of readings which he edited under the title *The Common Market: Progress and Controversy* (Englewood Cliffs: Prentice Hall, 1964) pp. 1—27. In a later book, *European Economic Integration and the United States* (Washington: Brookings Institution, 1968) he undertook empirical studies designed to 'measure' some of the immediate and longer-run effects of the formation of the European Common Market on member and non-member countries.

André Marchal (1907—68) published two books on economic integration: *L'Europe solidaire* (Paris: Cujas, 1965) and *L'intégration territoriale* (Paris: Presses Universitaires de France, 1965). In the second book he raised the question whether regional integration will help or hinder the attainment of worldwide integration. He recognised that regional communities were suboptimal, but necessary stages in the eventual formation of a fully integrated world economy.

Michael Michaely (born 1928) presented in his article 'On Customs Unions and the Gains from Trade', *Economic Journal*, Vol. 75 (Sept 1965) pp. 577—83, a comparison of the arguments of earlier writers, especially Gehrels and Lipsey, and showed that their results can be reached without some of their highly restrictive assumptions. Thus, the proposition that the discriminatory abolition of duties on imports from union partners may result in a welfare gain even with a preponderance of trade diversion acquires more generality. In a recent article on 'The Assumptions of Jacob Viner's Theory of Customs Unions', *Journal of Inter-*

274 *A History of Thought on Economic Integration*

national Economics, Vol. 6 (Feb 1976) pp. 75—93, Michaely
provided the definitive interpretation of Viner's conceptual
framework and of the arguments of those who adopted, criticise
or modified it. Michaely demonstrated that Viner, although he
explicitly allowed for increasing cost of production, implicitly
argued as if constant cost prevailed and, accordingly, the transformation (or production-possibilities) curve between two good
were a straight line. In particular, Viner's statement 'that a
union could be either trade creating or trade diverting' would
hold 'only if constant costs are assumed' (p. 10). With a convex
transformation curve, the preferential removal of the tariff
would result in both some creation and some diversion of trade
in the same good. Michaely also confirmed what Meade and
Lipsey had correctly observed, that Viner had disregarded the
positive consumption effect of the removal of the duty and the
consequent reduction of the price. Viner had focused only on
the increase in the amount of commodities available, and thus
neglected the welfare increase implied in the fact that consumer
substituting a cheaper commodity for a dearer, chose to acquire
the goods in a different proportion (although they could have
had them in the original proportion). The consumption effect is
therefore a welfare gain separate from that of the production
effect.

   Charles A. Cooper (born 1933) and **Benton F. Massell** (born
1930) produced two joint articles, one 'Toward a General Theory
of Customs Unions for Developing Countries', *Journal of Political Economy*, Vol. 73 (Oct 1965) pp. 461—76, and the other or
'A New Look at Customs Union Theory', *Economic Journal*,
Vol. 75 (Dec 1965) pp. 742—7. In contrast with earlier writers
from Viner to Meade and Lipsey, who had analysed the
economic effects of a customs union as a discriminatory reduction of duties on imports from union partners while the duties
on imports from third countries remain unaltered, the 'new
look' assumes two steps to be taken: the first, a general, non-
discriminatory reduction (or abolition) of duties on *all* imports;
the second, a reimposition of duties only on imports from third
countries. All increases in consumer welfare are then clearly due
to the first step, whereas all trade diversion is due to the second
step — 'a substitution of the high-cost partner's goods for goods
from the lowest-cost world supplier'. If all benefits come from
the reduction or abolition of tariffs, and all harm from the dutie
on imports from third countries, why does a customs union
seem acceptable to government while a general tariff reduction
is not? Evidently there is a strong demand for protection, and an

expectation — perhaps justified — that preferential tariffs can satisfy this demand as well as or better than non-preferential tariffs. The authors explain, just as Johnson did in his article published also in 1965, the demand for protection by popular tastes for having things made 'at home'.

Jaroslav Vanek (born 1930) published a book on *General Equilibrium of International Discrimination* (Cambridge, Mass.: Harvard University Press, 1965). After the earlier attempts by Lipsey, and by Lipsey and Lancaster, this was the first comprehensive use of general-equilibrium analysis in the treatment of the effects of customs unions and other discriminating trading arrangements. Most of Vanek's analysis was carried out with the help of a model comprising only two goods and three countries; it could deal with terms-of-trade effects but not with the problem of complementarity.

Edward Joshua Mishan (born 1917), in a note on 'The Welfare Gains of a Trade-Diverting Customs Union Reinterpreted', *Economic Journal*, Vol. 76 (Sept 1966) pp. 669—72, registered several reasons for questioning the proposition that despite the unfavourable production effects of a trade-diverting customs union the net effects on welfare may still be positive. Mishan found Michaely's proof insufficient; although it rested on Kemp's and Samuelson's demonstrations that 'some foreign trade is better than no trade', it failed to take account of the restrictive assumptions which were underlying these demonstrations. There were possibilities of distributional changes that might not satisfy Scitovsky's compensation tests and, moreover, there might be opposite changes in welfare in the three countries combined, which to compare would be even less feasible.

Hirofumi Shibata (born 1929) published an essay on 'The Theory of Economic Unions: A Comparative Analysis of Customs Unions, Free Trade Areas and Tax Unions', in Carl S. Shoup, ed., *Fiscal Harmonization in Common Markets* (New York: Columbia University Press, 1967) Vol I, pp. 145—264. His major contribution is to the theory of free-trade areas. The effects of this form of economic integration are different from those derived from the establishment of a common external tariff, and new problems of 'trade deflection' are likely to arise, as imports from non-member countries would tend to enter the free-trade area via the member with the lowest external tariff.

Richard N. Cooper (born 1934) addressed himself largely to monetary questions [which will be reviewed in the next section], but in his book *The Economics of Interdependence: Economic Policy in the Atlantic Community*, (New York: McGraw-Hill,

1968) he offered observations on economic integration in
general. He considered defining an 'integrated area . . . in be-
havioral rather than legal terms'; for example, in an integrated
area' political pressure groups follow predominantly functional
rather than regional lines. Texan plumbers would speak primari
as plumbers, not as Texans' (p. 8). 'Even economic integration
can be defined in many ways. An area is defined as integrated if
it is characterized (*a*) "by the absence of various forms of discrimination" (Balassa), (*b*) "by the optimum of international
economic co-operation" (Tinbergen) or (*c*) "by factor price
equalization — uniform wages (except for differences in skills,
etc.), common interest rates on comparable financial assets, and
equal profits on comparable investments" (Tinbergen)' (p. 10).
These three tests, Cooper showed, are not consistent with one
another, and any one of them is difficult to meet in reality.

Murray C. Kemp (born 1926), in his book *The General Equil
brium Theory of Preferential Trading* (Amsterdam: North-
Holland Publishers, 1969), examined the effects on the pattern
of trade, the terms of trade, and the changes in welfare that are
likely to result from three kinds of trade arrangements: (1) a
preference club, in which members grant each other, but not to
outsiders, small reductions in duties on imports and in taxes,
chiefly on investment income, (2) a free-trade area among dissimilar countries, likely to specialise in different goods; and (3)
a customs union of similar countries. Kemp's general-equilibriur
analysis, limited to a model of three countries, two factors and
two goods, follows that of Vanek's book (1965) for the case of
immobile factors, but extends it when international mobility of
capital is assumed. Like Meade, Kemp concluded that welfare
gains are far more certain from small changes than from large;
thus, one partner of a preference club surely gains — the one
competing with the outside world — while the other stands to
lose through worsened terms of trade, though the gain will
exceed the loss. With mobility of capital, the gainer will gain
even more, because of capital inflows at lower rates. Kemp
examines also the joint optimisation of tariffs and taxes; since
the gains from potential changes in the terms of trade and the
gains from potential changes in the terms of foreign loans and
investments are interrelated, the aim at a genuine optimum mus
take account of both.

James Rae Melvin (born 1938), in 'Comments on the Theory
of Customs Unions', *Manchester School of Economics and Soci
Studies*, Vol. 37 (June 1969) pp. 161—8, examined the significance which induced changes in the terms of trade may have for

the effects of trade-diverting customs unions. The recognition that trade diversion may still be consistent with a welfare gain to the country abolishing its intra-union tariffs had been based on the assumption of unchanged terms of trade. Melvin now showed that, in so far as the old tariff had improved the terms of trade, the probability of gains from joining a trade-diverting customs union would be smaller. If the tariff had been 'optimal', the customs union would reduce welfare.

Nicholas Kaldor (born 1908), later Lord Kaldor, in an article on 'The Truth about the Dynamic Effects', *New Statesmen*, 12 Mar 1971, compares the slow progress of economic integration in the European Community with that of the United States. Producers of engineering goods in the larger EEC countries were selling chiefly in their home market and very little in the other countries of the 'common' market. Purchases of such goods were made overwhelmingly (75·5 per cent in Italy, 84·3 per cent in France, 89·9 per cent in Germany) from domestic producers and minimally (2·1 per cent in Italy, 2·8 per cent in France, 9·8 per cent in Germany) from other EEC countries. This is in sharp contrast with market shares in the United States, where purchases of out-of-state products are almost one-half of the purchases from producers within the state.

Imre Vajda (1900—69), Hungarian socialist, published in English an essay 'Integration, Economic Union and the National State', in Imre Vajda and Mihaly Simai, eds, *Foreign Trade in a Planned Economy* (Cambridge: Cambridge University Press, 1971) pp. 29—44. He compared the economic integration of capitalist and socialist countries. The former concentrates 'on the integration of the market', the latter 'on the co-ordination of plans' (p. 31). Although Vajda did not deny the contribution which 'market integration' has made to economic welfare, he stresses the importance of selective 'production and development integration' (p. 35), with its important function of redistributing income within and among the integrated countries. Nevertheless, market integration should be applied also to 'socialist international division of labour' (p. 42). While this division of labour 'need not necessarily be directed towards total integration', 'a more planned and institutionalized co-operation should be achieved' in the 'sectors which determine technical progress'. However, the Socialist countries' CMEA should abandon 'the trend towards "closedness" ' and replace it 'by a wider, continental and eventually global attitude' (p. 42).

Jagdish Bhagwati (born 1934) published a useful note on 'Trade-Diverting Customs Unions and Welfare Improvement: A

Clarification', *Economic Journal*, Vol. 81 (Sept 1971) pp. 580—7, in which he translated Lipsey's analysis of trade-diverting customs unions into a general-equilibrium model. Allowing for variability in the pattern of production, he showed that it would be a sufficient condition for such unions to be welfare-reducing if 'the level of imports is fixed, and not that the pattern of consumption is fixed' (p. 580). [See, however, Harry Johnson, p. 268 above.]

Warner Max Corden (born 1927), in an article on 'Economies of Scale and Customs Union Theory', *Economic Journal*, Vol. 82 (May 1972) pp. 465—75, undertook to incorporate economies of scale systematically into the basic theory of customs unions. Staying within partial-equilibrium analysis and assuming that the member countries face given terms of trade with the rest of the world, he found Viner's concepts of trade creation and trade diversion fully operative, but he pointed to the importance of two other effects: a cost-reduction effect and a trade-suppression effect. If countries A and B form a customs union and B's formerly protected production is replaced by more efficiently produced imports from A, not only is there trade creation, but there may be an additional cost-reduction effect in A due to economies of scale, which would enable consumers in A to obtain their domestic supplies at lower costs. On the other hand, if, after formation of a customs union, Country B replaces cheaper but dutiable imports from non-member Country C with its domestic production which still is less efficient than production in C but has become domestically competitive with a given external tariff because of economies of scale that have lowered its costs, there will be a trade-suppression effect (as Viner had already called it in his 1950 book). In an article on 'Customs Union Theory and the Nonuniformity of Tariffs', *Journal of International Economics*, Vol. 6 (Feb 1976) pp. 99—106, Corden proposed the possibility of another, hitherto unnoticed, effect. If the tariff structures in countries forming a customs union had been non-uniform *ad valorem*, and hence distorted trade not only by reducing the total volume but also by distorting the commodity pattern of imports, the new union tariff would probably reduce the divergences in *ad valorem* duties. Hence, even if the customs union did not increase total trade, some benefits could be expected from the 'import-pattern effect' of greater uniformity of duties. The resulting increase in welfare would be separate from and independent of trade creation and trade diversion.

Melvyn B. Krauss (born 1938) wrote a survey article on

'Recent Developments in Customs Union Theory: An Interpretive Survey', *Journal of Economic Literature*, Vol. 10 (June 1972) pp. 413—36. His chief purpose was to interpret the theorems and theories found in the literature starting with Viner, to confirm some and refute others; but he had many novel things to say. He offered an interesting interpretation of 'the non-problem of the trade-diverting customs union that results in welfare improvement — the countercase to the alleged Vinerian "law" that trade diversion necessarily reduces welfare' (pp. 414—15); he recalled that 'the consumption effect need not always be positive' (p. 415); he held that 'once consumption effects are allowed for, labeling a customs union after its production effect is as arbitrary and un-illuminating as labeling it after its consumption effect' (p. 417); he divided the 'total gain' into three parts: the production element, the consumption element, and 'the government's element', the latter consisting of tariff revenues not transferred to consumers (p. 419); he chided economists for the 'misnomer perpetrated' by referring to induced efficiency and economies of scale as 'dynamic effects' (p. 419); he found that the positive production effects of trade creation and any associated 'economy-of-scale effects' should be treated as 'integral parts of the same phenomenon' (p. 421); he preferred to deal with redistributional effects not in terms of member countries or the union as a whole but, instead, of the 'particular groups' affected within countries — for example, the 'French farmers and German industrialists' enriched by the EEC 'at the expense of both their fellow countrymen and foreigners' (p. 421); he examined to what extent a 'terms-of-trade gain resulting from customs union' could provide an economic argument for it (p. 423); he found that the attainment of the supposedly desired 'public good' of producing domestically what could more cheaply be imported was a poor argument for a protection-yielding customs union, since direct subsidies would be more efficient than protection (p. 428); and he concluded, accordingly, that 'the public-good argument fails to provide a general economic argument for customs union, and thus reinforces the validity of the Vinerian approach that customs unions are best viewed as essentially non-economic institutions' (p. 430). Krauss saw three possibly rational arguments for seeking a customs union: as a 'necessary prelude to eventual full political union', as a mechanism to increase the income and wealth of one's own country at the expense of others (members or non-members), or as a mechanism for redistributing income to particular groups within one's own country, and he assigned two legitimate purposes to economic analysis of the effects of customs unions: either, if one assumes that the government sincerely desires to maximise the economic welfare of the country, to develop sound 'optimization procedures in support of government objectives' or, if one assumes 'government to be "irrational" or "non-economic" ', to assess 'the economic costs of such irrationality'. After all, 'an economist should no more expect the government to serve the public good as he sees it than he expects the industrial corporation or the trade union to serve the public good' (p. 434).

Petrus J. Verdoorn (born 1911) and Cornelis A. Van Bochove (born 1950), in an article on 'Measuring Integration Effects: A Survey', *European Economic Review*, Vol. 3 (Nov 1972) pp. 337—49, distinguished three methods of estimating the effects of integration: (*a*) a survey approach and Delphi technique (to obtain the views of experts who look into the future); (*b*) residual imputation (to find from statistical data of the past the residual attributable to integration after the ascertainable effect of other important changes, developments, or actions have been eliminated); and (*c*) the use of a suitable analytical model (appropriate for both *ex-ante* and *ex-post* estimates). Residual imputation has been of six major types: 1. Simple reconstructio of the trade matrix; 2. Import-demand equations with only one variable; 3. Import-demand equations based on multiple regression; 4. Modified reconstruction of the 'normal' trade matrix by a gravitation model; 5. Import-share analysis; and 6. Analysis of shares in apparent consumption. The authors appraised the com parative advantages of the methods and of some numerical results. They then present an analytical model in which price-elasticities of total import demand and price-volume elasticities of substitution between importables are the major terms, with the changes in tariff rates as exogenous variables. The elasticitie are either given from prior estimates or found by regressing the observed shifts in the trade flows on the changes in tariffs.

Fritz Machlup (born 1902) wrote on 'integration policies which actually hinder integration' in his address 'Integrations-hemmende Integrationspolitik', in Herbert Giersch, ed., *Bern-hard-Harms-Vorlesungen*, No. 5/6 (Kiel: Institut für Weltwirt-schaft, 1974) pp. 37—60. His main point was that sectoral integration and industrial — horizontal or vertical — integration may be inimical to general economic integration in that they achieve an allocation of resources that disregards their oppor-tunity cost. By circumventing the market and using non-com-petitive methods of pricing, productive services and intermediat products are steered into uses inconsistent with the principle of efficiency and economy.

Edwin M. Truman (born 1941) analysed 'The Effects of European Integration on the Production and Trade of Manufactured Products', in Bela Balassa, ed., *European Economic Integration* (Amsterdam: North Holland Publishing Company, 1975) pp. 3—40. He divided a country's total expenditure on 'apparent consumption' into three relative shares: on domestic products, on imports from bloc-partners, and on imports from other countries. With three 'basic shares', each showing either an increase or a decrease, six combinations are possible: (1) internal and external trade creation, (2) internal trade creation and external trade diversion, (3) internal trade diversion and external trade creation, (4) external trade diversion [to bloc countries] and external trade erosion [in favour of domestic production], (5) internal and external trade erosion, and (6) internal trade diversion [to non-bloc countries] and external trade erosion [in favour of domestic production]. The first three combinations show reduced shares, the other three increased shares, of expenditures on domestic production. Correcting actual expenditures for cyclical changes and for a time-variable, but assuming that nothing else 'happened to alter systematically the pattern of shares in the base year' (p. 8), Truman ascertained the changes in the three 'basic shares' for ten industrial sectors in both EEC and EFTA countries. The supposedly 'normal' effects of regional arrangements — internal trade creation with some external trade diversion — were found in less than 20 per cent of the (corrected) observations. A considerable number of observations yielded the verdict of trade erosion — an increase in the share of expenditures on domestic output — which surely cannot be attributed to the process of regional integration (p. 38).

Murray C. Kemp (born 1926) and **Henry Y. Wan, Jr.** (born 1931) supplied 'An Elementary Proposition Concerning the Formation of Customs Unions', *Journal of International Economics*, Vol. 6 (Feb 1976) pp. 95—7, in which they proved by set-theoretical methods that 'with any number of countries and commodities' and with complete freedom of countries to impose or increase tariffs and to form customs unions, 'there exists a common tariff vector and a system of lump-sum compensatory payments . . . such that each individual, whether a member of the union or not, is not worse off than before the formation of the union.' This implies 'that an incentive to form and enlarge customs unions persists until the world is one big customs union, that is, until world free trade prevails.' That the world has not

yet attained universal free trade 'must be explained in terms of
(1) the game-theoretic problems of choosing partners, dividing
the spoils, and enforcing agreements, and (2) the non-economic
objectives of nations.' There is also (3) inertia and ignorance,
which may be effective obstacles on the path towards worldwid
free trade.

MONETARY AND FISCAL INTEGRATION, 1923—76

Trade integration was the theme of the preceding section. We
are now turning to the literature on monetary and fiscal integration. Several of the contributors will be recognised as old friend
or at least old names, from the previous survey and some even
from the section before that. The appearance of writers in more
than one section testifies to the fact that the most widely noted
economists are not narrowly specialised — though there is nothing discreditable in an analyst concentrating on monetary and
fiscal problems. The survey will convey the impression that
differences of opinion are more pronounced on questions of
monetary integration than on matters of trade integration, at
least if the questions are oriented towards policy recommendations.

John Maynard Keynes (1883—1946) questioned the significance of an international monetary standard, first in his *Tract
on Monetary Reform* (London: Macmillan, 1923) and then in
his *Treatise on Money* (London: Macmillan, 1930). After talkin
about the international gold standard, he asked whether it is
really certain

> that the ideal standard is an international standard? It has
> been usual to assume that the answer is so obviously in the
> affirmative as to need no argument. . . . The conveniences an
> facilities which an international standard offers to foreign
> trade and foreign investment is thought sufficient to clinch
> the matter. The lack of international standard of value is
> assumed to be just one more of these foolish hindrances to
> international mobility, such as tariffs, which can only serve
> to impoverish the whole world in the misguided attempt to
> benefit some separate part of it (1930, p. 301).

Keynes then proceeded to consider the issue in a chapter entitle
'The Problem of National Autonomy', in which he stressed the
advantages of a system in which 'the Central Bank is free to vary
both the rate of foreign exchange and its market-rate of interest
(p. 362). He suggested that the national goals of higher levels of

employment and production were more important than exchange
stability.

Dag Hammarskjöld (1905—61), Swedish economist and later
Secretary General of the United Nations, wrote a 'Note on a Desintegrated, Provisional Monetary Standard as a Basis of Stabilization', in Joint Committee, Carnegie Endowment—International
Chamber of Commerce, *The Improvement of Commercial
Relations between Nations and the Problems of Monetary
Stabilization* (Paris: International Chamber of Commerce, 1936)
pp. 384—96. He raised the question 'whether alterations in the
rates of exchange are to remain a result of financial crises — for
various reasons considered morally more or less objectionable —
or are to be effected according to fixed rules and acknowledged
as the perfectly natural results of changes in economic conditions
that they are' (p. 385). He found that 'structural changes . . . are
of a kind that warrants a high degree of elasticity in the exchange
system enabling smooth adjustments of the rates of exchange'
(p. 387). He proposed the formation of groups of countries
which would alter their mutual exchange rates only with the
consent of, or at least after consultation with, the other members.
The smaller countries should fix 'the value of their currencies in
relation to one or more other currencies' and 'form blocks centered round world currencies which would remain free in relation
to one another and to gold' (p. 390). Hammarskjöld believed
that 'the central banks have proved their ability to manage a free
currency and they have not yielded to the temptation to let the
rates of exchange slip in an arbitrary way'; he held 'that in some
respects complete freedom is more binding than agreements'
(p. 392). [It should be noted that the memorandum was produced in 1936.]

Robert Triffin (born 1911) was a prolific contributor to the
discussion of monetary arrangements consistent with economic
integration. He was one of the earliest ot warn of the defects of
the Bretton Woods system. In his article 'National Central Banking and the International Economy', *Review of Economic
Studies*, Vol. 14 (No. 36, 1946—7) pp. 53—75, he pointed to the
delays in adjustment which may result from the operations of
the International Monetary Fund; he examined the diagnosis of
'fundamental disequilibrium' (p. 72) and its cure through price
deflation or currency devaluation. In his article 'Aspects de la
Reconstruction Monétaire de l'Europe', *Revue d'Economie
Politique*, Vol. 60 (Jan—Feb 1950) pp. 5—36, Triffin proposed
the creation of a European Clearing System with lines of credit
for the member countries, rapid liberalisation of quantitative

restrictions on imports and foreign exchange, and correction of unrealistic exchange rates. In his book *Europe and the Money Muddle: From Bilateralism to Near-Convertibility, 1947—1956* (New Haven: Yale University Press, 1957), he contrasted the performance of the European Payments Union with that of the International Monetary Fund and claimed the superiority of the regional over the universal approach to multilateralism in payments and trade.

James Edward Meade (born 1907) presented the most methodical analysis of international adjustment in his book *The Balance of Payments* (London: Oxford University Press, 1951) pp. 151—260. He described the processes of adjustment through variable exchange rates and through variable wage rates, and compared the mechanisms of the gold standard, the adjustable peg, and the free exchange market. When, in later years, he applied his analysis to the conditions prevailing in most countries, he concluded that a system of sliding exchange rates — somewhere between the adjustable peg and freely flexible rates — would be the most efficient choice. He presented his arguments in several publications; among them are his article (justly called a 'classic paper') on 'The Balance of Payments Problem of a European Free Trade Area', *Economic Journal*, Vol. 67 (Sept 1957) pp. 379—96; and two other influential articles, 'The International Monetary Mechanism' and 'Exchange-Rate Flexibility', *Three Banks Review*, No. 63 (Sept 1964) pp. 3—25, and No. 70 (June 1966) pp. 3—27. As a member of the *Study Group on Economic and Monetary Union: European Economic Integration and Monetary Unification* (Brussels: Commission of the European Communities, 1973) Meade contributed two papers, published in Part II (pp. 89—105). In one of them, on 'European Monetary Union', he warned that Monetary Union 'set up as an objective in its own right' would make the 'basic objectives of Economic Union more difficult . . . to attain' (p. 89). The successful operation of currency integration presupposes '(a) a centrally integrated monetary and fiscal policy, (b) a co-ordinated wage flexibility, and (c) a highly developed regional policy'. Since wage rates are not flexible downward, 'it would be foolish' and 'disastrous' to try to fix exchange rates, either within the Union or between it and countries outside, and thus submit to the necessity of monetary deflation to adjust to a variety of conditions (p. 90).

Fritz Neumark (born 1900) published a report on 'Die budgetären und steuerlichen Aspekte einer wirtschaftlichen Integration', in *Aspects financiers et fiscaux de l'intégration économique*

internationale, Travaux de l'Institut International de Finances
Publiques, Neuvième Session, Francfort, 1953 (The Hague: W.
P. van Stockum et Fils, 1953) pp. 21—53. Later he was respon-
sible for, and evidently the chief author of, the *Report of the
Fiscal and Financial Committee* of the European Economic
Community Commission (Brussels, 1963). It was published in an
English translation as Book II of *The EEC Reports on Tax Harmonization: The Report of the Fiscal and Financial Committee
and the Reports of the Sub-Groups A, B, and C* (Amsterdam:
International Bureau of Fiscal Documentation, 1963) pp. 92—
156. The task of the Neumark Committee was to study 'if and
to what extent the differences' between the financial systems of
the member countries 'hinder the establishment . . . of conditions analogous to those of an internal market' and 'to what
extent it is possible to eliminate these differences' (p. 98). The
Neumark Report examined the disparities in 'the so-called overall
tax burden', in 'the composition of public expenditures', and in
'the composition of tax systems' (p. 106). It made proposals 'for
the qualitative and quantitative harmonization of certain particular taxes' (p. 118), in particular, personal and corporate income taxes, special excise duties, general turnover taxes, taxes
on the transfer of capital, on motor vehicles and transport, on
special types of income, and regarding the problem of the size
of taxes on companies and the withholding of taxes on dividends
(pp. 118—44). It compared the distorting effects of using the
origin principle and the destination principle (pp. 145—9), discussed the general problems of budget policy and a timetable of
measures for tax-harmonisation. With regard to the most controversial questions, the Neumark Report made it clear that the
destination principle operated like a quasi-tariff on imports,
largely because of systematic undercompensation by the tax
rebates of exporting countries. It recommended that in the case
of general turnover taxes the destination principle be abandoned
in favour of the origin principle, but that it could be retained in
the case of specific excises on goods in internal EEC-trade and
in all trade with third countries. Finally, the adoption of a value-
added tax by all member countries of the Community was
suggested.

   Carl S. Shoup (born 1902) investigated some of the implications for fiscal harmonisation of tax-collection systems when
countries form a customs union. In an article on 'Taxation
Aspects of International Economic Integration', in *Aspects
financiers et fiscaux de l'intégration économique internationale*,
Travaux de l'Institut International de Finances Publiques, Neu-

vième Session, Francfort, 1953 (The Hague: W. P. van Stockum et Fils, 1953) pp. 89—107, he argued that the technical tax requisites for a workable internal-revenue system under economic integration in many cases 'are more concerned with the stag at which the tax is levied and the general level of rates, than with complete uniformity of rates from member to member, or complete uniformity in kinds of taxes imposed' (p. 102). He also analysed the economic effects of applying the 'origin principle' or the 'destination principle' of taxation within the union when members collect alternative internal revenues such as sales taxes, excise taxes, profits taxes, or payroll taxes.

Robert Marjolin (born 1911), an efficient protagonist of European trade integration, contributed also to the cause of monetary integration, especially in connection with the European Payments Union. In an article on 'The European Trade and Payments System: A Study in Co-operation', *Lloyds Bank Review*, n.s. No. 31 (Jan 1954) pp. 1—15, he described the mult lateral clearing system aided by 'compensation through time' (p. 3). This implies delayed clearing, or credit, facilities until a country's payments position turns round from deficit to surplus. With the aid of grants and credits by the United States, balances could be settled through gold transfers and dollar payments. The 'purpose of EPU credits is precisely to make the foreign currency reserves of central banks less insufficient, and thus partially to fulfill the role previously played by the banking system' (p. 9). According to Marjolin, 'freedom of trade is impossible without adequate multilateral payments arrangements' (p. 12).

Gottfried Haberler (born 1900) discussed several times the question of the kind of monetary arrangements most appropriate to facilitate economic integration. In his essay 'Die wirtschaftliche Integration Europas', in Erwin Beckerath *et al.*, eds, *Wirtschaftsfragen der freien Welt* [Festschrift for Chancellor Ludwig Erhard] (Frankfurt a.M.: Fritz Knapp, 1957) pp. 521—30, he stressed that the three objectives (*a*) free trade or fixed tariffs; (*b*) independent monetary policies aiming at full employment pursued with different resoluteness and hence different rates of inflation; and (*c*) stable exchange rates, are incompatible in the long run (pp. 524—5).

Tibor Scitovsky (born 1910) produced an important article on 'The Theory of the Balance of Payments and the Problem of a Common European Currency', *Kyklos*, Vol. 10 (No. 1, 1957) pp. 18—44). He held that the full benefits of a common Western European market could be had only if it secured an efficient geographic distribution of investment. This required that economic relations should no longer be disturbed and disrupted by trade restrictions, exchange controls, or exchange-rate revisions — which in effect means the need for a common currency, where market forces, without the aid of deliberate economic policy, secure balance in international payments within the Community (pp. 18—19). In a common-currency area, like the United States, interstate payments balance is maintained or quickly restored through 'equilibrating flows of capital' thanks to a 'completely integrated securities market' and, when this is insufficient, through the investment effects of interest differentials, through income effects of any remaining balances, through geographic distribution of Federal Government expenditures compensating for imbalances of private payments, and finally through 'classical' monetary policies of the District Reserve Banks (which hold almost a 100 per cent reserve in Federal securities, accepted by all other reserve banks of the system). On the basis of this theory, Scitovsky discussed the problem of European currency union and found that 'a common all-European capital market and a common all-European employment policy would be prime requisites' (p. 32), that 'unco-ordinated national employment policies' would be too costly both in terms of government expenditures needed and in terms of foreign exchange lost (p. 34). Accordingly, he prescribed a 'supranational authority' with powers to tax, to issue securities accepted by all European central banks, to take over from national governments all responsibility for fiscal policy, to co-ordinate monetary policies, and to invest in the infrastructure (public utilities, transport system, etc.) in the member countries. Since conflicts of national goals with Community goals are unavoidable, but unbalancing policies of national central banks must be ruled out, the solution is to 'prohibit (or severely restrict) the purchase of government securities by central banks'. The 'securities issued by the supranational employment authority and by other supranational agencies would serve as central-bank reserves suitable for settling intra-union accounts; and the continued activity of the supranational agencies, coupled with the ban on central-bank expansion based on national government securities, would bring about a gradual increase in the reserve ratios of central banks in relation to payments within the currency union' (pp. 37—8).

James C. Ingram (born 1922) wrote a widely noted and often quoted article on 'State and Regional Payments Mechanisms', *Quarterly Journal of Economics*, Vol. 73 (Nov 1959) pp. 619—32, in which he contrasted interstate payments in the United States with payments among member countries of a customs union. In his view, capital inflows into any one state of the United States cause no transfer problems because accommodating counterflows through commercial banks acquiring generally accepted assets (claims) cushion the immediate impact, and real transfers of goods may readily follow the financial transfers with no price effects and hardly any income effects. Different nations however, neither have sufficient holdings in generally (internationally) acceptable securities for banks to accomplish an accommodating counterflow of claims; nor are sufficiently open to use the purchasing power received for imports without going first through adjustments of prices and incomes. Since the capital market plays a strategic role in the smoothening of financial transfers and in financing imbalances of payments, the creation of an integrated capital market is of the essence, and this presupposes the removal of restrictions on capital movements.

Robert A. Mundell (born 1932) created the concept on an 'optimum currency area', meaning the territory (of one or more countries) most suitable for use of a single currency or for linking several currencies through interconvertibility at fixed exchange rates. In his article, 'A Theory of Optimum Currency Areas', *American Economic Review*, Vol. 51 (Sept 1961) pp. 657—65, he held that the currency area was optimal if it coincided with a region within which productive factors were mobile while their movements to and from other regions were restricted. Flexibility of foreign-exchange rates may serve to offset the consequences which immobility of factors has on adjustment and stabilisation; flexible rates are therefore appropriate for currencies of different regions but not within a region with internal mobility. Among other arguments against a world of many small currency areas, Mundell points to the costs of revaluations, the thinness of foreign-exchange markets, and the absence of 'money illusion' on the part of labour unions in small currency areas. Consistent with this point of view, Mundell saw great advantages in European monetary integration with fixed exchange rates among European currencies. In his essay 'The International Monetary System and the European Region' in *L'union monétaire en Europe* [ed. Alexander Swoboda] (Geneva: Institut Universitaire de Hautes Etudes Internationales, 1971) pp. 45—67, Mundell held that 'regional monetary integration' would be more easily attained than worldwide monetary integration and would help to attain the latter eventually (pp. 55—6). Three categories of provisions make up monetary integration: (1) 'currency provisions', such as elimination of exchange-

rate margins, abandonment of parity changes, and creation of a
currency-bloc currency; (2) 'credit provisions', such as swaps,
lending, and reserve pooling; and (3) 'policy provisions', such as
harmonisation of monetary and budgetary policy, centralisation
of the capital market, and a common wages policy (p. 63). The
first step, however, for European monetary integration would
be 'the creation of a European Monetary Fund . . . with a genera-
lized liability analogous to the SDRs, e.g., a European Currency
Unit' (p. 66).

Fritz Machlup (born 1902) rejected the view that one could
regard either fixed or flexible exchange rates as preferable
regardless of other choices concerning monetary policy. In his
pamphlet *Plans for Reform of the International Monetary System*
(Princeton: International Finance Section, Princeton University,
1st ed. 1962, 2nd ed. 1964), he stated that fixed rates are suitable for countries which 'subordinate their monetary policy to
the requirements of external balance', whereas countries which
pursue other objectives, such as employment, interest, or growth
targets, must in consistency opt for flexible rates (1st ed., p. 61,
2nd ed. p. 84). In his essay 'Nationalism, Provincialism, Fixed
Exchange Rates, and Monetary Union', in Wolfgang Schmitz,
ed., *Convertibility, Multilaterialism, and Freedom* [Festschrift
for Reinhard Kamitz] (Vienna and New York: Springer Verlag,
1972) pp. 265—73, Machlup stressed the difficulties of monetary
unification in Europe, where each country has its separate
national central bank, in contrast with the United States, where
none of the twelve districts of the Federal Reserve System co-
incides with any of the fifty states, and none of the states could
influence monetary policy (pp. 270—3).

Gottfried Bombach (born 1919) explored the problem of
optimal international division of labour with structurally different systems of taxation, in a study on *Das Problem der optimalen
internationalen Arbeitsteilung bei unterschiedlicher Struktur der
Steuersysteme: Bestimmungslandprinzip versus Ursprungsland-
prinzip* (Düsseldorf: Verlag Stahleisen, 1962). He showed the
destination principle of border-tax arrangements to be unsound,
and argued for applying the origin principle, which is less distorting. The system of border tax adjustments as practiced by
France was shown to warp competition and divert trade into un-
economic channels, with a consequent distortion of the locational structure of industry. Since, under present conditions, shifting and incidence of direct and indirect taxes are not essentially
different, the higher share of indirect taxes in France is no valid
argument for applying the destination principle. Adjustments in

exchange rates, possibly effective in offsetting differences in the general level of taxation, cannot correct the distortions caused by structural differences in taxes and border tax arrangements (p. 25).

Hans Möller (born 1915) prepared in 1962 for the EEC Commission a study on the 'Origin and Destination Principles', which was later published under the title 'Ursprungs- und Bestimmungslandprinzip', *Finanzarchiv*, Vol. 27 (June 1968) pp. 385—458. He examined the effects of taxes on foreign trade, first without movements and then with movements of productive factors. He concluded that the distinction between the origin principle and the destination principle is significant for selective taxes only, but not for general taxes on all products in proportion to their values (p. 422). However, when factor movements play an important role, the differential effects of the two principles of indirect taxes cannot be evaluated if the effects of public expenditures are not taken into account (pp. 428, 442).

Peter B. Kenen (born 1932), in an article 'Toward an Atlantic Capital Market, *Lloyds Bank Review*, p. 69 (July 1963) pp. 15—30, emphasised the advantages of 'financial integration'. A policy of 'financial autarky', especially in France, has led to a 'paucity of trading' in Continental capital markets, making bonds less liquid than they are in New York or London, and constricting both the demand for existing securities and the supply of new ones (p. 27). In a paper 'Toward a Supranational Monetary System', in Giulio Pontecorvo, Robert P. Shay, and Albert Hart, eds, *Issues in Banking and Monetary Analysis* (New York: Holt, Rinehart and Winston, 1967) pp. 209—26, Kenen held that a realignment of aims and instruments under a managed world-currency system could induce countries to pursue measures of adjustment that could be co-ordinated with the policies of other countries. One 'cannot define an "optimum policy mix" for a single country or group of countries without first articulating a consistent constellation of national and international objectives' (p. 224). Kenen advocated discretionary management by a supra-national authority. In another paper, 'The Theory of Optimum Currency Areas: An Eclectic View', in Robert A. Mundell and Alexander K. Swoboda, *Monetary Problems of the International Economy* (Chicago: University of Chicago Press, 1969) pp. 41—60, Kenen found Mundell's major criterion of optimality in the delineation of a currency area — internal mobility and external immobility of labour — to be inadequate and proposed as an alternative the degree of diversification in production. 'Fixed rates . . . are most appropriate — or least inappropriate —

to well-diversified national economies' (p. 54). He concluded that 'the principal developed countries' should rarely resort to changes in exchange rates, while 'the less developed countries, being less diversified and less well equipped with policy instruments, should make more frequent changes or perhaps resort to full flexibility'.

Ronald I. McKinnon (born 1935) suggested a criterion for determining the optimality of a currency area different from that proposed by Mundell. In an article on 'Optimum Currency Areas', *American Economic Review*, Vol. 53 (Sept 1963) pp. 717—25, he gave to the 'openness' of the economy (region) the decisive role, and defined an economy as open if its ratio of [internationally or interregionally] tradable to non-tradable goods was relatively large. He reasoned that, as one moved from closed to open economies, flexible exchange rates were less effective in ensuring external balance and more damaging to internal stability of the price level. A small and open country would therefore be well advised to peg its currency to those of its neighbours.

Clara K. Sullivan (born 1916) wrote a book on *The Search for Tax Principles in the European Economic Community* (Cambridge, Mass.: Law School of Harvard University, 1963) and contributed three chapters to Carl S. Shoup, ed., *Fiscal Harmonization in Common Markets* (New York: Columbia University Press, 1967), Vol. II, pp. 1—206. The chapters deal with indirect taxation in the European Community and the United Kingdom, and with the 'Potential Rates of Value-Added Tax' in the community.

Douglas Dosser (born 1927) published an article on the 'Welfare Effects of Tax Unions', *Review of Economic Studies*, Vol. 31 (June 1964) pp. 179—84, the main points of which were included in his 'Economic Analysis of Tax Harmonization', Chapter II of Carl S. Shoup, ed., *Fiscal Harmonization in Common Markets* (New York: Columbia University Press, 1967) Vol. I, pp. 1—144. In this chapter he distinguished between 'tax union' and 'customs union' (p. 11); between 'equalized formal rates', 'equalized effective rates' and 'equivalent taxes' (pp. 31—41); between the 'equalization approach' and the 'differential approach' to harmonisation, the former often 'irrespective of the economic effects' (p. 31), the latter 'choosing appropriate differentials in tax rates' (p. 89); and, of course, between the 'destination principle' and the 'origin principle' of taxing tradable goods, the former taxing imports and exempting exports, the latter taxing exports and exempting imports (p. 48). He analysed first the production effects alone, then the production and consumption effects together; and he showed the differences between regarding 'second-best' allocative efficiency according to Meade and according to Lipsey and Lancaster (p. 83). After treating allocative efficiency he dealt with the stabilisation aspects (p. 93), and the growth aspects of fiscal harmonisation (p. 107), and finally with the harmonisation of government expenditure (p. 116) and with the effects on the international mobility of factors (p. 121) In a later contribution, a comment on 'Community Budget and the Member-States Budgets', in Part II of the report of the *Study Group on Economic and Monetary Union: European Economic Integration and Monetary Unification* (Brussels: Commission of the European Communities, 1973) pp. 45—53, Dosser discussed the role, size, and realisation of a Community budget. He stressed three aspects: (1) conceivable economies of scale in the provision of public goods, (2) assistance to ailing regions within the Community, and (3) long-term regional redistribution. He visualised a gradual transition from national corporation taxes to a European one, with a simultaneous unification of corporation law.

John H. Williamson (born 1937) coined a name for a new system of exchange-rate flexibility, in his Princeton Essay No. 50, *The Crawling Peg* (Princeton: International Finance Section, 1965). According to his proposal, countries should agree 'that any changes in par value needed to correct a "fundamental disequilibrium" would be carried out gradually, at a maximum rate of 1/26 of 1 per cent per week, rather than by a sudden discrete jump' (p. 2). Thus,

> at any given time, the exchange rates of all countries with convertible currencies would be fixed within a narrow range [but] certain countries . . . would have a range that altered, in a preannounced manner, from week to week. Central banks would intervene in the market to stabilize the rate when it approached its current limits. The incentive to transfer funds out of a currency undergoing devaluation . . . would be neutralized by interest-rate differentials (p. 2).

Central banks might keep better discipline if rapid exchange-rate adjustment were excluded (p. 11); moreover, gradual adjustment would avoid 'overshooting' (p. 15). In his Princeton Essay No. 90, *The Choice of a Pivot for Parities* (Princeton: International Finance Section, 1971) Williamson criticised the passive role of the United States during the late 1960s, when it failed to correct the overvaluation of the dollar on the theory that the world's currencies, though *de jure* on a gold pivot, were *de facto* moving on a dollar pivot, which gave the United States no chance to devalue the dollar *vis-à-vis* other currencies (p. 4). Williamson proposed to make the gold-SDR the pivot on which all currencies could turn as new parities were desired. He also proposed a novel rule for determining the need for the creation of additional SDRs for reserve purposes:

> The optimal rate of SDR creation is that which will hold constant the value of the gold-SDR unit in terms of an appropriately weighted average of currencies. An excess of devaluations over revaluations is evidence of a reserve shortage that demands increased SDR creation, while an excess of revaluations over devaluations is evidence that on the average countries are seeking to repel imported inflation, so that the rate of SDR creation needs to be cut back (p. 19).

As a co-rapporteur with Giovanni Magnifico, Williamson produced a report on *European Monetary Integration* (London: Federal Trust for Education and Research, February 1972), recommending the creation of a European currency which would for several years be used as a parallel standard and/or a means of payments together with national currencies, but could gradually replace the separate currencies to become the common currency in the European Community. [See also Chapter 6].

Stephen Marris (born 1930) produced Princeton Essay No. 80 on *The Bürgenstock Communiqué: A Critical Examination of the Case for Limited Flexibility of Exchange Rates* (Princeton: International Finance Section, 1970). His major concern was with the question of the practicability of a 'discretionary band-and-crawl system' (pp. 33—42). In the context, however, Marris raised the question of how, in a system in which most countries were pegging or otherwise managing their exchange rates *vis-à-vis* the US dollar, the dollar could be given the same flexibility that other currencies were to have. He proposed that parities be established not in terms of gold but instead in terms of the Special Drawing Right, the new international reserve medium (pp. 48—50). [This 'Marris Heresy', the proposal to use the SDR rather than gold as the common denominator for national currencies, though first regarded as far ahead of its time, was soon to become an official orthodoxy.]

Herbert G. Grubel (born 1934), in a note on 'The Theory of Optimum Currency Areas', *Canadian Journal of Economics*, Vol. III (May 1970) pp. 318—24, proposed to regard a currency area (fixed-exchange-rate area) as optimal if its welfare gains from a possibly larger real income in the long run exceed the

welfare losses that are due to possibly reduced stability of income over time and to reduced economic independence of the
countries or provinces joined in the mutual pegging of their
currencies.

Harry G. Johnson (born 1923) made so many contributions
to the discussion of monetary integration that any selection for
annotation here cannot help but be arbitrary. In his article on
'Problems of European Monetary Union', *Journal of World Trad
Law*, Vol. 5 (July—Aug 1971) pp. 377—87, he commented
critically on the Barre Plan and Werner Report. [See Chapter 6.]
He saw two reasons behind the attempt of the EC Commission
to design an approach to monetary union in several stages: (1)
'to persuade, cajole, or blackmail the members . . . into the adop
tion of central co-ordination of monetary and financial policies'
(p. 383); and (2) to escape from 'dollar domination' by creating
a rival international currency (p. 373). Johnson saw the common
European money as 'an outward symbol, of, but not a prerequisi
for, effective economic integration' (p. 383); he considered completely rigid exchange rates as impossible, abruptly adjustable
rates as harmful, and floating rates as the only practical solution.
Any movement towards monetary unification would presuppose
'surrender of autonomy in monetary policy'. As the European
countries procrastinate in creating a common currency and an
integrated capital market, they perpetuate the much disliked
dollar domination. From another of Johnson's papers, 'The
Exchange Rate Question for a United Europe: Internal Flexibility and External Rigidity versus External Flexibility and Internal Rigidity', in the conference proceedings edited by Alexander
K. Swoboda, *Europe and the Evolution of the International
Monetary System* (Leiden: A. W. Sijthoff, 1973) pp. 81—91,
two statements are reproduced here:

> The question of relevance . . . is whether there will be greater
> divergences between the average of the European countries
> (or . . . [their] aspirations and tolerances) and the United
> States, or among the European countries themselves.

And

> If . . . the United States adopts policies that will result in a
> return to reasonable stability of American prices, the Europea
> countries may well prefer to retain the domestic policy auto-
> nomy they have enjoyed over the postwar period on the basis
> of their ability to change their exchange rates against both the
> United States and their fellow-European countries together,

while of course continuing to pay lip-service to the common currency ideal but contriving in practice to make only glacial progress towards it (p. 91).

John Marcus Fleming (1911—76), besides many other contributions to timely questions of international monetary arrangements, wrote an article 'An Exchange Rate Unification', *Economic Journal*, Vol. 81 (Sept 1971) pp. 467—88. He pointed to the dangers of participating in a fixed-exchange-rate area arising from the 'certainty' that 'in the absence of perfect competition in product and factor markets, . . . developments would occur from time to time that pushed the relative cost levels . . . out of line, and even some that tended to push them progressively further and further out of line' (pp. 467—8). Differences in 'unemployment/inflation relationships' in the member countries would lead to a common rate of price inflation 'higher than that preferred by the surplus members' and to a level of unemployment in the deficit members higher than they would tolerate if they were free to adjust their exchange rates (p. 469). After examining the factors that could mitigate or aggravate the unavoidable 'disequilibria', and after evaluating the benefits and costs of unalterable rates, Fleming warned 'that if adherence to a unified exchange rate area were found to lead to excessive hardships, reactions might ensue leading not only to the abandonment of exchange rate unification but even to a rejection of other forms of economic integration among participating countries' (p. 484).

Fred Hirsch (born 1931), author of the volume *Money International* (London: Allen Lane, The Penguin Press, 1967; enlarged edition New York: Doubleday, 1969), published an incisive evaluation of 'The Political Economics of European Monetary Integration', *The World Today* [London] Vol. 28 (Oct 1972) pp. 424—33. He regarded the commitments to European monetary union as having 'been taken on in ignorance of their implications or for purposes of political posturing' and as 'bound to conflict with "true" objectives to which economic and political forces will give overriding priority' (p. 425). The members of the EEC need 'more exchange flexibility rather than less'; 'the exchange rate has proved not a sufficient but still a necessary instrument of international adjustment' and 'is likely to remain so as long as "money illusion" persists — i.e., as long as it is easier to adjust real living standards through changes in money prices than through direct reductions in money incomes' (p. 426). Hirsch does not question the general view that 'once a certain degree of integration of economic activity is reached, the advantages of exchange unification outweigh the disadvantages' (p. 429). However, even *within* countries that degree has not always been reached. Thus, 'when the economies of the present EEC countries are significantly more integrated with each other than are England and Scotland today', that would be the time for an exchange-rate or currency union (p. 430). Hirsch finally cogitated over the true or imagined reasons for the pertinacious political campaign for European monetary union.

Robert G. Hawkins (born 1936) contributed a paper on 'Intra-EEC Capital Movements and Domestic Financial Markets', in Fritz Machlup, Walter S. Salant, and Lorie Tarshis, eds, *International Mobility and Movements of Capital* (New York: Columbia University Press, 1972) pp. 51–78. He found 'little convincing evidence that financial markets of the EEC countries became very much more integrated during the first decade of the EEC'. Indeed, the evidence shows 'a noticeable disintegration after 1967' (p. 77), due primarily to restrictions by governments trying to maintain fixed exchange rates but to continue 'independent' credit policies.

Warner Max Corden (born 1927) wrote the Princeton Essay No. 93, on *Monetary Integration* (Princeton: International Finance Section, 1972). He defined monetary integration as the combination between 'exchange-rate union' and market convertibility, that is, 'the permanent absence of all exchange controls, whether for current or capital transactions, within the area', allowing therefore for 'capital-market integration' (p. 2). He distinguished between 'complete exchange-rate union' (with a 'union central bank', enforcing strict surveillance and close co-ordination of policies, managing the common reserve pool and eventually taking over all national central banks) and a 'pseudo-exchange-rate union' (where members are committed to maintain fixed exchange rates *vis-à-vis* the currencies of all other members, but may be unable to do so since their policies are insufficiently co-ordinated). Exchange-rate union imposes on its members 'departures from internal balance' and acceptance of non-optimal policies with regard to employment and price level, unless the countries can institute wage flexibility, labour-market integration, and labour mobility throughout the union. Trade integration may strengthen or weaken the case for fixed exchange rates — since tariffs can no longer be used to help in coping with payments deficits. Capital-market integration, limited to the union, will benefit member countries if it creates trade in securities, and will injure them if it diverts such flows (pp. 25–8). The hope that capital mobility will always help the maintenance of both internal and external balance is not warranted. Fiscal integration is not a prerequisite for monetary integration, but 'efficient short-term management may require some harmonisation or control of over-all budgetary policies' (p. 41).

Bela Balassa (born 1928) contributed a paper on 'Monetary Integration in the European Common Market' to the conference proceedings edited by Alexander K. Swoboda, *Europe and the Evolution of the International Monetary System* (Leiden: A. W. Sijthoff, 1973) pp. 93—128. Although Balassa regarded 'unalterable fixity of parities' as 'the hallmark of monetary integration' (p. 101), he realised that 'central decision-making on monetary and fiscal policy . . . and the acceptance of the policy implications of fixed exchange rates for individual regions' (p. 103) were prerequisites of a permanent commitment to fixed parities. Deep-seated differences in national political attitudes among European countries make effective co-ordination in monetary policy most unlikely (p. 105). If unalterable parities are thus excluded, one has to choose among different systems of flexibility. To Balassa 'the continued application of adjustable pegs does not appear to be an appropriate solution for the European Common Market' (p. 119). He proposes 'the adoption of a system of crawling pegs', a narrowing of the bands around the pegs, the establishment of an exchange-stabilisation fund, and creation of a common currency which could 'assume functions presently fulfilled by national currencies and the US dollar' (p. 128).

Peter M. Oppenheimer (born 1938) examined the possibility and desirability of establishing a common currency for the European Community and of approaching such a currency union by stipulating fixed exchange rates among the members' separate currencies. In an essay on 'The Problem of Monetary Union', in Douglas Evans, ed., *Britain in the EEC* (London: Victor Gollancz, 1973) pp. 99—128, Oppenheimer looked into the possible substitutes for exchange-rate flexibility as an instrument for adjustment. He found that control of domestic cost levels (wage-and-price controls), mobility of labour and capital, and regional aid through fiscal transfers (subsidies and direct investments) are ineffective or insufficient. Hence, countries cannot do without adjustments of exchange rates. Oppenheimer argued that

> history shows no clear movement towards larger currency areas. The past hundred years have seen, on balance, a growing integration of the world economy. Trade has expanded

considerably faster than output. Communications have been
revolutionized. The multi-national corporation has appeared
on the scene. Yet in the monetary sphere arrangements are
much less unified today than they were under the pre-1914
gold standard . . . The factors which have led to this result are
familiar. They include the development of central-banking
techniques, the rise of trade unions, the acceptance of government responsibility for full employment in the wake of the
Keynesian revolution, decolonization and, probably, the
accelerated pace of technological change (p. 127).

In an article on 'Monetary Union: A Survey of the Main Issues',
De Economist [Amsterdam] Vol. 122 (Nov 1974) pp. 22—48,
Oppenheimer stressed that an 'exchange-rate union' would
require members to surrender a key instrument of economic
policy, without receiving compensatory benefits, inasmuch as
currency speculation, exchange risks, and the high cost of money
changing would not be eliminated. Hence, a looser form of
monetary association, without commitment to fixed rates, is
more appropriate under current monetary conditons.

E. Victor Morgan (born 1915), in his article 'Regional Problems and Common Currencies', *Lloyds Bank Review*, No. 110
(Oct 1973) pp. 19—30, found that the problem of a country's
depressed areas staying depressed for a long time was closely
connected with the fact that, with downward rigidities of wage
rates and product prices, unemployment in these areas was difficult to reduce; even with generous fiscal aid from the national
government, and, with a common currency for the entire nation,
there was no way of resorting to exchange-rate adjustments
(p. 26). As long as it is unlikely that the European Community
could provide sufficient fiscal aid to a depressed member
country, it will remain important for members to avoid joining a
monetary union. The 'retention of national currencies with some
flexibility in exchange rates could help to prevent temporary
setbacks, at the national level, from turning into chronic depression' (p. 30).

Raymond Barre (born 1924), in various reports and memoranda written as Vice President of the European Commission, and in his essay 'L'intégration économique et monétaire
européenne' in *La monnaie et l'économie de notre temps:
Mélanges en l'honneur de Professeur Emile James* (Paris: Cujas,
1974) pp. 1—13, set forth the steps towards the establishment
of a monetary union, beginning with a narrowing of the margins
for permissible fluctuations of exchange rates around fixed

parities. While he admitted that it would be 'illusory' to think of irrevocably fixed parities in the near future (p. 6), he insisted on stability of exchange rates as a necessary condition for 'the functioning of the common market', 'the security of transactions, the optimal guide for capital movements, and the development of intracommunity investments' (p. 7). Margins of fluctuations between any two currencies of member countries should be smaller than those *vis-à-vis* the dollar; interventions in the exchange market should be in community currencies (rather than dollars) and, eventually, in a European monetary unit defined as a fixed quantity of gold; and massive flows of foreign capital should be dealt with by concerted actions of the monetary authorities (p. 6).

CONCLUDING REMARK

In my attempt to bring this survey forward, as far as possible, to the publication of this book, I happened to end it with a flagrant contrast of opinions. The tenets of the last economist reviewed clash rather strikingly with several of the preceding ones. I could have avoided the conspicuous exhibition of conflict by moving this and some other annotations back to Chapter 6, inasmuch as they include proposals for action. Considering, however, that the differences in the plans for action go back to differences in assumptions and value judgements which pervade much of the economic theory on the subject, I have left the arrangement as it is. Ending on a note of disharmony or dissonance had not been my design, but it may, after all, serve a good purpose: to make it quite clear that the economic profession has not reached a consensus on monetary integration.

Index

This book can serve three objectives rarely attained in a single volume: it is a monograph on a timely economic problem, a textbook in international economics, and a bibliographical reference book.

The author conceives economic integration as the process of making increasing use of potential – existing or emerging – opportunities for efficient division of labour in geographical areas extending from individual nations to multinational regions and the entire world. Consequently, virtually all propositions on economic integration are firmly based on the general theory of international trade. The effects of modifying, extending or restricting interregional and intraregional movements of products and factors of production cannot be fully understood without comprehension of international trade theory. Unlike most modern expositors, who present that theory largely with the aid of algebraic and geometric arguments, Fritz Machlup writes in plain English, using not a single graph or equation. Lucidity and elegance of exposition do not depend on the use of mathematics.

Another feature of this volume that may appeal to teachers and students is its division into a survey of ideas and a separate review of the authors. Chapter 4 disentangles the main strands of the ideas on the extension of geographic division of labour but avoids references to authors and their writings. Chapters 6 to 9, on the other hand, review or annotate over 200 books and articles by 159 authors. This device may suggest to enterprising teachers the use of open-book examinations, requiring students to trace particular arguments or propositions found in Chapter 4 to their authors reviewed in later chapters.